The Knopf C...
to American ...

Robert Bishop & William C. Ketchum, Jr.
Series Consultants

A Chanticleer Press Edition

Chairs, Tables, Sofas & Beds

Marvin D. Schwartz

With photographs by Chun Y. Lai

Alfred A. Knopf, New York

This is a Borzoi Book
Published by Alfred A. Knopf, Inc.

Prepared and produced by
Chanticleer Press, Inc., New York.

Color reproductions by Nievergelt Repro AG, Zurich,
Switzerland. Type set in Century Expanded by Dix Type Inc.,
Syracuse, New York. Printed and bound by Dai Nippon Printing
Co., Ltd., Tokyo, Japan.

First Printing

Library of Congress Catalog Number: 82-47846
ISBN: 0-394-71269-2

Contents

Acknowledgments

Many people were kind enough to assist in the preparation of this book. I want to express my appreciation to all the antiques shops, individuals, and institutions for making their collections available to us, and in particular Margaret Nolan and the staff of the Photograph and Slide Library at The Metropolitan Museum of Art in New York City; Alberta M. Brandt at the Henry Francis du Pont Winterthur Museum in Delaware; Bernard and S. Dean Levy, Inc., in New York City; and John Ott, director of the Shaker Community in Pittsfield, Massachusetts. Holman J. Swinney, director of the Margaret Woodbury Strong Museum in Rochester, New York, allowed us to photograph objects in the museum's collection, and Lawrence Belles, former chief curator of collections, generously helped in the preparation for the photography. Chun Y. Lai spent half a year photographing most of the furniture in this guide.

Robert Bishop deserves special thanks for helping to launch the project; he also reviewed the manuscript and made many useful suggestions. William C. Ketchum, Jr., also commented on the manuscript, provided invaluable help in selecting the pieces to be photographed, and compiled the price guide. John Kremitske skillfully copy-edited the text. The following individuals kindly contributed to the compilation of the price guide: Frederick DiMaio of Inglenook Antiques in New York City; Dean Failey of Christie's, New York; and Chris Kennedy of American Decorative Arts in Northampton, Massachusetts.

Much of the credit for this book goes to Paul Steiner and his staff at Chanticleer Press. Special thanks are due to Gudrun Buettner and Susan Costello, who developed the idea for this series; Carol Nehring, who supervised the art and layouts; Helga Lose and John Holliday, who saw the book through production. Most of all, I am indebted to Michael Goldman, who, with the help of Constance V. Mersel, edited and coordinated this guide through its completion. Finally, I am grateful to Charles Elliott, senior editor at Alfred A. Knopf, for his editorial advice and encouragement.

About the Author, Photographer, and Consultants

Marvin D. Schwartz
Besides serving as curator of decorative arts at the Brooklyn Museum from 1954 to 1968, Marvin D. Schwartz has lectured and organized exhibitions at The Metropolitan Museum of Art, Detroit Institute of Arts, and other museums around the country. Mr. Schwartz has also taught courses in the decorative arts and acted as an advisor for state restoration projects in Alabama. He is the author of *American Furniture from Pilgrim to Chippendale* and collectors' guides to glass, ceramics, silver, and clocks. He has also co-authored *The New York Times Book of Antiques*, *History of American Porcelain*, and, most recently, *The Furniture of John Henry Belter and the Rococo Revival*. He also wrote a weekly column about antiques for *The New York Times* and presently is the New York editor of *Antique Monthly*.

Chun Y. Lai
Chun Y. Lai is a New York-based freelance photographer specializing in antiques and architecture. His photographs have been featured in many national magazines, including *Antiques*, and in *The Catalog of World Antiques*.

Robert Bishop
Director of the Museum of American Folk Art in New York City, consultant Robert Bishop is author of more than 30 books, among them *How To Know American Antique Furniture*. He established the first master's degree program in folk art studies at New York University. Dr. Bishop is on the editorial boards of *Art & Antiques*, *Horizon Magazine*, and *Antique Monthly*.

William C. Ketchum, Jr.
A member of the faculty of The New School for Social Research, consultant William C. Ketchum, Jr., is also a guest curator at the Museum of American Folk Art in New York City. Dr. Ketchum has written 17 books, including *The Catalog of American Antiques*, and is a contributing editor of *Antique Monthly*.

Preface

Since chairs and tables have always been the most common types of furniture and usually set the tone of the furnishings of an age, it is hardly surprising that they comprise one of the most popular fields of collecting. But even though everyone is familiar with these objects—whether antique or of more recent vintage—most people cannot evaluate them. This book is therefore designed to help readers identify and judge the wide range of American seating furniture—chairs, sofas, benches, and stools—as well as beds and tables found in antiques shops, flea markets, or even in their own homes.

American chairs and tables are both remarkably consistent in construction and diverse in appearance. Their design is characterized by boldness and clarity, exemplified in the most elaborate pieces as well as in plain country work and modern examples. The basic forms and construction of wooden chairs and tables have changed little from the 17th century to today—the period covered in this book. During these centuries, however, shifting tastes in decoration and proportions have resulted in pieces that are greatly varied in appearance. It is interesting to note that this variety parallels a similar diversity in ancient furniture: in Egypt, for instance, chairs also ranged from simple forms made of plain narrow boards to highly decorative examples with carved backs and animal legs.

This guide covers American furniture made primarily with the mortise-and-tenon technique: that is, chairs, sofas, stools, and other forms of seating as well as beds and tables. Since chairs are generally the best key to style and the most widely collected form, they are given the broadest coverage. A companion volume presents case, or storage, furniture—chests, cupboards, desks, and other forms—made with more complex cabinetry techniques.

Today American furniture of every type and period is collected by a growing number of people. In the past, connoisseurs would most often limit their collections to 17th- and 18th-century high-style furniture. While such pieces are still the most sought after, examples from the 19th and 20th centuries—from country and Victorian to Colonial Revival and Art Deco styles—are now avidly collected as well. Though not technically antiques, pieces from these later periods are nonetheless stocked by many antiques shops, with the hope and expectation that these will become the antiques of the future.

Each illustrated entry in this guide describes in detail a representative object; tells where, when, and of what materials it was made; identifies prevalent variations; and provides historical background along with practical hints on what to look for and what to avoid. These hints are summarized in a general essay on How to Recognize Authentic Pieces, which includes information on fakes, reproductions, and altered pieces.

The Price Guide in the back of the book lists current prices for all types of furniture illustrated. The high prices given for some pieces may be the result either of their rarity and fine construction or of their great popularity; on the other hand, low prices often provide clues to undervalued areas that may be worth investigating. This guide should help a collector make prudent selections in building a distinctive collection of American furniture.

A Simple Way to Identify Furniture

Although chairs, tables, and related forms are functional pieces, their designs are astonishingly varied, ranging from the traditional to the latest fashions, from simple to elaborate, and from original designs to revivals and reproductions. To help collectors identify style and period, we have chosen 347 representative examples for full picture-and-text coverage. The selection includes not only the most commonly available designs and styles, but also some rare examples necessary to an understanding of the development of American furniture. The color plates and accompanying text are organized in a visual sequence based on type (e.g., all chairs are grouped together) and shape (e.g., all slat-back chairs are together), so that beginning collectors can find a piece quickly without knowing its style, maker, or date. For collectors who may want to refer directly to entries in a particular style, we also give a List of Plates by Style.

Because it is impossible to illustrate every chair, sofa, bed, stool, and table design plus its variations, this guide is also designed to assist you in identifying pieces that are not shown. The illustrated introductory essay called American Furniture Styles provides background information to help identify any table or piece of seating furniture. In addition, a Checklist for Identifying Styles offers a quick way of ascertaining the distinctive features of a style. The illustrated Glossary defines special terms used in this guide. The following sections provide additional information for an understanding of chairs and other joinery forms: How to Recognize Authentic Pieces; Joinery Construction; and the Upholstery Guide. Using all these tools—photographs, descriptions, essays, illustrations, and charts—both the beginner and the connoisseur will find furniture collecting easier and, with a little luck, a rewarding pastime.

American Furniture Styles

This survey of American furniture styles describes the major changes in taste that have taken place over the past 350 years. It concentrates on high-style furniture—that is, pieces that followed the newest fashions and were the clearest expressions of them. Emphasis is given to joiners' works, such as chairs and tables, since their basically simple construction allowed them to be readily adapted to new styles.

Collectors should realize, however, that at any given moment high-style and traditional furnishings were produced simultaneously. The contrast between fashionable and so-called country works, which tended to be more conservative, partially explains this variety of styles. Since, in many cases, styles or their elements continued to be utilized long after they were fashionable, any given range of years for a particular style is somewhat arbitrary. For instance, when the Queen Anne style came into fashion about 1725, the William and Mary style was still often employed, and an even earlier form, the slat-back chair, also remained popular. Several styles sometimes coexisted in a house or room, or even in a single piece of furniture.

It is also important to remember that much American furniture, particularly during the first 200 years, was produced when craftsmen in this country were not leaders or innovators but talented followers and adaptors primarily of English styles. Over the centuries it took less and less time for these styles to travel across the Atlantic. American design during the Colonial era was as much as two generations behind fashionable English efforts. This lag was reduced in the 19th century at the same time that French influence became equally important, and the time lapse almost disappeared in the 20th century when various Continental trends were transmitted within a few years.

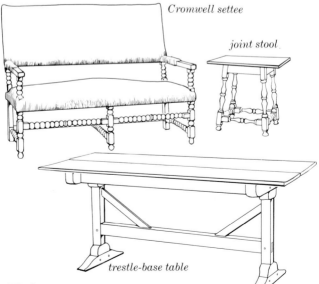

Cromwell settee

joint stool

trestle-base table

Pilgrim Style: 17th Century

The first style that became fashionable in the English settlements in America is popularly known as the Pilgrim style. It encompassed various designs derived chiefly from medieval, Renaissance, and 17th-century English models. It dates from about 1640 to 1690; earlier designs from the first half of the century have not been found. Furniture was massive, rectilinear, and sturdy. Oak was the predominant wood, and elements were relatively thick and turned on lathes, simple devices for rotating wood while it is cut with a chisel. Because the basic construction technique they used was the simple mortise-and-tenon joint, 17th-century craftsmen were called joiners.

Most early American homes had few chairs. Generally massive, and therefore called Great chairs, they were reserved for senior members of the household and important guests. Others sat on small joint stools, benches, or chests. Many chairs were made entirely of turned posts and spindles. They had rush seats and derived from medieval English designs. The simpler version is called a Carver chair, and the more complex type a Brewster chair, both named after founding fathers of Massachusetts. Massive slat-back chairs were a common variation of the turned-post form. The Wainscot chair, with its solid wooden back and simply turned columnar legs, was based on an Elizabethan model. Another early design is the Cromwell, or Farthingale, chair, which was upholstered either in needlework or leather, and on occasion was made into an elongated settee.

Tables varied greatly in size and shape. Trestle-base and gate-leg models were common. Another type has a rectangular top on turned legs joined by low stretchers; the skirt may have a drawer. Smaller tables also served as stools, while some larger ones with tilt tops doubled as chairs.

paneled cradle

gate-leg table

Wainscot chair

William and Mary Style: 1690–1725

Named after the king and queen of England, who reigned jointly from 1689 to 1694, the William and Mary style was introduced in America at the end of the 17th century as a New World version of the Baroque style that had swept Europe earlier in the century. Its elaborate decoration reflected a new taste for elegance. As in the Baroque style, classical motifs were interpreted inventively; this is seen most clearly in scroll, spiral, and columnar leg shapes as well as scroll, or Spanish, feet. Richly decorative surfaces, veneered or painted, became desirable, and thus walnut and maple replaced oak as major woods. Baluster, vase, ball, and ring turnings became more slender and crisp.

Chair designs reflect this style most dramatically. Chair elements became thinner and more highly embellished. Backs were tall and narrow, caned or upholstered in leather, or else fitted with split bannisters turned in classical vase shapes. Cresting rails were usually carved elaborately and set on elegantly turned stiles. Seats were most often made of cane or rush, or upholstered in leather. Though side chairs were more common, some examples had curved or molded arms. Wing, or easy, chairs as well as daybeds that were like chairs with extended seats were introduced in this period.

Elegant interiors included small tables that were new in form and function. Gate-leg tables, reduced in size at the start of the 18th century, seem to have been the most popular table form; their many sizes indicate they were used for various purposes. Another type of drop-leaf design was the butterfly table, named for the shape of its leaf supports. One form of table had canted legs; another variation, with a rectangular top and delicate proportions, is now commonly called a tavern table. Tea tables and dressing tables were also introduced.

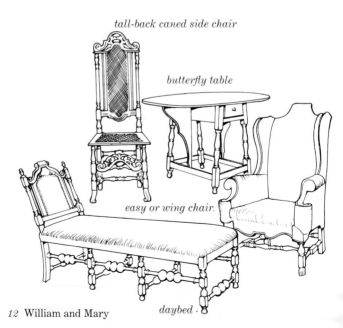

tall-back caned side chair

butterfly table

easy or wing chair.

daybed

Queen Anne Style: 1725–1750

For American furniture, the 18th century might be said to begin about 1725, when a radical shift took place to what is called the Queen Anne style (even though that ruler had died in 1714). As the restrained first phase of Rococo influence on 18th-century American design, the Queen Anne style was characterized by greater delicacy and sophistication than previous styles, as well as by elegantly curving forms and distinctive regional variations. Woods were richly finished and carved: walnut was most popular, along with cherry and maple; imported mahogany began to be favored toward 1750. Of great importance was the introduction of the cabriole leg. Whereas the turned William and Mary leg had a certain monumentality, the cabriole leg gave furniture a more human scale.

The chair is most representative of the new Queen Anne style. Besides cabriole legs, chairs had yoke-shaped top rails with down-curving ends, solid vase-shaped splats, and horseshoe-shaped seats, all curving yet restrained. This basic form is thought to have been an adaptation of a Chinese model. Delicate carved details included the popular shell motif.

Finely detailed candlestands and tea tables were common, often on tripod cabriole bases and sometimes with tilt tops to save space. The game table with a hinged folding top, and some forms related to dining, such as large drop-leaf tables and side or serving tables, were introduced.

Upholstered sofas and settees, relatively rare, evolved from earlier benches. Low-post beds were most common, but some beds had high posts and canopies.

It is difficult to date the Queen Anne style precisely since it sometimes blended with the William and Mary and, later, Chippendale styles. Some Queen Anne pieces, particularly rural examples, were executed close to the time of the Revolution.

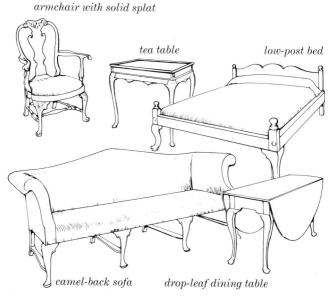

armchair with solid splat

tea table

low-post bed

camel-back sofa

drop-leaf dining table

Queen Anne

Chippendale Style: 1750–1780

Chippendale design, closely related to Queen Anne forms, was the second, more elaborate phase of the Rococo style in 18th-century America. Named for the London cabinetmaker Thomas Chippendale, who published *The Gentleman and Cabinet-Maker's Director* in 1754, the American version of the style was more conservative than its English counterpart, reflecting earlier 18th-century trends that were already out of style in London. Thus, the claw-and-ball foot, a popular feature of American Chippendale design, was too old-fashioned to be illustrated by Chippendale, whose designs were declared to be in the French, Gothic, and Chinese tastes.

Chippendale created a number of designs with cabriole legs, but generally ending in scroll feet. He also adopted straight-sided, or Marlborough, legs from Chinese models, as well as fretwork in a variety of Chinese and Gothic patterns. American Chippendale furniture, whether simple or elaborate, was much lighter in its proportions than Queen Anne designs. Forms did not change much but became more ornamental. Mahogany was the favored wood, though walnut, cherry, and maple were used for less costly pieces. Chairs had intricately carved pierced slats, yoke-shaped top rails ending in distinctive turned-up ears, stiles sometimes carved in foliate patterns, and straight-sided seats. Another popular Chippendale chair design was the ladder-back, with its series of scrolled horizontal slats.

Sofas, settees, and easy chairs had curving Rococo lines and rich imported upholstery. Tables were made in a greater range of sizes, shapes, and carved decoration than before. Tea tables and card tables were common, frequently having shaped tops. A new form was the drop-leaf Pembroke table.

The Queen Anne and Chippendale styles share many Rococo elements, such as the cabriole leg, so at times it is difficult to

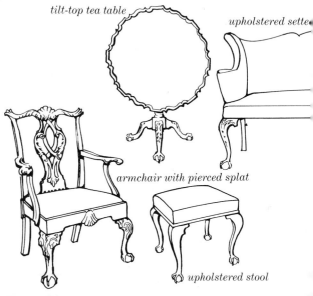

tilt-top tea table

upholstered settee

armchair with pierced splat

upholstered stool

distinguish between them. Restrained American designs were influenced not only by Chippendale's French-inspired Rococo decoration, but also by the classical trend most evident in England in the furniture of William Kent and the Palladian architecture of the early 18th century. Regional preferences became more apparent, despite the wide availability of design books: cabinetmakers from Newport, Rhode Island, for instance, were generally conservative and closely followed the classical style, using fluted and reeded columns and legs; at the other extreme, Philadelphia craftsmen produced the most elaborately carved Rococo pieces. New centers such as Charleston, South Carolina, also evolved distinctive versions of the style. Regional differences aside, American Chippendale furniture was consistent and elegant, not merely a provincial adaptation of its English namesake.

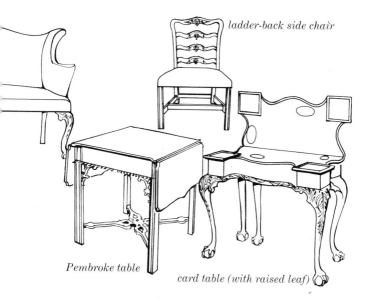

ladder-back side chair

Pembroke table

card table (with raised leaf)

Federal Style: 1780–1820

The Rococo style began to go out of fashion as the Revolution transformed the Colonies into a young republic during the Federal era. The Rococo was gradually overshadowed in the 1780s by Neoclassicism. Literally a renewal of classicism, the new style was a reaction to Rococo exuberance. The direct inspiration for this European style was the excavation of ancient monuments in Herculaneum, Pompeii, and elsewhere. By the 1770s Neoclassicism had become a dominant style in England and France. In England, the architects and designers Robert and James Adam introduced the new style.

Besides the use of ancient ornament, Neoclassicism was characterized by a delicacy of decoration and scale. Its simple geometric shapes were supported on characteristic tapered columnar legs. Classical decorative motifs such as the patera, bellflower, thunderbolt, sheaf of wheat, and vase of flowers were executed in low relief, veneers, inlays, or paint. In the American version, patriotic symbols often appeared as ornament, either painted, carved, or cast on hardware.

It is difficult to determine how much American cabinetmakers depended on the widely available design books of the period. Hepplewhite's *Cabinet-Maker and Upholsterer's Guide* (1788) and Sheraton's *Cabinet-Maker and Upholsterer's Drawing Book* (1791–94) are the best known, and although these were not the only design books, there has been a tendency to divide American furniture of the Federal era into Hepplewhite or Sheraton design. This incorrectly assumes that there are substantial differences between them.

In its second phase, Federal design gradually shifted as American furnituremakers followed newer approaches to classicism, including a more literal borrowing of Greco-Roman forms. It is not easy to discern whether the influence on

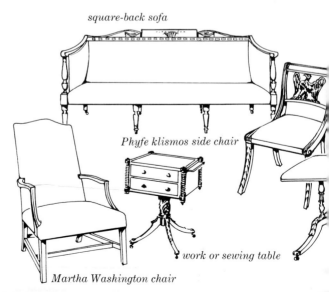

square-back sofa

Phyfe klismos side chair

work or sewing table

Martha Washington chair

American craftsmen came directly from France or from English sources based on French models. The main French influence came from furniture designs by Napoleon's architects, Charles Percier and Pierre Fontaine. Napoleon's official style was as Roman as the titles he adopted for himself—first "consul" and then "emperor." Napoleonic designs were plagiarized by English publishers, giving American craftsmen easy access to them. The American results were restrained versions equally influenced by English Regency-period furniture (1811–20).

An important factor in American Neoclassicism was the change in the way pieces were produced: designs were simpler and executed more quickly than ever before. New forms included the work (or sewing) table, used for storing small objects. As separate dining rooms became more common, makers developed tables for them, including large dining tables that could sometimes be extended or dismantled into smaller tables. Side tables were used both for serving and as decoration in halls and parlors. Shield-back, oval-back, and square-back chairs displayed a greater lightness than earlier designs and had either a center splat carved in a classical motif, such as the urn-and-feather, or a series of columns. Upholstered-back, or Martha Washington, chairs were also popular.

Chair designs after 1800 were heavier and based more closely on the ancient klismos model, with a thick curved top rail and usually a carved horizontal slat across the back. Sofa designs became more delicate and simple, with straight-topped or curved backs. The classical Grecian couch, as echoed in the French récamier, was popularly used as a daybed. The most stylish examples of American Neoclassicism were produced by Duncan Phyfe, who was influenced by Sheraton and later by classical French designs. American furniture of the late Federal period, continuing into the 1820s, overlapped with Empire designs.

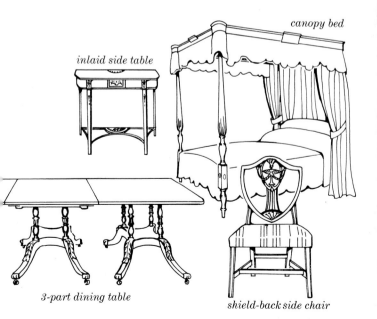

canopy bed

inlaid side table

3-part dining table

shield-back side chair

Empire Style: 1815–1840
Empire design, first introduced in Paris at the start of the 19th
century, did not become popular in America until about 1815.
The delicacy of the earlier Neoclassicism gave way to heavier
classical forms with more emphasis on outline than on carved
detail. As the style of the Napoleonic empire, it was a revival of
Roman (and Greek) forms that were adaptable to 19th-century
living. Roman-inspired symbols, furniture, and even hairdos
were part of an ambitious scheme to relate Napoleon to Emperor
Augustus as the French government was transformed from a
republic into an empire. Adopted in dozens of countries during
the first decades of the 19th century, Empire design did not go
completely out of fashion until mid-century.
The style, which was appropriate for furnishings for all classes of
society, could be well done whether its execution was very
elegant and costly or very plain and inexpensive. Empire
furnishings, with their undulating scrolls balancing heavy
geometric shapes, complemented the Greek Revival architecture
of the period. Ornament was carved in high relief; inlays were
abandoned in favor of stenciling and gilded brass or bronze
decoration. Other pieces were kept simple by omitting carving
and emphasizing overall line. Richly grained mahogany or
rosewood, veneers, and marble were common.
A French emigré, Charles-Honoré Lannuier, was one of the first
cabinetmakers to introduce the style in America. Working in
New York between 1803 and 1819, he combined belated Louis
XVI and early Empire designs. His gilded caryatids on tables
and chairs provided an elegance that had great appeal;
other cabinetmakers tempered this stylishness with great
restraint.
Inspiration for Empire forms was derived from ancient models
illustrated in a number of contemporary publications. Periodicals

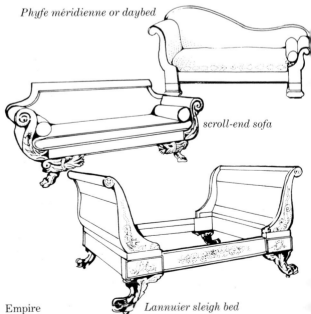

Phyfe méridienne or daybed

scroll-end sofa

Lannuier sleigh bed

and books printed in London provided such designs, some adapted or plagiarized from French sources, others based on the work of prominent English designers such as Thomas Hope. Klismos chairs, scroll-end sofas, ornamental center tables, sleigh beds, and récamiers and méridiennes (the last two being daybed forms) were all widely available in simple as well as elaborate models. While Duncan Phyfe's workshop produced restrained but elegant Empire designs in the 1820s and 1830s, more flamboyant pieces with lavishly carved details were executed in Philadelphia and Boston. Later American design books from the beginning of the Victorian period, such as those by John Hall of Baltimore (1840) and Robert Conner of New York (1842), still included Empire designs.

Because fashionable Empire furnishings were made at every price level, there was a significant democratization of fashion after 1820. By the 1830s, an expanding market had created a nationwide industry—based on machine production—that began to replace craftsmen's workshops. The output included simple veneered pieces as well as furniture for "cottage use," meaning painted furniture for modest homes. The public could also choose among such other popular pieces as Sheraton painted Fancy furniture, Windsor chairs, and a wide variety of country designs.

mirrored pier or console table

window seat

painted klismos side chair

marble-topped center table

Country Furniture: 1690–1850

"Country furniture" is the term used to describe most simple designs made between the late 17th and mid-19th centuries. The American equivalent of European provincial furniture, it combines fashionable and more conservative elements. Country furniture is so named because it was generally thought to have been made by rural artisans who simplified sophisticated urban designs to economize and to suit rural interiors. Recent research has shown, however, that some of it was made in cities: for example, William Savery, a Philadelphia cabinetmaker who produced some elegant Chippendale furniture, also made pieces that were country in spirit.

Decoration was minimized, so that pieces could be made easily and inexpensively. In spite of their limitations, country craftsmen worked with ingenuity and good taste. Painted surfaces were popular since pine and maple, the most common woods, needed protection, and painted colors were more appealing than the natural color of such woods. Country furniture often combined several styles. For instance, turned legs in the William and Mary style were used long after they had gone out of fashion; they were more easily crafted than cabriole legs, which are relatively rare on country pieces. Straight-sided legs were also popular. Solid splats were favored for Chippendale as well as Queen Anne chairs. Carved ornament was schematized, so that shell motifs were fanlike and fluting became a series of wide ridges. Windsor and slat-back chairs were common; the latter, a 17th-century form, persisted even into the 19th century, when Shaker craftsmen adapted it. Dating country work is difficult because little of it is documented. Country furniture was sometimes made at the same time as stylish urban versions of the same designs, but also as long as 50 years after fashions had changed.

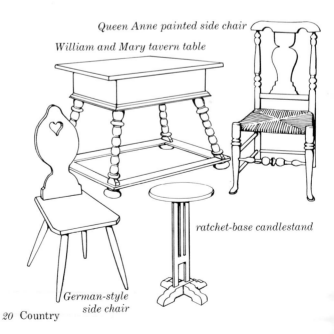

Queen Anne painted side chair

William and Mary tavern table

ratchet-base candlestand

German-style side chair

Shaker Furniture: 1790–1900

Shaker furniture is perhaps the finest type of country design. The Shakers, so named for the movements they made in their ritual dance, were a celibate religious sect living in rural communities in New York, Massachusetts, and half a dozen other states. These communities depended on agriculture and various craft industries. From the late 18th to the mid-19th century, Shaker craftsmen treated their work as part of their religious duties and created furniture designs as distinctive as the architecture, dress, and lifestyle of their society.

Simplicity and utility were hallmarks of this furniture: function governed form and all unnecessary ornament was omitted. Forms were based on simple 18th-century designs—Windsor and slat-back chairs, plain tables, benches, and low-post beds—as well as on some Sheraton designs. Furniture was made for domestic use and work; the seed industry, for instance, was a mainstay of Shaker communities, and tables for sorting seeds were popular. Pine and maple were the woods most commonly used; surfaces were unadorned, and turned elements were slender.

The heyday of Shaker furniture production lasted from about 1820 to 1870; except for chairs, production decreased after 1870. At first all pieces were used in their own community houses, but by mid-century more and more were made for public sale, partly because the shrinking membership of the sect made additional pieces unnecessary within the communities. Shaker population had declined drastically by 1900, and very little Shaker furniture has been made since then.

sewing table

slat-back side chair

bench

cradle

Shaker

Windsor Chairs: 1730–1830

One of the most popular of all American chairs is the Windsor. It originated in England early in the 18th century, and was first common around the town of Windsor. Beginning about 1730, American craftsmen developed their own distinctive versions. The classic models were made until about 1830, and mass-produced variations and reproductions of this enduring form have been produced ever since.

Windsors are all-wood chairs with interlocking parts that were delicately turned or simply cut. The back was made of turned or whittled spindles enclosed by a curving or straight rail. The solid seat was shaped to fit the body. Legs were turned, set at an angle, and reinforced by turned stretchers. Lightweight, comfortable, and sturdy, these chairs were also inexpensive and easy to make. One reason for their sturdiness was that parts were made of green wood, which later shrank until the joints were tight.

Colonial craftsmen, not content with English forms, created Windsors that varied greatly in the shape of the back, seat, and legs. Six basic models are generally distinguished: the low-back, or captain's, chair, with a flat semicircular top rail set on short spindles and doubling as an armrest; the hoop-back, a modification of the low-back with an arched addition topping the central portion; the comb-back, also based on the low-back, with a row of spindles extending well above the arm rail and fitting into a serpentine top rail; the fan-back, a side chair with a serpentine top rail like the comb-back, but no dividing arm rail, so that the back consists of long spindles flanked on each side by a heavier turned stile; the continuous-arm, with arms and arched top rail made from a single piece of bentwood, but no midrail; and the loop-back, a side chair with a sharply bowed back rail enclosing long spindles.

low-back or captain's chair

comb-back chair

loop-back chair with writing arm

Among other variations are the addition of writing arms or of angled braces behind the back. Legs were turned in a variety of shapes. The pattern of turnings and the thickness of legs are clues to the date and geographical origin of a chair. Vase-shaped turnings were used more often before the Revolution, and bamboo shapes afterward.

In the early 19th century many Windsors were made in chair factories. These often incorporated Sheraton-style elements such as a wide top rail; many were called arrow-back or rod-back Windsors, depending on the shape of their spindles. Models with a rectangular projection above a wide top rail are called step-down Windsors. Late 18th- and early 19th-century Windsor forms were also adapted for stools and settees.

Windsors were made of several woods so that the most suitable timber could be used for a particular purpose. Soft pine generally served for seats; strong and flexible hickory, ash, or birch was used for spindles and rails; solid maple was carved into legs. Since different woods had contrasting colors and grains, the chairs were usually painted solid green, red, black, yellow, or white; such paint also protected the wood.

Windsors captured a large market because of their simple grace and durability. Made and used throughout the Colonies, they were found in farmhouses and country homes as well as in city dwellings, and were used both indoors and outdoors. George Washington had a set on the porch of Mount Vernon that is still there, and in Philadelphia members of the Continental Congress sat in Windsors. Though tastes have changed, the popularity of the Windsor form remains almost undiminished.

settee

hoop-back chair

fan-back chair

loop-back chair

19th-Century Revival Styles: 1840–1900

To understand 19th-century furniture design, it is important to note the new character of its historical inspiration. While 18th-century makers often embellished their pieces with classical, Gothic, or even Oriental motifs, these details were used solely for ornamental purposes. However, beginning in the Federal and, in particular, Empire periods, designers were more intent on adapting ancient forms to modern needs and on evoking the civilization that had produced them. This general historic awareness was particularly important between 1840 and 1900, as designers turned to more than half a dozen earlier styles for inspiration.

This is usually called the Victorian period, after the long-reigning British queen who has become a symbol of the fashions and attitudes that prevailed during much of the 19th century on both sides of the Atlantic. The term "Victorian" may, however, cause some confusion, for although there was some consistency in the historical basis of design throughout that period, the revival styles varied markedly in their sources and in their fidelity to them.

Gothic Revival Style: 1840–1880

The Gothic Revival is the first of several mid-19th-century styles explicitly labeled "revival," and the most complex to explain, since it reflects two distinctive approaches. The first was purely decorative, with details garnered from historic ornament. The second and later approach was that of designers seeking simple and functional forms, following the aesthetic theories of William Morris, the English designer and social reformer who advocated straightforward furniture design in the medieval crafts tradition.

The renewed interest in Gothic furniture evident in England in the 1830s arose in America about 1840. American examples made

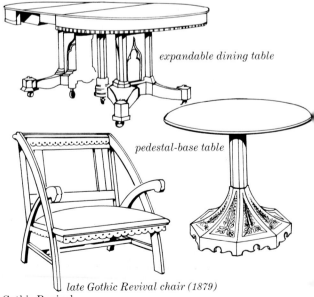

expandable dining table

pedestal-base table

late Gothic Revival chair (1879)

between 1840 and 1860 were embellished with tracery and other Gothic carving such as quatrefoils and trefoils; they were sometimes designed by architects and meant to be used in the Gothic Revival homes of the period. The rose window and pointed arch, for instance, became the basis of a number of designs for the tall backs of chairs. Because the Gothic style was so extravagant and fanciful, designers in the 1850s turned to congenial alternative styles, including Norman, Romanesque, and, most often, Elizabethan Revival.

The Gothic style was revived again in examples made in the 1870s. Though smaller in scale and more delicate in detail than the originals, these display a more authentic simplicity than do earlier 19th-century examples. Furthermore, at the turn of the century and into the early 20th century, a limited amount of Gothic-style furniture was produced that might actually be confused with genuine medieval work.

Furniture production in the 19th century was more often traditional than innovative, despite the increase in mechanization. During the first half of the century, however, production was somewhat simplified as pieces were deliberately designed to be more easily executed. Gothic Revival pieces, for example, had turned or cutout elements that were simply made. Bold details enhanced plain surfaces that were usually walnut, cherry, or oak, or sometimes mahogany or rosewood.

settee with 3-arch back

Elizabethan Revival side chair

armchair with tracery back

side chair with rose-window back

Rococo Revival Style: 1840–1870

The Rococo Revival style was not introduced in America until about 1840, though it was illustrated in earlier English design books. It became the dominant mid-century style and lasted through the 1860s. Referred to at that time as the Louis XIV style—though it is even closer to the Louis XV style—the 19th-century Rococo style is easily distinguished from its 18th-century counterpart by its boldness. Ornament was carved in higher relief and usually rendered more realistically than on 18th-century models, and the forms themselves are distinctly 19th-century in taste. The most notable American expression of the Rococo Revival style was the work of John Henry Belter of New York. His was one of several workshops using laminated wood for intricately carved Rococo forms.

Rosewood, mahogany, and walnut were the favored woods during the Rococo Revival. The style is characterized by richly carved ornament—roses, leaves, grapes, scrolls, and shells—on curving forms inspired by 18th-century French Rococo furniture. Craftsmen produced it all over America, but pieces from New York, Boston, and Philadelphia are the best documented. The style was most commonly used for parlor and bedroom furniture; elaborate parlor sets included sofas or settees, chairs, center tables, and accessory forms. Center and side tables often had marble tops and scalloped shapes. The tête-à-tête, or conversational sofa, was a popular new form. All furnishings were made in exaggerated curving shapes. Many chairs had balloon-shaped backs and, like most Rococo Revival pieces, cabriole legs. Upholstery, frequently tufted, became an important feature as concern for comfort grew and inner springs were perfected. The Rococo style was also popular for forms cast in iron and used outdoors.

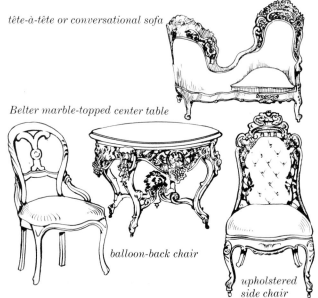

tête-à-tête or conversational sofa

Belter marble-topped center table

balloon-back chair

upholstered side chair

Renaissance Revival Styles: 1850–1880

The Renaissance Revival style is often considered a reaction to the Rococo, even though it was in use as early as 1850. It is characterized by an eclectic use of both Renaissance and 18th-century Neoclassical motifs on straight-lined forms loosely based on 16th-century French models. Porcelain, bronze, or mother-of-pearl plaques were popular embellishments on pieces with inscribed, linear classical motifs. Furniture from the 1870s ranged from works made in shops employing skilled craftsmen to the products of large midwestern factories. The New York shops, in particular, produced work with elegant detail and elaborate inlays, while the factories, centered primarily in Grand Rapids, manufactured pieces with turned and cut elements that could be produced more readily in volume and at lower cost. Since the Renaissance Revival style was based on rectangular shapes and prominent motifs, it could be successfully interpreted with either type of production.

Walnut was the most popular wood, with some veneer introduced as surface decoration. Light woods were favored in reaction to the prevailing dark woods of the Empire and Rococo Revival styles. Common motifs were flowers, fruit, cartouches, medallions, contoured panels, caryatids, scrolls, classical busts, and animal heads, as well as architectural elements, usually without any structural intent, such as pediments, columns, and balusters. Upholstery was prominently featured on chairs and sofas. Ornament from the then current Louis XVI Revival—popular with elegant New York cabinetmakers, who favored ebonizing and ormolu—was sometimes incorporated in the work of the 1860s. The Neo-Grec (or Neo-Greek) and Egyptian Revival styles were elaborate and exotic substyles of the Renaissance Revival.

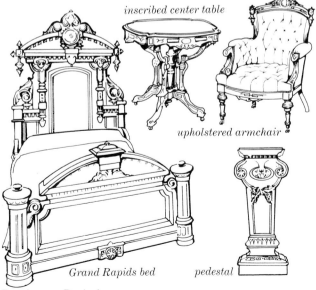

inscribed center table

upholstered armchair

Grand Rapids bed   *pedestal*

Renaissance Revival

Eastlake Style: 1870–1890
The Eastlake style was conceived in reaction to the excesses of the preceding historic revivals. Named for Charles Lock Eastlake, an influential English architect, author, and lecturer who advocated design reform, the style eventually encompassed much shoddy or overly elaborate American furniture that he would have abhorred. In his book *Hints on Household Taste* (1868; published in America in 1872), Eastlake decried the poor construction, overblown designs, and the ornate decoration of Victorian furniture. He called for a return to careful craftsmanship, honest use of materials, and reconsideration of the basic relationship between form and function. He emphasized bold 17th-century forms, sometimes combined with Renaissance and medieval borrowings, to produce simple sturdy furniture.

Because classical motifs had become overly familiar, new sources of ornament, particularly Middle Eastern and Far Eastern, were sought. Eastlake emphasized the beauty of wood grains, favoring oak and cherry, as well as rosewood or walnut if not obscured by dark varnish. In spite of his suggestions, however, many American furnituremakers used ebonized wood for Oriental decoration on otherwise essentially Eastlake pieces. Eastlake forms were strongly rectilinear and had geometric ornament, turnings, brackets, trestles, and incised linear decoration—all easily executed with machines. Eastlake designs were displayed at the Philadelphia Centennial Exhibition in 1876 and remained popular until about 1890. The first glimpses of modernism can be seen in Eastlake reforms and other reactions against the poor quality of Victorian design.

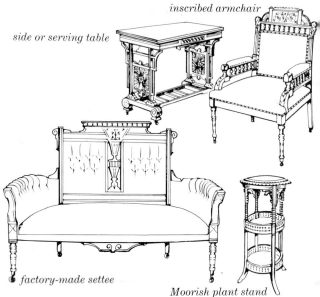

inscribed armchair

side or serving table

factory-made settee

Moorish plant stand

19th-Century Innovations: Patent Furniture, Wicker, Cast Iron, and Bentwood

One trend in 19th-century furniture design that does not easily fit into the sequence of stylistic evolution was the growing use of patented innovations and new materials. As early as the 1820s, patents were obtained for furniture that folded, swiveled, reclined, or converted into other forms. Another innovation was the platform rocking chair, which was able to rock in place. New construction techniques included the lamination process perfected by John Henry Belter.

Cast iron was used for components of some patented pieces as well as for outdoor furniture; the latter was produced in a variety of styles by the rapidly growing foundries around the country. By the 1850s iron inner springs were used to make upholstered seats more comfortable. Cushioned chairs and sofas with metal frames as well as tubular-brass beds were popular at the end of the century.

Wicker furniture—made of rattan, bamboo, willow, and various exotic materials—was imported from the Orient before 1840 and has been widely produced in America ever since. The most elaborate wicker designs were made in the last decades of the 19th century, when new machines were developed for weaving and shaping rattan and for bending wooden frames. Bentwood was another innovative furniture material, and imported pieces, made primarily in Austria-Hungary, became a staple of American homes. Other new materials for furniture included animal horns as well as bark-covered stumps and branches, all expressing the late 19th-century American yearning for rusticity and the wilderness.

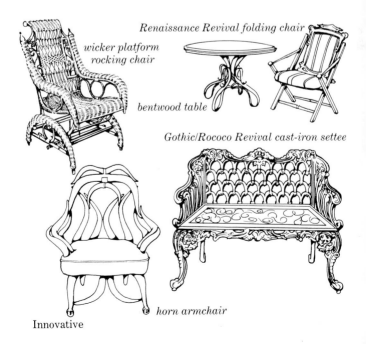

wicker platform rocking chair

Renaissance Revival folding chair

bentwood table

Gothic/Rococo Revival cast-iron settee

horn armchair

Innovative

Late 19th-Century Revival Styles: 1880–1900

Trends affecting furniture design in the 1880s and 1890s were complex. While the Eastlake approach was adopted by many makers, there was also renewed interest in styles of the past. Previous mid-century revival furniture, however, was dismissed as inauthentic by many designers and their patrons. Historic styles were now carefully studied and collecting antiques became a serious pursuit in America. Architects of the grandest homes of the era (in the so-called Beaux Arts style), inspired by Europe's more palatial buildings, designed or commissioned equally grand furnishings for their interiors, from Renaissance-style Savonarola chairs to Louis XVI-style beds and settees. This taste for period furniture inspired large manufacturers to produce faithful adaptations of European models as well as of American designs from the Pilgrim to Federal eras. Begun in the 1880s and peaking about 1920, this highly nationalistic re-creation of early American designs is known as the Colonial Revival.

Art Nouveau: 1895–1910

By the end of the century a new French movement, Art Nouveau, began influencing American furniture design. This style was characterized by fine traditional craftsmanship and sinuous, elongated forms. American designers were inspired to incorporate Art Nouveau relief ornament—whiplash curves, stylized flowers, and other organic forms—but rarely created entire designs in the style. Art Nouveau decoration sometimes appeared on furniture mass-produced in Grand Rapids, as well as on pieces by Arts and Crafts designers.

Mission, Arts and Crafts, and Colonial Revival Styles: 1900–1925

A more distinctive and influential tendency on the American scene at the beginning of the century was the Mission style. The

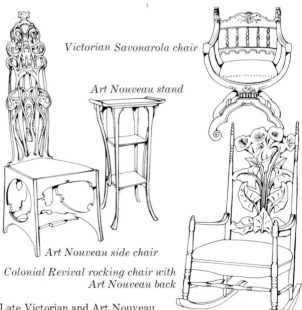

Victorian Savonarola chair

Art Nouveau stand

Art Nouveau side chair

Colonial Revival rocking chair with Art Nouveau back

style was originally associated with furniture supposedly housed in the old Franciscan missions of California. Seen as a revival of medieval and other primarily functional designs, the Mission style was the major American expression of the Arts and Crafts style that had evolved in England.

Oak was the favored wood and forms were rectilinear and as strictly functional as possible. Simple construction with obvious signs of handwork, such as exposed mortise-and-tenon joints, was a hallmark of the Mission style.

Chair and settee backs were usually constructed of a series of flat vertical or horizontal boards. The most important designs were by the furnituremaker Gustav Stickley, who was also the publisher of a magazine, *The Craftsman*, which popularized the new style. Stickley had some fine competitors, including several of his brothers. Much Mission-style work, obviously mass-produced, was not well designed. A special, more decorative group of pieces was made by artist-craftsmen belonging to the Arts and Crafts societies of the beginning of the century.

Another important trend was architect-designed furniture, such as that by Frank Lloyd Wright and by Charles and Henry Greene, which often combined Mission, Arts and Crafts, and sometimes even Art Nouveau elements.

Oak was also favored for the vast quantity of mass-produced furniture of the beginning of the century, particularly in Grand Rapids. Individual pieces were eclectic in style, with medieval, Renaissance, and 18th-century European features all combined in some designs. Other pieces, part of the continuing Colonial Revival that began in the 1880s, were based on American models from the 17th to early 19th centuries; this popular style persists in much of the furniture manufactured today. Accidentally or deliberately, Colonial designs were modified according to the tastes of any given decade.

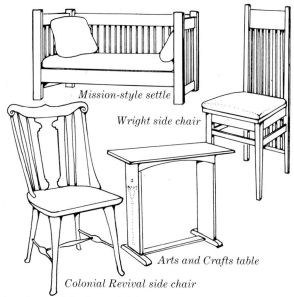

Mission-style settle

Wright side chair

Arts and Crafts table

Colonial Revival side chair

Mission, Arts and Crafts, and Colonial Revival

Art Deco and Modern Styles: 1925–1950

The modern movement in furniture design began in the late 19th century with the emergence of the Arts and Crafts movement in England and Art Nouveau in France. During the 1920s, two important decorative styles evolved, Bauhaus and Art Deco, which reflect, in part, radical innovations in painting and sculpture.

Art Deco was named for the influential Exposition Internationale des Arts Décoratifs et Industriels Modernes, held in Paris in 1925. Though it spread to other countries, Art Deco was a distinctively French response to the postwar demand for luxurious objects and fine craftsmanship. French designers utilized lavish materials and such rich, traditional decorative techniques as inlay and veneer on streamlined geometric forms. The style had a strong impact in America during the 1930s, but in a popularized version using less elegant materials and more dramatic forms. These designs often combined the sleek geometric shapes of French Art Deco with functional innovations and new materials such as the tubular steel that was an important part of Bauhaus design; such later variations are sometimes called Art Moderne.

The most advanced and inventive American Art Deco designs were developed by leading architects, interior decorators, and industrial designers. Large manufacturers and department stores helped acquaint the public with this streamlined style, which persisted in America well into the 1940s and was used for everything from overstuffed armchairs and sofas to kitchen and bedroom furnishings. One new form, the coffee, or cocktail, table, was usually lacquered or topped by blue mirrored glass, a distinctively American type of decoration.

The other important trend in 20th-century decorative arts derived from the Bauhaus, a school of art and design founded in

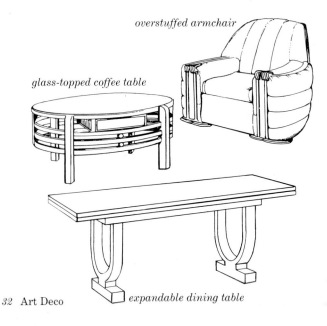

overstuffed armchair

glass-topped coffee table

expandable dining table

Germany in 1919. More innovative than Art Deco, Bauhaus design, also known as the International style, focused on new industrial materials, machine production, and severely functional forms totally unrelated to those of the past. Many of its finest designers, including Marcel Breuer and Ludwig Mies van der Rohe, emigrated to America when the rise of Hitler closed the Bauhaus, and their designs were particularly influential here. The tubular-steel chair with cantilevered seat became a symbol of the modern age, and was much imitated by American manufacturers.

Designers of the 1940s took Bauhaus design as a point of departure for their own innovative work. Epitomizing this approach were Charles Eames's revolutionary plywood or plastic chairs, molded to the shape of the human body. Because the innovations of Bauhaus design have become virtually synonymous with modern design, furniture in this style is called "modern" in this guide.

Bauhaus design was also influential in Denmark, Sweden, and Finland, where modernism was combined with a strong handicraft tradition and the designs of peasant furniture. The Scandinavian modern style was highly influential in America, where various designers and some commercial manufacturers adopted it.

Since 1945 another new movement in furniture design has developed. "Studio" furniture—so named because it is handmade in artists' studios—revives the traditional emphasis on handsome wooden surfaces and fine craftsmanship. Working in highly individualistic styles, artists have created forms that range from the traditional and practical to the inventive and, sometimes, amusingly fanciful.

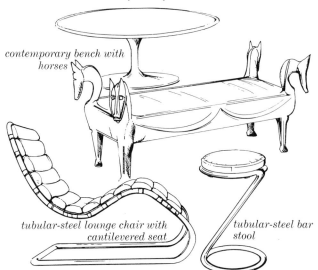

plastic pedestal-base table

contemporary bench with horses

tubular-steel lounge chair with cantilevered seat

tubular-steel bar stool

Modern

Parts of Furniture

Side Chair

yoke-shaped top rail

ea[r]

pierced splat

stile

lower rail

seat

seat rail or skirt

leg

stretcher

foot

Sofa

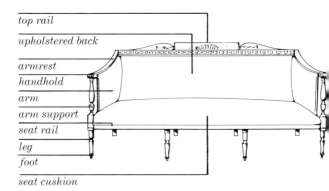

top rail

upholstered back

armrest

handhold

arm

arm support

seat rail

leg

foot

seat cushion

Table

top

leaf joint

leaf

skirt

leaf support

leg

stretcher

foot

pul[l]

drawe[r]

Upholstered Armchair

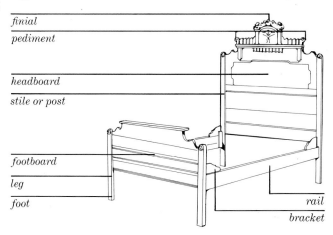

cresting

upholstered back

stile

handhold   arm

arm support

upholstered seat (over inner springs)

knee

leg

seat rail or skirt

caster

Pedestal-base Stand

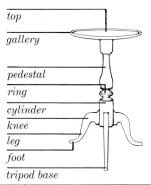

top

gallery

pedestal

ring

cylinder

knee

leg

foot

tripod base

Stool

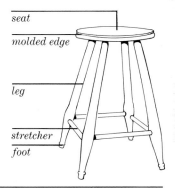

seat

molded edge

leg

stretcher

foot

Bed

finial

pediment

headboard

stile or post

footboard

leg

foot

rail

bracket

Feet and Turnings

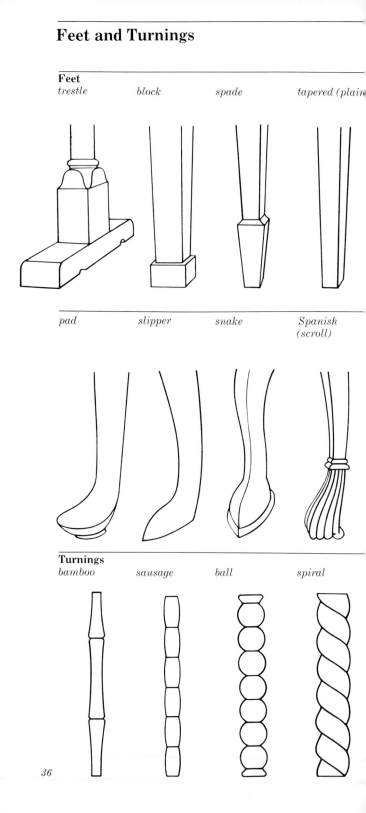

Feet

trestle *block* *spade* *tapered (plain)*

pad *slipper* *snake* *Spanish (scroll)*

Turnings

bamboo *sausage* *ball* *spiral*

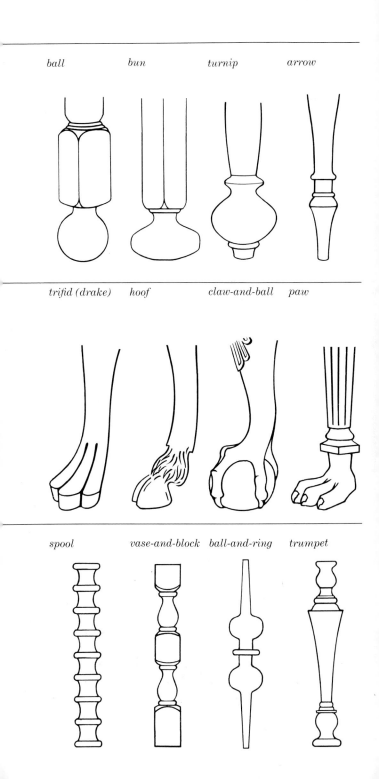

ball   *bun*   *turnip*   *arrow*

trifid (drake)   *hoof*   *claw-and-ball*   *paw*

spool   *vase-and-block*   *ball-and-ring*   *trumpet*

Joinery Construction

The construction of American chairs, tables, and related furniture has remained essentially consistent despite more than three centuries of radical changes in design. The methods have at times been simplified, made more sophisticated, or else speeded up by the introduction of new machines, but such modifications have had little effect on the basic techniques for interlocking the parts of a chair or table.

The Colonial Tradition

The mortise-and-tenon joint, used since ancient times and introduced in America by the first settlers, is the primary method for constructing wooden chairs, tables, sofas, beds, and related forms. Early craftsmen, who depended totally on this kind of joint, were called joiners. This versatile technique involves the joining of a horizontal element, generally a rail, to a vertical element, usually a stile. The end of one piece is cut into the shape of a thin rectangular projection, or tenon, that fits into a corresponding hole, or mortise, chiseled into the other piece. In the Colonial period, mortise-and-tenon joints were most often pinned together with wooden pegs for added strength, while nails or glue became more common for the reinforcement of joints in the 19th and 20th centuries.

Beginning in the Pilgrim period, many American chairs and tables had turned stiles and rails connected by mortise-and-tenon joints. These parts were turned on a lathe, a device for rotating a piece of wood while various cutting tools are applied to it. Turning as well as sawing, planing, and finishing wood were all done by hand in the 17th and 18th centuries. Carved forms were fashioned from thick pieces of wood or were produced by applying shaped pieces to complete a curved contour. An early type of bentwood, used for the looped back rails of Windsor chairs, was made by steaming and soaking pliable woods such as hickory, ash, or birch and bending them into shape. Dovetail joints—connecting two pieces of wood by means of a row of interlocking toothlike projections—were employed primarily on chests and other storage furniture, as well as on the drawers and pedestal bases of many tables.

The introduction of the curved cabriole leg with the Queen Anne style radically altered the appearance of American furniture, particularly chairs, but not the basic construction. Gracefully curved legs, rails, and stiles, however, required skillful carving. Moreover, while earlier seats were made of woven rush or splint, Queen Anne seats were usually stuffed with horsehair and upholstered over the seat rails, or upholstered over a separate frame that was slipped within the rails. These seats were supported by reinforcements such as corner blocks or an entire inner frame. The vase-shaped back splats of Queen Anne and Chippendale chairs were grooved into the top rail and set into a special "shoe" added to the back of the rear seat rail. It is often difficult to locate the joinings on more sophisticated furniture produced after about 1725, because such pieces became more elaborate and decorative, and signs of construction were carefully camouflaged.

Wrought-iron nails, screws, and hardware were infrequently used on Colonial joiners' work, with the following exceptions: nails to attach upholstery to chairs and sofas; screws (concealed by colored beeswax) to connect arms to chair and sofa frames; and screws for securing most tabletops to bases or legs, for attaching knobs, and for holding the hinges of drop leaves or swinging supports. Brass pulls, usually consisting of a back plate and bail handle, were used on table drawers.

Table construction departed from the mortise-and-tenon technique when a table's function required an additional element, such as drawers, that needed dovetail construction. Drop leaves were supported by a variety of devices: small boards that pulled out horizontally from the skirt; gate legs or swing legs (sometimes a fifth leg on card tables); or hinged butterfly-wing supports. Such leaves required metal hinges, and the supports needed special joints that would allow them to swing out. Tilt tops also required metal or wooden hinges; some tilt tops, set on a small square box called a birdcage, could be rotated when horizontal. Tilt-top and other small 18th-century tables usually had carved pedestal bases into which three legs were dovetailed.

19th-century Innovations

Throughout the 19th century, traditional furnituremaking techniques were mechanized to speed production and reduce the responsibilities of individual workmen. Machines to make mortises, tenons, and dovetails in quantity were among the devices that increasingly standardized the details of factory furniture as the century progressed. Dowels—round pegs glued into holes within two pieces of wood that were to be joined— were sometimes used on less expensive furniture because they were a cheap and easy, though weaker, method of joinery. The major shift, however, was in design and machinery rather than in basic construction. Beginning in the Federal period, designs were simplified; geometric shapes, straight-sided legs, and flat decoration instead of carving all led to easier production.

The one important structural change involved upholstered seats. About 1830, for greater comfort, iron inner springs began to be added to seats and to some upholstered backrests as well as bed mattresses. Used increasingly ever since, inner springs affected the overall design of chairs and sofas, which took on an overstuffed appearance. At about the same time, a change occurred in dining tables: new kinds of wooden or metal mechanisms were devised to enlarge their top surfaces. One Empire form, for instance, had a columnar base that split in half so that leaves could be inserted in the top. Later in the century, some tables included a spring mechanism that allowed a board to pop up into place when the top divided.

Furniture production during the last century varied from factory to factory and from decade to decade. In general, the manufacturing process was shortened as mass production developed; however, few details of these changes have been recorded. Many patents were granted for a variety of machines to facilitate production, but it is difficult to tell how much these machines were actually used. In 1860, a published description of one major furniture factory reported that more than 80 machines were in use there "for turning, sawing, planing, jointing, mortising, tenoning, and boring, besides machines for a variety of miscellaneous uses." Machines were also used to produce molding, flat carving, linear decoration, and simple inlay, generally in regular patterns. Toward the end of the 19th century, machine-made nails and screws were increasingly used in inexpensive furniture.

A major innovation was the laminated wood technique used during the Rococo Revival by a number of makers, most notably John Henry Belter, who perfected this process. Laminated wooden backs often replaced the conventional stiles and rails; a thin solid back, pressed into shape, was attached to a chair or sofa. Though used initially for elegant pieces, laminated wood was revived later in the century in the form of plywood utilized for inexpensive furniture.

The general trends in 19th-century furniture production did not always apply to cabinetmakers who worked in small traditional shops. Yet even many of these craftsmen modified traditional techniques to simplify their work. Thus, although some Colonial Revival designs from just after the turn of the century were faithfully executed in the 18th-century manner, others were carried out with such shortcuts as metal braces and applied or machine-made ornament. This range of traditional and mechanized production techniques is also clearly evident in Mission-style furniture, made either largely by hand (following the approach of the Arts and Crafts movement) or else by machine.

Construction methods varied greatly for Art Deco and modern furniture, which for the most part benefited aesthetically from an industrial or machine-made look. Some craftsmen still worked in small shops, particularly in New York, and continued to utilize many traditional procedures. But most pieces were made in large factories, where time-saving mechanical devices were used extensively on middle- and lower-priced furniture, but much less on pieces of the finest quality. Innovative materials required special production techniques: for instance, plywood was produced by a mechanized laminating process; tubular metal was soldered or welded in metalworking shops or factories; and after the Second World War, molded plastic and fiberglass were produced for furniture by factories specializing in those materials.

How to Recognize Authentic Pieces

To determine the authenticity of a piece of antique furniture, a collector must examine a variety of details. To gain the necessary background, the novice should begin by studying the pieces illustrated in this guide as well as those in museums. Essential is a knowledge of the basic lines, proportions, and distinctive components of a particular style, all of which are covered in the essay on American Furniture Styles and in the Checklist for Identifying Styles.

Caution should be balanced with openmindedness; the latter is vital, since an unusual and even exciting variation, though authentic, may put off the overly cautious collector. There are exceptions to every rule in judging furniture, and an unusual detail may prove acceptable if it is not anachronistic and if the other elements of the piece are consistent with the basic style.

Reproductions
The manufacture of reproductions has been a legitimate business for about a century. They are generally easy to recognize. The authentic lines and proportions characteristic of each period have rarely been duplicated convincingly. Modern construction techniques and inaccurate or poorly executed details also reveal a reproduction. A handsome gate-leg table, for instance, may look impressive until you notice that its turned legs are a bit too thin, the edges of its top too plain, and the feet insufficiently worn, telling you that it is actually a 1920s reproduction rather than the early 18th-century piece it appeared to be. On the other hand, many reproductions, particularly Colonial Revival examples, have a charm of their own once they are recognized as reproductions.

Fakes
Most fakes are harder to detect as they are intended to deceive through feigned signs of age and concealed evidence of their recent manufacture. Rare and valuable pieces are most often faked; 19th- and 20th-century designs attract fakers much less frequently. Except for some extremely well-made examples, most fakes display a telltale inconsistency or other indication of recent manufacture. Even a maker's label can be faked by using an advertisement from an old newspaper (the signs of this trick are the printing on the reverse and the small-size type), while other "old labels" have been fabricated in other ways.

Altered pieces
Far more common than outright fakes, altered pieces of furniture range from those that have been honestly repaired or restored to those deliberately altered to enhance their value. Restoration can be so extensive that a piece may hardly qualify as an antique anymore. If repairs are minor and well done, an object need not be rejected, but its value will probably be lower. Pieces may also be altered to suit contemporary tastes: for instance, bed rails may be shortened or lengthened to make a bed more salable; and large dining tables and canopy beds may be cut down. Since carving, inlay, or other decoration tends to increase the value of a piece, these have sometimes been added later. Such decoration is generally less skillfully done than that on original pieces, but it may be difficult to detect if added early on.

Other examples of altered pieces are those that have been "married"—that is, assembled with antique parts from other pieces. Since all the parts, in such cases, will have the plausible signs of age, the indications of fakery will be inconsistencies in woods, construction techniques, and decorative details.

Reproductions, fakes, and altered pieces are among the serious pitfalls in collecting antique furniture, but with experience a collector should be able to detect the deficiencies in such pieces. Close and continued scrutiny, using eyes and hands, will disclose the telltale signs of problems. The details to be examined when evaluating the authenticity of a piece of furniture are woods, construction and execution, tool marks, screws and nails, patina, and signs of wear.

Woods
The kinds of wood used in a piece of furniture are a valuable clue to its authenticity and geographical origin, since wood is a prominent aspect of style and period taste. Most furniture has primary and secondary woods, the latter being used for bracing and unseen structural parts.
Certain woods were commonly used for each style and, though there are exceptions, the presence of an unusual wood should make you cautious. (The Checklist for Identifying Styles includes the major woods favored for each style.) Though some kinds of furniture, particularly Windsor chairs and painted furniture, combined several woods throughout, the presence of different woods or wood textures usually indicates that some parts are replacements.
Secondary woods can be a clue to the national origin of a 17th- or 18th-century piece, since inexpensive local softwoods were then used for concealed elements. Secondary woods thus help to distinguish early American pieces from their European counterparts: oak, for instance, was used frequently by English and Continental furnituremakers, but rarely by American craftsmen.
In addition, certain secondary woods help to establish a specific geographical origin of a piece because they are associated with a particular American city or region.
Unfortunately, some secondary woods may at times be difficult to identify unless examined in a laboratory. Also, secondary woods are of little help in identifying later 19th- and 20th-century furniture, since by the 1830s pine had largely replaced the variety of local secondary woods in major furnituremaking centers around the country.

Construction and Execution
Since craftsmen of any given period utilized fairly standard procedures, the construction techniques, decoration, tool marks, and screws and nails provide some of the clearest means of dating and authenticating a piece.

Joinings
Early mortise-and-tenon joints, which were cut and chiseled by hand, are therefore more irregular than later machine-made examples. Tenons were relatively large, precisely fitted into the mortise holes, and usually pinned with pegs for added strength.
After 1800, glue was generally used instead of pegs; this was a gelatinous animal or vegetable glue, which is usually less visible than is the synthetic white glue developed in the 20th century.
Early dovetail joints have larger teeth than the tiny, evenly spaced machine-cut joints of the 19th and 20th centuries.
42 Visible scribe marks, made with awls to measure and lay out bot

dovetail and mortise-and-tenon joints, are another indication of early handiwork.

Turnings

The turnings on 17th- and 18th-century furniture tend to vary subtly in detail, so that no two hand-turned elements are exactly alike. Later examples made on machine-powered lathes are crisper, often smaller in scale, and more regular in pattern.

Carving

Carving should be deep on 17th- and 18th-century furniture, since thick wood, from which areas were cut away, was employed. Flat carving on a Chippendale piece, for instance, may indicate that it was added later to increase the desirability of the piece.

Recent carving tends to be either too simplified or else too complex in detail.

The claw-and-ball feet found on Chippendale furniture reveal the difference between authentic and reproduced or faked carving. Genuine 18th-century American feet are modeled on a bird's or a dragon's claw, but imaginatively simplified, whereas Colonial Revival examples from the early 20th century are more stiffly schematic, lacking the vitality of the originals.

The carving on claw-and-ball feet also conveys the difference between American and English work: the English carved claw is rendered more faithfully and realistically.

Handmade moldings, reeding, and fluting appear uneven in comparison with those made by machines, particularly when viewed down the length of the ridges.

Tool Marks

The smooth surface produced by a rotary plane and the curving marks made by a circular saw are signs of reproductions or alterations made after 1830 when found on furniture that would appear to to have been made before that date.

Plane Marks

Since early craftsmen planed by hand, a slight unevenness or slight ridges should be visible on planed surfaces. This is most apparent on unfinished surfaces such as the undersides of tabletops or of chair or settee seats. This unevenness can also be discerned on some finished surfaces when light strikes them at the proper angle. If you pass your hand over the surface, you will feel subtle undulations; later pieces were made perfectly smooth by power-driven rotary planes.

Saw Marks

Saw marks, found on undersurfaces that have not been planed smooth, provide another dating clue. Early saw marks are straight and parallel. The rotary circular saw, which became common about 1830, left curved marks that are a sure sign of post-Federal work.

Because they were often hand-sawed, early boards generally vary slightly in width or thickness. Since wood was plentiful during the Colonial period, tabletops and other large flat surfaces were often made of a single plank, sometimes as much as a yard wide. Tops made from narrower boards (under 20″) may indicate later work.

Screws, Nails, and Hinges

Screws, nails, and other hardware—made by hand of wrought iron before about 1800—are not common on joiners' work such as chairs and tables but, when found, provide important clues to the date of a piece.

Nails
Early nails have squarish, unevenly tapered shanks and large, imperfectly rounded heads. Machine-cut nails, used from about 1810 to 1870, have a rectangular, unhammered body tapering only on two sides, so that their flat tip is as wide as the head. Machine-made steel-wire nails, with the familiar round head and body, were not perfected until the 1880s, but then supplanted earlier types.

Screws
17th- and 18th-century screws had an uneven spiral thread, blunt end, and only a slight taper. Machine-cut screws, used in the first half of the 19th century, had a more even thread and a round head. Modern screws, recognizable by their uniform thread and pointed end, became common after 1850.

Screws and nails were concealed by colored beeswax in the 18th century and by wooden plugs in the 19th century.

Modern screws or nails may indicate that a piece was made after the mid-19th century, or that the element they attach is a replacement.

Hinges
Screws or nails securing a hinge are more likely to have been replaced than those with a structural function.

If additional screw or nail holes are found near a hinge, the hinge or the element it holds, such as a drop leaf, may be a replacement.

Early iron or brass hinges, compared with machine-made hardware, have rough surfaces and imperfect outlines.

Patina and Signs of Age
Antique furniture displays subtle as well as highly visible signs of age from years of use and exposure to air. Patina, worn surfaces, and shrinkage are primary indications of authenticity.

Patina and Paint
The soft mellow look — or patina — that finished wood acquires from years of polishing and gentle friction is highly desirable on antique furniture and impossible to reproduce exactly, since no dye or stain can duplicate it. Its darkened tone varies from the orange-brown of walnut to the golden honey of maple.

Unfinished woods acquire their own special complexion from age. From exposure to air and dirt, woods on the undersides of tables or drawers develop a smoky gray color that cannot be accurately duplicated, though fakers sometimes try to create this darkening by painting new wood with a uniform gray wash.

The original paint found on much country furniture, Windsors, and Sheraton Fancy chairs also acquires a look of age. The overall color darkens, and gilded or stenciled touches become more subdued. Old paint frequently becomes brittle and crazed from the evaporation of its natural oils; new paint is more flexible and can be scraped off more easily. The crackled look of old paint is sometimes faked, but simulated cracks are generally larger and more widely spaced.

If the stain on one element differs in color from that on the rest
of the piece, this may indicate that the element is a replacement.

although varied hues can simply result from the distinctive grains of different pieces of wood.

Signs of Wear

Authentic signs of wear, another proof of age, normally range from minor scratches on fine, carefully preserved pieces to gouges and chips on heavily used pieces.

Wear should not be uniform throughout a piece, but rather most evident on those areas most handled and exposed to damage.

On tables, tops become scored and slightly warped, and their edges and corners become rounded or bruised. Table legs will be worn from contact with shoes and chairs, and their feet may be completely worn away.

Chairs and other seating show some of the same signs of wear as tables. Top rails, backrests, arms, and handholds are particularly prone to wear. The upper surfaces of stretchers should be well worn from shoes that have rested on them. Carving will be smoothed or possibly chipped on its raised surfaces and edges.

Most fakes have artificial signs of wear, created with anything from sandpaper to chains; such damage generally looks freshly made or is unconvincingly distributed.

Wormholes

Although undesirable, wormholes are usually interpreted as a sign of old age. However, they may have been made recently, either by worms or with a drill. Fake holes are generally straighter than the meandering pathways created naturally by worms. Wormholes are rarer on American pieces than on European furniture. In some humid areas of New England, however, worm damage was more common.

Shrinkage

Another indicator of age in furniture is shrinkage, since over the decades wood contracts across the grain. A circular tabletop, for instance, will eventually become somewhat oval and as much as half an inch longer in the direction of the grain. Similarly, round legs or stiles will become oval in cross section.

Another result of shrinkage is the cracking, or sometimes buckling, of veneer because of the contracting of the base wood to which it is glued, as seen, for example, in the veneered tabletop on the cover of this guide.

How to Use This Guide

Successful collectors of American furniture rely on a combination of related skills: a knowledge of the major styles and periods, an understanding of how furniture is made, and an awareness of current marketplace activity. The simple steps outlined below should enable you to identify, date, and evaluate the pieces you find at antiques shops, auctions, flea markets, yard sales, and perhaps even in your own attic.

Preparation
1. Turn to the Visual Key (pp. 50–55) to become familiar with the way pieces of furniture in this guide are organized. There are 11 basic groups, including 4 groups each of chairs and tables, the most widely produced and collected forms of furniture.
Elongated seating forms such as sofas, settees, daybeds, and benches comprise another section. Beds and cradles form another group, as do stools.
2. Become acquainted with the brief essays preceding each group, which discuss the history of the forms illustrated and provide basic collecting hints.
3. Consult Information-at-a-Glance (p. 48) for an explanation of the separate headings used in the entries and the type of information given under each.

Using the Color Plates to Identify Your Piece
1. Find the symbol in the Visual Key that most resembles the piece of furniture you wish to identify. Then turn to the entry numbers listed above it.
2. Continue the visual comparison by narrowing your choice to a single color plate. The title of the entry identifies the style. Then read the Description, Materials, and Dimensions pertaining to the object illustrated. If your piece does not match it exactly, read the Variations section within the description as well as the rest of the entry to see if your piece is a common variation. Remember that almost any chair shown may have variants with or without arms, rockers, stretchers, or a given seat material; since these are optional elements, they are not listed as variations. The remainder of the entry tells when and where the piece was made, and provides a historical note on the type as well as hints on what to look for and what to avoid.
3. Look in the Price Guide under the entry number for the market value of this type of piece.
4. Be sure to read the section How to Recognize Authentic Pieces (pp. 41–45) for ways to identify fakes, reproductions, and altered pieces.

Using the Style Checklist as a Guide
If you do not find an illustrated example or a listed variation that roughly matches your piece, try to identify its style and use this information to evaluate your example.
1. Turn to the color plate that most closely resembles your piece and note its style. Then refer to the Checklist for Identifying Styles (pp. 426–429) to see whether the characteristic elements, woods, proportions, and decoration of that style match those of your example. To double-check this identification, turn to the essay entitled American Furniture Styles (pp. 10–33) and read the section on the appropriate style to see whether its description or illustrations apply to your piece.
2. Then refer to the List of Plates by Style (pp. 430–431) or the Index to find other objects in this style. Turn to all of the plates listed, including those of other types of furniture. For instance, if you are trying to identify a Federal sofa, examine Federal chairs

or other forms of seating as well; you may find a chair closer to it in style than any of the sofas illustrated. You may then be able to use the information in this chair entry to identify your sofa. Once you find the illustrated piece (or pieces) that looks most like your object, read the Description and Comment; these will tell you which elements of the example illustrated are most important to its identification and value. If your piece also displays these elements, refer to the Price Guide for the value of this related piece. You may have to adjust this price, since it is for a different type of furniture and some types are less common and thus more valuable than others. The essays in the Price Guide give you general guidelines that will help you estimate the value of your piece accordingly.

3. If your piece has a maker's mark, check the Index for an illustrated object bearing this maker's name; the Description and Comment concerning it may apply to your piece, and the price range may help you to estimate its value.

Developing Your Expertise

1. Begin by reading the essay on American Furniture Styles. The major styles are illustrated with drawings of representative pieces, making it easy for you to recognize those elements characteristic of each style and to see how the styles are related and how they differ. In addition, the Checklist for Identifying Styles summarizes the most important features of each.

2. Familiarize yourself with the basic terminology used in this guide. The illustrated glossary defines important terms, and drawings in the section on Parts of Furniture picture typical elements of chairs, sofas, stools, beds, and tables.

3. Become acquainted with construction techniques by reading the sections on Joinery Construction and How to Recognize Authentic Pieces. These will help you detect alterations, reproductions, and outright fakes.

4. If you are especially interested in the furniture of a particular period, turn to the List of Plates by Style, which includes all the pieces in this guide.

5. Visit museums. Being familiar with the very best examples will help you to develop connoisseurship, that is, a sense of style, a practiced eye, and the ability to distinguish exceptional from commonplace pieces. To find the collections near you, check the section on Public Collections (pp. 438–439).

6. Consult the Bibliography for books on the period or types of furniture that most interest you.

7. Read the section on Where to Buy Antique Furniture (pp. 453–455), which describes the major sources of antiques and explains how to buy at auction.

Information-at-a-Glance

Each numbered entry in this guide consists of a color plate and a descriptive text giving the facts needed for identifying the piece. The entry title gives the style and furniture type of the object pictured. The entry number is repeated in the Price Guide and in cross references throughout the book.

Description
The description covers the elements and decorative details of the particular object, starting at the top and continuing down to the legs and feet. (Technical terms are defined in the Glossary, and the most common are also illustrated in the Parts of Furniture section.) In the description, a section called Variations notes commonly occurring differences in shape and decoration. Construction is not described unless it is unusual; the construction techniques used for most of the furniture in this guide are explained in the essay on Joinery Construction. Throughout the descriptions and other parts of the entries, there are nontechnical terms that have special meaning when applied to furniture. "Light proportions" means that the parts of an object are relatively slender or delicate; "heavy proportions" indicates that the parts are relatively thick, making the piece look bulky. Pieces in any given style may have decoration that ranges from simple to complex; "restrained" describes decoration that is limited, subdued, or moderated; "elaborate" characterizes decoration that is generous, detailed, or possibly ornate for the style.

Materials and Dimensions
This section lists the woods, type of upholstery, applied decoration, paint, and other materials used in the object shown. Primary woods are listed first, followed by secondary woods used for concealed elements. Dimensions are given specifically for the object illustrated. They are measured in inches and at the widest or tallest point, and are given for height, length, and depth (or width for beds), with the following exception: chair dimensions are of overall height and seat height, the latter being measured to the top of the seat rail or seat upholstery, whichever is higher. Since virtually no two handmade pieces, even those by the same maker, have exactly the same measurements, the dimensions given here should be used only as a general guide.

Locality and Period
This category indicates where the example shown was made and its approximate date of manufacture. The maker, manufacturer, or designer, if known, is also given. Although a specific maker and locality may be listed, variations were probably made by other craftsmen in other areas. The phrase "throughout the United States" means that the type of object illustrated might have been made in any of the cities or areas that were furnituremaking centers during that period. For a piece made before 1850, such centers were located east of the Mississippi.

Comment
This section discusses the history of the type of object shown and how it may be identified. It may also give the origin of its name or additional information about the maker, locality, or dating.

Hints for Collectors
Here are collecting tips such as how to evaluate the type of furniture illustrated, what labels to look for, telltale signs that distinguish authentic pieces from fakes, reproductions, or
revivals, and advice on buying and maintaining such a piece.

Chairs, Tables, Sofas & Beds

Visual Key

The furniture in this guide is divided into 11 groups. For each, a symbol appears at left, along with descriptions of the types of pieces within that group. Symbols of pieces representing subgroups are shown at right, with plate numbers indicated above them. The group symbol is repeated on the opening page of the section concerning those pieces and in the Price Guide.

Slat-back and Spindle-back Chairs (*Plates 1–42*)
These simple traditional chairs have horizontal slats or vertical spindles on their backs. Generally of rural origin, they include some of the earliest American chair forms. The 4 subgroups are, from left to right: 1) slat-backs, such as early country, Shaker, Mission-style, and Sheraton painted Fancy chairs; 2) spindle-backs with flat top rails, such as Windsor, bannister-back, Carver, and Brewster chairs; 3) spindle-back Windsors with curved top rails; 4) low spindle-backs, including Windsor, Shaker, and country corner chairs.

Splat-back, Shield-back, and Related Chairs (*Plates 43–82*)
This group includes fashionable chairs with carved splats, shields, and other back designs that date primarily from the 18th and early 19th centuries. The 4 subgroups are, from left to right: 1) chairs with horizontal, vertical, or diagonal slats, including Federal square-backs, Empire balloon-backs, and klismos chairs; 2) chairs with solid splats, mostly Queen Anne; 3) chairs with pierced splats, mostly Chippendale; 4) Federal chairs with shield backs.

Wicker, Bentwood, and Metal Chairs (*Plates 83–105*)
Here are chairs made of innovative materials—wicker, bentwood, and metal—that became popular in the 19th century. The 4 subgroups are, from left to right: 1) bentwood chairs; 2) wicker chairs, including bamboo and China Trade examples; 3) 19th-century iron chairs, including rocking, folding, and cast-iron examples; 4) simpler metal chairs, primarily 20th-century.

Upholstered-back and Related Wooden-back Chairs
(*Plates 106–159*)
This section includes not only upholstered-back chairs but also stylish wooden-back examples related to them. The 4 subgroups are, from left to right: 1) wooden-back chairs, from the Pilgrim era to modern times; 2) chairs with rectangular upholstered backs, primarily 19th-century; 3) chairs with curved upholstered backs, primarily 19th-century; 4) fully upholstered easy chairs or armchairs, from Queen Anne to Art Deco.

How the Color Plates Are Organized

Chairs are organized in 4 sections according to the shape of their backs, their most prominent and significant feature. Elements such as arms, rockers, stretchers, and various seat materials do not affect the group arrangements. Tables are also organized in 4 sections—arranged first by function and second by shape, so that tables of widely differing design and size are often put in the same category if serving the same function. Sofas, settees, daybeds, and benches are gathered in one section. Beds and cradles also form a single group, as do stools.

| *1–12, 39–42* | *13–22, 29–30, 35–38* | *24–28* | *23, 31–34* |

| *43–50, 71–72, 74, 79–80* | *51–63, 73* | *64–70, 81–82* | *75–78* |

| *83, 92* | *84–89, 91* | *93–96* | *90, 97–105* |

| *109, 111–115, 117, 131–133, 135, 137, 139, 141, 153* | *106–108, 110, 122–130, 134, 138, 140* | *116, 118–121, 136* | *142–152, 154–159* |

Sofas, Daybeds, Settees, Settles, and Benches
(Plates 160–201)
This section includes all elongated forms of seating. The 6 subgroups are, from left to right: 1) sofas; 2) short asymmetrical settees, sometimes called méridiennes; 3) daybeds, pieces for reclining that have a long seat and a single raised end; 4) 2-seat settees, including wicker, metal, and modern examples, as well as tête-à-têtes; and below, 5) long settees, with wooden backs made of spindles or slats; 6) benches and settles, including country benches, window seats, and storage settles (rural benches usually with a tall solid back and skirt).

Stools *(Plates 202–215)*
The stools comprising this section are the simplest type of seating, since they have neither arms nor back. The 4 subgroups are, from left to right: 1) plain country stools; 2) fashionable designs; 3) tall piano and bar stools; 4) squat 20th-century forms, including ottomans.

Beds and Cradles *(Plates 216–241)*
Furniture for sleeping ranges from small cradles to oversize double beds. The 5 subgroups are, from left to right: 1) low-post country beds and simple daybeds; 2) canopy beds, in stylish designs from the Chippendale to Victorian eras; 3) elaborate 19th-century beds, usually with tall headboards and fashionable decoration; 4) metal beds, including turn-of-the-century cast-iron and brass beds as well as a modern tubular-steel design; and below, 5) cradles and cribs.

161–179 *180–181* *183–185, 195* *160, 186–189,*
196–198

190–194 *182, 199–201*

202–204 *205–209* *210–211, 215* *212–214*

222–226 *227–230* *221, 231–237* *238–241*

216–220

Drop-leaf and Tilt-top Tables *(Plates 242–267)*

Tables included here have drop leaves, tilt tops, or concealed leaves; these were designed to save space and served many purposes, depending on their size. The 4 subgroups are, from left to right: 1) tables with rectangular drop leaves, including dining, work, Pembroke, and small library tables; 2) tables with curved drop leaves, generally used for dining; 3) tilt-top tables, including chair-tables, tea tables, and candlestands; 4) tables with concealed leaves that pull out from under the top.

Library, Tavern, Console, Side, Tea, and Card Tables
(Plates 268–297)

This section includes a variety of tables designed for specific purposes. The 6 subgroups are, from left to right: 1) large rectangular library tables with paired trestle or pedestal bases; 2) rectangular tavern and simple dining tables, sometimes with drawers; 3) console tables, to be placed against a wall for decoration; 4) side, serving, and seed tables, for serving food and drink or for other purposes; and below, 5) 18th-century tea tables, with a rectangular or round top for serving tea; 6) card tables with hinged tops that swing open for playing cards or other games.

Center, Coffee, End, and Related Tables *(Plates 298–317)*

These decorative tables range from elaborate medium-size center tables to small coffee and end tables. The 4 subgroups are, from left to right: 1) center tables with legs; 2) center and expandable dining tables with pedestal or platform bases; 3) center or all-purpose tables made of metal, glass, or wicker; 4) 20th-century coffee and end tables.

Stands, Pedestals, Work, Sewing, and Other Small Tables
(Plates 318–347)

The 4 subgroups of small tables in this section are, from left to right: 1) low or tall stands with legs, designed to hold plants or other objects; 2) pedestal-base stands, including candlestands and pedestals for displaying artworks; 3) small occasional and serving tables; 4) sewing or work tables with drawers or compartments to hold sewing or other small household articles.

Slat-back and Spindle-back Chairs

 Simple American chairs range from plain slat-back and Windsor chairs, used in farmhouses all over the Colonies and later the young Republic, to somewhat more elaborate examples such as Sheraton painted Fancy chairs and turn-of-the-century revival designs. All of these so-called country chairs and related examples have backs made of slats or spindles, plain stiles or turned posts, and seats of splint, rush, woven tape, or solid wood. Though related to European models, these time-honored forms are quintessentially American.

Slat-back Chairs

Chairs with flat slats—rectangular rails usually set horizontally across a chair's back—span the 17th to 20th centuries. The type is best represented by the slat-back chairs made in 19th-century Shaker communities, where craftsmen perfected the simplification of the traditional form. The great restraint and yet subtle nuances of Shaker chairs distinguish them from less simple but similar chairs made by other 19th-century rural craftsmen and factories.

Generally thick on earlier chairs, slats became thinner and sometimes curved in the 18th century. Beginning in the Federal period, makers of Sheraton painted Fancy chairs stylishly transformed vertical or horizontal slats into Neoclassical forms to be embellished with painted decoration. Throughout the 19th century, slats were usually thin and finely shaped, except for more rustic pieces. Turn-of-the-century chairmakers working in the Mission style, reacting against the elaborate furniture of the Victorian period, returned to traditional construction techniques and plain slat-back designs.

Spindle-back Chairs

The second important type of country chair is that with a back consisting of spindles, which are slender, turned or whittled elements that generally taper toward the ends. Spindle-back chairs also span the centuries; among the earliest American chairs are so-called Carver and Brewster chairs, which have prominent spindles and heavy posts. Thicker turned spindles, or balusters, were used on subsequent William and Mary chairs. Thin vertical spindles are the hallmark of all the various forms of the lightweight, sturdy Windsor chairs made during the 18th and 19th centuries. Sheraton painted Fancy chairs also sometimes incorporated turned spindles. And in the late 19th and early 20th centuries, Pilgrim-period and Windsor designs were sources of inspiration for manufacturers producing chairs in substantial quantity—usually in oak—for a mass market.

Collecting Hints

Country and other simple chairs are difficult to date because their forms remained so consistent over the decades. As is evident in the following pages, similar designs made a century apart may, for instance, differ only slightly in the thickness of slats or the kind of turnings on legs; thus close inspection and comparison is recommended. Collectors should look for traces of fashionable trends, which can sometimes be spotted on conservative designs and may help date them. Whether strictly traditional or moderately stylish, these chairs tend to be well constructed and sturdy. Many were painted, and pieces with original paint are highly desirable. Once regarded by collectors as crude or primitive, most of the simple forms shown in this section are much sought after today by those who appreciate their subtle variations and sturdy construction.

Shaker rocking chair

Description
Rocking chair with top rail arched on upper edge and straight on bottom. 2 lower back rails concealed by tape panel. Stiles topped by pointed finials. Tape seat looped over rails, with front legs projecting above them. Straight cylindrical legs braced by pairs of plain tapered stretchers in front and at sides; single stretcher in rear. Rockers plain and thin. *Variations:* Top rail may be a plain rod. Taping may be used in various complementary colors. Rocking chairs often have arms.

Materials and Dimensions
Birch. Tape seat and back. Height: 43″; 15½″ to seat.

Locality and Period
Probably New York State. c. 1860–80. Similar designs produced in New England.

Comment
Shaker furniture was produced at Shaker religious communities all over the country beginning in the early 19th century. Important Shaker villages were located in New York State near Albany and the Massachusetts border, and the chair shown here may have come from one of these locales. This simple design may have been made for sale outside the community, as so many chairs were, or it may have been used in a Shaker setting.

Hints for Collectors
Some examples made for outside sale were marked with metal mounts attached to rear legs. Shaker design is typically practical and very simple, but other furnituremakers also created plain everyday furniture. Characteristics of Shaker simplicity are stiles without turnings, simple slats, and unadorned designs that echo 18th-century models.

2 Shaker dining chair

Description
Low-back side chair with single horizontal back slat, or top rail, arched on top and straight on bottom. Tapered cylindrical posts, serving as stiles and rear legs. Acorn finials. Tape seat. Front legs project slightly above straight seat rails and taper toward floor. Stretchers plain and rod-shaped, used in pairs in front and on sides, with single one in rear. *Variations:* Low-back Shaker chairs may have 2 back slats. Seat may be made of rush or splint.

Materials and Dimensions
Maple and ash or hickory. Tape seat. Height: 21″; 18″ to seat.

Locality and Period
New York State or New England. c. 1840–50.

Comment
Shaker design was marked by simplicity, practicality, and respect for good traditional design. The chair shown here is based on the 18th-century slat-back chair (7), but stripped down to its essentials. There are no ring turnings on the posts or stretchers, no unnecessary carving on the slat. This austerity distinguishes Shaker designs from other interpretations of traditional forms.

Hints for Collectors
Many comparatively simple late 19th-century chairs were not made by the Shakers, but most have extra details or frills the Shakers avoided. Distributed widely when made and collected extensively since the 1930s, Shaker furnishings can be found all over the country. Check stained examples carefully for flaws or signs of undue wear that may be covered over. This chair bears a Shaker stamp on a rear leg.

3 Shaker side chair

Description
Side chair with turned posts and 3-slat back. Plain rear posts topped by simple egg-shaped finials. Slats relatively thin, slightly curved on top, and straight-bottomed. Legs and feet plain. Tape seat. Plain stretchers paired on 3 sides and single in rear. *Variations:* Height may vary. Seats may be made from splint. Feet are often tapered. Some Shaker chairs slant backward slightly; others have a maple button fitted into the bottom of the rear legs to enable the sitter to tilt the chair.

Materials and Dimensions
Maple. Painted red. Tape seat. Height: 39½″; 17″ to seat.

Locality and Period
New York State or New England. c. 1870–80.

Comment
Shaker furniture from the early 19th century was made solely for use within the Shaker community, but by the last quarter of the century more and more pieces were made for sale to the public. These austere and functional pieces not only suited the spirit of Shaker philosophy, which called for simplicity, but also satisfied the requirements of those aesthetic reformers who advocated a return to unembellished, forthright design in the decorative arts.

Hints for Collectors
In a brochure from the 1870s, Shaker salesmen warned potential buyers about competitors whose furniture imitated Shaker wares but was less well made. Today's buyers should continue to heed this warning, since many of these imitations and other, more recent Shaker-inspired pieces are still mistaken for the real thing. Authentic pieces will show wear, particularly on the slats, stretchers, and bottoms of the feet.

4 Child's slat-back highchair

Description
Child's highchair with 2 arched slats across back and plain turned posts. Rear posts ending in egg-shaped finials with button tops; front posts rounded at top. Plain rounded arms. Tape seat. Plain stretchers paired on every side. Tapered feet. *Variations:* Turned parts in delicate ring patterns. While slats generally form the back, some later versions use spindles. Rush or splint seats are more typical.

Materials and Dimensions
Ash and maple. Tape seat. Height: 37½"; 21" to seat.

Locality and Period
New England. c. 1740-1800.

Comment
Children's highchairs of this type were made over a long period. A simple turned-post design most often indicates a chair was made in the 18th, or possibly the 19th, century; earlier models have thicker, more complex posts. The tape seat on the chair shown here is presumably a 19th-century replacement for the rush or splint seat that would have been used in the 18th century.

Hints for Collectors
This early form, first made in the 17th century, is often difficult to date because it was continually used over a long period of time. The simplicity of the posts suggests the piece shown here might well be of later date, yet the plainness of the arched slats relates it more strongly to earlier documented works. Such pieces should be examined carefully because this form has frequently been copied since the 1920s. Few rush, splint, or tape seats are original because such surfaces wear out and are replaced in short time.

5 Slat-back rocking chair

Description
Rocking chair with 4 slats on back and plain turned posts topped by onion-shaped finials; slats arched slightly on top. Arms are flat planks cut in curved contours ending in scrolls, with turned supports that pass through seat rails into plain side stretchers. Splint seat. Front stretcher turned in ball-and-ring design. Plain legs, rear ones being straight extensions of rear posts. Tapered feet mortised into thick, relatively short rockers. *Variations:* Some turned posts are more elaborate. Slats may be cut in more intricate patterns.

Materials and Dimensions
Maple and hickory. Splint seat. Height: 45″; 17″ to seat.

Locality and Period
New England. c. 1800–50.

Comment
The slat-back rocking chair was popular over a long period, from the 17th century to as late as 1880, when slat-back Shaker rocking chairs were made. One theory—the shorter the rockers, the earlier the chair—is refuted in an example like this chair, where the character of the turnings and the length of the arms suggest a later date. Moreover, the fact that the arms here are ⅔ the length of the seat (inspiring some experts to call this a "hoop-skirt rocker") suggests the chair was made closer to 1850 than 1750.

Hints for Collectors
Because slat-back chairs were popular for more than 200 years, they are readily available today; but beware of reproductions. Sharply turned posts and sharp-edged rockers may be signs of recent manufacture. Rocking chairs made by adding rockers to earlier chairs are not as highly valued as original ones.

6 Shaker armchair

Description
Armchair with 5 slats arched on top and straight on bottom.
Back stiles cylindrical and smooth, ending in elongated ovoid
finials. Flat arms with rounded edges, curving out in middle and
ending in applied mushroom-shaped handholds. Arms resting on
upper ends of simply turned front stiles. Rectangular tape seat
covering rails. Plain cylindrical legs. Thin paired stretchers in
front and on sides; single one in rear. *Variations:* Finials,
armrests, and other details may vary. Seats may be splint,
wicker, or cane. Rear legs may have ball-and-socket feet,
allowing a sitter to tilt back.

Materials and Dimensions
Maple. Tape seat. Height: 50½"; 17½" to seat.

Locality and Period
New England or New York. c. 1840–80.

Comment
Dating Shaker chairs is difficult because the same general
designs were produced from the 1840s until the early 1900s. One
distinctive type, however, was a bentwood chair patented by the
Shakers in 1874.

Hints for Collectors
A branded mark or metal Shaker mount constitutes definite
identification, but some Shaker chairs may lack such a mark.
Simplicity of details and overall design, as well as subtle touches
like the elongated finials and mushroom-cap handholds on this
chair, are valid signatures of Shaker craftsmanship. These
furnishings can be found not only in New York and in
Massachusetts, which had active Shaker communities and
craftsmen, but also in other parts of the country where Shaker
salesmen distributed their wares.

William and Mary slat-back side chair

Description
Side chair with turned stiles, or rear posts, topped by ball-and-vase finials. 4 slats with arched tops and straight bottoms, diminishing in width from top to bottom. Rush seat. Front legs turned in elaborate pattern similar to stiles, with bun feet; back legs plain round stumps. Single front stretcher of modified ball-and-ring pattern; plain paired stretchers on sides, single one in rear. *Variations:* Turned parts may vary in pattern, with slightly thinner proportions typical of New Jersey. Many later 18th-century examples have lighter proportions. Splint seats were also used.

Materials and Dimensions
Maple. Painted brown. Rush seat. Height: 45½"; 16" to seat.

Locality and Period
Delaware Valley, Pennsylvania. c. 1720–40. Variations made in other areas.

Comment
American craftsmen continued making turned-post chairs well into the 18th century; these later examples often have proportions influenced by the Queen Anne and Chippendale styles. Although simple pieces like this are generally considered "country," such examples were sometimes made in cities.

Hints for Collectors
Many chairs like the one shown here were originally painted. Repainting is usually undesirable because it conceals charming details and the attractive patina that comes with wear. A glossy surface can also detract from the basic lines of a design. Turned-post chairs have been much copied during the past 60 years, and new chairs might be confused with older ones. Note that turnings tend to be sharper on recent pieces.

William and Mary slat-back side chair

Description
High-back side chair with 5 arched horizontal slats, graduated in width and mortised into plain cylindrical stiles. Stiles slightly tapered to top and ending in globular finials. Rectangular rush seat covering rails on all sides. Plain rear legs continuations of rear stiles. Front legs turned simply with single ball near top; ball feet. Paired stretchers on sides, single one in front and at rear; front stretcher turned in ball-and-ring pattern. *Variations:* Back slats may range from 3 to 6. Legs may be turned in other patterns. Slat-back chairs by Philadelphia craftsmen often have cabriole legs.

Materials and Dimensions
Maple. Painted black. Rush seat. Height: 45½"; 16" to seat.

Locality and Period
Delaware Valley, Pennsylvania. c. 1720–40. Related designs made throughout the Colonies.

Comment
Slat-back chairs, also known as ladder-backs, were first introduced in the 17th century. During the 18th century, they became lighter in proportions, as in the chair shown here. Though this rural design was used throughout the Colonies, the arched slats and ball feet seen here are characteristic of chairs from the Delaware Valley in Pennsylvania, an area where English rather than German influence was strong.

Hints for Collectors
This design was frequently reproduced in the 1920s. While it is often easy to recognize reproductions by the lack of pegs at the junctures of slats and stiles, the uniform size of their slats, and their very simple turned elements, some better-made imitations are more difficult to detect.

9 Slat-back Great chair

Description
Armchair with 4 heavy stiles turned in ball-and-ring pattern.
Front stiles topped by flattened dome finials; rear stiles with
egg-shaped finials. 3 heavy back slats arched on top and flat on
the bottom. Arms sloping toward front and vase-turned at ends.
Rush seat. Paired stretchers on 3 sides and single stretcher in
rear; front stretchers with vase-turned ends. *Variations:* Overall
height varies. Turnings on posts may be ball-and-ring or other
patterns. Slats vary in width. Arms may be level; some rare
examples have no arms. Splint seats. Great chairs with spindles
rather than slats are called Carver chairs (38).

Materials and Dimensions
Maple and hickory. Painted black. Rush seat. Height: 42½"; 17"
to seat.

Locality and Period
Connecticut. c. 1700–10. Related examples made in other areas.

Comment
Turned-post chairs with slat backs, a traditional form that can be
traced back to the Middle Ages, were produced in America from
the Pilgrim period to the 19th century. Called Great chairs when
massive, these practical chairs were favored by people who were
not influenced by changing fashions.

Hints for Collectors
An important indication of the age of chairs is their proportions,
particularly the size of the slats—larger slats being
characteristic of earlier pieces. During the 18th century lighter
proportions were favored, and 19th-century examples feature
more delicate details. Prime signs of recent reproductions and
fakes are sharp edges at the turnings, lack of wear, and
simplified construction rather than mortise-and-tenon joints.

Federal comb-back rocking chair

Description
Rocking chair topped by comb consisting of curved panel over row of 4 simple spindles; eagle painted on top panel. Flared stiles flattened at top, and round with ring turnings above seat. 3 rectangular back slats of graduated width. Arms curving down from stiles to scrolled handholds resting on turned supports. Horseshoe-shaped seat. Front legs turned in elaborate ring pattern; plain cylindrical rear legs. Single turned front stretcher; paired plain stretchers on sides, single one in rear. Broad rockers. *Variations:* Back slats may be cut in complex patterns. Detailing may be more elaborate. Combs are often omitted. Rush seats.

Materials and Dimensions
Maple and pine. Painted and grained. Height: 44″; 15½″ to seat.

Locality and Period
Possibly Midwest. c. 1830–60.

Comment
Simple variations of Sheraton painted Fancy chairs, such as the one shown here, were usually made at workshops in the South and Midwest, but without documentation it is difficult to attribute a piece to a specific shop or area. The plain back and elaborate turnings on the front legs here suggest this was the work of a small midwestern shop rather than a more fashionable earlier craftsman.

Hints for Collectors
Collectors who appreciate folk art should look for simple furniture like this in shops and at country auctions in the South and Midwest. Examples that turn up in shops in the Northeast and on the West Coast are usually higher-priced. Simple designs with bold details have the most charm.

Mission-style side chair

Description
Side chair with back topped by plain wide rail mortised into straight square stiles terminating above rail. 3 vertical slats enclosed by upper and lower rails. Seat straight-sided, widening at front, with flat wide boards framing central caned area; seat skirt plain and straight. Front legs straight and tapered; rear legs curving back slightly. H-pattern stretchers. *Variations:* Backs may have 2–7 vertical slats. Seats are most often solid wood or upholstered in leather.

Materials and Dimensions
Oak. Cane seat. Height: 36″; 18″ to seat.

Locality and Period
Possibly Grand Rapids. c. 1900–15. Also made throughout the United States.

Comment
Oak furniture with simple lines was an important result of the Arts and Crafts movement. Furniture magazines of the period rarely credited Gustav Stickley—now regarded as the creator of the Mission style—but instead cited other small manufacturers who supposedly based their designs on examples discovered in Spanish missions in California. Whatever the origin, Mission design was very popular from about 1900 to 1915. Manufacturers in Grand Rapids, the center for oak furniture, made large numbers of elaborate pieces that seldom followed Stickley's simple designs.

Hints for Collectors
Within the limited confines of the Mission oak style, designers created some appealing variations. The simple pieces range from dull to attractively plain, depending on how slats are placed and whether such details of construction as tenons are exposed.

Child's rustic rocking chair

Description
Child's rocking chair made of rough-hewn wood. Simple rectangular back with straight stiles and rails framing pair of spindles mortised into rails. Splint seat covering seat rails. Single stretchers on all sides reinforcing straight legs, which have rockers set into them. *Variations:* Elements may be more slender and bark-covered. Less finished wood may give chairs a more rustic look.

Materials and Dimensions
Hickory. Splint seat. Height: 19½"; 11½" to seat.

Locality and Period
Rural areas of New York State. c. 1900–15.

Comment
Rustic furniture came into fashion at the turn of the century when many affluent families built hunting and fishing lodges in mountain areas such as the Adirondacks. Soon it was adapted as practical furnishings for suburban porches and sun parlors. The idea of using rough lumber for making furniture was not new in the 19th century; there were descriptions and renderings of this kind of furniture in 18th-century books on gardens. Interest in rustic furniture was spurred, however, by the Arts and Crafts movement about the turn of the century. Rustic pieces were made by amateurs as well as in professional shops.

Hints for Collectors
In certain parts of the country, particularly the West, there was a trend toward simple rough furniture in the mid-19th century; such western pieces can be confused with later pieces like the chair shown here. In general, while the earlier pieces were rather clumsily crafted, they were not as deliberately rough-surfaced as so-called Adirondack furnishings (*see also* 265).

13 Windsor/Sheraton painted Fancy side chair

Description
Painted side chair with back topped by curving wide rail having straight upper edge and rounded ends, and painted with flowers, leaves, and fruit. Stiles flaring out, flattened in upper section and rounded below. Lower back rail straight-edged and curved, with painted floral decoration. Row of 4 turned spindles between lower back rail and seat; egg-shaped turnings on spindles. Seat surface curving from back to front, with curved sides. Legs slanting out; front ones bamboo-turned. Single plain rod stretchers. *Variations:* Backs range from standard Sheraton designs to those with broad, more deeply curved top rails, like this model. Spindles may be arrow-shaped (20). Painted decoration and colors vary.

Materials and Dimensions
Maple, ash, and pine. Painted. Height: 32½″; 16¾″ to seat.

Locality and Period
Possibly Pennsylvania. c. 1830–50. Also made in other parts of the country.

Comment
Windsor and Sheraton painted Fancy designs were combined by a number of early 19th-century furnituremakers. The top panel, simple seat, and bamboo-turned legs on the chair shown here are elements well suited to the limited mass production of chair factories in this period. Chairs with rows of short spindles were often made in Pennsylvania and the South.

Hints for Collectors
Beware of painted decoration that has been "refreshed." Inspect pieces to determine if painted patterns are original, or at least original in style. Check painted surfaces for concealed repairs; if done poorly, they may not last.

Windsor/Sheraton painted Fancy side chairs

Description
Painted side chairs with turned top rail having wide center panel
flanked by rings and flattened balls. Horizontal slats, upper one
with center oval flanked by scrolls; lower slat straight. 3 slender
turned spindles between lower slat and seat. Stiles cut flat in
upper section, rounded and ring-turned at spindle level.
Horseshoe-shaped seat. Front legs turned in ball-and-ring
pattern; bamboo-turned rear legs. Single stretchers on all sides,
higher in front and at rear, with front stretcher turned in ball-
and-vase pattern. Tapered feet. *Variations:* Painted chairs range
from simple Windsors in traditional designs to those based on
fashionable Sheraton patterns.

Materials and Dimensions
Maple and pine. Painted. Height: 33″; 17″ to seat.

Locality and Period
Throughout the United States. c. 1820–50.

Comment
In the first half of the 19th century, chairs like the one shown
here were made in the South and Midwest as well as in older
centers of the Northeast. This example combines Windsor and
Sheraton elements. Such combinations are frequently difficult to
date with precision because they remained popular for almost
50 years.

Hints for Collectors
Much painted furniture available today hardly looks as it did 150
years ago: restoration has frequently distorted painted designs
and individual motifs. Such chairs have sometimes been
repainted by artists who loosely interpreted original designs;
these can be detected by comparing them to documented
examples.

15 Colonial Revival side chair

Description
Side chair with wide, elaborately curved, symmetrical top rail embellished with wood and mother-of-pearl inlay. Between top rail and curved lower back rail are 8 spindles turned in ball-and-ring pattern with bulbous centers. Stiles round and plain. 2 curved brackets connecting stiles to solid seat, which is hollowed in center, concave on sides, and convex in front and at rear. Front legs turned, tapered, and flared out to feet; rear legs tapered and slightly flared back. 3 stretchers in front turned to match back spindles; 3 plain stretchers on each side, single one in rear. *Variations:* Spindles may be turned in many patterns. Overall design may be closer to Sheraton or Windsor models, with simpler back rails. Such chairs were more often made of oak.

Materials and Dimensions
Mahogany and pine. Mother-of-pearl and wood inlay. Height: 38″; 17½″ to seat.

Locality and Period
New York, Grand Rapids, or other furniture centers. c. 1900–10.

Comment
Turn-of-the-century chairs with spindle backs based on Windsor models were usually made in oak. Occasionally finer woods, like the mahogany of the chair shown here, were used for bedroom or dining room sets combining a wide variety of styles.

Hints for Collectors
Eclectic turn-of-the-century furniture offers collectors a rich array of designs, from simple and traditional to gaudy and trendy. Study a piece to see if its balance of styles is successful. The mahogany and inlays on this chair make it unusual and perhaps more desirable to collectors.

16 Colonial Revival press-back rocking chair

Description
Rocking chair combining turned posts, broad horizontal rails, and thin tapering spindles. Elaborate finials crown turned stiles. Top rail scalloped and decorated in floral and cattail pattern. Curved middle rail and floral lower slat joined with simply turned spindles. Curved arms terminate in floral disks. Slats of scalloped wood set under arms. Front skirt of upholstered seat decorated with floral design. Front legs, arm supports, and front stretcher ring-turned; rear legs and side stretchers plain and tapered. Plain rockers. *Variations:* Turned and cut parts exist in numerous combinations. Splats may be wider; rails plain or embellished with a variety of floral or foliate reliefs.

Materials and Dimensions
Oak. Modern fabric upholstery. Height: 48″; 17″ to seat.

Locality and Period
Grand Rapids or other furniture centers. c. 1900–10.

Comment
Called press-back because its decoration was pressed in rather than carved, the chair design shown here combines Pilgrim-style turned stiles (7) and Windsor spindles (25). Such hybrid interpretations of traditional designs were typical of the Colonial Revival style at the turn of the century.

Hints for Collectors
As the value of turn-of-the-century oak furniture has increased in recent years, a certain amount of it has been restored. Often the original designs are altered when that is the easy solution to restoring damaged furniture. If the design of a piece is stylistically puzzling, it should be examined closely for evidence of later changes.

Boston or Salem rocking chair

Description
High-back rocking chair topped by wide panel with scrolled and gilded ends. Panel decorated with 2 stenciled cornucopias flanking bowl of fruit. Curved stiles flanking 7 plain turned spindles tapering to top rail. Arms rod-shaped, tapering to back; 3 short spindles supporting each arm. Seat concave in center and curved on all sides. Bamboo-turned stump legs tapered at top. Single turned stretchers on all sides. Simple rockers. Gilded incised rings on spindles, legs, and front stretchers. *Variations:* Seats may be more elaborately shaped, with scrolled front and curved rear edge. Arms may also be scrolled.

Materials and Dimensions
Maple and pine. Painted and gilded. Height: 42½"; 18½" to seat.

Locality and Period
Throughout the United States. c. 1820–50.

Comment
Though commonly called Salem or Boston rockers, chairs like the one shown here were made in many places. Among factories producing such chairs, Hitchcock (Connecticut) was one of the most important. Differences between a Hitchcock chair and this example include the simplicity of the arms and seat shown here, which suggest that this chair was the creation of a small shop using traditional methods.

Hints for Collectors
Consider the basic design and details of rocking chairs before choosing one: this chair, for example, is charmingly primitive, while others have more graceful seats and finely turned legs and arm supports.

Colonial Revival press-back side chair

Description
Side chair having turned stiles joined by wide, curving top panel with pressed scroll decoration. Stiles turned in elaborate ring pattern and topped by ball finials. 6 slender, elaborately turned spindles on back. Bent brackets reinforcing stiles. Seat with caned center and wide wooden frame. Tapered legs turned in ring design, terminating in flattened ball feet. Paired stretchers on all sides; front pair turned in elongated ball-and-ring design. *Variations:* Pressed ornament may combine various 17th- and 18th-century chair motifs. Wide top rail may be repeated as a lower back slat.

Materials and Dimensions
Oak. Cane seat. Height: 43½″; 18½″ to seat.

Locality and Period
Grand Rapids or other furniture centers. c. 1900.

Comment
At the turn of the century, Grand Rapids manufacturers and their counterparts elsewhere in the country mass-produced durable oak furniture. Designs inspired by historic models were used separately or in varied combinations. The chair shown here mixes 3 styles: Pilgrim, Windsor, and Sheraton Fancy.

Hints for Collectors
In the 1960s some collectors began buying turn-of-the-century oak furniture with pressed and turned decoration, regarding it as amusingly homely or as a whimsical response to functional modern design. By now the style has become popular enough to warrant reproduction. Although labels do not always add appreciable value to pieces in this category, they do add historical interest.

19 Windsor/Sheraton side chair

Description
Painted side chair with rectangular back topped by broad curved panel decorated with stenciled fruit. Stiles curved back, flat at top, and rounded near seat. Back spindles tapered; turned in ball pattern just below midpoint. Seat concave on sides and in center, convex at front and rear edges. Legs bamboo-shaped, flaring out from seat. Single bamboo-shaped stretchers set low on sides and at midlevel in front and rear. *Variations:* The balance between Sheraton and Windsor details may vary. Some rare armchairs were made, featuring rod-shaped or turned arms. The painted or stenciled decoration varies considerably.

Materials and Dimensions
Maple and pine. Painted. Height: 29½″; 14½″ to seat.

Locality and Period
Throughout the United States. c. 1820–40.

Comment
Chairs like the one shown here, combining Windsor and Sheraton elements, were produced in the early 19th century, particularly by small workshops and chair factories in Pennsylvania and the South. Painted decoration was applied with stencils more often than freehand. The design motifs most commonly painted on top rail panels were fruit, patriotic symbols such as the eagle, and landscape vignettes.

Hints for Collectors
Painted furniture presents special, challenging considerations, since paint may conceal unwelcome repairs. It is also difficult at times to determine whether the paint is original—and if it is not, to detect the original color.

Windsor/Sheraton side chairs

Description
Side chairs with broad curved panel as top rail, plain rectangular in left example, and with double step-down at right. Stiles flattened in front on top portions, rounded below; stiles flaring back toward top rail. 3 arrowlike spindles at left; 7 thin rod spindles tapering slightly toward top at right. Seat hollowed in center, with convex front and rear edges and concave sides. Legs and front stretcher bamboo-turned; thin turned stretchers set lower on sides and at midlevel in rear.

Materials and Dimensions
Left: birch and pine, painted black. Height: 33″; 18″ to seat.
Right: maple and pine. Height: 34″; 17″ to seat.

Locality and Period
Probably New England. c. 1800–40. Variations made in other regions.

Comment
Adapting the Windsor chair to current fashions was a popular practice in the early 19th century. Sheraton elements, such as the solid panels used as top rails on the chairs shown here, were often added to such traditional Windsor features as the spindles (at right), seat, and legs of these chairs. The arrow-back Windsor at left is a late design that particularly reflects the Neoclassicism then fashionable at every economic and social level. Chairs like these often appear in the background of folk portraits painted in rural areas, and were probably made at local factories.

Hints for Collectors
Windsor chairs are attractive to collectors because of their wide variety of designs, from the timeless classic to the briefly fashionable. These chairs, for instance, are fine examples of traditional country work combined with more stylish outlines.

Windsor fan-back side chair

Description
Fan-back side chair with serpentine curved rail topping 7
whittled spindles; stiles 3-part and vase-turned. Saddle seat
shallow and peaking in front. Vase-turned legs reinforced by
bulbous H-shaped stretchers. *Variations:* Some cresting rails are
plain or carved in relief at ends. Spindles may be turned rather
than whittled by hand. Turned stiles may be more or less
elaborate. Painted various colors. Turnings are often more
pronounced than on this example.

Materials and Dimensions
Maple and pine. Painted white. Height: 38″; 16″ to seat.

Locality and Period
New England or Mid-Atlantic region. c. 1770–1800.

Comment
Fan-backs are very much like comb-backs, except that comb-
backs are in 2 distinct sections. Some fan-backs were made
before the Revolution; whittled spindles and vase-shaped legs
are characteristic of these early examples, most likely made in a
craftsman's shop rather than a chair factory. However, there are
similar examples from a later date, about 1800. Dating is a
challenge because the temptation to consider related designs as
evolutionary steps has been refuted by some marked works
bearing the stamps of makers active either earlier or later than
one might expect.

Hints for Collectors
Paint that is crackling may not always be old. To check if paint is
original, look for former colors under the seat and at the joining
of legs and stretchers, where paint remover may not have
reached. White was a popular color for 18th-century Windsors.

Windsor comb-back armchair

Description
Comb-back armchair topped by serpentine curved rail ending in scrolls. 9 back spindles intersected by center rail terminating as arms with flattened curved handholds. Arms supported on vase-turned balusters and short spindles. Seat shield-shaped and peaking in front. Legs elaborately turned in ring-vase-cylinder pattern. Short arrow feet. H-shaped stretchers; center stretcher turned in ball-and-ring pattern. *Variations:* Legs may be turned in simpler forms and terminate in plainer feet. Scroll ends on top rail can be cut simply or carved in relief pattern. Spindles may be plain or decorated with turnings.

Materials and Dimensions
Maple with pine seat. Painted black. Height: 37″; 18″ to seat.

Locality and Period
Philadelphia. c. 1760–80.

Comment
The turned legs, feet, and stretchers of the chair shown here are signs of a Philadelphia origin that relate it to the earliest surviving Windsor chairs. The back reinforced with the center rail is an early Windsor form popularly called a comb-back. A chair with the same flat cresting rail but no midrail is called a fan-back.

Hints for Collectors
Authentic early designs like this are rare. In general, these Windsors were originally painted (in the 1920s there was a tendency to remove the paint). Black was popular, but early advertisements indicate a full range of colors. Check spindles closely for cracks not readily evident under paint. Though adding paint was once frowned upon, a growing group of collectors and museum curators believe in restoring paint whenever possible.

23 Windsor low-back armchair with writing arm

Description
Low-back armchair with curving top rail having rounded cresting at center. One side ending in flat circular writing arm covering shallow drawer with curved front; other arm rail extending to scrolled handhold. Top rail and writing extension mortised into row of 13 whittled spindles running between vase-and-ring-turned arm supports at ends, with 2 balusters slanting out from projections on seat to support drawer. Shield-shaped seat with peaked front. Vase-and-ring-turned legs reinforced by H-pattern turned stretchers with bulbous centers and tapered ends. Plain tapered feet. *Variations:* Writing-arm Windsors often have comb backs (22). Legs may be bamboo-turned. Low-back Windsors without writing arms are called captain's chairs.

Materials and Dimensions
Tulip, maple, and chestnut. Painted. Height: 31⅛"; 17" to seat.

Locality and Period
Made by Anthony Steel, Philadelphia. c. 1790–1815.

Comment
Writing-arm Windsors are very rare, and the well-executed piece shown here, bearing the mark of Philadelphia chairmaker Anthony Steel, is an important example. The maker's mark enables us to date the chair more accurately than is possible with most ordinary Windsors. Vase-turned legs like these were once thought to have been earlier than bamboo-turned ones, but this chair proves they actually coexisted.

Hints for Collectors
Anyone lucky enough to find an authentic writing-arm Windsor should acquire it regardless of condition. However, spindles are breakable and often have been replaced, and the quality of the design and detailing of the replacements varies widely.

Windsor hoop-back armchair

Description
Hoop-back armchair with back divided horizontally into 2
sections by center rail that also forms arms. 7 central spindles
mortised into top rail and divided by center rail: spindles
bulbous-contoured below rail, straight above. Arms end in
knuckle-molded handholds resting on 2 short spindles and vase-
turned support. Seat shield-shaped and concave. Vase-turned
legs reinforced by H-pattern turned stretchers. *Variations:* Plain
arms and seat. Spindles may be boldly curved or subtly tapered,
whittled with little attention to detail or more precisely
fashioned.

Materials and Dimensions
Maple and pine. Painted black. Height: 37½"; 16½" to seat.

Locality and Period
Connecticut. c. 1800. Variations made throughout the Northeast.

Comment
Hoop-backs were popular enough to lead the artist Robert Edge
Pine to use the chairs—but with bamboo-shaped legs—in his
celebrated painting of the signing of the Declaration of
Independence. The thinness of the vase-turned legs in the
example shown here suggests a Connecticut origin; and if so, it
was most likely made closer to 1800 than the year of the signing.

Hints for Collectors
The original black paint visible on this chair verifies its
authenticity and good condition, proving that original paint has
indeed survived on some early Windsors. Since more recent
paint can very well look old, check the underside carefully for
former colors not covered by later coats. Good old paint like this
should not be removed as it is part of a Windsor's history.

Description

Continuous-arm, arch-back armchair with arched rail and arms
fashioned from single flat piece of wood, terminating in simple
curved handholds; 9 spindles spanning back, 2 short spindles and
vase-turned baluster supporting each arm. Saddle seat peaking
at center in front. Legs vase-turned. Stretchers H-shaped and
bulbous; rings flanking bulb of center stretcher. *Variations:*
Braced back. Legs may be more or less elaborately turned.

Materials and Dimensions

Pine and ash. Painted black. Height: 37½″; 18½″ to seat.

Locality and Period

Rhode Island. c. 1760–1800.

Comment

Precisely dating the piece shown here is difficult, since Windsor
forms were used over a long period. It is also challenging to
localize this type because 18th-century examples were produced
throughout New England and Pennsylvania. However, Rhode
Island examples have heavier, more pronounced turnings than
those found in northern New England. Spindles as simple as
those on this chair look as if they were whittled in a craftsman's
shop rather than turned in a chair factory, so an early date and
Rhode Island origin are likely.

Hints for Collectors

This is one of the designs that was made best in small workshops;
later copies are rarely successful. Lighter proportions and
fancier spindles should raise suspicions about authenticity. This
Windsor may originally have been painted green, a prevalent
18th-century color that should be preserved when found. When
restoring original color, look for traces of it in cracks and at
joints where the stripper may not have reached.

Windsor braced loop-back armchair

Description
Armchair with loop back enclosing 9 vase-turned spindles,
backed by 2 matching diagonal braces. Braces set into projecting
piece on back of seat. Curved arms mortised into back and
attached to upholstered seat by short spindles and slanted vase-
turned supports. Legs vase-turned. H-shaped stretchers in
bulbous forms; center stretcher with 2 rings. *Variations:* Seats
are not usually upholstered. Similar mortised arms may be made
of mahogany. Arms are often flat; spindles plain and tapered.
Braces are not always used.

Materials and Dimensions
Maple, hickory, and pine. Leather upholstery with brass tacks.
Height: 37½"; 16" to seat.

Locality and Period
Rhode Island. c. 1770–80.

Comment
The design shown here features the bold, heavy turned legs
characteristic of Rhode Island craftsmanship. Chairs with
separate arms like this were invented because they were
probably easier to make than were those having arms and back
rails made from one continuous piece of wood (25). Windsors
were made in early chair factories, but too little is known about
these factories to distinguish their output from that of smaller
workshops. Collectors now consider Rhode Island Windsors as
distinctive as their Philadelphia cousins.

Hints for Collectors
Most upholstered Windsors have lost their fabric over the years.
Check an uncovered Windsor for tack holes at the back and
around the bottom of the seat to see whether it originally
had upholstery.

Description
Rocking chair with continuous loop back enclosing 9 bamboo-turned spindles. Arms mortised into loop, with bamboo-shaped arm supports. Saddle seat relatively flat. Legs bamboo-turned and braced by H-shaped stretchers; side stretchers with bulbous centers; center stretcher bamboo-turned. Rockers are plain, cut slats. *Variations:* Loop may be balloon-shaped or more subtly curved. Legs may be vase-turned, though bamboo design is more common. Stretchers are sometimes X-shaped.

Materials and Dimensions
Hickory, maple, ash, and pine. Painted. Height: 33¾"; 18" to seat.

Locality and Period
New England. c. 1780–1820.

Comment
The rocking chair is a common form that was introduced in the late 18th century or possibly somewhat earlier. (Its invention is sometimes credited to Benjamin Franklin, but that is an unfounded myth.) Like all Windsors, the Windsor rocking chair is a simple form that is sturdy and practical.

Hints for Collectors
Windsors are popular today and readily available in shops and at country auctions. Since many country chairs were converted to rocking chairs in the 19th century, it is difficult to be sure that a rocking chair has not been altered. One clue to authenticity is the width of the legs: original rocking chairs often have thicker legs than ordinary Windsors. More often than not, Windsors have had their paint stripped, so chairs with original paint like the one shown here are prized.

Windsor loop-back side chair

Description
Loop-back side chair with 9 bamboo-turned spindles and back curved in almost keyhole shape. Saddle seat peaking in center at front. Bamboo-shaped legs reinforced with bulbous H-pattern stretchers. Surface covered with black paint. *Variations:* Legs may be vase-turned and of varied thickness.

Materials and Dimensions
Ash. Pine seat. Painted black. Height: 37½″; 18½″ to seat.

Locality and Period
New England, possibly Connecticut. c. 1780–1810.

Comment
Simply constructed and sturdy, Windsors were partially made of green wood that contracted as it aged so that spindles became more tightly secured after a few months. Loop-back chairs, a popular form toward the end of the 18th century, are found all over the country. Early factories may well have produced chairs of the design shown here, since the parts were turned and there was no difficulty in using a factory setup for their production. Chairs with bamboo-turned legs, as in this example, though more difficult to place geographically than chairs with vase-turned legs, are equally graceful and distinctive.

Hints for Collectors
This design has been reproduced frequently, and one way of checking its authenticity is to examine the legs closely. In reproductions the turnings are just a bit crisper, or more keenly defined, because mechanical means of production brought less subtle results. The seat bottoms also look more finished on the copies, and seats may be made of several pieces of wood. Reproductions are generally lighter in overall proportion than are the early examples.

Windsor rod-back side chair

Description
Tall rod-back side chair with straight top rail pierced by 7 thin
spindles. Stiles plain and round, flaring out from seat and
continued just above top rail. Seat saddle-shaped, curving at
sides and rear, and peaking in front. Legs bamboo-turned and
flaring out. Stretchers bamboo-turned and H-shaped. *Variations:*
Rod-back Windsors generally have lower backs. Some have
paired top rails, suggesting the influence of the Sheraton Fancy
chair.

Materials and Dimensions
Ash and pine. Height: 52″; 17½″ to seat.

Locality and Period
Throughout the United States. c. 1820–30.

Comment
American chairmakers produced about a dozen general types of
Windsors, though no sources for specific designs are known. The
distinctive interpretation of a simple early 19th-century Windsor
chair design shown here is evidence of the endless variety
possible within the standard Windsor forms. The unusual height
of the back must have been intended for decorative purposes,
since there is no functional reason for it.

Hints for Collectors
The authenticity of unusual variants should always be
questioned. Often the novelty results from a misunderstanding of
an early design by a later craftsman or maker of reproductions.
This chair looks authentic: the turned parts resemble those on
early examples, though with different proportions; the seat is
shaped and curved like those on standard period examples.

Windsor rod-back side chair

Description
Rod-back side chair with bamboo-turned parts. Straight top rail and parallel lower rail create space for panel of alternating short spindles and oval ornaments. Stiles flare out from seat to top rail, with 7 spindles conforming to curve of stiles. Saddle-shaped seat hollowed at center. Legs reinforced by stretchers on each side. *Variations:* Back panel may have row of short spindles or a solid surface that may be decorated. Legs may be turned in the Sheraton style. Often painted black, green, or red; sometimes grained.

Materials and Dimensions
Pine and ash. Height: 36″; 17″ to seat.

Locality and Period
Probably Connecticut, but elsewhere in New England as well. c. 1800–20.

Comment
The rod-back, or birdcage (a more recent term), Windsor was introduced at the beginning of the 19th century, when Sheraton influence affected ordinary as well as elegant furniture production. Similar examples found with Connecticut makers' names branded underneath the seat suggest that the chair shown here was the product of a rural Connecticut chairmaker.

Hints for Collectors
Beware of reproductions: though this type of Windsor chair was not often reproduced in the late 19th century, it became a much copied design at the beginning of the 20th century. Some older originals have painted surfaces, and such pieces should be carefully inspected for paint-concealed repairs and replacements.

Shaker revolving chair or revolver

Description
Revolving chair with back topped by curved narrow rail mortised onto 7 turned spindles set into flat, round seat. Seat attached to cylinder set into a larger wooden cylinder to allow it to revolve. Cylinder mechanism fitted onto platform consisting of round top supported by 4 canted legs turned in Sheraton-style ring pattern. Single plain rod stretchers. *Variations:* Heights vary. Pedestal bases are also used. Wooden spindles are sometimes replaced by metal ones.

Materials and Dimensions
Pine, ash, and maple. Iron mechanism. Height: 27½″; 18½″ to seat.

Locality and Period
Massachusetts or New York. c. 1830–70.

Comment
The revolving chair, also known as a revolver, was invented by the Shakers and typifies their basic furniture philosophy. Although primarily a functional chair, the design of the revolver shown here borrowed and simplified elements from 2 traditional chairs: the back resembles that of the Windsor captain's chair (23); and the legs are turned in a pattern found on Sheraton painted Fancy chairs (14). Supposedly first made in New Hampshire, revolvers were also made in Shaker communities in Massachusetts and New York.

Hints for Collectors
Revolvers were made almost exclusively by the Shakers. Not all simple 19th-century furniture was made by the Shakers, however, so if you are asked to pay a premium for a Shaker item, verify its origins by comparing it with museum examples.

Windsor highchair

Description
Highchair with thick top rail arched on top and curving around
seat to serve as flat arms. Top rail resting on 6 spindles tapered
toward tops. Flat seat straight in front and curved at back.
Flaring legs bamboo-turned, tapered at tops and feet. Single
front and rear stretchers higher than side stretchers. *Variations:*
A variation of the so-called captain's chair (23), this type of
highchair is sometimes more elaborate, with more spindles, a
shaped seat, and thinner legs. Children's chairs may be either
low or high enough to be used at a dining table.

Materials and Dimensions
Maple and pine. Height: 31″; 24″ to seat.

Locality and Period
Throughout the United States. c. 1820–40.

Comment
Windsor chairs were widely made from the mid-18th to mid-19th
century. Their sturdiness made them ideal children's seating.
The example shown here, sometimes called a firehouse chair, is
difficult to date: though basically a simple early design, its
tapered spindles and fairly thick legs suggest a 19th-century
dating.

Hints for Collectors
Generally inexpensive, 19th-century Windsors may be used in
both rural and urban settings. Such children's chairs are easier to
find than more fashionable Chippendale or Federal models. They
are among the sturdiest chairs ever made, yet it is wise to check
for splits thoroughly, since replacing damaged elements can be
costly. Firehouse chairs mass-produced since the turn of the
century usually have more elaborate turnings than originals.

Description
Corner chair with flat top rail curving toward rounded handholds, with molding over center of rail serving as backrest. Top rail supported by 3 baluster-turned stiles that continue below rectangular rush seat as block-and-vase-turned legs. Front leg terminating in scrolled Spanish foot, other 3 with plain bun feet. Paired stretchers on all sides; vase-and-ring-turned on 2 front sides, plain in rear. *Variations:* Baluster-shaped supports may be turned in various patterns. Stretchers may be single and more boldly turned.

Materials and Dimensions
Maple. Rush seat. Height: 29½"; 18" to seat.

Locality and Period
Possibly New York; also throughout New England. c. 1710–60.

Comment
Besides being used in corners, corner chairs were ideal desk chairs, and many of the more elegant designs were made to hold chamber pots. The rush-seated country version shown here, however, could not have held a pot since its seat cannot be lifted. Turned legs are a William and Mary trait that continued to be used in simple country chair designs after the mid-18th century, long after the Queen Anne style became fashionable.

Hints for Collectors
Early country corner chairs are both useful and comfortable. Though basically sturdy, the joints of seat rails may become loose from continual use. Check stretchers for breaks hidden under stain or paint. Corner chairs, while popular in the 18th century, are relatively rare today, thus making them more expensive than ordinary chairs.

Queen Anne country corner chair

Description
Corner chair with flat top rail curving toward scrolled handholds. Molding over center of top rail serving as backrest. Top rail supported by 3 turned stiles that continue below rectangular rush seat as block-and-vase-turned legs. Paired turned stretchers on all sides; flat bun feet. *Variations:* Legs may be elaborately turned (combining William and Mary with Queen Anne elements) or vase-turned with spherical sections and pad feet.

Materials and Dimensions
Maple and ash. Rush seat. Height: 30½″; 19″ to seat.

Locality and Period
New England. c. 1730–60.

Comment
Rural chairs such as the one shown here were particularly favored in New England, but similar examples came from other Colonies. Judging by the top rail, the chair shown here may have been made about 1740–50, but the basic design was used for almost a century. While this example has turned legs thick enough to be considered early, simpler variants with more slender legs and curved seats were made later in the century.

Hints for Collectors
Although many variations of 18th-century origin do exist, the basic type was much reproduced in the 1920s and 1930s. If copies show convincing wear on the turnings, they can be easily confused with originals. Note that 20th-century versions have more delicate turnings and sharper edges on the top rail molding, and the latter may be secured by screws.

35 William and Mary bannister-back armchair

Description
Bannister-back armchair with wide double-arched top and lower back rails. Turned stiles topped by button finials. 4 turned baluster-shaped slats flat in front and curved on sides and back. Arms slightly curved, terminating in scroll-shaped handholds just beyond front stiles. Rush seat wider in front. Front legs turned in double-ball-and-ring pattern, ending in bun feet; rear legs plain and round. Paired stretchers in front and on sides, single one in rear; front pair turned in double-ball pattern. *Variations:* Back rails are sometimes carved, and the lower one is often straight. Surfaces may be painted. Seat may be splint-covered. Spanish feet are sometimes used in front.

Materials and Dimensions
Ash and maple. Rush seat. Height: 46½″; 16″ to seat.

Locality and Period
New England. c. 1700–20.

Comment
William and Mary chairs range from elaborately carved examples to those made with simply cut and turned parts. The bannister back was a common form in which elaborate detailing was easily achieved. The example shown here, typical of New England craftsmanship, is elegant because of its restrained turnings, even though it has no carving. The comparatively large scale of this chair is characteristic of the style. The term "bannister" is a corruption of "baluster."

Hints for Collectors
This kind of early chair might well have replacement parts, which lessen the value of a piece but are tolerable as long as the restoration has been done well. Proper replacements may be hard to find for damaged rails, balusters, or stretchers.

36 William and Mary bannister-back side chair

Description
Bannister-back side chair with back topped by carved arched scroll resting on molded top rail. 4 baluster-shaped slats flat in front and curved on sides and back. Lower rail curved on bottom and set high above seat. Stiles turned to match balusters and topped by vase-and-ball finials. Rectangular rush seat. Front legs turned in vase-and-block pattern, terminating in button feet. Rear legs plain and square. Turned stretchers high across front, lower across rear, and lowest on sides. *Variations:* The cresting and finials on the back may vary: cresting may have fuller leaf designs, and finials are often simpler.

Materials and Dimensions
Ash and maple. Painted black. Rush seat. Height: 46½″; 16″ to seat.

Locality and Period
New England. c. 1690–1720.

Comment
Tall-back chairs were introduced in the American Colonies toward the end of the 17th century. Simpler versions of English designs of a few decades earlier, such American chairs in the William and Mary style were subtle combinations of turned elements and carved details that achieved an air of Baroque elegance. Black paint was used to simulate ebony, which was very fashionable in 17th-century Europe.

Hints for Collectors
Check to see that the flat sides of balusters face the front, since they are sometimes reversed on restored examples. Painted furniture should be carefully examined for replaced parts concealed under the paint. Note that the feet on the chair shown here have been worn down with age.

Description
Armchair made of turned stiles and rails with inscribed ring decoration. Heavy back stiles crowned by bold finials. Paired top rails, midrail, and seat rail enclose 2 rows of baluster-shaped spindles filling back area. Armrests mortised into front and back posts, with rows of spindles like those on back mortised into arms and seat rails. Front posts topped by squat orbs. Plank seat framed by turned rails, with single rows of short spindles at sides and 2 longer rows in front. 4 posts continuing below seat as plain legs. Paired stretchers at front and sides, single lower one in rear. *Variations:* Brewster chairs range from plain models to those with single or double rows of balusters all around.

Materials and Dimensions
Maple and walnut. Stained black. Height: 47″; 19½″ to seat.

Locality and Period
Made by Wallace Nutting, Massachusetts. c. 1920–30.

Comment
Wallace Nutting was a well-known antiques scholar and maker of reproductions who changed some details intentionally so that his pieces would be recognized as reproductions. On the Brewster chair shown here, the top rail has an unusual bulge at its center, the legs are longer, and turnings sharper than on an original. Authentic Brewster chairs are quite rare.

Hints for Collectors
Wallace Nutting's reproductions are in great demand, and some labeled examples have sold for as much as originals. Other reproductions, however, are sometimes made with artificial signs of wear.

Pilgrim-style Great or Carver chair

Description
Armchair made of ring-turned stiles and rails, with front and
rear stiles continuing as legs below rush seat. Front stiles topped
by 2-part, flattened ball finials; rear stiles topped by pointed
finials in melon or acorn shape. 2 turned back rails enclosing 3
thick tapered spindles. Flattened arms with curved outer edges.
Stretchers paired on 3 sides and single in rear, turned like back
rails. *Variations:* Pattern of turnings, number of back rails, and
height of front stiles vary, but thickness remains the same. Arms
may be turned; rare examples without arms. Splint seats were
sometimes used, but rush seats were more common.

Materials and Dimensions
Maple. Rush seat. Height: 43½″; 17½″ to seat.

Locality and Period
Massachusetts, Connecticut, or New York. c. 1650–90.

Comment
Called Great chairs in 17th-century American household
inventories because of the size, the type of chair shown here had
been made centuries earlier in northern Europe. American
examples are often called Carver chairs, after John Carver, first
governor of Massachusetts Bay Colony, whose spindle-back
Great chair now sits in Pilgrim Hall in Plymouth, Massachusetts.
Carver chairs have fewer spindles than Brewster chairs.

Hints for Collectors
Look for signs of wear to distinguish original Great chairs from
reproductions. Since such signs can be faked, however, beware
of excessive and uniform unevenness of surfaces. Reproductions
as well as later 18th-century versions often have lighter
proportions: posts are more slender and seats narrower.

Sheraton painted Fancy armchair

Description
Painted armchair in klismos shape with rectangular top panel concave in center and decorated with oval cartouche of harbor scene flanked by 2 cornucopias. Horizontal center slat pierced with swag-and-tassel motifs flanking center oval with painted flowers. Lower back rail decorated with stars. Straight-sided stiles curving back and projecting above top panel, with painted scrolls near tops. Flat-sided arms curving to concave supports. Seat straight-sided, widening in front, and caned; straight front skirt with stenciled Greek key design. Front legs tapered saber forms with panel of painted stars above and scrolls at feet; rear legs plain and flared back. Simple paired rod stretchers in front and on sides, single in rear. *Variations:* Slats are often simpler. Painted decoration may be more geometric.

Materials and Dimensions
Maple and pine. Painted. Cane seat. Height: 33½″; 17″ to seat.

Locality and Period
Probably Baltimore. c. 1800–20. Variations from other centers.

Comment
The chair shown here is often called a Sheraton painted Fancy, an extremely popular form all over the country at the beginning of the 19th century. The painted scene and overall elegance of its decoration suggest that it was made in Baltimore, where the most elaborate furniture painting was done.

Hints for Collectors
Painted furniture is appealing but more vulnerable than furniture with plain surfaces. Check painted surfaces carefully for concealed defects. Keep painted pieces in places that do not get too dry or too damp. Restoring painted decoration is difficult and should only be undertaken by professionals.

Sheraton painted Fancy side chair

Description
Side chair with gilded and stenciled decoration. Rectangular top panel curving in toward center and decorated with landscape framed by gold border. 2 tiers of horizontal slats consisting of 3 rows of balls enclosed by rails. Stiles curving back and flaring out, with rounded tops, flattened fronts, and ring-turned lower section. Horseshoe-shaped rush seat framed by continuous bent rail. Turned front legs tapered and flared to small ball feet. Plain rear legs straight and tapered. Front stretcher matches lower back slat; plain round stretchers paired at sides and single in rear. *Variations:* Painted decoration differs from piece to piece. Slats may be thicker or solid; legs straight and simpler.

Materials and Dimensions
Maple and pine. Rush seat. Painted and stenciled. Height: 33¼"; 17" to seat.

Locality and Period
Made in New England for *Cleopatra's Barge* of Salem. c. 1816. Similar chairs made in other furniture centers.

Comment
Most Sheraton painted Fancy chairs were made of simply turned parts, allowing them to be factory-made. Sometimes, however, painted decoration was very elaborate. Elegant examples were often painted in Baltimore or New York, but the light proportions of the chair shown here suggest a New England origin.

Hints for Collectors
Painted chairs present the conservation problems of both furniture and paintings. Many have been retouched, sometimes radically; beware of shiny paint and delicately detailed brushwork.

41 Sheraton painted Fancy side chair

Description
Painted side chair with wide top panel slightly concave at center, bearing stenciled flower-bowl design and outline borders. Stiles, projecting above top panel and curving back slightly, are flat-fronted near top and rounded just above seat rail, then continue below as plain rear legs; stiles decorated with gilded rings and outline borders. Narrow straight slat connecting midpoints of stiles. Rush seat covering rails that are mortised into stiles and front legs; rounded tops of front legs protruding above seat. Round legs, with gilded rings, tapering to plain feet. Paired thin rod stretchers in front and on sides, single one in rear, with gilded rings on front pair. *Variations:* Stenciled decoration is often more complex. Back slats may be broader or cut in classical patterns such as vases or garlands.

Materials and Dimensions
Maple. Painted and stenciled. Rush seat. Height: 32½"; 17" to seat.

Locality and Period
C. Robinson, Rochester (stamped on back of top slat). c. 1860. Similar chairs made throughout the United States.

Comment
The example shown here is one of the latest Sheraton painted Fancy chairs, and its late date is evident in its simplicity. Except for the style of its painted decoration, this factory product is not too different from reproductions made beginning about 1920.

Hints for Collectors
This authentic but late Sheraton painted Fancy chair could be a perfect addition to a collection or a stylistic liability. Its overall design is early, yet its plainness and lack of detail might look jarring in a room filled with earlier pieces.

Sheraton painted Fancy side chair

Description
Painted side chair with back topped by horizontally striped panel
curving back and scrolled above. Rectangular stiles with leaf-
painted scrolled ends, broadening and curving into seat rails.
Back consisting of colonnade of 3 tapered pilasters with long leaf-
painted Corinthian capitals, set on raised back seat rail. Small
sloping brackets joining stiles and side seat rails. Straight-sided
cane seats widening toward down-curving front. Straight skirt
with stenciled cornucopia motif in front center, rosettes at front
corners, and scrolls on sides. Saber-shaped front legs with
stenciled waterleaf decoration and square feet; plain, tapered
rear legs flaring back. *Variations:* Chairs may have horizontal
back slats and simpler legs.

Materials and Dimensions
Maple. Painted and stenciled. Cane seat. Height: 35″; 17½″ to
seat.

Locality and Period
Marked "Holden's" (either Asa Holden of New York or Joshua
Holden of Boston). c. 1820.

Comment
The chair shown here is similar to Thomas Sheraton's most
sophisticated creations based on the Greco-Roman klismos form.
Such chairs were the height of fashion in the early 19th century.

Hints for Collectors
Fashionable painted furniture is a challenging field for collectors.
Some examples turn up in country shops for low prices while
other pieces are found in leading galleries at high prices. Painted
pieces can be confusing, since repainting done decades later may
be deceptively good.

Splat-back, Shield-back, and Related Chairs

Chairs with carved wooden backs, epitomizing fashionable design in many periods but most of all during the 18th and early 19th centuries, are among the finest examples of American craftsmanship. The backs, flamboyant expressions of style more than features of comfort, have carved splats or curving slats framed by straight or curving rails and stiles. Most have upholstered seats, appropriately stylish legs, and, often, arms. Elegant examples were made of mahogany, but many others were of local woods such as maple or cherry. Later in the 19th and the early 20th centuries, craftsman frequently revived the traditional wooden-back chair.

Splat-back Chairs

The solid vase-shaped splat—a flat, vertical element in the center of a chair back—is an essential part, along with cabriole legs, of 18th-century Queen Anne chairs. This basic design was also used for country versions that combine turned parts with more typical carved Baroque elements, as well as for turn-of-the-century Colonial Revival pieces. The Chippendale splat, usually pierced in elegant Rococo patterns, evolved from the Queen Anne splat and was most often topped by a yoke-shaped rail with turned-up ends. American interpretations were either elaborately carved by craftsmen in major furniture centers such as Philadelphia, New York, or Rhode Island or else adapted in less complex versions for rural production. Chippendale designs were also revived about 1900–20: some Colonial Revival examples are simplified transformations of the originals into oak; others, made of mahogany, generally have more elaborate and delicate detailing.

Shield-back and Other Chair Designs

The wooden-back chair remained a symbol of fashion in the Federal era (1780–1820). Backs evolved into simpler, more restrained patterns in the prevailing Neoclassical style. Shield-backs still curve, but with less exuberance than pre-Revolutionary models, and the legs are straight and tapered rather than in the curving cabriole shape. Some of the most graceful Federal chairs, based on the Greco-Roman klismos chair and on Sheraton designs, were made by the New York cabinetmaker Duncan Phyfe (43–44) and his competitors. The klismos model was later translated into Empire designs with curved center rails or vase-shaped splats and Rococo Revival designs with balloon-shaped backs. Such Empire chairs and other furnishings were also made in China and exported to America during the first half of the 19th century. By the mid-19th century, producers of fashionable pieces turned to more elaborate, upholstered-back furniture, but restrained, wooden-back Gothic Revival, Renaissance Revival, and Eastlake chairs were still produced. Some early 20th-century chairs had carved splats, such as those done in the Arts and Crafts style by the California architects Charles and Henry Greene (81–82) and other designers who returned to traditional American forms.

Collecting Hints

Because high-style chairs with finely carved wooden backs have traditionally been among the most sought-after American antiques, later craftsmen have reproduced or faked them. Such copies are often difficult to identify: beware of examples with improper proportions, flat carving, modern construction techniques, and insufficient wear.

Description
Matching side chairs in klismos shape with straight-sided back curving outward from seat to curved rectangular top rail. Top rail with reeds tied by ribbons in bow-knot motif. Reeded stiles and lower rails enclosing X-shaped slats. Stiles vase-shaped below lower rails. Cane seat horseshoe-shaped; seat rails curved and reeded. Round front legs tapered and reeded, with plain tapered feet. Plain rear legs flared back from seat to floor. *Variations:* Top rail may be carved with other Neoclassical motifs besides the ribbons and reeds shown here, such as cornucopias or stylized depictions of lightning. Back rails and stiles may be plain. Unusual examples have splats with lyre, harp, or eagle designs.

Materials and Dimensions
Mahogany. Cane seat. Height: 31½"; 16" to seat.

Locality and Period
Probably by Duncan Phyfe, New York. c. 1800.

Comment
This elegant Sheraton design is similar to a group of pieces known to be by Duncan Phyfe. The carving and X-shapes on the back resemble decoration on chairs that Phyfe sold to the Bayard family of New York. Even if these chairs were made by one of Phyfe's competitors, they would probably date from about the same period as the Bayard pieces.

Hints for Collectors
Sheraton designs made by Duncan Phyfe and his New York competitors have been copied since the late 19th century. Checking on quality of details is important: carving, for instance, should be crisp and well executed, and proportions proper for the piece and period.

Federal arm- and side chairs

Description
Matching arm- and side chairs in klismos shape. Back topped by rectangular rail curving into center. Reeded stiles curved back toward top rail and vase-shaped between seat and center rail. Arched slats forming curved X, with rosette at center. Fluted arms curving away from rear stiles to vase-shaped front supports. Horseshoe-shaped cane seat with reeded rails; cushions tied to stiles. Cabriole front legs with leaf carving and ormolu lion's-paw feet; plain rear legs flaring back to tapered feet. *Variations:* Straight-sided seats are also used. Backs sometimes have lyre, harp, or eagle splats. Top rails may be plain or decorated with leaves, wheat sheaves, thunderbolts, or cornucopias.

Materials and Dimensions
Mahogany and pine. Cane seats with cushions. Ormolu feet. Height: 32½"; 18" to seat.

Locality and Period
Probably by Duncan Phyfe, New York. c. 1800.

Comment
The restrained rectangular backs on the chairs shown here were inspired by Sheraton designs, but they are most often associated with Duncan Phyfe and his New York workshop. Phyfe was not, however, the only cabinetmaker to use the designs attributed to him; other New York craftsmen also turned out similar chairs.

Hints for Collectors
Fine reproductions of Phyfe-style chairs from the beginning of this century are sometimes confused with originals. But even the best copies have flatter carving, sharper reeding, and less curved elements than the originals.

Empire side chair

Description
Side chair in klismos shape. Rectangular top rail with rounded upper edge, curving in at center. Molded stiles thicken as they curve into side seat rails. 2 curving scrolled rails, joining midpoints of stiles, are connected by central turned disk. Plain legs with concave profile; molding of front legs similar to stiles and seat rails. *Variations:* Philadelphia and Boston examples are more elaborate, with shell or radiating floral patterns on top panels. Legs may have lion's-paw feet.

Materials and Dimensions
Mahogany. Modern fabric upholstery. Height: 33″; 17½″ to seat.

Locality and Period
New York. c. 1815–30. A popular type made throughout the East.

Comment
The klismos form, introduced at the beginning of the 19th century, is most often associated with Duncan Phyfe, who made more chairs of this type than any other identified maker. It was particularly common in New York, Phyfe's home. The design was soon simplified, but heavier-proportioned details persisted on chairs made for the popular market and for clients who preferred carved ornament. The Empire style was one of the first in which the contrast between refined and vulgar tastes became evident.

Hints for Collectors
Empire designs were revived at the turn of the century, and the simple later examples can easily be confused with originals. Later models were generally taller, with darker wood, sharp-edged turned details, and 20th-century screws or nails.

Empire side chair

Description
Side chair in klismos shape. Rectangular top rail with rounded upper edge, curving in at center. Rectangular rail curving up in center and set midway across tapered stiles, which curve toward seat. Upholstered seat widening toward front. Front seat rail rounded. Legs rectangular and tapered, curving in below seat and then flaring out to feet. *Variations:* Top rail and midrail on some klismos chairs are embellished with carved classical motifs. More complex versions, often attributed to Duncan Phyfe, are slightly shorter and usually have reeded stiles and legs.

Materials and Dimensions
Tiger maple and pine. Modern silk damask with Empire-style pattern. Height: 31″; 18″ to seat.

Locality and Period
Probably New York, but possibly Philadelphia or Boston. c. 1810–40.

Comment
Classical forms based on ancient prototypes were popular from 1800 to 1840. Chairs of this type were often part of furniture sets that included armchairs, sofas, center tables, and sometimes console tables. The simple yet imposing lines of Empire furnishings made such pieces fitting for the Greek Revival houses of the period.

Hints for Collectors
Tiger maple, a rare wood that was popular in the early 19th century, was a particularly good medium for Empire designs, which often featured graining as a decorative element. Chairs like the one shown here were made in sets, and it is possible to find matched groups of 6 or 8, generally selling at a premium.

Eastlake side chair

Description

Side chair with arched top rail including a veneered walnut burl
panel framed by an inscribed line. Lower edge of top rail cut in
series of 4 arches resting on 3 short turned spindles set in curved
middle rail; bottom rail curved similarly. Stiles rounded in front
and on top, flaring out from seat. Curved, inscribed side braces
mortised into stiles and seat rails. Circular cane seat; narrow
inscribed front skirt. Front legs and paired stretchers turned;
plain rear legs flaring back. Paired plain stretchers on sides and
single one in rear. *Variations:* Overall outline may be simpler,
with plainer rectangular back and seat.

Materials and Dimensions

Ash. Walnut burl veneer. Cane seat. Height: 37¾"; 17½" to seat.

Locality and Period

Throughout the United States. c. 1875–90.

Comment

Eastlake-style furniture was mass-produced in factories all over
the country in the late 19th century; it was both simply made and
distinctive. The inscribed decoration on the chair shown here is a
Renaissance Revival motif; the turned legs are Sheraton (14).
Such combinations of styles were typical of popular inexpensive
designs of the period.

Hints for Collectors

Stenciled names on seat bottoms sometimes identify makers, but
most Eastlake chairs were unmarked. Since prices for perfect
and damaged examples of this kind of chair are often about the
same, it is advisable to look for one in excellent condition.
Fortunately, they are relatively common and sometimes found in
sets of 4 or 6.

China Trade armchair

Description

Armchair with wide top rail having curved ends and relief carving, suggesting flora, and ending in scrolls. Stiles rectangular and slightly curved, with incised lines near seat. Horizontal rail, connecting midpoints of stiles, carved with leafy scrolls. Arms curving down from tops of stiles to scrolled handholds; arm supports curving in, then out, to join tops of front legs. Straight-edged cane seat widening at front; seat rails with carved rectangles. Front legs saber-shaped, with inscribed disks at rail level and carved lines below; plain rear legs flaring back. *Variations:* Chinese chairs made for the American market followed a variety of Sheraton and Empire designs.

Materials and Dimensions

Oriental rosewood. Cane seat. Height: 33½"; 18" to seat.

Locality and Period

China, made for export to the American market. c. 1840.

Comment

Chinese furniture meant for the American market and based on Western styles is distinguishable by its woods, such as the Oriental rosewood of the Empire chair shown here, and by its Orientalized details, such as the linear relief carving on the top rail.

Hints for Collectors

China Trade furniture may well be confusing to collectors; though its overall designs follow Western prototypes, its unusual decorative details may lead beginning collectors to think it eccentric or even fake. While rare, examples do turn up, particularly in areas that were important centers of the China trade. Such furniture offers a relatively untouched area for sophisticated collectors.

Rococo Revival balloon-back side chair

Description
Side chair with curved open back. Top rail with center panel of projecting pillow-shaped section flanked by 3 dots arranged vertically on each side. Curved lower back rail with raised center section. Curved braces, or low arms, arching from stiles to center of side rails of upholstered seat. Front legs simple and cabriole, ending in tapered feet; plain rear legs flaring back. *Variations:* Curved back is often close to balloon shape, with boldly curved stiles and top rail. Top rail may have carved floral or leaf cresting. Rosewood was the most fashionable wood; cherry and walnut were often used in pieces of lesser quality.

Materials and Dimensions
Boxwood. Modern needlework seat. Inner-spring construction. Height: 34″; 17″ to seat.

Locality and Period
Throughout the United States. c. 1840–60.

Comment
Small side chairs with balloon-shaped backs evolved from Empire models with similar curved backs and classical leaf or scroll ornamentation. While there is no documentation for the theory, the side braces have been interpreted as low arms necessitated by the huge skirts women wore in the 1840–60 period. Chairs of boxwood, rather than rosewood, with simple panel ornaments such as the example shown here, were very likely made in furniture factories rather than fine cabinetry shops.

Hints for Collectors
Very common during the Rococo Revival period, balloon-back chairs were made with a wide variety of carved and molded decoration. Make sure a slat or stile has not been replaced, and beware of shoddy repairs concealed by dark staining.

Rococo Revival balloon-back side chair

Description
Side chair with balloon-shaped open back; top rail molded, curved, and edged with carved flora. Stiles are molded and curved continuations of top rail. Lower back rail curving up to carved flower at center. Curved braces, or low arms, arching down from stiles to side rails of upholstered seat. Front seat rail slightly bowed, with floral carving at center; side and rear seat rails forming continuous curve. Front legs plain cabriole, carved at knees; plain rear legs flaring back. *Variations:* This popular type was made with or without carving; the range is broad, from plain to elaborately decorated.

Materials and Dimensions
Walnut and pine. Modern upholstery. Inner-spring construction. Height: 33½″; 17″ to seat.

Locality and Period
Throughout the United States. c. 1840–70.

Comment
Rococo Revival chairs like the one shown here developed from earlier klismos-shape designs that were simply modified according to the new taste. The curves are Rococo, but not precisely like those of any 18th-century model, and the use of springs in the seat is a mid-19th-century innovation. Made with varying degrees of refinement and at several price levels, such chairs attested to an awareness of current fashions in all classes of society. This particular design was modestly priced.

Hints for Collectors
Balloon-back chairs were reproduced in the 1930s, but details were flatter and overall size smaller. Original examples are relatively common and inexpensive. Also, unlike most Victorian chairs, they can often be obtained in matching sets of 6 to 8.

Empire side chair

Description
Side chair in klismos shape. Vase-shaped splat between broad, curved top rail and narrow lower rail. Back flared backward from seat to top rail, with round stiles flattened on front side. Cane seat enclosed by curved rails mortised into stiles. Flat front stretcher; paired spindle stretchers on sides, single spindle in rear. Ring-turned, tapered front legs with ball feet; plain rear legs, tapered feet. *Variations:* Top rail may be closer to typical rectangular klismos form and have a deeper curve. Splat may be replaced by one or more horizontal bars across the back. Painted black or grained. Upholstered seat instead of caning.

Materials and Dimensions
Tiger maple and ash. Cane seat. Height: 34″; 18″ to seat.

Locality and Period
New England, probably Massachusetts. c. 1820–40.

Comment
This simple design is based on 2 Sheraton designs, the Fancy chair and the klismos, the latter inspired by an ancient Greco-Roman chair with a curved back and straight top rail. The broad top rail of the chair shown here has scalloped motifs that resemble Rococo Revival designs prevalent in the 1830s.

Hints for Collectors
A very popular design in their time, Empire chairs of this type are easily located; it is therefore wise to look for those in very good condition. Any with spliced legs and replaced splats or seat rails should be avoided. Because this type of simple chair was often acquired in sets of 6 or more, some sets have survived intact. Since variations are relatively minor, chairs with different backs can be used together harmoniously.

Empire armchair

Description
Armchair in klismos shape. Wide top rail protruding at center of upper edge, flanked by curved ends, and having double-arched lower edge. Broad vase-shaped splat. Stiles curving down to seat, with narrow straight rails framing upholstered center. Arms curving down from top rail in continuous loop, ending in scroll at side seat rail. Front legs in modified cabriole shape with rounded fronts; plain rear legs flaring back. *Variations:* Back may be simpler, with plain curved panel as top rail. Front legs are sometimes turned. Seat may be caned. Splat may be shorter, set into a lower rail.

Materials and Dimensions
Mahogany and mahogany veneer over pine. Fabric upholstery. Height: 33"; 17½" to seat.

Locality and Period
Probably New England. c. 1830–45.

Comment
The Empire style, introduced at the beginning of the 19th-century, remained a popular American design tendency into the middle of the century. Its architectural equivalent, the Greek Revival style, was seen in many mid-19th-century houses. The arched and curved top panel and wide vase-shaped splat on the chair shown here suggest a date after 1830, although the contour of the back is in the spirit of the klismos designs made popular by Duncan Phyfe early in the century.

Hints for Collectors
Chairs like this were meant to be sturdy functional pieces and, if damaged, they are easily repaired. Moreover, they can often be obtained quite reasonably, particularly from country dealers and smaller auction houses.

Queen Anne country side chair

Description
Painted side chair with curved top rail dipping in center to form crown for vase-shaped splat. Splat resting on straight lower rail. Flat stiles curving back slightly toward top. Seat upholstered in leather, covering seat rails. Front legs turned in elaborate ball-and-block pattern, with scroll, or Spanish, feet; rear legs flared and plain. Front stretcher with unusual 3-ball design; side and rear stretchers plain. *Variations:* Seats can be rush. Some legs are subtle variations of type seen in this example or of cabriole design. Stretchers with standard ball-and-ring designs were used on all kinds of chairs made in the New York–Connecticut area.

Materials and Dimensions
Maple. Painted black. Leather seat. Height: 40″; 18½″ to seat.

Locality and Period
New England, probably Connecticut. c. 1740–1820.

Comment
Rural designs are often hard to localize, but the chair shown here appears to be of Connecticut origin because of the shape of the back stiles and front stretcher. Chairs such as this one, combining the turned legs of the William and Mary style and the curved back of the Queen Anne style, were used over a long period. Although some were made very early, a later group dates from the Federal era.

Hints for Collectors
Country Queen Anne chairs are in demand today and many repaired or reproduction pieces are on the market. A good example that has not been restored or is not a copy should have an overall look of age, with the edges of stretchers smoothed by use and the paint worn.

Queen Anne country side chair

Description
Painted side chair with curved top rail dipping in center. Vase-shaped splat resting on curved lower back rail. Turned stiles baluster-shaped at splat level and plain round stumps below. Straight seat rails covered by rush seat. Front legs with vase-turned upper section over cabriole lower part terminating in pointed trifid feet. Single ball-and-ring-turned stretcher in front, with pairs of plain round stretchers on other sides. *Variations:* Top rail may be carved or yoke-shaped above a tall back. Seat may be upholstered in leather or fabric. Legs and stretchers may have a variety of turnings.

Materials and Dimensions
Ash and maple. Painted black. Rush seat. Height: 40″; 18½″ to seat.

Locality and Period
New Jersey. c. 1750.

Comment
The combination of carved and turned parts in this type of chair, a mixture of William and Mary and Queen Anne styles, is characteristic of rural cabinetmaking. While this often indicates a relatively early example, other similar country pieces—simpler in detail and construction, with delicate moldings on back rails—were made after the Revolution.

Hints for Collectors
Black was the most common color for painted side chairs; the gold rings on this chair look like added details that were favored after the Revolution. Since paint may conceal repairs and replacements, it is wise to inspect painted surfaces. Painted country side chairs like this are relatively common, though not always in acceptable condition.

Description
Side chair with curved top rail having straight top edge, rounded corners, and double-arched bottom edge. Simple vase-shaped splat. Rectangular stiles, deeper than wide, continuing below seat as plain stump rear legs. Rectangular seat with leather-upholstered frame set into plain straight rails. Plain front legs curved slightly, their contour and feet suggesting animal legs and paws. Single rectangular stretchers on all sides, front and rear ones set high. *Variations:* Designs may be closer to 18th-century models, with back, splat, and legs more gracefully curved.

Materials and Dimensions
Oak. Leather upholstery. Height: 37″; 18″ to seat.

Locality and Period
Grand Rapids or other major furniture centers. c. 1900–20.

Comment
Turn-of-the-century oak furniture was made in a variety of eclectic designs based on historical models, as well as in the more innovative Mission style. The basic inspiration for the chair shown here was American Queen Anne designs; but to make it sturdy and inexpensive, as well as appealing to the public of 1910, the adaptation is quite loose.

Hints for Collectors
Colonial Revival furniture from the 1900–20 period often closely followed 18th-century models, with only incidental minor variations. Revival pieces continued to be made after 1920, but with more prominent, deliberate changes reflecting the tastes and proportions prevailing during each decade. "Early American" furniture manufacturers today produce Queen Anne pieces with smaller seats, thinner legs, and less detailing.

Queen Anne leather-back side chair

Description
Side chair with yoke-shaped top rail rounded at ends. Straight
stiles flat in front, rounded behind, and tapered toward top.
Straight-sided splat covered in leather, with brass tacks
reinforcing upholstery; splat set into shoe on rear seat rail.
Straight-sided seat widening toward front, with leather
upholstery covering seat rails and bordered with tacks. Cabriole
front legs with plain pad feet; square rear legs flaring back. 4
single stretchers simply turned; rear one raised. *Variations:*
Most Queen Anne chairs have solid vase-shaped splats without
upholstery. Back stiles may curve more.

Materials and Dimensions
Maple. Leather upholstery. Brass tacks. Height: 41½″; 18″ to
seat.

Locality and Period
New England. c. 1730–50.

Comment
New England chair designs are usually more restrained than
those from other parts of the country. The Queen Anne example
shown here has straight stiles that are more severe than most, a
trait more common in New England chairs (particularly those
from Connecticut or New Hampshire) than in those from the
Mid-Atlantic states. The presence of stretchers is another clue to
this chair's New England origin.

Hints for Collectors
The full range of American Queen Anne chairs, from the
restrained to the elaborate, has been extensively reproduced
since the turn of the century. Very tall backs as well as legs with
ungainly carved details on the feet and the knee brackets are
signs of reproductions.

57 Colonial Revival side chair

Description
Side chair with yoke-shaped top rail slightly arched at center and curved at ends. Stiles curving in, then slightly out, continuing down to form rear legs below seat. Vase-shaped splat. Leather-upholstered seat slipped between straight rails and enclosed by half-round molding. Cabriole front legs terminating in pad feet; plain rectangular rear legs flared back. *Variations:* Queen Anne Revival chairs made of oak usually have taller backs and straight stiles. Fabric upholstery is more common than leather.

Materials and Dimensions
Oak and pine. Leather upholstery. Height: 37½"; 19" to seat.

Locality and Period
Grand Rapids. c. 1900–15. Variants made elsewhere.

Comment
Colonial Revival designs from the turn of the century frequently differed more markedly from the originals than does the chair shown here, in which the proportions and gently curved legs and back stiles are quite close to 18th-century models. This chair does differ from the originals in that oak was not much used by the elegant American workshops that produced Queen Anne furniture. Also, details on this chair have been simplified so that it could be mass-produced. Grand Rapids was the center for factory-made furniture, particularly in oak.

Hints for Collectors
Turn-of-the-century Colonial Revival designs, many offering graceful lines and excellent construction, are all but ignored by most collectors and are inexpensive. This is an area in which research is just beginning, and collectors' interest is bound to grow as these pieces become better understood.

58 Georgian Revival side chair

Description
Tall-back side chair with yoke-shaped top rail curving in at ends.
Stiles subtly curving and rounded. Vase-shaped splat inlaid in
leaf design. Seat with upholstered frame slipped inside curved
rails. Seat rails curved down at center; front rail with applied
leaf decoration. Cabriole front legs cut in 3 sections, with claw-
and-ball feet. Plain rear legs curving back. *Variations:* Queen
Anne, Chippendale, and Sheraton designs were also adapted to
suit turn-of-the-century taste.

Materials and Dimensions
Mahogany and pine. Satinwood inlay. Original fabric upholstery.
Height: 46½"; 20" to seat.

Locality and Period
Throughout the United States. c. 1900–20.

Comment
At the beginning of this century, many manufacturers
interpreted traditional American as well as English and French
forms. The chair shown here was inspired by Georgian designs,
though it is taller and more slender and has more elaborate
curves than typical 18th-century models. The inlay pattern is
based on a later Hepplewhite model sometimes used in this
country.

Hints for Collectors
Revivals of 18th-century furniture designs just after the turn of
the century were often made by the finest manufacturers. The
chairs are often taller than early examples, and the shaping of
the rails is more complex. They have inner braces reinforced
with screws and metal plates that were not used in the 18th
century. Look for fine details and craftsmanship and avoid the
many shoddy examples.

59 Queen Anne side chair

Description
Side chair with yoke-shaped top rail embellished with central carved shell; rounded ends mortised into stiles. Stiles flat in front and rounded behind, curving in and back out just above seat. Center splat vase-shaped and set into shoe on rear seat rail. Seat horseshoe-shaped. Cabriole front legs with carved shells on knees, terminating in claw-and-ball feet; rear legs slightly flared, chamfered stumps. Single turned stretchers, with front one recessed and rear one set higher. *Variations:* Some Rhode Island chairs have flat stretchers. Claw-and-ball feet may be less squat.

Materials and Dimensions
Walnut. Modern fabric upholstery. Height: 38½″; 17″ to seat.

Locality and Period
Rhode Island. c. 1740–60. Related designs produced in New York and Pennsylvania.

Comment
Elegant Queen Anne chairs, like the one shown here, are often embellished with carved shells on the top rail and on the knees of cabriole legs. Curved backs like this one were made in Pennsylvania and New York as well as Rhode Island, and each region followed a particular English precedent. This chair's graceful lines reflect the new Rococo style that became so important in elaborate mid-18th-century craftsmanship.

Hints for Collectors
Fine Queen Anne chairs are among the most costly American furnishings as well as the rarest. Examples with restrained detail are more common than elegant ones like this chair, which combines claw-and-ball feet, associated with Chippendale designs, with a Queen Anne back and overall lines.

Queen Anne corner chair

Description
Corner chair with 2-part back crowned by additional upper section, or comb. Top rail with curved ends and indented center. Vase-shaped upper splat repeated in 2 taller splats of lower section of back. Flat-topped curving rail doubling as arms, with extra molding in center section. Stiles on comb curved in typical Queen Anne pattern; stiles on lower back turned in baluster design. Seat almost diamond-shaped with curved front corner. Front leg cabriole; 3 side and rear legs straight and round; all terminating in pad feet. Crossed turned stretchers. *Variations:* Comb is unusual; more often top rail continues as arms. Seat rail may be more elegantly curved. Pierced splats and elaborate carving on knees in Chippendale examples. No stretchers on elegant pieces made in Mid-Atlantic region.

Materials and Dimensions
Mahogany. Reproduction damask upholstery. Height: 48½"; 18" to seat.

Locality and Period
Rhode Island. c. 1740–60.

Comment
Rhode Island, particularly Newport, is associated with elegant but restrained design. The corner chair shown here is simple yet rich in subtle detail, such as the top rail with its wonderful curve. Some corner chairs have deep skirts designed to conceal chamber pots within (61), when the chair was placed in the corner of a room rather than at a desk.

Hints for Collectors
Craftsmanship as fine as that found on this chair is quite rare. Since this is an expensive piece, it is doubly important to check for repaired or replaced legs and splats.

Chippendale corner chair

Description
Corner chair with curved, flat top rail with plain molding at center; arms ending in rounded handholds. 3 vase-turned stiles separated by 2 wide urn-shaped splats slanting backward. Straight-sided rectangular seat having leather-upholstered frame slipped inside flat seat rails with rounded rear corner. Seat rails extending into deep cusped panels. 3 plain cabriole legs with claw-and-ball feet; rear leg plain stump. *Variations:* Such deep seat rails are rarely found nowadays, since many corner chairs, originally meant to conceal chamber pots, have been modified. Curved seat rails are common. Splats are often pierced.

Materials and Dimensions
Mahogany and cherry. Leather seat. Height: 30¾"; 18¾" to seat.

Locality and Period
New York. c. 1760–70.

Comment
Corner chairs (in early records also called roundabouts) were used at desks or in corners. While examples with solid splats are usually considered Queen Anne, the claw-and-ball feet and elaborate splat outline of the chair shown here make it more appropriately Chippendale. The design of its feet and turned stiles leads to a New York attribution.

Hints for Collectors
The original function of a particular corner chair may be surmised by lifting its upholstered seat and looking for traces of an inner support for a chamber pot. If a corner chair originally had a deep skirt that was later cut off, the bottom edge of the rail will likely be sharp or rough.

Chippendale armchair

Description
Armchair with yoke-shaped top rail turned up at ends. Solid vase-shaped splat. Stiles tapered and flaring out from seat. Double-curved arms spooned out near stiles; curved supports set back from front seat rail. Handholds flat and scroll-shaped. Straight-sided seat widening in front; front seat rail with applied gadrooned molding in front. Cabriole front legs with claw-and-ball feet; rear legs plain stumps. *Variations:* Splats are often pierced. Some have shells carved on the top rail and on the knees of the cabriole legs.

Materials and Dimensions
Mahogany. Pine corner blocks under seat. Modern fabric upholstery. Height: 38″; 17½″ to seat.

Locality and Period
New York. c. 1760–70.

Comment
New York Chippendale chair designs are often restrained, with solid splats in place of the more showy pierced splats. Other characteristic New York features seen here are: the spooning of the arms, the use of flat scroll handholds instead of knuckle carving, and the angle of the talons on the claw-and-ball feet. Chippendale chairs like the one shown here relate more to earlier Georgian models than to those in the Chippendale design book.

Hints for Collectors
Consider the regional origins of pieces when forming a collection. New York and Philadelphia pieces fit better together than do New York and Boston examples. Since this Chippendale model was much reproduced in the early 1900s, be sure that proportions are correct and the feet are well carved with proper detailing.

Queen Anne armchair

Description
Armchair with solid vase-shaped splat veneered to provide extra-lively surface graining. Yoke-shaped top rail with projecting molded ears and carved shell in center. Straight-sided seat. Stiles slanting out and tapering from seat to top rail. Seat rails cut out along lower edge. Arms, scooped out on top near stiles, with molded knuckles and curved supports. Front legs cabriole with trifid feet. Rear legs plain rounded stumps flaring back to plain feet. *Variations:* Curved top rails (in Queen Anne style) may be used with pierced splats and claw-and-ball feet. Legs may have leaf or shell carving. Mahogany was also used.

Materials and Dimensions
Walnut and walnut veneer over pine. Modern upholstery. Height: 43″; 19″ to seat.

Locality and Period
Probably Pennsylvania. c. 1740–50.

Comment
The broad scale, scooped arms, trifid feet, and plain stump rear legs all suggest the chair shown here was made in Pennsylvania. A certain elegance is apparent in the details of furniture made in Pennsylvania, particularly Philadelphia, during the decades preceding the Revolution. This armchair is considered transitional because the top rail with projecting corners, or ears, is associated with Chippendale chairs, while the solid splat and trifid feet are Queen Anne elements.

Hints for Collectors
Elaborate Queen Anne chairs are in great demand and quite costly. Elegant details are not often imitated with success. A few fakes have turned up in this pattern, with the back often a little too high and with obvious distressing to suggest wear and age.

Colonial Revival armchair

Description
Armchair with yoke-shaped top rail having arched center.
Pierced splat with overlapping Gothic arches above a distorted
trefoil. Stiles flat in lower section and molded above arms, flaring
out toward top. Thick straight-sided arms, curving in and then
out into knuckle handholds; arm supports curved, recessed from
front, and set into side seat rails. Upholstered seat widening
toward front; straight-edged front rail having arched skirt with
applied shell in center. Cabriole front legs with leaf-carved knees
and claw-and-ball feet; plain stump rear legs flaring back.
Variations: Any number of 18th-century splat designs were used
interchangeably on revival chairs.

Materials and Dimensions
Mahogany. Fabric upholstery. Height: 40½″; 19″ to seat.

Locality and Period
Throughout the United States. c. 1900–20.

Comment
The basis of the revival design shown here is an 18th-century
Philadelphia Chippendale model (65). The splat differs, however:
the arches are clumsier because of added details, and the trefoil
beneath is distorted. The arms, simpler than those on 18th-
century examples, are not so smoothly joined to the stiles. Other
signs that this is a turn-of-the-century piece are its flatly carved
shell and its clumsy claw-and-ball feet.

Hints for Collectors
Since Colonial Revival designs are free variations of 18th-century
models, collectors should understand their relationship to the
originals. Though at first glance revival pieces seem more
elaborate than early models, they are actually disarmingly simple
in detail and execution.

Chippendale side chair

Description

Side chair with yoke-shaped top rail curving up at ends, with foliate carving above splat. Splat pierced and carved in interlacing pattern of Gothic arches and trefoil; splat set into shoe on rear seat rail. Stiles flat-sided but with rounded edges. Seat widening toward front, enclosing upholstered slip seat. Seat rails plain and straight. Legs straight and molded. 4 stretchers flat and straight. *Variations:* Straight legs may have applied fretwork in Chinese Chippendale style. Splats are sometimes more restrained, with less carving. Front seat rail may have carved accents.

Materials and Dimensions

Mahogany. Modern fabric upholstery. Height: 36½"; 17½" to seat.

Locality and Period

Philadelphia. c. 1765.

Comment

Since pre-Revolutionary Philadelphia furniture is usually associated with elaborate designs, collectors sometimes overlook the more restrained pieces made there. The back of the chair shown here is elegantly executed, but its legs and seat reflect a more restrained approach. These plain legs are close to those used at the time on elegant chairs from London.

Hints for Collectors

Chippendale chairs, ranging from restrained to elaborate, are readily available, but avoid splats requiring repair and legs with cracks, and be wary of turn-of-the-century reproductions. Collectors appraising plain Chippendale chairs, particularly those without carved details, should check for sharp edges and crude construction—sure signs of a reproduction.

Chippendale side chair

Description
Side chair with yoke-shaped top rail curving down at ends,
carved with delicate foliate ornament; at center, ribbon-bordered
circle formed with top of splat. Splat in pierced pattern with fine
leaf carvings draped across 4 interlacing vertical bands. Stiles
flaring slightly to top rail, with round molded edges. Seat
widening toward front. Plain seat rails with molded top lip
enclosing upholstered slip seat. Cabriole front legs with leaf-
carved knees and claw-and-ball feet; rear legs plain stumps.
Variations: Carving may be more elaborate on some examples,
simpler on others.

Materials and Dimensions
Mahogany. Modern fabric upholstery. Height: 37″; 18″ to seat.

Locality and Period
Philadelphia. c. 1760.

Comment
In Philadelphia, the largest American city during the decades
before the Revolution, the affluent upper class admired
fashionable furnishings. Thomas Chippendale's design book
reached the city shortly after it was published, but Philadelphia
society evidently preferred simpler and stronger adaptations of
its designs. The chair shown here, for example, has legs with less
carving than Chippendale suggested. Claw-and-ball feet, which
had gone out of fashion in London by this time, continued to be
popular in the Colonies.

Hints for Collectors
The hallmark of fine American design was its sensitive
combination of fashionable and conservative elements. Collectors
should look for pieces, such as this one, that blend these
tendencies with subtlety.

Chippendale side chair

Description
Side chair with molded, yoke-shaped top rail with curved projecting center embellished with a shell; rail ends molded in scroll pattern. Stiles plain and tapered. Pierced vase-shaped splat relatively plain, with low-relief scrolls on upper section. Splat fitted into shoe set in rear seat rail. Front legs cabriole, terminating in claw-and-ball feet. Plain, flared rear legs, square at top and bottom, chamfered round in center. Stretchers with vase, ring, and block turnings. *Variations:* Splat and front legs may be elaborately carved with foliate or scroll designs. Stretchers are generally absent on chairs made outside Massachusetts.

Materials and Dimensions
Mahogany. Pine or ash in seat. Modern damask upholstery in Rococo pattern. Height: 37½"; 18" to seat.

Locality and Period
Massachusetts. c. 1765.

Comment
In the decade before the Revolution, Chippendale design was the basis of elegant furniture, but interpreted differently in each region of Colonial America. This chair represents the more restrained side of Massachusetts furniture: carving is minimal, but curves are generous and sensitively introduced. The delicate claw-and-ball feet with prominent claws are characteristic of Massachusetts work, as is the presence of stretchers.

Hints for Collectors
Because Chippendale splats are fragile, they should be carefully examined for cracks. Clumsily rendered piercing is a sign that a splat may be a replacement. Repaired legs can be a source of problems; look for saw lines and screw marks to spot them.

Chippendale side chair

Description
Side chair with molded, yoke-shaped top rail having central carved shell flanked by leaves. Stiles plain and tapered. Splat pierced in diamond-and-scroll pattern. Splat fitted into shoe set in rear seat rail. Straight-sided seat widening toward front; seat rails with rounded molding along top edges. Slip seat upholstered. Cabriole front legs with carved shells on knees; claw-and-ball front feet. Plain rear legs flaring back. *Variations:* Splats are sometimes thicker, with carved as well as cutout details. Leaf rather than shell motif on top rail and knees of legs.

Materials and Dimensions
Mahogany, oak, and white pine. Modern upholstery. Height: 40″; 18″ to seat.

Locality and Period
New York. c. 1760–80.

Comment
New York Chippendale chairs generally have claw-and-ball feet on which the claws have straight-lined talons; the curving feet of the chair shown here are similar to some made by the New York cabinetmaker Gilbert Ash. Carved shells are a conservative motif on American Chippendale furniture, since they are throwbacks to the Queen Anne style; here they are combined with an elaborately pierced splat in the latest fashion of the day.

Hints for Collectors
Proportions are generally reliable guides to authenticity. Vintage Chippendale reproductions and fakes made at the beginning of this century, often confused with originals, are comparatively slender and tall, and their claw-and-ball feet are more flatly carved. Check cabriole legs to see if they are later replacements, cracked, or repaired.

Chippendale country side chair

Description
Painted side chair with vase-shaped pierced splat terminating at lower rail; overall painted linear decoration. Top rail gently curved. Stiles curve in from top rail to rush seat, then out from seat to floor. Front legs turned in vase-ring-block pattern above scroll feet; rear legs plain and flaring back. Front stretcher in ball-and-ring pattern; 5 side and rear stretchers more subtly turned. *Variations:* Pierced splat design varies. Legs can be straight or turned in a variety of patterns. Stain was often used to simulate mahogany. Pine and cherry were also used. Seats may be of splint or fabric.

Materials and Dimensions
Maple. Painted black. Rush seat. Height: 38″; 18″ to seat.

Locality and Period
Connecticut. c. 1750–80.

Comment
Conservative rural designs like that shown here are arousing more and more interest these days. Turned legs, associated with the earlier William and Mary style, were later used in country workshops, where turning was preferred to carving because it took less skill. This chair's ingeniously simple pierced splat was known in more sophisticated versions of the Queen Anne style, but it was most firmly associated with the Chippendale style, which dominates in this chair.

Hints for Collectors
A variation on a popular form, this type of chair should be examined closely, since paint might conceal major problems. If there are cracks or breaks in the legs or splat, repairs are not easy. To determine if paint or stain is original, examine worn areas where you might see traces of old colors.

Chippendale country side chair

Description
Side chair with yoke-shaped cresting rail, its center arched above
fanlike shell motif scored with fine ridges. Vase-shaped splat
pierced in scroll, heart, and modified diamond pattern and set on
molded lower rail high above seat. Stiles straight-edged and
molded, curving back above seat and continuing down as plain
rear legs flaring out below. Rectangular seat widening in front;
bottom edge of front and side rails cut in double curve, rear rail
plain, and front skirt having carved center shell. Front legs
straight and molded, mortised into seat rails. Single molded
stretchers in front and on sides, slender turned one in rear.
Variations: Rural Chippendale designs may have plainer straight
legs, rush seats, and pierced splats in varied patterns.

Materials and Dimensions
Maple. Original crewel upholstery. Height: 44⅞"; 17½" to seat.

Locality and Period
Probably by Major John Dunlap, New Hampshire. c. 1775.

Comment
Families of cabinetmakers like the Dunlaps of New Hampshire
produced distinctive furniture that balanced traditional with
fashionable designs. The chair shown here is tall and narrow-
backed like an earlier William and Mary example (109), but the
shaping of its top rail, its molded front legs, and its pierced splat
were inspired by Chippendale designs, though adapted to the
taste of the Dunlaps and their clientele.

Hints for Collectors
Dunlap furniture is rare, but the Chippendale products of other
rural cabinetmakers are often available and should not be
overlooked. Matching sets are particularly desirable.

Chippendale ladder-back side chair

Description
Side chair with molded back stiles flaring out toward top and enclosing 4 rails in scroll pattern with center circles. Slip seat straight-sided, narrowing at rear. Plain straight, or Marlborough, legs reinforced by 4 plain stretchers; rear legs flaring to feet. *Variations:* Legs are often molded or fluted. Back rails may be arranged in a different, but equally curving, pattern. Some examples have center rosettes on rails—a sign of work by Daniel Trotter, a Philadelphia craftsman known for ladder-backs.

Materials and Dimensions
Mahogany and pine. Modern fabric upholstery. Height: 38½"; 18" to seat.

Locality and Period
Philadelphia, but widely adopted type. c. 1770–1800.

Comment
The ladder-back, a modern name for a chair called a scrolled-splat in early furniture design books, was one of the popular Chippendale forms after the Revolution. Martha Washington purchased a group of these chairs in Philadelphia about 1783 that can still be seen in the Washington home at Mount Vernon. One Mount Vernon chair bears the label of Jonathan Gostelowe, a Philadelphia cabinetmaker.

Hints for Collectors
To evaluate simple designs like this, study the subtle details. Even the simplest examples have molded stiles, carved back rails with overlapping scrolls, or other finely crafted elements not found on 19th-century reproductions. Philadelphia pieces frequently have seat rails mortised into the rear legs, so that the narrow rectangular tenons show behind the rear legs.

Description

Painted square-back armchair with straight stiles and rails framing urn-and-column splat painted in contrasting colors. Arms curving down from back stiles into front supports continuing down as tapered front legs. Cane seat straight-sided. Plain rear legs flaring back. Front stretcher recessed and mortised into side stretchers. *Variations:* Painted Federal chairs may have oval backs. Black or white was the usual ground color, with other color accents used for details.

Materials and Dimensions

Maple. Painted black, with multihued details. Cane seat. Height: 36″; 18″ to seat.

Locality and Period

Made by John and Thomas Seymour, Boston. c. 1800.

Comment

Painted Federal-period furniture is rare. Painted furniture in fashionable Neoclassical designs was introduced in England in the 1760s by Robert Adam. The chair shown here is a variation of a design in Thomas Sheraton's *Drawing Book* (1790–94). A side chair in the same design, bearing the Seymour label, is the basis for the attribution of this armchair. John Seymour and other Boston cabinetmakers were among the most fashionable craftsmen in the young Republic.

Hints for Collectors

Except for a few labeled pieces, painted furniture such as this elegant example can be difficult to identify. Very little distinguishes English from American work on the most fashionable level. One must rely mainly on the type of wood used: maple, for example, was used more often by American than by English craftsmen.

Description
Side chair with rectangular back. Top rail inscribed in floral pattern. Solid vase-shaped splat with inscribed decoration set into curved lower rim of top rail. Lower rail straight. Molded stiles. Angular braces supporting back. Rectangular cane seat with flat molded rails rounded at front corners; projecting front skirt with inscribed lines. Front legs turned in elaborate ball-and-ring pattern, ending in bun feet; rear legs square and plain. Paired stretchers on front and sides, single one in rear; front stretchers turned. *Variations:* Pedimented top rails and more elaborately decorated splats also occur.

Materials and Dimensions
Walnut and walnut veneer. Cane seat. Height: 35″; 17″ to seat.

Locality and Period
Throughout the United States. c. 1880–90.

Comment
Furniture in the Eastlake style ranges from very simple to elegant. This type of chair was mass-produced by large chair factories that sought to keep abreast of the changing tastes and fashions of the day. The turned legs and rectangular back of the chair shown here are inspired by Sheraton Fancy chairs of the 1810–30 period. While the design conforms to Charles Eastlake's principle of simplicity, the use of walnut veneers is a pretentious touch that would not have appealed to him.

Hints for Collectors
Except for rare labeled pieces by Herter Brothers and others, interest in Eastlake-style furniture is fairly limited, so it is a field that is worth the attention of adventurous collectors willing to study this influential style. Eastlake furniture is easy to find and generally inexpensive.

Renaissance Revival side chair

Description
Side chair with arched top rail crowned by small curved
pediment. Straight stiles with corbels at top and curved
pedestal-like segments at juncture with arched lower back rail.
Pattern repeated within back, framing cross-shaped splat with
octagonal pattern in center. Cane seat. Front seat rail curving
out, its skirt having inscribed curved corners. Curved center
brace connects seat rail to front stretcher and ends in globular
drop. Front legs columnar; rear legs plain and flaring back. Plain
stretchers on front and sides. *Variations:* Wooden-back chairs
were made with cane or solid wood seats, and in a variety of
simple classical designs with pierced or solid wooden backs.

Materials and Dimensions
Walnut. Cane seat. Height: 41¼"; 16" to seat.

Locality and Period
Possibly designed by James Renwick, New York. c. 1865.

Comment
Renaissance Revival furnishings were used in Italianate villas
and other classically inspired houses. Chairs with solid or pierced
wooden backs and cane or wooden seats were designed for use in
entrance halls. The chair shown here has been attributed to the
architect James Renwick because it came from a house Renwick
designed in New Jersey, and mid-19th-century architects often
designed some or all of the furnishings for houses they designed.

Hints for Collectors
Attributable architect-designed furnishings are uncommon prior
to the early 20th century. Any piece associated with a well-
known 19th-century architect is of greater interest and value
than undocumented examples.

75 Federal shield-back side chair

Description
Side chair having molded, open shield back with delicate leaf carving at center of arched top rail. Splat consisting of flat classical urn with streaming garlands spanning oval medallion, set atop 5 curved vertical bands ending in relief-carved fanlike patera. Plain curved stiles join back to flaring rear legs. Seat frame concealed by upholstery fastened with tacks in garland pattern. Front legs straight and tapered. Plain flat stretchers, with front one recessed. *Variations:* Inlaid decoration is often combined with flat carving or used as a replacement for it. Legs are sometimes more elaborate.

Materials and Dimensions
Mahogany. Ash or oak in seat frame. Reproduction silk damask upholstery. Brass tacks. Height: 37½"; 18" to seat.

Locality and Period
Rhode Island. c. 1800–20. Similar designs made elsewhere throughout the eastern United States.

Comment
The shield-back chair is most often associated with George Hepplewhite's designs. Distinctive interpretations are often found in certain cities or areas. Providence and Newport cabinetmakers were among the most frequent users of the kind of shield shown here, featuring a flat urn in the upper splat.

Hints for Collectors
Carefully examine chairs with very plain legs, since early reproductions of designs like this were often used in dining rooms, where legs would not ordinarily have been visible under a table. Splats that have been repaired are likely to come apart again, particularly if complex and delicate.

Federal truncated shield-back side chair

Description
Side chair with truncated, flat-topped shield-shaped back.
Central section of splat cut in diamond-and-pointed-oval pattern,
flanked by cutout triple-loop motifs, all resting on solid arc at
bottom of shield. Plain curved stiles connecting back to flaring
rear legs. Seat upholstery extending over curved rails. Front
legs straight and tapered toward feet. *Variations:* Shield-backs
are often embellished with inlaid or delicately carved
Neoclassical motifs. The full-shield back with an arched top is
more common.

Materials and Dimensions
Mahogany. Pine blocks under seat. Reproduction silk damask
upholstery. Height: 34½″; 18½″ to seat.

Locality and Period
Rhode Island. c. 1790–1810. Variants also produced in New
York.

Comment
The truncated shield-back is a rare design used in New York and
Providence. The chair shown here is closest to one attributed to
Thomas Howard, a Providence cabinetmaker. The basic design
was probably adapted from a chair with an upholstered shield-
shaped back illustrated in George Hepplewhite's *Cabinet-Maker
and Upholsterer's Guide* (1788).

Hints for Collectors
Unusual forms are often considered by collectors to be less
desirable than more typical ones, so one may find some fine
pieces that have been overlooked because atypical. Beware,
however, of examples that are unusual merely because they are
late variations or reproductions.

Federal shield-back side chair

Description
Side chair with shield back made of interlacing elements in a heart-shaped pattern. 3 splats with delicately carved capitals. Center splat broad, elaborate, and inlaid with bellflowers, ending in 7 branches at top; inlaid patera at base of splats. Straight-sided seat. Straight front legs tapered and molded. Curved stiles join shield to rear legs, which are square and flared back to plain feet. Flat stretchers. *Variations:* Backs may be more shieldlike, with splats carved in shallow relief or cut in vase shape. Splats may be columnar. Carved or inlaid classical details. Elaborate legs ending in projecting feet.

Materials and Dimensions
Mahogany. Ash in seat. Modern fabric upholstery. Height: 38¾"; 17" to seat.

Locality and Period
Baltimore or elsewhere in the Mid-Atlantic region. c. 1790–1800.

Comment
Heart-shaped shield-back chairs were featured in both the Hepplewhite and Sheraton design books of the 1780s and 1790s, and the Hepplewhite design was used extensively. The delicate inlays and carving on this chair relate it to Baltimore cabinetry, the most elegant of the post-Revolutionary era. The use of ornamentation in this basically simple design is representative of the finest Federal-era craftsmanship.

Hints for Collectors
After decades of neglect, Federal furniture is once more highly appreciated, and consequently prices have been rising. Collectors should expect to pay a substantial sum for a piece of this delicacy and condition.

Federal shield-back side chair

Description
Side chair with shield back topped by arched rail with convex molding; corners of rail carved with drapery swags hung from center of splat and continuing across to stiles. Splat with carved urn atop pedestal. Grapes and grape leaves on quarter-round base of splat and on 2 flanking splats radiating from base. Curved stiles set on curved braces, continuing below seat as plain, flared rear legs. Seat upholstered over rails, straight on 3 sides and curved in front. Tapered front legs with ebony-veneered spade feet; grapes and leaves carved on legs. *Variations:* Most shield-backs have curving splats but no urn. Inlay is more common than carving. Thin curved arms on narrow supports may be used.

Materials and Dimensions
Mahogany and ebony. Maple, ash, and pine as secondary woods. Height: 38¼″; 17″ to seat.

Locality and Period
Carving attributed to Samuel McIntire, Salem, Massachusetts. c. 1795.

Comment
Salem was a major center for fine cabinetmakers, supported by an affluent shipowner clientele during the early Federal era. The Hepplewhite-style shield-back chair shown here, elegantly executed and embellished with superb carving attributed to Samuel McIntire, is a masterful example of Neoclassical design.

Hints for Collectors
Fine chairs like this one are rare, but simpler shield-backs are readily available. Such chairs can be graceful even when not embellished with fine carving.

Description

Square-back armchair with straight molded top rail crowned by rectangular, fluted center panel. Straight molded stiles broadening just above seat. Stiles enclosing 5 pointed and fluted arches between 4 reeded columns with turned capitals and square bases. Molded lower back rail. Arms, projecting from side of stiles, are flat-sided, molded, and curved out; scrolled handholds ending in carved rosettes. Molded arm supports curving down to join side seat rails. Seat upholstered over curved rails and outlined in brass tacks. Front legs tapered, reeded columnar forms, with spade feet; plain tapered rear legs flaring back. *Variations:* Splats may be vase-shaped. Top panels sometimes display carved sunbursts or garlands.

Materials and Dimensions

Mahogany and ash. Cherry and pine secondary woods. Modern silk upholstery. Brass tacks. Height: 34¾"; 16½" to seat.

Locality and Period

Possibly by Slover and Taylor, New York. c. 1800–10. Similar designs by other fashionable cabinetmakers.

Comment

Chairs like the one shown here, called square-backs in early records, were produced by Slover and Taylor and other fashionable New York cabinetmakers. Designs from the same city tend to be similar; this chair resembles a number of other New York examples.

Hints for Collectors

Square-back chairs like this were reproduced for turn-of-the-century dining room sets. Check the rosettes and reeding carefully: rosettes without precisely detailed leaves or petals make a piece suspect, as should flat reeding.

Gothic Revival side chair

Description
Side chair with back slanting toward flat top rail cut into arcade of 4 pointed Gothic arches along its bottom edge. Arches supported by 3 slender rectangular columns widening toward curved lower rail. Straight-sided seat widening in front; cushion (upholstery removed here) with springs; seat rails straight and simply veneered. Front legs made from flat boards cut in cabriole contour, with scrolled knees and tapered feet; plain rear legs flaring back. *Variations:* Top rail may have piercework trefoils cut into it. Legs and back may be straight.

Materials and Dimensions
Mahogany, mahogany veneer, and pine. Fabric-upholstered cushion with inner springs. Height: 33½"; 17½" to seat.

Locality and Period
Possibly by J. and J. W. Meeks, New York. c. 1840–60.

Comment
The simple Gothic Revival chair shown here is more closely related to early 19th-century Gothic designs by English makers such as Thomas Sheraton and George Smith than to the more romantic Gothic designs introduced by American architects of the period. This must have been a popular design, since similar chairs appear in a contemporary engraving of Abraham Lincoln and his War Council, and there are also labeled examples by 2 New York makers, Roux and Meeks. The seat cushion with inner springs is a sign the chair was made after 1840.

Hints for Collectors
Gothic Revival side chairs like this were originally made in sets of as many as 12. A patient collector may be able to assemble a reasonably matched set. Since they were made in different workshops, individual examples may vary in woods and details.

Arts and Crafts armchair

Description
Low-back armchair with rectangular top rail flaring out slightly at ends, contrasting square pegs at joints, and flat central section projecting down. Straight rectangular stiles. Splat with wide center slat flanked by pairs of narrow curved slats; center decorated with inlaid flora and pierced holes; small rectangles joining slats. Arms curving out from stiles; stepped handholds with reinforcing pegs; curved spline connecting arm and support. Upholstered seat widening at front, with plain rails and double-curve brackets at front corners. Straight legs. Metal feet. Thin H-pattern stretchers. *Variations:* Splat may be solid wood or leather-upholstered. Stretchers may be set lower, as in Oriental style.

Materials and Dimensions
Mahogany. Ebony pegs and splines. Fruitwood inlay. Metal feet. Fabric upholstery. Height: 34"; 17" to seat.

Locality and Period
Designed by Charles Sumner Greene, Pasadena. 1907.

Comment
Charles Sumner Greene, of the architectural firm Greene and Greene, worked in California at the beginning of the century and designed Arts and Crafts furniture for houses built by him and his brother in southern California.

Hints for Collectors
The Arts and Crafts and Mission styles flourished in California with a distinctive flavor, but output was small. California designers less well known than Greene and Greene also worked in these styles, and their less expensive pieces offer collectors potential opportunities in this up-and-coming field.

Arts and Crafts armchair

Description
Armchair with rectangular top rail in stepped-arch outline, with square ebony pegs and inlaid flora and leaves. Straight stiles thickening toward seat. 3-part splat, the wide center pierced with vertical opening in rolling-pin shape and stepped outline repeated in 2 narrow strips flanking main section; small horizontal ebony bars join sides to center. Seat widening at front, with plain rails and leather upholstery. Arms curving out and tapering to rounded handholds; arm supports continuing as front legs. Straight legs with pegs at seat rail. Low thin stretchers in H-pattern. *Variations:* Other designs of the time also combined Mission and Oriental forms.

Materials and Dimensions
Mahogany. Ebony pegs. Fruitwood and gemstone inlay. Leather seat. Height: 42″; 18½″ to seat.

Locality and Period
Designed by Charles Sumner Greene, Pasadena. 1909.

Comment
The architects Charles Sumner Greene and Henry Mather Greene designed and supervised the production of distinctive furniture that fused Oriental, English Arts and Crafts, and Mission-style elements. Other designers combined similar elements, but never with such sculptural simplicity and subtle richness of detail.

Hints for Collectors
Greene and Greene furniture is uncommon because of its limited, commissioned production. If a piece does come on the market, its price should equal or exceed that paid for any Arts and Crafts furniture. Ebony pegs and splines, such as those on the chair shown here, are a hallmark of Greene and Greene work.

Wicker, Bentwood, and Metal Chairs

Many new materials and production techniques for furniture, and for chairs in particular, were either introduced or popularized during the 19th century, largely as a result of industrial advances and increasing middle-class demand. Wicker, bentwood, and various metals answered a growing need for practical, inexpensive furnishings. Their success was so marked and lasting that furniture using these materials is still produced and vintage examples are eagerly sought by collectors.

Wicker

Wicker—a term that covers such materials as rattan, willow, reed, and various grasses—has been used for furniture since ancient times, but only in the 19th century did it become truly popular. Beginning in the early 19th century, imported Oriental wicker designs inspired American manufacturers to make such furniture, for both indoor and outdoor use. In the mid-19th century, wicker designs were generally simple and utilitarian; but by the 1880s and 1890s—when new machines for shaping rattan and bending wooden frames gave skilled craftsmen new resources—designs became more intricate and fanciful. Again in the 20th century, wicker designs reverted to simpler shapes, but their popularity waned. Wicker furniture should be evaluated primarily by design and condition, rather than age.

Bentwood

Bentwood furnishings were made primarily in Central Europe and imported to America, where they became a familiar part of American interiors. Bentwood is made by steaming and bending wooden cylinders into sturdy curvilinear shapes. The major manufacturer, beginning just before 1840, was the firm established by Michael Thonet in Austria-Hungary. Bentwood chairs made today can be distinguished from early pieces by their less sturdy construction.

Metal, Plastic, and Fiberglass

Metal furniture, which had been made in limited quantity for centuries, gained great popularity with the advent of the Industrial Age. Cast-iron furniture, primarily for outdoor use, was produced in foundries around the country from the 1840s through the end of the century. Rococo Revival floral patterns and, later, Neoclassical motifs were common decoration. Cast iron was also used for a wide variety of patented rocking chairs. Portable folding chairs, a highly successful 19th-century invention, were sometimes made of iron or steel. From about the turn of the century, many purely functional chairs were made in metal: the so-called ice-cream parlor chairs, made of iron wire, are good examples of such sturdy, economical designs. Metal wire was used by Harry Bertoia, who designed some of the most popular modern chairs for the manufacturer Hans Knoll in the 1950s. Thicker steel (or aluminum) tubes, frequently chrome-plated, were used for many significant modern chair designs of the 1920s to 1940s. American designers of simple tubular-metal chairs often followed the lead of the innovative Bauhaus designers. Others created equally simple but more traditional forms in the Art Deco spirit, using metal as much for its color and texture as for its strength and durability. Plastic and fiberglass are other new furniture materials that have become important in the past 40 years because they can be shaped to suit the human form, as discovered by Charles Eames, who designed some of the best-known of these chairs.

Turn-of-the-century bentwood side chair

Description
Side chair made of cylindrical bentwood. Balloon-shaped back with 3 loops of bentwood inserted in overlapping balloon pattern. Stiles continuing as flared rear legs. Curved side braces join seat and back. Circular cane seat. Ring of bentwood serving as stretchers, a little below seat. Cylindrical front legs tapered and flared out to floor. *Variations:* Back splats are seldom as elaborate as this one. Seats are often made of plain wood or plywood, sometimes slightly contoured.

Materials and Dimensions
Ash and beech bentwood. Cane seat. Height: 35"; 19" to seat.

Locality and Period
Probably Austria-Hungary, possibly made for the American market by Thonet Brothers. c. 1900.

Comment
The process of producing bentwood was developed in the second quarter of the 19th century and is still used today. Furniture made by Thonet Brothers or Kohn in Austria-Hungary was shipped all over the world and was much advertised in America. The triple-looped splat of the unlabeled chair shown here suggests a turn-of-the-century date, even though its circular stretcher resembles those used on chairs advertised by Thonet as early as 1874. Thonet designs are sometimes considered forerunners of Art Nouveau.

Hints for Collectors
Made in large quantity, bentwood furniture is still readily available. Paper labels commonly applied to bentwood chairs have rarely survived, but it is still worth checking for them inside the seat frame for accurate dating and identification.

Victorian wicker rocking chair

Description
Rocking armchair with wicker back and legs, and wooden seat frame and rockers. Border in loop pattern framing back and arms. Back divided into 4 panels of repeated diamond motif ending at top in loops. 4 short panels under each arm. Seat caned in center. Straight legs with diagonal braces filled with loops. X-shaped stretchers with curved center braces. *Variations:* Wicker design evolved from plain early patterns to extravagant branching patterns during the second half of the 19th century.

Materials and Dimensions
Wicker (rattan), wood, and cane. Height: 39″; 16″ to seat.

Locality and Period
New England. c. 1860–90. Similar designs made in other regions.

Comment
Wicker furniture was introduced on the American scene just before the mid-19th century. At least one example was shown at the New York Crystal Palace Exhibition of 1853. Although best known as outdoor or patio furniture, wicker was used for flashy accent pieces in elegant parlors during the 1880s. Wicker styles followed the fashions of the day: early designs are plain and functional; at the turn of the century wicker forms became more fanciful and elaborate.

Hints for Collectors
Wicker furniture like the chair shown here was sometimes originally painted brown or green, but it has since become fashionable to paint it in a wide spectrum of colors. Removing undesirable paint is possible but difficult, and many collectors repaint early examples in proper period colors. Prices for wicker are generally based on design and condition, rather than age.

Child's Victorian wicker rocking chair

Description
Child's rocking chair made from wicker, with border of interlocking circles along top and sides; border narrowing to simple double band along arms and arm supports. Straight stiles. Openwork pattern of back depicts fan set at 45° angle. Broad twisted loops fill spaces on back and below armrests. Cane seat with wooden frame, curved on sides and front. Straight wooden legs wrapped in wicker; brackets filled with loops. Plain rockers. *Variations:* Simpler overall design and details. Bold twisted looping is more likely to occur on pre-1880 examples.

Materials and Dimensions
Wicker (rattan and willow) and maple. Cane seat. Height: 24″; 10½″ to seat.

Locality and Period
Throughout the United States. c. 1880–1900.

Comment
Little of the early wicker furniture made in America before 1850 has survived. The borders of the rocking chair shown here are reminiscent of early examples illustrated in the 1851 guidebook to the London Crystal Palace Exhibition and in *Godey's Lady's Book* of the period. The whimsical fan motif on the backrest relates this chair to designs of the late 1870s and 1880s, when Japanese decorative prints became an aesthetic influence.

Hints for Collectors
Most 19th-century wicker furniture is surprisingly simple and functional. Surviving catalogues of American retailers or manufacturers of wicker furnishings make it possible to date pieces illustrated in them. While seriously damaged wicker affects the value of a piece, replacement of the cane seat does not, since original seats are rarely found.

China Trade bamboo armchair

Description
Armchair with framework of bamboo stalks and interior detailing of thin bamboo shoots. Arched top rail crowning upper 3-part panel with octagonal center ornament. Central part of back, enclosed by rails and stiles, consisting of narrow panels flanking center octagon, all decorated with bamboo shoots in linear patterns. Arms curving down from back stiles, filled in with panels decorated with shoots. Cane seat bamboo-framed; seat rails made from 3 tiers of bamboo, topping 2 panels in front. Straight front legs with parallel bars on inside; rear legs flaring back. Single thin rod stretcher on each side. *Variations:* Back and arm panels come in a wide array of sizes and patterns.

Materials and Dimensions
Bamboo. Cane seat. Height: 35⅞"; 19" to seat.

Locality and Period
China, made for export to the American market. c. 1810–20.

Comment
Widespread interest in Chinese furniture began in the West in the early 18th century. Bamboo furniture like the chair shown here combines Chinese and Western elements in designs that are both Neoclassical and Oriental. Such chairs were imported from China in the early 19th century, following the lead of the British Prince Regent, who used them at his seaside residence in Brighton.

Hints for Collectors
Bamboo furniture has been imported to America for 2 centuries, and some recent products may be mistaken for antiques. New models are generally simpler and less carefully constructed. Check surfaces for wear or damage hidden by varnish.

Description
Wedge-shaped wicker corner chair with 2-sided latticework back.
Both top rails beaded and sweepingly curved, twisting around
top of straight center stile and ending in scroll. Taller half of
back with open panel edged by scrolls; shorter half with scrolls
enclosing lattice panel. Straight lower back rails with hanging
looped scrolls. Cane seat framed in wood, with beaded rim.
Saber-shaped legs reinforced with lacy scroll brackets and
straight cross stretchers. *Variations:* Wicker scrolls were added
or omitted with great freedom. Top rails and seat rim do not
usually have beaded edging (called rat-tail). Similar chairs were
made with more asymmetrical designs.

Materials and Dimensions
Wicker (rattan), hickory, and pine. Cane seat. Height: 35"; 17" to
seat.

Locality and Period
Throughout the United States. c. 1890–1915.

Comment
Wickerwork, consisting of rattan or willow, has been used for
furniture since the mid-19th century, or earlier. Although early
examples were relatively simple, the last quarter of the 19th
century saw the creation of elaborately detailed wicker pieces
which, like the chair shown here, often displayed some kinship to
Art Nouveau design.

Hints for Collectors
Makers' paper labels are sometimes found on older wicker chairs.
In the late 19th century wicker chairs were not usually painted;
white wicker is a recent trend. Early wicker is often found in a
damaged state and may require extensive and expensive repairs.

Late Victorian wicker armchair

Description
Wicker armchair with flat top rail curving to flared stiles topped
by cord-wrapped globe finials. Top rail and stiles covered in
herringbone-patterned wicker and enclosing rectangular panel of
heart-shaped scrolls. Side and lower back panels covered with
solid-woven wicker curving around seat. Cane seat with curved
sides and wooden frame. Legs flaring out. Front legs with
applied wicker decoration in scroll-and-ball pattern; plain rear
legs braced by simple brackets. Plain cross stretchers.
Variations: Wicker may be woven in a variety of designs, often
with more complex scrollwork. Legs may often be much simpler.

Materials and Dimensions
Wicker. Hardwood. Cane seat. Painted white. Height: 37½";
15" to seat.

Locality and Period
Throughout the United States. c. 1890.

Comment
Wicker is an exotic material usually from the Orient. Prompted
by the success of imported wicker furniture, American
manufacturers began adopting it during the 1840s for both indoor
and outdoor use. The earliest was apparently the plainest, but by
the 1890s it was being made in intricate and showy, as well as
simple, patterns.

Hints for Collectors
Some wicker furniture has been revitalized by having its worn
materials stripped off, so check for signs of such restoration. If a
wicker piece is worn and fraying, bring it to a professional
wicker restorer.

Child's Art Deco wicker armchair

Description
Painted reed armchair with straight top rail covered by several reed tubes bound in 4 places by flat rattan in contrasting color. Reeds curved around to cover straight stiles, arms, arm supports, and front legs, with intermittent wrapped rattan reinforcement. Back has midrail at arm level and another rail at seat; grillwork of vertical reed tubes with rattan binding forms back, seat, sides of arms, and long skirt all around. Thick wooden stretchers and diagonal leg braces. *Variations:* Solid rows of reeds may conceal framing. Similar designs have cushions.

Materials and Dimensions
Reeds and rattan. Wood. Painted. Height: 24½″; 10½″ to seat.

Locality and Period
Factories throughout the United States. c. 1925–50.

Comment
Wicker, the generic name for furniture made of reeds, rattan, and willow, was produced by American manufacturers since about 1840. Simple functional designs were made in the 19th century and became popular again in the Art Deco era, when the chair shown here was produced. Some examples from the period also use thin willow boughs in curving designs.

Hints for Collectors
Wicker and related materials were used for a wide variety of forms: chairs are the most readily available, but tables, plant stands, and shelves are also common. 20th-century wicker furniture can often be found at garage sales and in shops specializing in inexpensive furnishings. Similar, less sturdy designs still imported from the Orient differ from earlier American products in their overall design and glossy surfaces.

Eastlake folding armchair

Description
Folding armchair with turned, simulated-bamboo frame
enclosing steel webbing (originally covered in fabric). Cone-
shaped finials on top of straight stiles and at ends of upper rail.
Armrests attached to stiles midway above seat and supported on
angled front legs. Rectangular seat pinned to slanting front legs.
Flared rear legs. Front feet tapering and slightly curved. Front
stretcher joined to seat by 2 vertical rods. *Variations:* Turnings
may be less bamboolike. Webbed back panel may be taller.

Materials and Dimensions
Maple. Steel webbing. Height: 34″; 17½″ to seat.

Locality and Period
Made by George Hunzinger and Sons, New York. c. 1876–1900.
Similar designs by other American makers.

Comment
Hunzinger had patented several folding chairs in the 1860s, but
did not obtain a patent for a steel-mesh model until 1876. It
represents an interesting reaction to the overstuffed furniture
commonly viewed as typical of the Victorian period. Designers
saw comfort as a primary objective but attempted to achieve it
by rather different means, as in the chair shown here. The
textile-covered mesh pioneered by Hunzinger became as
much a hallmark of late 19th-century design as the overstuffed
iron-spring construction had been of earlier Victorian designs.

Hints for Collectors
Hunzinger chairs are frequently marked, so that it is possible to
form a collection of various models by this important designer.
Some are more practical than others, but all are distinctive
expressions of middle-class taste. Beware of chairs in poor
condition, since the mesh would be difficult to repair.

Turn-of-the-century highchair

Description
Highchair with rectangular back and plain round stiles topped by
grooved ball finials. Round top and center rails enclosing 5
turned spindles with grooved ball centers. Wicker-mesh back
panel framed by center and lower rail and 2 wicker-wrapped
spindles. Flat arms with curved edges and flattened knobs above
supports; 4 knobbed spindles matching those on back are set
beneath armrest. Cane seat with thick rails. Round legs tapered
at ends and flaring out toward floor. Front footrest. Paired
stretchers on sides; single one front and back. *Variations:*
Turned parts may be more complex; stiles and legs may be ring-
turned. Footrest is sometimes absent.

Materials and Dimensions
Oak. Cane seat. Wicker mesh. Height: 41¼"; 24½" to seat.

Locality and Period
Probably made in the Midwest. c. 1890–1910.

Comment
Large American factories made a great volume of sturdy oak
furniture. Borrowing elements from many historic styles,
designers produced popular lines attractive to a mass market but
scorned by aesthetes. The chair shown here displays an
eclecticism that has not yet been fully traced or appreciated.

Hints for Collectors
Oak furniture of this period is generally sturdy enough to be in
good condition after 70 or 80 years of regular use. Moreover,
most forms are common enough so that it is not necessary to buy
damaged or repaired pieces. Restored wicker or caned areas,
however, do not seriously devalue a piece. Since oak pieces are
mostly acquired for utilitarian purposes, collectors often overlook
changes in overall design or in details.

Turn-of-the-century bentwood highchair

Description
Highchair with back rail and stiles made from single loop of
bentwood enclosing egg-shaped caned panel on back. Arms
consisting of a movable outer ring attached to back stiles and
fitted with tray, and fixed inner arms curving down to form front
legs. Circular cane seat attached to 4 plain stiles flaring out to
feet. Plain circular stretcher with flat footrest attached.
Variations: Diverse shapes were used for backrests and seats.

Materials and Dimensions
Ash bentwood. Cane seat and back. Cast-iron mounts. Height:
37"; 21" to seat.

Locality and Period
Probably Austria-Hungary. c. 1900.

Comment
Bentwood furniture became popular in 19th-century America,
but there is little proof that any of it was made here. Thonet
Brothers and Kohn, two important manufacturers with factories
in Austria-Hungary, had wide distribution in the United States.
At the turn of the century bentwood suited the spirit of Art
Nouveau, though it was meant to be functional rather than
decorative. Bentwood is a sturdy material suitable for utilitarian
furniture. Highchairs, like the one shown here, and other kinds
of children's furniture were among the popular bentwood forms.

Hints for Collectors
Design—as much as wear—distinguishes early from more recent
bentwood pieces. In cross section, bentwood cylinders are
generally circular in the earliest designs and oval or quite flat in
newer pieces.

Description

Spring armchair with upholstered back framed in cast iron; upholstered headrest above pierced cast-iron panel. Lower back a flattened curved oval. Cast-iron arms with curved wooden armrests. Circular seat (upholstery removed) set on cylindrical post over 8 curved, springlike iron straps attached to 4 iron legs; casters. *Variations:* Since this is a patented design, there are only minor changes among examples.

Materials and Dimensions

Cast iron. Laminated wood (probably maple). Original upholstery. Height: 43″; 17″ to seat.

Locality and Period

Made by the American Chair Company, Utica, New York. Patented 1849; produced for several decades thereafter. Similar models by other manufacturers.

Comment

A dozen or more patents for new kinds of rocking chairs were issued in the mid-19th century. Patents protected designs from piracy but did not necessarily lead to extensive production. Patented in 1849 by Thomas Warren, the spring chair shown here made use of cast iron and laminated wood, new materials of the period. A major accomplishment of American ingenuity, this design was exhibited in 1851 at the Crystal Palace Exhibition in London.

Hints for Collectors

Patent furniture is an interesting specialty. Examples often bear marks or labels. Remember that the term "patent" is sometimes applied today to mechanical furnishings that were never actually registered with the U.S. Patent Office. If damaged, the mechanism of a spring chair may be difficult to repair.

94 Renaissance Revival folding iron armchair

Description
Iron-framed folding armchair with 3 tufted velvet cushions.
Adjustable back topped by pierced arched rail. Caned back
panel. Stiles hinged to seat frame. U-shaped legs swing out from
top of back when fully reclined. Arms projecting from stiles are
straight and upholstered in velvet. Curved arm supports with
mechanism to adjust angle of back. Frame cantilevered forward
from seat to serve as adjustable footrest. Legs curving out to
casters; flat stretchers on all sides. *Variations:* Shape of iron
frame varies. Wooden top rail may be omitted.

Materials and Dimensions
Iron. Walnut. Cane backrest. Original velvet cushions. Iron
casters. Height: 46½″ (upright); 16″ to seat.

Locality and Period
Designed by C. B. Sheldon for Marks Adjustable Folding Chair
Co., New York. Patented 1876. Similar designs patented by
other manufacturers.

Comment
A remarkable number of folding chairs were produced and
patented in the 1870s, many with interesting innovations. The
chair shown here can be folded up compactly, and its patent
document described it as useful for invalids because of its
adjustable back and footrest. The decorative wooden top rail,
Renaissance Revival in style, is a conservative detail on an
otherwise advanced design.

Hints for Collectors
Folding chairs, produced by numerous makers in the 1870s and
1880s, are often marked with makers' names and with patent
dates and numbers. Such chairs are preferable because they are
easier to date and document.

Rococo Revival cast-iron side chair

Description
Cast-iron side chair with elaborate grape-and-leaf piercework forming the arched back that wraps around rear of pierced seat. Legs in leaf-tendril-grape pattern, with flared leaf-shaped feet. Iron rod stretchers between front and rear legs. *Variations:* Grape-and-leaf patterns were painted in a variety of colors. Renaissance Revival motifs were also used for cast-iron pieces in the 1860s and 1870s.

Materials and Dimensions
Cast iron. Painted white. Height: 29″; 15½″ to seat.

Locality and Period
Throughout the United States. c. 1840–70.

Comment
Iron furniture was cast in foundries all over the country during the second half of the 19th century. While much of it imitated rustic wooden furniture, many pieces had naturalistic grape-and-leaf patterns in the Rococo Revival style. Both indoor and outdoor furniture was produced, though the popularity of indoor pieces was brief. Most cast-iron garden furniture, like the chair shown here, was originally painted in dark colors, particularly green, brown, and gray. It was often placed in large cemeteries on the outskirts of populous American cities such as Boston and New York.

Hints for Collectors
Some cast-iron pieces have a maker's name cast directly into the seat or applied as a medallion on the back. Careful examination of unpainted corners or worn areas may reveal a chair's original color; but detection is often made difficult by layers of protective lead that were in many cases applied to iron furniture.

Late Victorian cast-iron armchair

Description
Cast-iron armchair with back topped by flower-and-scroll crest over flat top rail extending into slanting arms. Back panel with delicate lyre, foliate scrolls, and floral garland. Scrolls repeated under arms; handholds curled. Seat intricately pierced, framed by rails with leaf border; skirt under seat decorated with foliate scrolls. Modified cabriole legs bearing floral relief ornament. X-shaped cross stretchers. Foliate pad feet. *Variations:* Cast-iron furniture also came with other delicate Neoclassical motifs such as columns and various architectural elements. Chairs were usually painted green, gray, brown, or other dark colors.

Materials and Dimensions
Cast iron. Painted white. Height: 32½"; 15" to seat.

Locality and Period
Throughout the United States. c. 1880–1910.

Comment
Cast-iron furniture became popular in the 1840s and continued to be made into the first decade of the 20th century. The delicacy of the scrolls, lyre, and floral patterns on the chair shown here is characteristic of ironwork made after 1875, as are the chair's lighter proportions. Delicate Neoclassical designs such as the lyre on this chair were often used on such late cast-iron pieces.

Hints for Collectors
Whereas white is today a popular color for cast-iron furniture, it was not used often in the 19th century; pieces were generally painted in relatively dark colors. Check for traces of the original color behind the skirt or inside the legs, where new paint may not have reached. To avoid rust, keep chairs well painted.

Turn-of-the-century iron-wire side chair

Description
Side chair with looped iron-wire back and legs; curved stiles twisted into open splat consisting of 2 circles, a center spiral, and an inverted vase-shaped outline. Circular oak seat framed by iron band. Legs formed of double twists of wire reminiscent of cabriole shape; wire loops forming pad feet. Single wire stretchers on each side forming a square. *Variations:* Back designs of twisted wire are sometimes more intricate. Legs may be more elaborate. Seats may be metal instead of oak. Stretchers may be crossed.

Materials and Dimensions
Iron and iron wire. Oak seat. Height: 34¼"; 17¼" to seat.

Locality and Period
Throughout the United States. c. 1900–20.

Comment
The design of the chair shown here resembles one illustrated in a patent from the early 1900s. A number of manufacturers made such wire chairs; because they were used in public places like restaurants and cafés, they became known as ice-cream parlor chairs. They resulted from the quest for functional furniture during the late 19th and early 20th centuries. Similar pieces were made for garden use, though the seats of those were generally made of metal instead of wood.

Hints for Collectors
Wire chairs are sturdy and, if damaged, easily repaired. The patterns of backs and legs vary subtly from model to model, and an interesting collection of variants could be put together. But collectors trying to form a matching set may have difficulty finding several chairs exactly alike.

Turn-of-the-century iron-wire armchair

Description
Tall armchair with looped iron-wire back and legs. Curved stiles twisted in center to form splat consisting of 2 circles, a center spiral, and an inverted vase-shaped outline. Wooden armrests on wire supports set into iron band circling plywood seat. Modified cabriole legs made from paired wires twisted together in lower segment, ending in loop feet and fastened to seat frame by tacks. *Variations:* Wire backs may be twisted into heart-shaped splat or other designs. Legs may be twisted in more complex patterns.

Materials and Dimensions
Iron and plywood. Painted white. Height: 41½″; 24¾″ to seat.

Locality and Period
Throughout the United States. c. 1900–30.

Comment
Simple wire-and-plywood chairs like the one shown here were often used in turn-of-the-century ice-cream parlors, restaurants, and pool halls. Although designed mainly to be sturdy and functional, these chairs could be quite graceful. Elements of this design, such as the modified cabriole legs and the vase-shaped splat, were loosely based on Queen Anne wooden models (59).

Hints for Collectors
Ice-cream parlor chairs are inexpensive and readily available in shops around the country. Though most wire chairs were painted in a variety of colors, many were left unpainted because gray iron and golden oak seats went well with the oak tables of the period. Since plywood can warp or buckle, check the seats before buying.

Modern steel-wire side chairs

Description
Group of side chairs with backs and seats shaped from wire
lattice in small grid pattern. Concave backs with arched tops and
straight-edged sides slanting in. Seats concave with straight
sides, curved fronts, hollowed centers, and vinyl-covered pads.
Tubular 2-part base bolted to seat and welded to 2 pairs of
squared U-shaped legs. *Variations:* This design may have overall
vinyl or cotton upholstery. Chairs may be chrome-plated or
vinyl-coated in a variety of colors (usually for outdoor use). A
child's version is also made.

Materials and Dimensions
Welded steel wire and tubing. Vinyl-coated or chrome-plated.
Vinyl seat covers. Height: 30″; 18″ to seat.

Locality and Period
Designed by Harry Bertoia for Knoll International, New York.
First made in 1952, and still in production.

Comment
In 1950 Hans Knoll, one of the leading manufacturers of modern
furniture in the United States, commissioned the prominent
American metalsmith and sculptor Harry Bertoia to design

several chairs. Bertoia's designs transcended the barrier between decorative and functional design that had marked the 1920s and 1930s; his objects balanced successfully between sculpture and furniture. The chair shown here, one of the masterpieces of recent American furniture design, is a practical form that is also a significant aesthetic expression of the 1950s. The most important influence on Knoll furniture was Bauhaus design, and like the creations of the Bauhaus, many Knoll designs were conceived by leading artists, sculptors, and architects. Besides Bertoia, Knoll has produced well-known designs by Ludwig Mies van der Rohe, Marcel Breuer, Eero Saarinen, and Hans Wegner.

Hints for Collectors

Modern objects from the 1950s and later can be a fascinating collecting specialty. While some of these designs became outdated within just a few years, the finest remain as fresh and striking as when they were first made. Since most Knoll designs are still in production, it is often difficult to date a particular piece. Some designs have been affected by subtle changes over the years—such as various surface coatings and upholstery materials—which provide clues to dating these modern classics.

Modern steel-wire armchair

Description
Armchair with back, seat, and arms shaped from a single rectangular sheet of wire lattice; curved corners serve as crest of back, front of seat, and armrests. Wire is exposed except for seat, which is upholstered in cotton and widens toward front. 2 sets of squared U-shaped legs bolted to sides of seat. *Variations.* Harry Bertoia designed a line of wire-lattice chairs for Knoll International, which included the so-called diamond chair shown here as well as a smaller version. Diamond chairs may have overall upholstery. Vinyl upholstery is also used.

Materials and Dimensions
Welded steel wire and tubing. Chrome-plated. Cotton seat cover Height: 30½"; 17" to seat.

Locality and Period
Designed by Harry Bertoia for Knoll International, New York. First made in 1952, and still in production.

Comment
Harry Bertoia designed the diamond chair, as the example shown here is called, for the manufacturer Hans Knoll, who commissioned it for his line of artist-designed chairs. Not all were as successful as this chair, in which Bertoia transformed abstract form into practical furniture. Bertoia's concept of using wire lattice is disarmingly simple, but the subtly contoured wire back is actually quite ingenious.

Hints for Collectors
Beware of imitations of this design, which are often imperfectly shaped and poorly constructed. Look for Knoll labels, often found on upholstery, though these sometimes fall off or are removed.

Description
Armchair with molded fiberglass body contoured to fit human form. Arched back curving into projecting arms; straight front edge of arms forming U-shape with edge of seat. All edges with smooth curved lips. Fiberglass seat rests on 4 slanting iron-rod legs braced by V-shaped wire loops converging in square at center. Capped feet. *Variations:* Wire-mesh models with openwork backs were also made.

Materials and Dimensions
Fiberglass and iron. Height: 33½"; 17½" to seat.

Locality and Period
Designed by Charles Eames for Herman Miller, Inc., Zeeland, Michigan. Introduced in 1951.

Comment
The designs of Charles Eames had a profound influence on innovative modern American furniture. The chair shown here is characteristic of Eames's approach, which utilized new materials and Bauhaus functionalism to produce typically American modern works. Eames was one of several American designers working for pioneering manufacturers such as Herman Miller and Hans Knoll, and his modern furniture is particularly prized by collectors.

Hints for Collectors
Fiberglass is a modern material that is prone to damage, so check a chair for cracks and chips. Designs like that shown here look good only if in perfect condition; damaged chairs look shabby. Imitations of this subtly molded form may look like originals at first glance, but are usually shallower and not as nicely shaped.

Modern tubular-steel roundabout armchair

Description
Round armchair with deep-curved back serving as armrest and flaring out from seat. Upholstered back sectioned vertically, set a few inches above seat on 3 tubular stiles continuing as legs; fourth leg screwed to front seat rail. Round upholstered seat circled by wide metal band to which legs are welded. Legs attached to similar reinforcing band slightly above floor; straight tubular legs ending in ring feet. *Variations:* Steel chairs were made in other restrained, more geometric shapes.

Materials and Dimensions
Chrome-plated tubular and flat steel. Imitation leather upholstery. Height: 30″; 19″ to seat.

Locality and Period
This and similar steel chairs were made throughout the United States. c. 1935–55.

Comment
Simple furniture designs in steel were introduced in the 1920s, and continued to be ᵣ ade into the 1950s. Beginning in the 1930s, there was a broader use of steel, adapting traditional designs as well as inventing new forms. The chair shown here is a fine example of a modern adaptation of an early 18th-century type (roundabouts were used in the Dutch colonies; *see also* 61) in new materials. The effect is striking and quite surprising, one of the aims of much industrial design since the 1930s.

Hints for Collectors
Traditional designs updated in modern materials comprise a fascinating development that might provide the basis of an interesting collection. Tracing the original owners of fine 20th-century furniture is an important step toward identifying the maker of a custom-made, unlabeled piece.

Description
Side chair with upholstered rectangular back and seat on tubular metal frame; back vertically sectioned. Stiles with double-ring finials. Legs with double rings at stretcher joints and feet. Thin stretchers low and straight on sides and in rear, higher and curved in front. *Variations:* Tubular elements may be undecorated. Other early forms were also updated in metal.

Materials and Dimensions
Anodized aluminum. Imitation leather upholstery. Height: 32½"; 17" to seat.

Locality and Period
Designed by Warren MacArthur, United States. c. 1935. Similar chairs by other designers.

Comment
The use of modern materials in adapting traditional designs started in the 1920s. In the example shown here, the rings used as decoration at junctures of stiles and rails are vaguely reminiscent of the bamboo turnings on some late 18th-century Sheraton chairs. The new materials and Sheraton motif work well together for a witty effect, doubly subtle because the rings also look like pipe joints.

Hints for Collectors
Furniture of the 1930s has been attracting more and more interest, but it is a difficult field because little research has yet been done, few pieces bear makers' marks, and many designs were made in limited quantity. Some furnishings may be illustrated in contemporary decorating magazines or factory catalogues.

Modern tubular-steel side chair

Description
Side chair with tubular-steel frame forming back, seat, and legs. Backrest and seat made of bent pine upholstered in plastic. Back slanting away from seat toward flat top rail; seat curving up from back and down toward tubular front seat rail. Legs reinforced by tube stretchers on sides at floor level. *Variations:* The seat may be cantilevered from a floor support continuing as front legs. Steel may be uncoated or chrome-plated. Some mass-produced models have seats and backs made with plain boards upholstered in canvas or imitation leather.

Materials and Dimensions
Tubular steel painted black. Pine. Plastic seat and backrest. Height: 33″; 17½″ to seat.

Locality and Period
Throughout the United States. c. 1925–40.

Comment
Tubular-steel chairs, introduced by Ludwig Mies van der Rohe and Marcel Breuer in designs made for the Bauhaus in Germany, were adapted by avant-garde designers on both sides of the Atlantic during the 1920s and 1930s. Their pure functionalism was considered revolutionary. In the American chair shown here, steel and plastic were used in a simple design that was quite new in spirit, but not as daring as examples with cantilevered seats.

Hints for Collectors
In 20th-century furniture, the names of certain designers ensure that specific pieces will be recognized as having lasting significance. Simple, austere designs by major architects such as Mies van der Rohe and Breuer are much preferred by collectors over the many popularized variations by lesser-known designers.

Modern tubular-steel armchair

Description
Armchair with tubular-steel frame and cushions upholstered in imitation leather. Straight-sided back cushion concave and rounded at top corners, supported by 2 flat stiles and by arms. Tubular-steel arms curving out horizontally from back cushion, then down in front to become arm supports and legs, in a single continuous loop ending as floor-level stabilizer that parallels outline of seat. Thick cushioned seat, straight-edged in front and curved at rear, with border of welting. *Variations:* Cushions may be thinner. Arms may be omitted.

Materials and Dimensions
Tubular steel. Chrome-plated. Imitation leather. Height: 30"; 17" to seat.

Locality and Period
Throughout the United States. c. 1930–40.

Comment
Tubular-steel furniture by Bauhaus designers of the 1920s inspired American manufacturers to mass-produce similar designs during the 1930s. Moderately priced pieces like the chair shown here retained many of the innovations of the Bauhaus models. The use of new materials and simple functional designs separates this kind of furniture from the more traditionally oriented Art Deco pieces of the period.

Hints for Collectors
The thick seat cushion of this chair clearly differentiates it from the airy, daringly cantilevered examples associated with Marcel Breuer and other major figures. Though it may be a clumsy misinterpretation of the original designs, it is a charming expression of the era.

Upholstered-back and Related Wooden-back Chairs

Chairs with upholstered backs and seats provide the fullest expression of fashion and comfort; examples in this section span 300 years and virtually every American style. Most represent styles of the Victorian era, when the largest number of upholstered chairs were made; these include fine pieces made by influential craftsmen as well as popularized mass-produced versions. This section also includes related wooden-back chairs designed with equal emphasis on stylishness.

The earliest fashionable chairs were only occasionally upholstered, in either leather or needlework. By the mid-18th century, upholstery was more commonly used on chairs meant to be both impressive and comfortable. Wing chairs and upholstered-back Chippendale armchairs were covered in elegant fabrics; their ample upholstered frames and carved legs were shaped to suit the taste of the period. Among fine Federal-era examples are so-called Martha Washington, or lolling, chairs. Another type of Federal upholstered armchair is based on the Louis XVI *bergère*.

Chairmakers in the 19th century kept abreast of the latest fashions and newest means of providing comfort. They turned from traditional American models to a succession of European historical styles, altered to suit production techniques of the period. Gothic Revival, Renaissance Revival, and Rococo Revival chairs have upholstered seats, reinforced with inner springs, and either cushioned or openwork wooden backs. Among the finest revival chairs are those by John Henry Belter, whose lamination methods and curving Rococo designs were much imitated. The quest for greater comfort and convenience led to many designs for folding chairs, platform rocking chairs, and various patented innovations. Less concerned with high fashion than popular appeal, many manufacturers turned to mass-produced carpet upholstery and new materials such as plywood; these were economical and particularly appropriate for lower-priced Eastlake chairs. Whereas elaborate carving was all-important on Gothic Revival and Rococo Revival chairs, inscribed linear decoration was more characteristic of Renaissance Revival and Eastlake designs.

Fully upholstered, or overstuffed, chairs were introduced in the 1880s, but were produced in greatest quantity in the Art Deco years. Other upholstered chairs, as well as related examples without upholstery, were later produced in the Art Nouveau, Mission, and modern styles.

The chairs in this section range from some of the rarest and most valuable (for example, Cromwell and Wainscot chairs) to such widely available examples as mass-produced upholstered Victorian pieces and Art Deco kitchen chairs. These later chairs have been attracting more and more collectors because they are generally inexpensive, comfortable, and evocative of their periods. The quality of carved or inscribed decoration on the exposed woodwork of an upholstered chair is usually a gauge of its value. Original upholstery is rare, particularly on older pieces. When replacing upholstery, make certain the pattern and material are appropriate to the style of the chair (*see* p. 432).

Empire side chair

Description
Side chair with arched top rail resting on upholstered back. Back flanked by columnar stiles having brass capitals and resting on lower back rail. Prominent seat frame with curved, overhanging outer edges and upholstered center. Tapered front legs with projecting feet; square rear legs flaring to feet. Plain stretchers reinforcing sides and rear. *Variations:* Gothic, Rococo, and Renaissance Revival elements may be used instead of classical columns and legs.

Materials and Dimensions
Mahogany. Modern velvet upholstery over iron-spring construction. Brass capitals. Height: 38½"; 18½" to seat.

Locality and Period
Probably New York. c. 1825–45. Similar designs made in other centers.

Comment
The Empire style was important in America from the time of its introduction from Paris in the early 19th century until mid-century, when the last Greek Revival houses were built. The prominent frame and narrow proportions of the chair shown here differ from earlier and heavier French-inspired models, suggesting a date after 1825. Classical but restrained, this design is of a bolder simplicity than were the Renaissance Revival chairs that followed in the 1850s and 1860s.

Hints for Collectors
A design as unusual as this one is apt to be overlooked in sales of assorted unattributed furniture. Resourceful collectors seek out the unusual and then track down documentation—such as manufacturers' advertisements and pictures of labeled works—to support attributions.

Art Nouveau side chair

Description
Side chair with rectangular, leather back panel topped by rail carved in symmetrical leaf-and-ribbon design. Upper stiles partly concealed by leather upholstery reinforced with brass tacks; rectangular lower stiles. Lower rail, set into stiles, carved in symmetrical snake design. Seat straight-sided, hollowed, and widening at front; upholstered over seat rails in leather reinforced with brass tacks. Shallow arched bracket with small central drop under front rail. Front legs straight and rectangular; cleft flaring feet. Rear legs plain and flaring back. H-pattern stretchers. *Variations:* Flat carving may be based on other Renaissance or exotic motifs. Chairs may have no upholstery.

Materials and Dimensions
Oak. Leather. Brass tacks. Height: 41″; 17¼″ to seat.

Locality and Period
Buffalo. c. 1900. Similar designs made in other centers.

Comment
Fashionable furniture from the turn of the century often had elongated proportions, frequently in the Art Nouveau manner of the chair shown here. Art Nouveau decoration was commonly used, but the carving on the chair shown here was inspired more by traditional Renaissance motifs, inventively interpreted and executed by a skilled craftsman.

Hints for Collectors
Collectors may find that turn-of-the-century furnishings like this chair remain interesting far longer than the more standard output of the larger factories. Art Nouveau furniture is much sought after, and prices for finer pieces have risen dramatically in recent years.

108 William and Mary leather-upholstered side chair

Description
Side chair with upholstered leather back. Arched top rail, with straight center section flanked by curves. Stiles, of same width and molded in same pattern as top rail, curving back from seat. Straight lower back rail enclosing leather back panel. Seat rectangular and upholstered over rails. Front legs turned in vase-and-block pattern, terminating in Spanish feet; rear legs plain and square. Front stretcher turned in ball-and-ring pattern; side and rear stretchers plain and rectangular. *Variations:* Leather back may be narrower, like a wide splat. Curve of back varies subtly. Cane back and seat are also used.

Materials and Dimensions
Maple. Original leather upholstery. Height: 45¾″; 18½″ to seat.

Locality and Period
New England. c. 1700–25.

Comment
Early leather-upholstered chairs like the one shown here, though sometimes called Boston chairs, appear to have been made all over New England. Turned legs and scroll feet—popularly called Spanish feet—were typical of William and Mary chairs. The curve of the back, however, is a refinement suggesting the chairmaker was aware of the more curving designs soon to be adapted to the Queen Anne style (53).

Hints for Collectors
William and Mary chairs are not readily found today, but when available they may not be very expensive. Very often, chairs of this period have been over-restored. Many reproductions were made in the 20th century. Original leather is very rare.

William and Mary caned side chair

Description
Side chair with arched, stepped top rail having carved openwork scrolls and molded borders. Stiles straight and finely molded. Back splat consisting of caned panel framed by 2 molded vertical slats, arched top rail, and straight lower rail joining stiles. Seat straight-sided, widening in front, and caned; scalloped skirt on front and sides. Front legs turned in vase-and-block pattern, with Spanish feet; flared rear legs with cylindrical segments interrupted by rectangular blocks. Front stretcher, set high, turned in ball-and-ring pattern; side stretchers turned in block-and-ring pattern and connected by tapered cross stretcher; plain tapered stretcher in rear. *Variations:* Top rail may be more richly carved; back splat may be carved. Stiles may be taller and turned.

Materials and Dimensions
Maple. Painted black. Caning. Height: 47½″; 18¾″ to seat.

Locality and Period
Massachusetts. c. 1710–30.

Comment
Though the chair shown here is basically William and Mary in style, its arched top rail suggests that the craftsman was aware of more fashionable elements soon to become dominant in the Queen Anne period. Other advanced elements are the scalloped skirt and ball-and-ring stretcher.

Hints for Collectors
The molded stiles and rails on the back of this chair, with their well-turned, nicely carved details, are signs of quality in early furniture. Too often, original stiles have been replaced by simple turned elements or plain wood.

Renaissance Revival side chair

Description
Side chair with upholstered back panel topped by pediment and flanked by inscribed columnar stiles. Lower rail with central ornament and inscribed linear decoration. Upholstered seat with curved rails. Front seat rail with applied central decoration. Front legs trumpet-shaped and columnar, with prominent capitals and arrow feet; rear legs round and flaring out. *Variations:* Inscribed decoration may be gilded. Proportions may be heavier. Seat cushions may lack iron springs.

Materials and Dimensions
Walnut. Reproduction silk damask upholstery over iron-spring construction. Height: 36½″; 17½″ to seat.

Locality and Period
Possibly from the Midwest. c. 1875–90.

Comment
Although the Renaissance Revival style was first seen in American furniture about 1850, examples like the one shown here, with narrow proportions and restrained decoration, are usually later variations made from about 1875 to 1890. Simple, inscribed linear decoration was introduced in the 1870s, when midwestern factories began to flourish. By 1876 these factories had become successful enough for a group of Grand Rapids makers to exhibit their turned and inscribed Renaissance furnishings at the Philadelphia Centennial Exposition.

Hints for Collectors
Upholstery may require restoration; this does not greatly devalue a piece, since few have original upholstery. Check very carefully the condition of the gilded surfaces that may often be found on Renaissance Revival furniture, since the restoration of gilding can be very expensive.

Child's Gothic Revival side chair

Description
Side chair with central section of back consisting of 3 sausage-turned spindles in a frame topped by leaf-carved decoration beneath pointed arch and finial. Back panel joined to turned stiles at 2 junctures on each side. Seat with spring construction upholstered in silk damask fastened by a row of brass tacks. Plain skirt. Round front legs columnar and tapered, with ball-and-ring-turned capitals and arrow feet; rear legs plain stumps, slightly flaring back. *Variations:* Gothic arched backs often have tracery splats in Gothic motifs. Legs range from Louis XVI-style columns to distinctively Gothic forms. Some have straight legs with applied tracery.

Materials and Dimensions
Walnut and pine. Modern upholstery, iron-spring construction, and brass tacks. Height: 35½"; 14" to seat.

Locality and Period
New York, Philadelphia, or Boston. c. 1840–60.

Comment
Gothic-inspired designs were popular from 1840 to 1860. Since Gothic-style villas—for which Gothic Revival furnishings were best suited—were often built in the countryside near larger cities, Gothic Revival pieces were usually made in these cities. Gothic and Elizabethan Revival designs are often closely related: for instance, the back spindles of the chair shown here might well have been used in an Elizabethan design.

Hints for Collectors
Since chairs usually have fairly standard seat heights, the fact that the seat here is only 14" high suggests it was made for a child. Original seat coverings for Gothic Revival chairs were often made of tapestry in small floral or geometric patterns.

Gothic Revival side chair

Description
Side chair with back in tracery design, topped by intricate
cresting. Arched back encloses trefoil motifs above an oval frame
filled with 3 quatrefoils supported by 2 columns. Stiles
elaborately turned, topped by vase-shaped finials with arrow-
shaped tips. Seat straight-sided and widening in front, built to
hold an upholstered frame. Front legs tapered toward bottom
and turned in columnar design; rear legs plain and curving back
to feet. *Variations:* Chairs show a wide range of Gothic details.
Stiles may be spiral-turned. Legs are often square and covered
with Gothic decoration.

Materials and Dimensions
Walnut. Pine seat frame. Height: 45½"; 14" to seat.

Locality and Period
Eastern United States. c. 1850.

Comment
Primarily Gothic in style, this chair also has elements that would
have been called Elizabethan in the 19th century, such as the
turned stiles and legs. The Gothic style was one of several
revived in reaction to Empire designs. Gothic Revival furniture
was generally used in the halls and libraries of late Greek
Revival, Italianate, and Gothic Revival houses of the period.

Hints for Collectors
The Gothic Revival style, popular from about 1840 to 1860, was
revived again after 1870. Later examples were most often made
of oak, in simpler designs closer to authentic Gothic furniture.
The early pieces, less truly Gothic, are more amusing. Both
types are available today.

Rococo Revival side chair

Description
Side chair topped by arched rail with carved foliate cresting and
turned pendants at ends. Rail crowns arcade of 4 scrolled arches
on 3 columns having Ionic capitals and leaf-carved lower sections;
tapered plinths resting on scroll-topped lower rail. Stiles ending
in scrolls and set on scrolled brackets joining backrest to rear
legs. Seat with curved sides, upholstered over springs; seat rails
curved below, front rail with molding continued onto front legs.
Front legs cabriole and molded, terminating in plain tapered
feet; rear legs plain and flaring back. *Variations:* Open backs
may be simpler, with a single flat slat, for instance. Arcade may
be more Gothic in style.

Materials and Dimensions
Rosewood. Original needlework upholstery over iron-spring
construction. Height: 34″; 17″ to seat.

Locality and Period
New York. c. 1855.

Comment
Many historical styles served as points of departure for furniture
design of the 1850s. The curved legs and the scrolls on the back
of the chair shown here are clearly elements based on 18th-
century Rococo design, but the arcade is a Gothic motif and the
original needlework is also Gothic in pattern.

Hints for Collectors
Unusual designs, such as this chair, continually turn up, and
collectors should be on the lookout for them. Original needlework
is rare and difficult to preserve; regular use of a fabric like this
would destroy it in 10 years or less.

Description
Revolving armchair with curved top rail in pediment design inscribed with linear scrolls, panels, and central shield. Vase-shaped pierced splat resting on shaped lower rail inscribed with scrolls and panels. Wide flat stiles flaring out from seat. Arms with brackets at rear and scrolled handholds; arm supports curved to join seat rails. Seat with curved sides, thin leather cushion fitted into rails, and elaborately cut and inscribed front skirt. Central metal support under seat fits into base joining 4 cutout slanting legs on casters. *Variations:* Backs are usually plainer, many with rows of vertical slats. Seats may be wooden, without upholstery.

Materials and Dimensions
Walnut and walnut burl. Leather upholstery. Cast-iron revolving mechanism with springs. Porcelain and iron casters. Height: 41″; 19″ to seat.

Locality and Period
Throughout the United States. c. 1875–90.

Comment
The pedestal-base revolving armchair was a late 19th-century innovation, preceded by early Shaker revolving chairs (31) and some piano stools (210, 211) that also turned. The chair shown here is a functional model embellished with Renaissance Revival details and inscribed linear decoration characteristic of the 1880s.

Hints for Collectors
Look for patent marks on revolving armchairs. Though not always used, when they occur they can help supply information about when and where a piece was made. To avoid expensive restoration, check the condition of the revolving mechanism.

Renaissance Revival armchair

Description
Armchair with pedimented back; scrolls inscribed at center and ends of top rail. Wide pierced splat. Stiles slanting into upholstered seat. Arms partly upholstered and curving out from stiles to scrolled handholds; inscribed supports mortised into tops of front legs. Upholstered seat flaring from back to curved front seat rail having grooved and hanging decoration. Front legs trumpet-turned columns; inscribed decoration on capitals and bases. Rear legs rectangular and curving back. *Variations:* Back may have solid splat. Stiles may be straight and veneered.

Materials and Dimensions
Walnut. Leather upholstery over spring construction. Brass tacks. Height: 37″; 18″ to seat.

Locality and Period
Possibly from the Midwest. c. 1870–85.

Comment
Renaissance Revival design was at its height in the 1870s, when fine small shops were producing elegantly carved chairs with ormolu and applied porcelain or ivory decoration. Furniture factories were making pieces in the style with simpler ornament, like the chair shown here. Examples with inscribed decoration, which came later than those with carved parts, were usually made in large factories in the Midwest, where Grand Rapids was one of the centers.

Hints for Collectors
Many Renaissance Revival chairs were set on casters. The overall lines may be altered if the casters are lost, so check feet for holes left by missing casters. Reupholstering can change the shape of a cushion when extra stuffing is added.

Rococo Revival side chair

Description
Upholstered side chair with curved back of laminated wood. Oval back cushion framed by piercework in grape-and-leaf pattern. Back crowned with carved floral cresting over scrolls. Wide upholstered seat. Undulating front and side seat rails with carved roses at center. Front legs cabriole and molded, with carved roses at knees and scrolls at feet; rear legs rounded on front and back faces but straight-sided, flaring out to feet. Brass and iron casters. *Variations:* Backs may be more elaborately carved or almost plain.

Materials and Dimensions
Rosewood and rosewood veneer. Brass and iron casters. Reproduction damask upholstery. Height: 38″; 15½″ to seat.

Locality and Period
Made by John Henry Belter, New York. c. 1845–65. Related designs by cabinetmakers in Boston and Philadelphia.

Comment
John Henry Belter, for whom this type of furniture is often named, was the most important American cabinetmaker working in the Rococo Revival style. He introduced and patented improved methods of lamination, used in his elegantly curving Rococo designs. Belter's competitors in New York, Boston, and Philadelphia followed him in using laminated wood for their ornate Rococo Revival designs.

Hints for Collectors
The difference in price between pieces by Belter and those by his competitors is great, so it is important to note that Belter's work has more layers of veneer—6 or more, while his rivals used 3 to 5—and his carving is more naturalistic. Some upholstered examples have paper labels beneath the seat.

Description

Side chair with laminated piercework back panel framed by rounded undulating stiles and carved top rail in single continuous scroll design; cresting with floral and fruit motifs. Scrolls frame central carved design of grapes, leaves, acorns, and thin scrolls. Wooden dowels connect back to upholstered seat, which has molded curving rails; front skirt with carved rose and scrolls at center. Front legs molded and cabriole, with carved roses at knees and scrolls at feet; plain rear legs. All legs on brass casters. *Variations:* Pierced backs are made in simpler designs. Back often has central upholstered panel.

Materials and Dimensions

Rosewood and possibly ash or oak. Brass casters. Fabric upholstery. Height: 37"; 16" to seat.

Locality and Period

Made by John Henry Belter, New York. c. 1845–65. Related designs by cabinetmakers in Boston and Philadelphia.

Comment

The Rococo Revival style, which flourished in America between 1840 and 1865, inspired some of the most elaborate furniture of the 19th century. The back of the chair shown here has 7 layers of veneer pressed into the curving outlines particularly favored during this period. The overall shape and carved motifs are based on 18th-century Rococo designs, but the leaves, fruit, and flowers are rendered more realistically.

Hints for Collectors

The finest Rococo Revival designs are much in demand. Works attributed to Belter command the highest prices, so check such an attribution carefully. Genuine Belter pieces have superior carving and very finely laminated wood.

Rococo Revival armchair

Description
Armchair with peanut-shaped upholstered back having molded
frame and carved floral cresting. Arms curving out from lower
back and upholstered to curved supports; arm supports
continuing below upholstered seat as upper part of elaborate
cabriole front legs with leaf carving on knees. Side seat rails
curving to front legs; undulating front rail carved in leaf-and-
ribbon motif. Flat-sided rear legs flaring back sharply.
Variations: Carving and shape of back may be simpler. Rare
examples with carved backs made from laminated wood in the
Belter manner (116).

Materials and Dimensions
Walnut and pine. Modern upholstery. Height: 43″; 15″ to seat.

Locality and Period
Throughout the United States. c. 1840–60.

Comment
The Rococo Revival style flourished throughout America as well
as in Europe, so it is sometimes difficult to ascertain the precise
origin of a piece. The simplicity of design and the elegant
carving of the chair shown here relate it to examples from the
New York area, but similar work was produced in furniture
shops throughout the United States.

Hints for Collectors
Good examples of this revival style are those pieces with
exaggerated lines emphasizing the Rococo curves. Pieces which
can be identified by labels are particularly prized. Labels can be
hard to find on 19th-century furniture: if, for example, the
upholstery on a chair is original, a paper label may be affixed to
the protective cloth under the seat.

Rococo Revival armchair

Description
Upholstered armchair with ormolu-decorated, ebonized frame. Egg-shaped back with cresting enclosed by scroll carving to which cabochon and floral ornament are applied; beaded border around molded frame of back. Short scroll-shaped stiles connecting backrest to seat. Arms curved and molded with scrolls at rear, upholstered in midsection. Arm supports curve down to knees of front legs. Upholstered seat with inner springs and curved sides. Front skirt with applied floral and leaf ornament. Cabriole front legs with scroll feet on casters. Plain rear legs flaring back. *Variations:* Ormolu-decorated and ebonized frames may be more ornate, in more traditional Rococo shapes.

Materials and Dimensions
Walnut. Ebonized. Ormolu mounts. Fabric upholstery over iron springs. Metal casters. Height: 40″; 17″ to seat.

Locality and Period
Made by Pottier and Stymus, New York. c. 1860.

Comment
Ebonized parlor sets with ormolu decoration were made in both the Rococo (Louis XV) and Neoclassical (Louis XVI) styles, particularly by prominent New York cabinetmakers such as Pottier and Stymus during the 1850s and 1860s. The oval back and decoration of the conservative chair shown here suggest a combination of both styles.

Hints for Collectors
Rococo Revival designs of the mid-19th century are heavier in proportion than slightly later versions, which were sometimes more faithful to 18th-century French models. Look for examples with fine details such as carving and ormolu mounts.

Renaissance Revival armchair

Description
Upholstered armchair with cushioned oval back encircled by broad molding and crowned by a cabochon and floral ornament; curved lower rail of back placed high above seat. Arms curving out from back and partly upholstered at center; curved arm supports set into side seat rails slightly back of front legs. Round upholstered seat outlined with tacks; front seat rail and arm supports inscribed with linear decoration. Front legs columnar and tapered, with prominent capitals and bases; front feet on casters. Rear legs flaring out to floor. *Variations:* Inscribed decoration may be more elaborate or gilded. Straight-sided backs were also popular.

Materials and Dimensions
Walnut. Needlepoint upholstery. Brass tacks. Height: 42″; 17″ to seat.

Locality and Period
Probably from the Midwest. c. 1870–90.

Comment
The oval back and columnar legs of the chair shown here were inspired by the Louis XVI style, which influenced fashionable cabinetmakers from the 1850s on. The chair's Eastlake-style inscribed decoration indicates, however, that it is a late Renaissance Revival piece. Its simple carving and overall plainness suggest that it was mass-produced.

Hints for Collectors
When selecting or trying to match Victorian furnishings, weigh the relative elegance or plainness of the various pieces. Beware of furniture that is unusually small for its type or has no naturalistic detailed decoration, for it may well be a 1930s reproduction of a 19th-century design.

121 Renaissance Revival miniature or child's armchair

Description
Upholstered armchair with oval back framed by double-molded edge with leaf cresting. Back resting on extensions of flared rear legs. Open arms partially upholstered. Arm supports, skirt, and legs with inscribed decoration. Upholstery outlined with brass tacks. Columnar front legs turned and carved; stumplike rear legs flaring back. *Variations:* Louis XVI-style miniature chairs such as this one were not as popular as those based on Louis XV models, which have curving front legs and backs that were more Rococo than Neoclassical.

Materials and Dimensions
Walnut. Modern velvet upholstery. Brass tacks. Height: 18¾"; 8" to seat.

Locality and Period
New Orleans. c. 1850–70. Similar designs made in other centers.

Comment
Miniature furniture is puzzling. It is popularly thought that such small pieces were made as samples; yet, as seen in the Louis XVI-style chair shown here, many are not true miniatures, with every detail scaled down proportionally. Here, for instance, the legs are too thick, the arms too thin, and the decoration oversized for a precise scale model. This piece was perhaps made for a child, or just for its charming effect. Though finely made, it does not show off craftsmanship as a scale-model sample might.

Hints for Collectors
Since some miniature pieces are recent copies, careful inspection is important. Signs of genuine wear are the best proof of age. The inscribed classical details, resembling those on some labeled New Orleans works, support the likelihood that this piece was made in New Orleans, as does its provenance.

Renaissance Revival armchair

Description
Upholstered armchair with curved top rail and small ebonized pediment. Back frame ebonized on outer rim and inscribed with linear designs. Straight stiles topped by round ears embellished with brass rosettes. Lower rail curving to seat and supported on short scrolled brackets continuing as rear legs. Arms straight and upholstered on top; scrolled handholds with brass rosettes in front. Arm supports curving into front legs; rosettes at level of seat rail. Deep upholstered seat with curved sides; skirt with incised gilded border and ebonized drop at front center. Front legs tapered columns; ringed feet on casters. Plain rear legs flaring out. *Variations:* Backs are sometimes more elaborate, with more complex pediments.

Materials and Dimensions
Walnut and pine. Ebonized and gilded. Brass rosettes. Iron casters. Modern fabric upholstery. Height: 42″; 17½″ to seat.

Locality and Period
Grand Rapids. c. 1870–80. Similar models made in other furniture centers.

Comment
Renaissance Revival chairs were made in midwestern factories and workshops in major cities that catered to an upper-middle-class trade. The factory products were often quite fashionable. The chair shown here has excellent lines and interesting details, but no elements that would have been costly to execute.

Hints for Collectors
Renaissance Revival chairs, which come in a wide variety of appealing designs, are usually moderately priced, highly serviceable pieces. Look for examples with unusual enamel or brass medallions on the top rails, often depicting classical figures.

Renaissance Revival armchair

Description
Armchair with rectangular back upholstered over center of top rail like a headrest; ends of top rail curved, with carved and gilded cornucopia festoons. Stiles topped by ormolu lion's heads and decorated with ebonized and gilded details. Horseshoe-shaped seat upholstered over springs; curved seat rails. Arms partly upholstered, ending in ebonized and gilded sphinx-head handholds; ormolu rosettes at seat level. Carved animal legs with hoof feet on casters. Rear legs flaring back and ending in plain rounded feet. *Variations:* Egyptian details may be replaced by Grecian or exotic motifs. (*See also* 179.)

Materials and Dimensions
Cherry and pine. Ebonized and gilded. Ormolu mounts. Modern velvet upholstery. Brass casters. Height: 42″; 17″ to seat.

Locality and Period
New York and other centers. c. 1870–85.

Comment
The chair shown here is in the Egyptian Revival style, which was part of the Renaissance Revival. This style flourished in the 1870s and 1880s, when interest in Egyptian art was heightened by news of the French archaeological excavations in Egypt. In the 1880s Egypt was still considered an exotic land, and ancient Egyptian art became a treasure trove for Western craftsmen. The designs adapted were generally classical: the sphinx heads with animal legs on this chair were inspired by Roman rather than Egyptian art.

Hints for Collectors
Check the condition of exotic pieces closely, since worn paint and gilding can mar a design and be costly to restore, and more extensive repairs may be impossible or prohibitive.

124 Renaissance Revival platform rocking chair

Description
Platform rocking chair with upholstered back topped by rail embellished with medallion and inscribed. Stiles curve to form side seat rails. Iron arms covered in fabric connect stiles and seat rails. Upholstered seat detached from front rail to permit movement. Front rail with center medallion and inscribed scrolls. Cutout legs flat-sided and concave. Plain rear stretcher; cutout side stretchers. Iron rocking mechanism. *Variations:* Platform rocking chairs may be set on a pedestal base. Simpler stretchers also used.

Materials and Dimensions
Mahogany. Iron rocking mechanism and arms. Needlework upholstery. Brass tacks. Height: 42″; 17″ to seat.

Locality and Period
Made by Theodore J. Palmer, New York. Patented 1870. c. 1870–85. Similar models patented by other manufacturers.

Comment
Rocking chairs were a popular American form and, beginning in the 1850s, various patented rockers were introduced. Curved metal arms like those on the chair shown here provide the leverage required for the rocking movement. The decoration on this chair shows Renaissance Revival influence, though the flatness of the top rail relates it to the Eastlake style.

Hints for Collectors
A stamped patent date does not necessarily mean that a piece was made on or even shortly after that date, but it does make it easier for a collector to learn more about a particular design by obtaining a copy of its patent description. Look for chairs with unusual rocking mechanisms like that concealed in this example.

Eastlake folding armchair with footrest

Description
Upholstered folding armchair with back frame continuing down
to serve as front legs. Top rail cut in modified pediment design.
Molded stiles continuing as front legs. Seat cantilevered out, its
side rails continuing behind to rear legs, which also support
adjustable mechanism for back. Arms bolted to stiles; curved
arm supports pinned to side seat rails. Detachable footrest,
covered in matching fabric, sits on own short legs and is hooked
to front of seat. Stretchers on back frame and rear support.
Variations: Some folding chairs have entirely plain frames and
more elegant upholstery.

Materials and Dimensions
Walnut and pine. Gilding. Wool scenic upholstery. Metal fittings.
Height: 42″; 16″ to seat.

Locality and Period
Made by P. J. Turcupile & Co., Brooklyn. Patented 1881.
c. 1881–95. Similar chairs patented by other American
manufacturers.

Comment
Folding chairs, often armchairs, were popular in the last quarter
of the 19th century. Utilitarian designs like the one shown here
were used as spare chairs in rooms usually furnished in the
Eastlake style. Many folding chairs were patented; they
evidently had great appeal in an era when innovation was
welcomed in every phase of production and design.

Hints for Collectors
Originally inexpensive, the folding chairs of this period are
comfortable and sturdy. Unusual types are beginning to attract
collectors and higher prices. Many can be identified by makers'
or patent marks usually found under the seat or on the back.

126 Eastlake folding armchair

Description
Upholstered folding armchair with rectangular back topped by cutout scrolls with ball finial. Curved top rail enclosing gallery of circles and knobbed spindles. Back upholstered with carpetlike fabric depicting Egyptian scene. Pair of lower back rails with 7 balls between them. Stiles curving back toward top and continuing below seat as curved rear legs. Upholstered seat attached to back by pins, allowing it to fold; seat straight-sided with rounded front corners. Armrests partly upholstered and pinned to stiles to permit folding. Arm supports continuing below seat as curved front legs. Turned stretchers in front and rear. *Variations:* Backs are usually straight-topped.

Materials and Dimensions
Walnut and oak. Carpet upholstery. Height: 37"; 14½" to seat.

Locality and Period
Made by E. W. Vaill, Worcester, Massachusetts. Patented 1877. c. 1877–95. Similar designs created by other manufacturers.

Comment
Folding chairs in the Eastlake style were particularly popular after 1875. A number of patents were issued for folding chairs, and several companies specialized in producing them. These were perfect spare chairs for the small parlors of many middle-class Victorian homes. The Egyptian theme, used earlier in Empire and Renaissance Revival furnishings (123, 179), was revived by popular interest in recent excavations; in the 1880s, for instance, an obelisk was erected in New York's Central Park.

Hints for Collectors
Upholstery, particularly when pictorial in pattern, as shown here, can be an integral part of a chair's design. In such cases, the upholstery should be in good condition.

Colonial Revival platform rocking chair

Description
Upholstered platform rocking chair with turned posts and rails.
Stiles ring-turned with bulbous finials. 2 uppermost rails on back
connected by turned H-shaped support; top rail partly covered in
carpet fabric. 2 lower back rails, upper one partly upholstered.
Armrest braces angled from back stiles to front seat rail; carpet-
covered armrests ending in brass caps and set on turned posts of
unequal lengths. Rectangular seat set on curved rockers, in turn
set on platform cut from flat planks and reinforced by turned
stretchers. Iron springs at joints between rockers and platform.
Metal casters. *Variations:* Mechanical improvements and
patented variants were made. Stiles may be inscribed planks.

Materials and Dimensions
Oak. Iron springs. Brass studs and caps. Modern carpet
upholstery. Metal casters. Height: 42″; 15″ to seat.

Locality and Period
Throughout the United States. c. 1900.

Comment
Platform rocking chairs, common during the second half of the
19th century, were made in factories all over the country. The
example shown here, with turned posts inspired by the Pilgrim
style, is made of oak, very popular at the turn of the century.
Carpet upholstery was used on lower-priced furniture from the
1850s to the early 1900s.

Hints for Collectors
Platform rocking chairs with original or period upholstery are
more desirable than those which have been recovered. Check
whether color, condition, and pattern of the material indicate
that it is of the period (*see* p. 432).

Renaissance Revival side chair

Description
Upholstered side chair with tufted back cushion framed by
elaborate rails and stiles with ring-and-block turnings and carved
disks. Cresting rail with carved female head centered in
pediment resting on simple turned top rail. 3 curving rails
project from each stile and end in freestanding side posts with
ball finials. Tufted upholstery ridge curving along rear of seat,
terminating in carved female heads. 2-part cushioned seat with
curved rear edge and straight sides and front. Canted front legs
turned and tapered with inscribed linear decoration and ball feet.
Plain rear legs flaring back. Turned front stretcher braced by 2
vertical turned rods attached underneath seat. *Variations:*
George Hunzinger made minor decorative changes in this design
from time to time.

Materials and Dimensions
Maple and other woods. Tufted upholstery. Height: 35″; 18″ to
seat.

Locality and Period
Made by George Hunzinger and Sons, New York. c. 1875–1900.

Comment
Hunzinger's design of the chair shown here is loosely based on
the folding chairs his firm originated (90). The turned elements,
inscribed decoration, and sculpted heads are in the late
Renaissance Revival style. Parlor sets often featured chairs like
this and matching settees.

Hints for Collectors
Hunzinger's chairs, settees, and other seating furniture are often
prominently marked with the company stamp and patent date.
Such markings are important because Hunzinger pieces now
command a premium.

Eastlake side chair

Description
Upholstered side chair with ebonized simulated-bamboo frame.
Top rail with cresting bar set above thin flanking bars hooked
through each end of projecting top rail. Straight stiles enclosing
tufted rectangular back cushion. Plain lower rail with 3
protruding rod stumps. Rectangular seat with partly exposed
rails. Straight turned legs, front pair on casters. Paired front
stretchers braced at center by thick post and 2 thin rods; single
turned side stretchers. *Variations:* Ebonized bamboo-turned
stiles and rails may be arranged differently.

Materials and Dimensions
Maple. Ebonized. Tufted damask upholstery. Metal casters.
Height: 34½"; 17" to seat.

Locality and Period
Throughout the United States. c. 1875–90.

Comment
The Oriental designs popular in the United States after 1870
were part of the Anglo-Japanese style, following English fashion
of that period. English influence on American design persisted
during most of the 19th century, particularly through Charles
Eastlake's book *Hints on Household Taste* (1868). Though
Japanese-influenced designs like the chair shown here may not
have appealed to Eastlake himself, they were inspired by the
work of compatriots such as Edward W. Godwin.

Hints for Collectors
Manufacturers' labels are rare on fine 19th-century furniture.
One must assume that a chair of this type was made in a major
city, possibly New York, by a manufacturer of fashionable
furniture. The turned decorative details on pieces like this are
easily broken and potentially expensive to repair.

Description
Side chair with rectangular upholstered back panel topped by flat rail set on a gallery of 9 short spindles. Back cushion reinforced by brass tacks. Lower back rail resting on X-shaped support. Stiles, topped by acorn finials, straight at gallery level and chamfered alongside back cushion. Projecting braces connect stiles to seat rails. Upholstered seat with molded edges, inner springs, and border of brass tacks. Front seat rail with gallery of 11 spindles below. Front legs with rectangular and spiral-turned sections; rear legs chamfered in front and flaring back. H-pattern stretchers. *Variations:* Galleries may have spindles in varied shapes. Legs may be plain.

Materials and Dimensions
Walnut. Imitation leather upholstery over iron inner springs. Brass tacks. Height: 39″; 18½″ to seat.

Locality and Period
Philadelphia, New York, or other furniture centers. c. 1875–90.

Comment
Charles Eastlake would probably have approved of the design of the chair shown here. So-called Eastlake furnishings that actually follow Eastlake's guiding tenet of simplicity as closely as does this chair are rare. American manufacturers tended to use fashionable new rectangular forms in designs more flamboyant than this, often featuring the inlaid or carved decoration that Eastlake criticized.

Hints for Collectors
Eastlake side chairs are quite common and collectors may be able to assemble a group of 4 to 8 matching examples at reasonable cost, though these may differ slightly in woods and details.

Eastlake plywood armchair

Description
Armchair with rectangular pierced back panel; pedimented top rail with pierced trefoil. Curved armrests and arm supports. Pierced plywood seat, continuation of back, attached to front rail. Front legs ring-turned; arrow feet. Plain rear legs flaring out to floor. Paired turned stretchers in front; plain pairs on sides and single one in rear. *Variations:* Different types of plywood were used. Within simple architectural frames, inscribed and pierced decoration in Gothic or Renaissance style varies.

Materials and Dimensions
Plywood, hickory, and ash. Height: 38″; 17½″ to seat.

Locality and Period
Made by Gardner and Company, New York. Patented 1872. c. 1872–95. Similar designs by other manufacturers.

Comment
Plywood, used for the back and seat of the example shown here, was often adopted for church and school seating. Many long benches were made of the material, popular from the 1870s through the turn of the century. Economical plywood chairs were often found in lower-class homes or public places. This design is a restrained interpretation of the Eastlake style, with pierced patterns as the main decoration.

Hints for Collectors
Mass-produced and inexpensive, plywood chairs were made in functional forms that relate them to other utilitarian furniture from the last quarter of the 19th century, such as bentwood, folding, and simple iron chairs. This straightforward functionalism often appeals to modern tastes. Though made in large numbers, such pieces are not commonly available today.

Description
Armchair with arched back panel cut in curved outlines; applied scroll-and-leaf carving on upper section enclosing carved mask. Back supported by flat central board joined to rear seat rail and by curved stiles also supporting arms. Rounded arms curve down at center and up to scrolled handholds; front arm supports and rear stiles curving to seat, then continuing down as flat-sided cabriole legs. Simple seat curves down in center; flat front skirt with double-curved edge. *Variations:* Designs may be closer to original Savonarola chairs, with legs crossing under seat. Backs may be more or less carved or else fabric-covered; some models have no backs. Chairs may fold.

Materials and Dimensions
Mahogany. Height: 39½"; 18" to seat.

Locality and Period
Probably Grand Rapids. c. 1890–1910. Similar designs made in other furniture centers.

Comment
After 1880 American furnituremakers began to closely follow Renaissance models (during the earlier Renaissance Revival, the inspiration was less direct). Savonarola chairs, sometimes called X-chairs because of their interlaced arms and legs, were named after a 15th-century Florentine monk who was martyred by the Medici and who was associated with this type of chair. The example shown here is a loose adaptation that was particularly in vogue at the turn of the century.

Hints for Collectors
Ingenious adaptations of medieval or Renaissance designs can form the basis of an unusual collection. Look for interesting carving on these relatively inexpensive pieces.

Modern laminated side chair

Description
Side chair with trapezoidal back rounded at corners and molded to curve in at center and out at sides. Curved back support is part of frame supporting seat. Rectangular seat with rounded corners, curving up at sides and down in rear and front to form central depression. Flat tapering legs bent under seat and flaring out. *Variations:* Metal legs may be used. Staining varies.

Materials and Dimensions
Laminated plywood, probably birch. Mahogany stain. Height: 26½"; 15½" to seat.

Locality and Period
Designed by Charles Eames. Produced in California, c. 1944; in Zeeland, Michigan, by Herman Miller, Inc., c. 1948–present.

Comment
Plywood, laminated and pressed into shape, has been well known for over a century. In the 1940s it was adopted by the American designer Charles Eames, who saw it as the ideal material for shaping chairs to the contours of the human body. Eames is particularly admired for distinctive designs like the chair shown here, though other designers had similar ideas at about the same time. However, his broadly proportioned chairs are so distinctive that their unauthorized imitations are regarded as counterfeits rather than legitimate reproductions.

Hints for Collectors
The sturdy Eames chairs rarely need serious restoration work. If something breaks, however, it may be difficult to repair; this is especially true of the backs, which are screwed to rear supports. Look for labels or other marks to historically document a particular chair. To identify unlabeled examples, check manufacturers' catalogues and magazines of the period.

Art Deco side chair

Description
Side chair with hexagonal back panel; narrow straight border framing inset diamond-shaped panel on top and chevron-shaped upholstered section below. Back supported by 3 stiles joined to seat rail and rear stretcher; 2 outer stiles narrow and angled. Rectangular seat with beveled corners; straight-sided rails framing cushion. Rectangular legs canted, with triangular tops; single stretchers on all sides. Front stretcher recessed; side stretchers with inner bracing continuing up legs. *Variations:* A wide variety of geometric shapes were used.

Materials and Dimensions
Oak. Fabric upholstery (originally imitation leather). Height: 37¾″; 17″ to seat.

Locality and Period
Designed by Frank Lloyd Wright, Chicago, for the Hotel Imperial, Tokyo. c. 1920. (Executed in Japan, c. 1935.)

Comment
American interest in the Art Deco style was first seen in designs by architects just before 1920. The type of design shown here, in which form is conceived without consideration for function, is very unusual. American designers tended to be more conservative, adapting traditional forms or conceiving new functional ones. This chair was devised by Frank Lloyd Wright for the dining room he designed in Tokyo's Imperial Hotel.

Hints for Collectors
Architect-designed furniture may often be documented by looking up original room plans and renderings or checking contemporary magazine articles describing the homes for which it was made. The available furniture in this field is limited, since it was usually custom-made in small quantities.

Child's Art Deco chair

Description
Small side chair with circular bentwood back (perisphere) enclosing obelisk-shaped (trylon) splat. Seat circular and plain. Plain cylindrical legs flaring out. Stretchers plain and thin. *Variations:* Other simple chair designs incorporate the symbols of the 1939 World's Fair. Other souvenir furniture has also been made using the official symbols or symbolic colors of expositions or notable events.

Materials and Dimensions
Bentwood (probably birch) and pine. Painted. Height: 19½″; 10½″ to seat.

Locality and Period
Throughout the United States. c. 1939–40.

Comment
Souvenir furniture, popular since the late 19th century, bears an identifying symbol or inscription, but convenient-sized plates or spoons were more common than furniture as souvenirs. The chair shown here is a modified Art Deco (or Art Moderne) design bearing the official symbols of the New York World's Fair of 1939, the geometric trylon and perisphere. The sleek lines of this design are hallmarks of most important works of the period, but the combination of the 2 Fair symbols in this chair back is a bit corny and far from the elegance of the best works in the style.

Hints for Collectors
Souvenir furniture is a field for collectors with a sense of humor, since these designs often feature a sentimentality that makes them quite amusing. Collectors specializing in World's Fair or other such memorabilia are willing to pay dearly for rare pieces, even if the designs are not to be taken seriously.

Description
Side chair with upholstered back rounded on top and straight on sides and bottom; back upholstery ending at partly exposed lower rail. Upholstered seat with curved sides. Front legs angled at corners of seat rails and ornamented with graduated arches; flared feet. Rear legs plain. H-pattern stretchers, side rails peaking in center. *Variations:* Legs may be cabriole. Reverse of backrest may be exposed, with upholstery edges often reinforced with rows of brass tacks. Back may reach down to seat. Top may be straight or more arched.

Materials and Dimensions
Walnut. Silk upholstery. Height: 36½″; 18½″ to seat.

Locality and Period
Designed by Eugene Schoen, New York. c. 1930. Variations by other designers.

Comment
Eugene Schoen, an architect and industrial designer, created the chair shown here for the nightclub of the ocean liner *S. S. Leviathan.* Designs like this first evolved in the mid-1920s, and variations appeared throughout the 1930s. Art Deco designers adapted traditional forms to the streamlined imagery of the period; for example, the tall back of this chair was inspired by 18th-century English models.

Hints for Collectors
While fine Art Deco designs such as this chair were made in limited quantity, others were produced in sizable numbers by major manufacturers and are thus more readily available. In collecting modern furniture, you should seek out appealing designs as much as makers' labels or marks.

Art Deco kitchen chair

Description
Painted side chair with back panel topped by rounded arch,
stepped sides, and pierced modified trefoil. Inscribed horseshoe-
shaped design painted red, looping from sides of top arch. Back
panel grooved into straight-sided stiles with rounded tops. Flat
seat with rounded front corners projecting over recessed rails
and front legs, both with inscribed painted borders. Front legs
rounded on 2 outer sides and flat behind; rectangular rear legs
flaring back. Plain H-pattern stretchers, with single rear
stretcher set higher. *Variations:* Back panel may be more
flamboyantly stepped and patterned in relief.

Materials and Dimensions
Pine. Painted. Height: 38½″; 18″ to seat.

Locality and Period
Throughout the United States. c. 1925–50.

Comment
Chairs and tables that loosely adapted the Art Deco style were
used from 1925 to 1950 in the kitchens of homes otherwise
traditionally furnished. The simple design shown here, with its
stepped outline and inscribed decoration, is a popularized version
of more elegant designs conceived in costlier materials for
parlors and bedrooms.

Hints for Collectors
Like many pieces of Art Deco pine furniture, this chair has been
repainted; few examples have their original paint, since they
underwent heavy daily use in rooms such as kitchens. If a chair
needs repainting, look for traces of its original colors or search
for similar designs with original paint in magazines such as
House Beautiful from the 1930s.

Modern side chair

Description
Side chair with rectangular upholstered back panel curving inward and set at an angle on plain cylindrical stiles. Seat upholstered and straight-sided. Seat rails plain, with side rails tapering to front. Legs cylindrical and plain, with front legs tapering toward feet. Rear legs braced by cylindrical bracket extending from side rails to feet. *Variations:* Legs and stiles may be square rather than round. Bracing may be attached to legs at higher point.

Materials and Dimensions
Pine. Finished with lacquer. Imitation leather upholstery. Height: 34½"; 18" to seat.

Locality and Period
Throughout the United States. c. 1935–55.

Comment
Beginning in the 1930s, a machine-made "modern" look became a prime objective of many American furniture designers. They were reacting against reliance on traditional techniques such as inlay and veneer by the finest Art Deco designers of the 1920s. But unlike the more radical Bauhaus designers in Germany, most American designers relied on updated historical forms. The chair shown here, for instance, made in a large factory in a typical "modern" style, is basically Empire in its lines.

Hints for Collectors
Unlike fine period furniture, which is generally enhanced by moderate wear, most modern pieces should look new, and their upkeep may require frequent, often troublesome restoration. For example, blond furniture mass-produced from the 1930s to 1950s was often finished with lacquer that, if restoration is needed, is hard to match exactly.

Art Deco side chair

Description
Side chair with curved rectangular back panel and plain tapered
stiles. Upholstered seat with plain rails, convex in rear, concave
in front, and straight along sides. Elliptical legs tapering to feet.
Variations: Back panel may be flattened or trimmed with a dark
color. Legs and stiles may be square.

Materials and Dimensions
Maple. Fabric upholstery. Height: 32″; 18″ to seat.

Locality and Period
Made by Heywood-Wakefield, Massachusetts. c. 1935–55.
Variations by other American manufacturers.

Comment
The sleek-lined yet luxurious French Art Deco designs of the
1920s were popularized and simplified during the 1930s and 1940s
by American manufacturers. Many experts prefer the term Art
Moderne for these later adaptations. Heywood-Wakefield, one of
the largest American furniture manufacturers, produced Art
Deco furnishings that were successful because its designers
understood the contemporary trend toward minimal
ornamentation and restrained design. Furniture like the chair
shown here, simple yet bold, differed from French models, which
were more elaborate in conception, construction, and use of
luxurious materials.

Hints for Collectors
Later Art Deco chairs such as this one are readily available at
very reasonable prices. Major manufacturers like Heywood-
Wakefield usually printed or branded their marks on their
products or used paper labels. Check manufacturers' catalogues
to date a piece, though not every design was illustrated.

140 Pilgrim-style Cromwell or Farthingale side chair

Description
Side chair with needlework back; top rail and upper stiles covered by upholstery. Lower stiles turned in ball-and-block pattern, flaring slightly backward below seat as plain rear legs. Rectangular seat with upholstery tacked over seat rails. Front legs turned in same pattern as back stiles. Single front stretcher ball-turned with center ring; paired side stretchers and single rear stretcher rectangular. *Variations:* Leather or wool upholstery is also used. Back stiles may be plain. Side stretchers may be turned.

Materials and Dimensions
Maple and oak. Original needlework upholstery based on carpet designs. Brass tacks. Height: 37″; 18″ to seat.

Locality and Period
New England, probably Boston. c. 1675.

Comment
Popularly called Cromwell chairs (after the 17th-century English leader Oliver Cromwell, during whose rule such chairs were supposedly used) or Farthingale chairs (after a type of Renaissance skirt), chairs like the one shown here were called turkeywork chairs in early American household inventories because of their needlework patterns based on "turkie" (Turkish) carpets. These were among the earliest American chairs, and surviving examples are remarkably similar in their turnings.

Hints for Collectors
American Cromwell chairs are exceedingly rare. Since many collectors may have difficulty distinguishing them from similar European examples (usually in walnut or cherry) and late 19th-century reproductions, they should be particularly cautious when buying these chairs and other Pilgrim-era furniture.

41 Pilgrim-style Wainscot chair

Description
Armchair with wooden back consisting of 2 vertical panels
framed by 2 rails and 3 stiles. Side stiles projecting above
straight top rail and curving back slightly. Arms, mortised into
side stiles, sloping down to columnar armrests. Rectangular
board seat shaped at edges and set on rails, with front and side
rails cut in double curve. Seat cushion in 17th-century style.
Columnar front legs with rings as capitals and bases; plain rear
legs. Low stretchers. Rectangular feet. *Variations:* Wainscot
chairs sometimes have carved backs. Turnings on the legs are
often more elaborate.

Materials and Dimensions
White oak. Modern cushion. Height: 41½"; 17¾" to seat.

Locality and Period
Connecticut. c. 1640–60.

Comment
Wainscot chairs were among the first American chairs; in fact,
the few documented examples were made by the first settlers
from England. Though based on 16th-century English models,
early American Wainscot chairs were surprisingly varied. Some
examples were elaborately carved like the elegant English
models, while others were quite simple, such as the chair shown
here, which still serves as the president's chair at Yale
University. Its columnar legs, in a style dating back to the
Renaissance, are particularly subtle.

Hints for Collectors
Authentic Wainscot chairs are extremely uncommon and seldom
come on the market. Since they have been much reproduced over
the past century, however, compare the proportions, wood type,
and carved details of such a chair with museum examples.

142 Queen Anne easy chair

Description
Easy, or wing, chair with vertical-cone arms on bare frame.
Arched top rail. Straight stiles slanting out from seat. Wings
mortised into stiles and tops of arms; arms made of flat rails
resting on rolled vertical supports. Straight-sided seat. Front
legs cabriole with pad feet, rear legs plain and flared back; all
reinforced with spindle-turned stretchers. *Variations:* Knees
may have simple carved shell decoration. Skirts may have curved
fronts in New England and Pennsylvania examples.

Materials and Dimensions
Maple frame. Mahogany base. Height: 49½"; 13" to seat.

Locality and Period
New England, probably Massachusetts. c. 1740–60.

Comment
Easy chairs were made throughout the American Colonies. The
straight front skirt and simple legs and stretchers on this chair
are characteristic of New England craftsmanship. The
combination of mahogany and maple, the design of the back, and
the rolled vertical supports for the arms are common elements in
New England (particularly Boston) easy chairs.

Hints for Collectors
Investigate the frame of a chair whenever possible, because
upholstered areas may conceal problems. Check the bottoms
of feet for appropriate wear. A good Queen Anne easy chair
should have a simple strong frame, with holes from earlier
upholstery. Reproduction fabrics for reupholstering are
available in many styles (*see* p. 432), and fragments of old fabric
found on the frame may make it possible to match early covering.

Description
Upholstered easy chair with top of back subtly arched.
Projecting wings almost at right angles to back, terminating in
arms made of vertical rolls. Seat has separate cushion with
straight front and tapered sides. Front legs cabriole, with sharp
vertical edges at corners and claw-and-ball feet; rear legs plain
and flared back. Front and side stretchers are turned; rear
stretcher rectangular. *Variations:* Straight, or Marlborough,
legs were also used; or straight tapered legs usually associated
with Federal design. Conical armrests may be horizontal.

Materials and Dimensions
Maple frame. Mahogany base. Modern silk damask upholstery in
Rococo floral pattern. Height: 47″; 19″ to seat.

Locality and Period
Rhode Island. c. 1755–65. Variations in other Colonies.

Comment
The easy chair, or wing chair, a form that flourished in America
throughout the 18th century, was inspired by late 17th-century
English models. Its wings were designed to protect the sitter
from drafts. According to early household inventories, these
chairs were used more often in bedrooms than in parlors. The
vertical rolled arm supports on the chair shown here are common
on New England chairs. The undercut claws of its feet are
characteristic of Newport furniture.

Hints for Collectors
Since only the legs are exposed to examination, it is important to
check the frame well to be sure it is solid. Ideally, it is wiser to
buy stripped-down frames. Inspect the legs for reasonable wear
and skillful carving; old legs were well carved, while recent
versions are rougher, as if sawed into shape.

Description
Easy chair with wings at right angles to back. Back with projecting center crest. Arms with horizontal rolls joined to conical front sections. Seat straight-sided. Front legs cabriole with trifid feet and with scrolls at knees; tongues overlap centers of knees. Rear legs plain rounded stumps. *Variations:* Top rail may be straight; wings may project at an angle. Plain cabriole legs often reinforced by stretchers.

Materials and Dimensions
Mahogany base. Oak frame. Upholstered in reproduction flamestitch needlework. Height: 49″; 17½″ to seat.

Locality and Period
Philadelphia. c. 1730–50.

Comment
Popularly called a wing chair, the easy chair is known in American examples from about 1710 until the 1820s or 1830s. Queen Anne examples, relatively rare, vary in the design of the upholstered frames as well as the legs. The angular wings and projecting center crest are associated with earlier designs in the William and Mary style. The horizontal roll of the arms, design of the front legs, and trifid foot are typical of Philadelphia craftsmanship. Easy chairs were widened and their backs lowered during the course of the 18th century.

Hints for Collectors
Although earlier 18th-century easy chairs are relatively rare, early 19th-century examples are common. Remodeling of a late chair to make it look earlier can be detected by careful examination of details of woods and joints. Examples with original fabric are very, very rare.

Chippendale upholstered armchair

Description
Armchair with upholstered back and open arms. Slanted back
with arched top. Padded arms rest on curved wooden supports
terminating at upholstered seat just above front legs. Front legs
straight and molded; rear legs plain and flaring back. 4 plain
stretchers. *Variations:* Earlier Queen Anne examples have
cabriole legs as well as seats and backs that are more curved.
More elaborate Chippendale versions were sometimes made,
often with claw-and-ball feet.

Materials and Dimensions
Mahogany base and arms. Maple frame. Silk damask upholstery
(modern copy of an 18th-century textile). Height: 40½"; 18" to
seat.

Locality and Period
New England, probably Massachusetts. c. 1765–75.

Comment
This is a restrained version of the chairs with upholstered backs
that appear in Thomas Chippendale's design book. The
proportions of the back and seat of the chair shown here are
characteristic of the Chippendale style, with its molded front legs
a popular interpretation of the Chinese-inspired straight, or
Marlborough, leg. The most elegant examples have flat-surfaced
legs to which carved ornament was applied. Later Federal
examples have taller backs and tapered legs (146).

Hints for Collectors
This type of chair can easily be faked, since some old legs may be
added to a later frame to make a convincing, good-looking
upholstered-back chair. Copies have flat details, which should not
be confused with the delicate moldings found on originals.

146 Federal upholstered Martha Washington armchair

Description
Armchair with tall upholstered back topped by wooden rail having rectangular center panel flanked by scrolled panels; center motif of carved drapery garlands against punchwork background, sides with carved crossed torches. Panels set above frieze of alternating plain and fluted segments. Stiles covered with upholstery that forms rectangular cushion outlined by brass tacks. Square arms sloping forward, with carved handholds. Baluster-shaped arm supports with leaf carving below. Seat straight on sides and at rear, bow-shaped in front, with upholstery over rails and brass-tack borders. Front legs square and tapered; plain rear legs flaring back. Casters on 4 legs. *Variations:* Upholstery may cover top rail. Simpler arms and round tapered legs are also common.

Materials and Dimensions
Mahogany. Horsehair upholstery. Brass tacks and casters. Height: 43"; 15" to seat.

Locality and Period
Carving attributed to Samuel McIntire, Salem, Massachusetts. c. 1805.

Comment
Federal upholstered-back armchairs like the one shown here are commonly called Martha Washington, or lolling, chairs. The form had been introduced much earlier in the 18th century, but was most popular in the Federal period, when it had tapered legs and a tall back.

Hints for Collectors
Beware of legs that are thin and very plain, and arms with little or no carving; these may be signs of a later copy. Unfinished wood under the upholstery should be darkened from age.

Modern upholstered bentwood armchair

Description
Armchair with upholstered back and seat in continuous sectioned shape; upholstery designed as series of horizontal panels. Arms and legs made from single curved loops of bentwood. *Variations:* Some versions have no upholstery, plainer lines, less angular back and seat, and legs that do not taper. Purist designs had simpler upholstery; the plush model shown here was made to have broader sales appeal.

Materials and Dimensions
Bentwood. Lacquered. Velvet upholstery over pine frame. Height: 43″; 19″ to seat.

Locality and Period
Made by Thonet Brothers, Austria or Czechoslovakia. c. 1932–45. Similar designs made in the United States.

Comment
Bentwood, introduced in the first half of the 19th century, has been used for furnituremaking ever since. The major manufacturer was the multinational firm founded in 1849 by Michael Thonet, a German designer who perfected the bentwood process. Still in existence, the firm has never stopped making the functional designs they popularized in the mid-19th century, but since the 1920s Thonet production has included more innovative furniture. The chair shown here is one of several Thonet designs carefully contoured to fit the human back.

Hints for Collectors
Check bentwood furniture for tiny cracks or damaged wood that might break from continued use. Some bentwood and related pieces have a label or maker's mark under the seat. Makers may also be identified by reference to manufacturers' catalogues or to documented examples in museums and books.

Art Deco leather-upholstered armchair

Description
Armchair with rectangular back, open arms, and green painted trim. Leather-covered back framed by wood. Plain straight arms resting on straight supports joined to side seat rails a few inches in from front. Front seat rail slightly curved; straight side and back rails frame seat cushion matching the back. Rear legs tapered and flaring back to floor. Front legs tapered and straight; painted feet. Iron scrolled braces attached under seat rail and on front legs. Single high stretchers on sides and in rear. *Variations:* Overall design may be simpler. Legs may not taper. Details may be painted in various colors.

Materials and Dimensions
Maple. Stained and painted. Leather upholstery. Iron scrolled braces. Height: 37″; 18″ to seat.

Locality and Period
Designed by Jules Bouy, New York. c. 1930. Variations made by other designers.

Comment
American Art Deco differed from the better-known French version in its simpler detailing. While Parisian furnituremakers of the 1920s and 1930s used sophisticated decorative techniques, American makers tended toward designs that could be executed more easily. Some were factory-made, while others, like the chair shown here, were produced in fairly limited quantities. (For a matching console table, *see* 276.)

Hints for Collectors
American Art Deco designers, at their best, successfully simplified forms to achieve elegant effects. Distinctive examples, like this chair, are much sought after and often costly.

Chippendale leather-upholstered armchair

Description
Armchair with rectangular back, seat, and open arms leather-covered and outlined with brass tacks. Molded, curved arm supports, continuations of molded handholds, joined to seat rails several inches from front of seat. Front legs straight-sided, tapering, and molded; rear legs simpler and flaring to feet. *Variations:* Some elegant early examples have curved top rails and legs that do not taper. Most later Federal examples have taller backs.

Materials and Dimensions
Mahogany. Pine frame. Modern leather upholstery. Brass tacks. Height: 35¼"; 18" to seat.

Locality and Period
Possibly made by Thomas Affleck, Philadelphia. c. 1790.

Comment
The chair shown here may be one of a set of chairs made by the Philadelphia cabinetmaker Thomas Affleck for the Senate and House of Representatives while Philadelphia was the nation's capital. The flat-topped back and tapering legs suggest a post-Revolutionary date of manufacture. The relatively heavy proportions of this unusual design show Chippendale inspiration. Leather was a popular upholstery material throughout the 18th century; decorative borders of tacks were often added to seats. Chairs with the original leather are very rare.

Hints for Collectors
When a chair of this kind is stripped of its upholstery, one can see if its design has been altered over the years. It is easier, however, to look at the overall stylistic lines and exposed details of the woodwork to judge whether the original design has been preserved.

Federal upholstered armchair or bergère

Description
Armchair with leather-upholstered back. Curving top rail continuing as arms that slope down to rounded handholds. Arm supports baluster-shaped and freestanding, set on rectangular segment topping front legs. Barrel-shaped back outlined in brass tacks, with rounded stiles and lower rail exposed behind. Separate seat cushion with curving sides. Flat seat rail curving from front legs around entire back; front seat rail bowed out. Columnar front legs tapered, with molded rings and round feet; rectangular rear legs flaring back. *Variations:* Frame is usually completely covered by upholstery, which may be fabric. Exposed rails may be carved in leaf designs.

Materials and Dimensions
Mahogany. Modern leather upholstery. Brass tacks. Height: 32"; 16" to seat.

Locality and Period
Attributed to George Bright, Boston. c. 1795.

Comment
The chair shown here is based on a Louis XVI *bergère;* the plainness of its frame is a sign of its Americanization. The attribution is based on the fact that the Boston cabinetmaker George Bright is known to have made a set of such chairs for the Massachusetts State House.

Hints for Collectors
This chair is one of 30 Bright made for the Massachusetts State House, but so far only a handful have turned up. Evidently they were sold sometime in the 19th century, and were probably purchased by prominent Boston families. At least a dozen of these fine chairs are still to be discovered.

Art Nouveau upholstered armchair

Description
Upholstered armchair with back topped by arched rail having carved floral cresting. Top rail curving to join flat sloping arms decorated with diamond-shaped marquetry panels of wood and brass; arms curving down at handholds, continuing as straight supports to top of front legs. Barrel-shaped back curves into sides of arms. Seat covered by cushion curved in back and straight-edged in front. Curved skirt embellished all around with panels of gilded glass enclosed by marquetry frame. Cylindrical legs reeded and tapered, set on brass claws holding glass balls. *Variations:* Art Nouveau decoration and Louis XVI chair design were frequently combined.

Materials and Dimensions
Maple. Varied wood and brass inlay. Glass panels. Brass and glass feet. Velvet upholstery. Height: 35½"; 17" to seat.

Locality and Period
Attributed to Tiffany Glass and Decorating Company, New York. c. 1890–1900.

Comment
Based on a Louis XVI *bergère*, the chair shown here is an excellent example of fine turn-of-the-century craftsmanship. The carving and inlay, as well as the overall construction, are clearly the product of able cabinetmakers working in a relatively traditional shop, such as Louis Comfort Tiffany's Glass and Decorating Company, rather than a factory.

Hints for Collectors
Although Tiffany chairs are rare, the products of other fine small shops are available. These well-made turn-of-the-century furnishings were often more eclectic than this elegantly restrained example.

Victorian upholstered horn armchair

Description
Upholstered armchair with pairs of steer horns framing upper back and serving as arms and legs; tips of horns serving as feet. Spring construction under back, sides, and seat. Single ivory finial (one missing). *Variations:* Back and sides without upholstery are common on horn chairs designed more for novel appearance than for comfort. Number of horns varies. Elk or deer antlers were also used.

Materials and Dimensions
Steer horns. Iron-spring construction under woolen twill covering. Ivory finial. Height: 38″; 17″ to seat.

Locality and Period
Made by F. M. Holmes, Boston. c. 1880. Variations made by other furnituremakers.

Comment
Horn chairs, a Victorian invention, were part of the fad for decorating with mementos of the wilderness—from elk antlers to elephant tusks or feet—that lasted from about the time of the purchase of Alaska (one source for horns) in the 1860s until after 1900. Presidents Abraham Lincoln and Theodore Roosevelt both received horn chairs as gifts. Though primarily a western invention, such chairs were made all over the country, as this example from Boston proves. Their design, quite suitable for the eclectic interiors of the 1880s and 1890s, has been related to the curvilinear motifs of Art Nouveau.

Hints for Collectors
Horn chairs range from ungainly, purely decorative examples to others as usable as the one shown here. These surprisingly sturdy chairs are available from time to time in shops specializing in odd or exotic furnishings.

Victorian platform rocking chair

Description
Platform rocking chair with back having 27 spindles; globular forms at top and bottom of spindles joined to suggest strands of beads. Rear spindles topped by hemispherical finials carved in rosette pattern; middle spindles ball-and-ring-turned. Padded seat; rails reeded on all sides. Seat set on pair of rockers attached to trestlelike platform by spring mechanism. Spiral-turned stretchers. *Variations:* Many manufacturers received patents for variations of the platform rocking chair. Hunzinger, better known for his folding chairs, made them in several designs.

Materials and Dimensions
Maple. Modern upholstery. Iron springs. Height: 32½″; 15″ to seat.

Locality and Period
Made by George Hunzinger, New York. c. 1880. Numerous similar designs by other American chairmakers.

Comment
Platform rocking chairs—made to rock only within a fixed area defined by their bases—were used in Victorian parlors and were popular at all social and economic levels. Their design reflected many of the fashions of the period. The rocking chair shown here was probably inspired by the Windsor chairs that returned to popularity with the Colonial Revival beginning in the 1880s.

Hints for Collectors
Because patented furniture frequently bears the patent date as well as number, it is possible to trace the original patent description for some examples. The spring mechanism should be examined with care, since a platform rocking chair in perfect condition often costs little or no more than a damaged one.

Art Deco bamboo armchair

Description
Bamboo armchair with plain rectangular back covered by large cushion with rounded corners and simple welting in contrasting pale color. Plain rectangular seat cushion. Arms made of 6 bamboo tubes bent into armrests and bases in trapezoidal shape with curving corners; arm structure reinforced by interior cross braces. Seat base made of 8 bamboo tubes bent into straight-fronted skirt with curving corners. *Variations:* Arms and skirts may be narrower. Cushions may be thinner and tufted.

Materials and Dimensions
Bamboo. Wooden frame. Heavy cotton upholstery. Height: 29″; 15½″ to seat.

Locality and Period
Possibly designed by Paul Frankl, New York. c. 1930–50. Similar designs made in New England and California.

Comment
Bamboo and wicker furnishings, intended primarily for porches, patios, or summer rooms, were made by factories all over the country, with the highest concentration located in New York and New England. Simple squat shapes were most typical of the 1930s; many designs were based on early 19th-century prototypes, while others, like the chair shown here, followed modern trends. This chair features the geometric lines characteristic of Art Deco. Many homes furnished in traditional styles had modern furniture outdoors.

Hints for Collectors
Bamboo furniture, both for indoor and outdoor use, is sturdy, utilitarian, and moderately priced. Many examples were styled in the modern idiom, since the material was easily bent into the simple geometric shapes characteristic of the 1920s to 1940s.

Mission-style rocking chair

Description
Rocking chair with rectangular components and thick upholstered cushions on back and seat. Plain plank slats set vertically into back and arm rails. Plain stiles. Arms slightly lower than back. Seat rails consisting of planks mortised into stiles; pegs, reinforcing tenons, visible on front stiles. Plain flat rockers, longer in rear. *Variations:* Vertical slats are sometimes narrower. Tenons may not be visible. The typical Mission-style rocking chair has no back cushion and is raised higher on stretcher-braced legs.

Materials and Dimensions
Oak. Floral fabric upholstery. Height: 29½"; 17" to seat.

Locality and Period
Made by Stickley Brothers, Grand Rapids. c. 1900–10. Similar chairs produced by other furnituremakers.

Comment
Simple oak furniture made at the turn of the century in the so-called Mission style, a fashionable variant of the Arts and Crafts style, appealed to those who spurned the more eclectic designs dominating the low-priced furniture market at that time. The leader in this field was Gustav Stickley, head of a New York firm called Craftsman Furniture. The chair shown here was made by 2 of his brothers, George and Albert, who formed the Stickley Brothers Company in Grand Rapids.

Hints for Collectors
Look for paper labels or metal tags on Mission-style oak furniture, since documented examples are the most valuable, though some unlabeled examples may be just as fine. Designs by the oldest Stickley brother, Gustav, are most prized. Also look for exposed tenons and pins on Stickley pieces.

Mission-style easy or Morris chair

Description
Easy chair with leather-upholstered cushion on slat back leaning away from seat; angle of back adjusted by moving wooden supporting rod held in place by knobs behind arms. Flat arms curving up and broadening from back to front. Arms supported by front and rear posts; horizontal rectangular panels enclosing 7 vertical slats. 2 brackets under each arm. Posts passing through arms. Wide front seat rail. Legs square and straight. *Variations.* Backs may have metal rails. Seat may have footrest. Width of slats may vary.

Materials and Dimensions
Oak. Leather cushions. Height: 36"; 10½" to seat.

Locality and Period
L. and J. G. Stickley, Fayetteville, New York. c. 1900–15.

Comment
Mission was the name given to a type of simple turn-of-the-century oak furniture supposedly inspired by furnishings from the Californian missions of Spanish Colonial times, though such originals no longer exist. Mission-style easy chairs––called Morris chairs if adjustable, after the famous chair by the English designer William Morris—are usually simple rectangular designs. Some mass-produced examples have slats with rounded edges or decoration applied as a concession to popular taste.

Hints for Collectors
Mass-produced Mission-style chairs, generally with applied decoration or carving, are more available than simple classics like this example. While all Mission-style furniture has become popular during the past decade, only finer pieces by craftsmen such as Gustav Stickley and his brothers bring high prices. The side slats and slanted arms add to the value of this chair.

Mission-style armchair

Description
Armchair with rectangular back panel supporting tufted cushion.
Arms made of broad flat boards with straight edges, resting on
solid sides; straight strips of molding applied to sides and
wrapped around legs. Solid wooden panel grooved into legs at
sides. Seat is rectangular panel holding cushion of same shape.
Rectangular legs with angled feet on metal casters. *Variations:*
Mission-style chairs, including those by Frank Lloyd Wright,
usually have side and back panels composed of rows of thin
vertical slats.

Materials and Dimensions
White oak. Fabric-upholstered cushions. Metal casters. Height:
33¼"; 10" to seat.

Locality and Period
Designed by Frank Lloyd Wright, Chicago. c. 1902.

Comment
Frank Lloyd Wright designed furniture as well as buildings: the
chair shown here was made for the house he designed for Francis
Little in Peoria, Illinois. Its rectilinear quality is typical of the
Mission style fashionable in the early 20th century; the solid
panels and subtle decorative moldings, however, foreshadow
tendencies that were later part of the Art Deco style. Thus,
where most Mission-style furnishings had simple functional
designs, this chair is more decorative. (For a stand also from the
Little house, *see* 336.)

Hints for Collectors
Though unusual, this chair displays the decorative quality
important during the first decades of this century. Fine early
Wright furniture, such as this chair, can be quite costly.

Art Deco overstuffed corner chair

Description
Corner chair entirely upholstered over wooden frame, with back cushion curving diagonally across square base. Back tufted in vertical ridges, with straight sides and welted edges. Seat curved in rear where it meets back cushion; 2 front edges perpendicular. Back rails perpendicular, forming triangle with back cushion. Skirt and base plain, with edges outlined in contrasting pale welting. Turned wooden feet. *Variations:* Upholstered Art Deco furniture was often made to suit room shapes, to look built-in or to divide rooms. Glossy solid fabrics were popular, sometimes with contrasting details.

Materials and Dimensions
Wooden frame. Maple feet. Velvet upholstery. Height: 24″; 16″ to seat.

Locality and Period
New York or any major furniture center. c. 1930–50.

Comment
Overstuffed furniture in geometric shapes was fashionable in the 1930s, reflecting current design trends. The notion of adapting simple, modern-looking shapes to traditional forms began in the 1920s, when Art Deco was first introduced, and continued into the 1930s and 1940s. The chair shown here, a striking updating of the Victorian upholstered corner chair and a good example of this modern approach, may well have been mass-produced or else made in an upholstery shop at moderate cost.

Hints for Collectors
A great deal of overstuffed furniture from the 1930s and 1940s is available and generally inexpensive, though not all of it is in a condition suitable for purchase. Upholstery can be costly to refurbish and appropriate textiles hard to find.

Art Deco overstuffed armchair

Description
Upholstered armchair in modified tub shape with back rail joined to slanting arms and topped by projecting roll all around. Arm supports straight and recessed from flat front. Rounded cushioned back; plain sides. Seat with separate cushion. Space between seat and feet concealed by upholstery and fabric skirt. Ebonized wooden legs cylindrical and tapered. *Variations:* Many subtle changes are apparent from example to example. Tufting may be used. Some tub-shaped chairs have simpler lines that are more clearly related to works by major Art Deco designers.

Materials and Dimensions
Oak and pine frame. Textured woolen upholstery. Height: 29″; 18½″ to seat.

Locality and Period
Throughout the United States. c. 1925–55.

Comment
Overstuffed armchairs were introduced in the late 19th century, when the first so-called turkey-spring chairs were invented. Early examples tend to have tufting in complex patterns, but in the 1920s, when sleek Art Deco lines became fashionable, tufting was often omitted to emphasize angularity. These chairs were either crafted by upholsterers operating as independent artisans or mass-produced in factories.

Hints for Collectors
Dating unlabeled overstuffed armchairs is challenging because the same designs were used over several decades and were easily adapted or copied. Examples with distinctive upholstery may be dated by their fabrics: for example, those with bold geometric or abstract floral patterns in the Art Deco style probably date from the 1925–40 period (*see* p. 432).

Sofas, Daybeds, Settees, Settles, and Benches

Sofas, daybeds, settees, settles, and benches are all elongated chairlike forms usually meant for two or more people. The largest category is sofas—long upholstered seating forms with arms. Shorter forms include daybeds—extended chairs used for lounging—and conversational sofas. Other related elongated types of seating are settees, settles, and benches. Settees are usually shorter than sofas, though some longer models with openwork wooden backs are also given the name. The term "settle" is most commonly applied to rural wooden benches with solid wooden backs and skirts or chestlike storage areas under the seats. Benches are long flat seats without backs or arms.

Sofas

Sofas were made as early as the 17th century, but these are exceedingly rare. The camel-back sofa, named for its arched back, was favored from the mid-18th to the early 19th century. The major difference among various camel-back designs is the legs: cabriole or Marlborough legs are common on Queen Anne and Chippendale examples, whereas tapered legs were used on Federal-era pieces. Delicate Neoclassical carving on exposed woodwork is a hallmark of other Federal sofas, but is less evident on country pieces of the same era. Empire sofas usually have large-scale decoration, scrolled arms, and sometimes dolphin legs or lion's-paw feet. Fashionable mid-19th-century sofas follow the same trends as chairs. The importance of upholstery on a sofa or settee depends on the style of the piece. Many high-style examples were initially upholstered in elegant fabrics, but such original materials have rarely survived. When choosing new upholstery, study period patterns to determine what is appropriate to the style of a piece (*see* p. 432). It is important to check the frame under the upholstery, particularly on valuable older sofas or settees, to make certain that all elements are original.

Daybeds and Conversational Sofas

Early daybeds are basically chairs with slanted backs and extended seats. Some Federal designs are based on ancient couches. Daybeds with one raised, often pillowlike end were produced throughout the 19th and 20th centuries. Asymmetrical settees, or méridiennes, were frequently made in Rococo Revival and Eastlake styles. Conversational sofas, or tête-à-têtes, having two seats facing in opposite directions and an S-shaped back, were also common in the Victorian period.

Settees, Settles, and Benches

Queen Anne and Chippendale two-seat settees made in the 18th century are rare, but Colonial Revival examples from about 1900–20 are fairly common. Sheraton painted Fancy settees often have backs divided into chairlike sections. Rocking settees or convertibles that open up as beds were designed in Sheraton and other styles. Shakers made open-back settees that were simplified versions of traditional designs. Craftsmen working in the Mission style favored oak settees with wooden or leather-upholstered seats and with vertical or horizontal slats on backs and under arms; longer versions were often called settles. Settees were also made of cast iron or wicker in the 19th and early 20th centuries. Tubular steel was used for Art Deco examples of the 1930s and 1940s. The variety of benches is great, ranging from simple country examples to elegant, high-style window seats.

Federal camel-back settee

Description
Camel-back settee with arched back upholstered over top rail, curved up slightly at ends. Sloping upholstered arms with scrolled tops. Exposed front arm supports topped by carved rosette; carved sunburst motif at seat rail level. Seat upholstered over front rail. Legs square and tapered. *Variations:* Top rail may be exposed and carved. Legs may be round and reeded.

Materials and Dimensions
Mahogany, maple, and white pine. Modern fabric upholstery. Height: 29″. Length: 45⅜″. Depth: 22½″.

Locality and Period
Carving attributed to Samuel McIntire, Salem, Massachusetts. c. 1800–10.

Comment
The curved lines of the settee shown here are a hallmark of Federal-era examples made in Salem, Massachusetts. While such designs were also executed elsewhere, a surprising number were made in Salem, with the most elaborate examples having carved top rails. The carving on this settee is limited, but its overall lines are as graceful as any on more elaborate examples. Much Salem furniture carving is attributed to Samuel McIntire, since it often resembles carved details on houses built by him.

Hints for Collectors
Line is of primary importance in Federal designs. Restrained examples like this settee, which retains the graceful lines but minimizes the kind of carved decoration found on more elaborate examples, offer collectors great elegance without the added ornamentation that can raise the price appreciably. Whenever possible, check the frame under the upholstery for replaced parts.

Chippendale camel-back sofa

Description
Camel-back sofa with arched back upholstered over top rail,
curving up slightly at ends. Horizontal rolls serving as armrests.
Arm supports slope forward and down to tops of corner legs.
Back, seat, and arms fully upholstered. Seat rails are simple
exposed boards. 3 cabriole front legs with leaf-and-scroll carving
at knees. Claw-and-ball feet. 3 round rear legs with wider tops
and feet. *Variations:* Rare examples may have exposed top rails.
Legs may be simpler and have stretchers.

Materials and Dimensions
Mahogany. Reproduction silk damask upholstery. Height: 36¼".
Length: 79¾". Depth: 33½".

Locality and Period
Philadelphia. c. 1775–80.

Comment
The sofa shown here is a masterpiece of 18th-century American
furnituremaking. Its overall design and superb details would be
enough to suggest its importance, but it is also documented as
originally owned by John Dickinson, a signer of the Declaration
of Independence. The fine carving on the front legs is deep and
typical of Philadelphia work.

Hints for Collectors
While a sofa like this, if it were on the market, would cost as
much as many houses, less elegant interpretations are available
around the country at lower prices. Chippendale sofas have been
much reproduced: beware of lighter proportions, flat carving,
and signs of modern tools—such as circular saw marks—on the
inner framework.

Chippendale camel-back sofa

Description
Long camel-back sofa with arched back upholstered over top rail,
curving up at ends. Horizontal rolls serving as armrests.
Upholstered arms slope down from scroll ends; front arm
supports curve down to tops of front legs. Straight-sided seat
upholstered over rails, with lower borders of tacks. 3 front legs
square and straight, with molding around bottom to form feet.
Rear legs plain and flared back. Each pair of front and rear legs
connected by flat stretchers, with long stretcher joining shorter
ones. *Variations:* Arched back may be steeper. Legs may be
plain without molding.

Materials and Dimensions
Mahogany. Modern fabric upholstery. Brass tacks. Height: 39½″.
Length: 97¾″. Depth: 33¼″.

Locality and Period
Philadelphia. c. 1770.

Comment
Commonly called camel-backs, sofas with arched backs were
popular in the Chippendale period. A relatively simple design for
the period, it was nevertheless furnished with elaborate
upholstery. The form was particularly favored in Philadelphia,
where some of the finest examples were produced. Straight
Marlborough legs with the molding added to articulate the feet
were called Chinese in Thomas Chippendale's design book.

Hints for Collectors
It is wise to examine the frame hidden under a sofa's upholstery,
particularly on a fully upholstered and valuable example like the
one shown here. A dealer should leave part of the back
uncovered or offer to strip a portion to enable a customer to
check the tack holes and aged wood of the frame.

Description
Sofa with straight top rail slanted down at ends; upholstery covers rail and stiles. Arms projecting straight out a few inches below top of back. Arm rails and sides upholstered. Arms supported by flat wooden posts exposed in front. Upholstered seat with separate rectangular cushion. Seat rail wide and exposed. Seat suspension consists of flat boards in grooved slats. Legs turned and columnar. Ball feet. *Variations:* Country sofas may be plainer, with square tapered legs rather than columnar ones. Back rail may be exposed.

Materials and Dimensions
Maple and pine. Modern upholstery. Height: 35″. Length: 77″. Depth: 27″.

Locality and Period
New England. c. 1820–40.

Comment
Many country furnishings, such as the Sheraton sofa shown here, were made in styles that had already gone out of fashion. Though heavy, the turned legs on this sofa are an example of the elegant details occasionally found on country pieces. This design is interesting because its fashionable elements are tempered by simple stained surfaces that betray its rural origin.

Hints for Collectors
"Country" is a catchall term that can be applied to furniture made anywhere and at any time. Check pieces to be sure that old-looking paint does not cover new lumber and that modern nails, screws, or tool marks are not present. Simple designs are easy to imitate, but modern imitators are not usually careful about details, which may be crude. Authentic country furniture, though simple, is not crude.

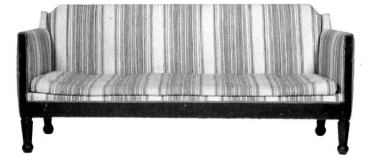

Federal square-back sofa

Description
Square-back sofa with fully upholstered back raised slightly in center. Arms curving down from top rail to exposed arm supports with upholstered sides. Arm supports vase-turned and set on small pedestals above front corner legs. Seat upholstered over front rail, with separate rectangular cushion. 4 front legs square and tapering; 4 rear legs flared back. *Variations:* The top rail may be exposed. Legs are frequently round and reeded (166). Arm supports and handholds may be carved.

Materials and Dimensions
Mahogany and pine. Modern upholstery. Height: 34″. Length: 72″. Depth: 24″.

Locality and Period
Philadelphia. c. 1795. Variations made in other centers.

Comment
Sheraton sofas with straight backs and vase-turned arm supports were produced in several American furnituremaking centers, particularly Boston and Philadelphia. Boston examples were usually more elaborate, while those from Philadelphia were restrained but elegant. The vase-turned arm supports on the sofa shown here are simpler versions of the elegant ones produced by 2 Philadelphia craftsmen, Henry Connelly and Ephraim Haines.

Hints for Collectors
Simple versions of elegant designs are quite appealing when their proportions and lines are good, as in this example. Such designs, however, may easily be reproductions, so look for proper signs of wear on arm supports and legs.

Federal square-back sofa

Description
Square-back sofa with fully upholstered, arched back.
Upholstered arms curving down to exposed scrolled handholds
resting on vase-turned supports. Seat with separate cushion
having curved front and back edges. 4 front legs columnar and
tapered; 4 rear legs plain, square, and flared back. *Variations:*
Arm supports and front legs may be carved or reeded. Shorter,
6-legged models were also made.

Materials and Dimensions
Mahogany and maple. Modern upholstery in Louis XVI-style
Neoclassical pattern. Height: 36″. Length: 78″. Depth: 26″.

Locality and Period
New England, probably Massachusetts. c. 1790–1800.

Comment
In early household records, the type of sofa shown here was
called a square-back sofa. Stylish but restrained, it is a
fashionable design that lacks the elaborate detailing of more
expensive examples. Its straight arms and tapered legs are
characteristic of designs inspired by the work of Thomas
Sheraton. The elegant legs and vase-turned arm supports relate
it to New England, particularly Massachusetts, designs.
Sheraton designs were more dependent on classical borrowings
than were contemporary Hepplewhite examples; they were also
closer to the Empire style that followed.

Hints for Collectors
Compared to Queen Anne, Chippendale, and even the finest
Victorian examples, most Federal sofas are reasonably priced.
Sheraton sofas like this were reproduced, but usually with more
ornamentation. Reproductions often have sharp moldings and,
sometimes, overly delicate legs.

166 Federal square-back sofa

Description
Square-back sofa having exposed top rail. Elaborately carved
center and side panels with punched background. Carved frieze
atop tufted upholstery of back. Arms flaring out from back.
Exposed wooden armrests sloping down to carved handholds,
with vase-turned supports set on leaf-carved bases. Thin seat
cushion. Plain skirt with curved ends. 4 front legs tapered
columns, with plain capitals and reeded main sections over
tapered cylindrical feet. 4 rear legs square and flared back.
Variations: The carving on the example shown here is the finest
known, but other Sheraton designs also have elegant carving.

Materials and Dimensions
Mahogany and birch. Modern tufted upholstery. Height: 40″.
Length: 84″. Depth: 25″.

Locality and Period
Carving attributed to Samuel McIntire, Salem, Massachusetts.
c. 1800–10.

Comment
The square-back is a Sheraton design that was interpreted by
many American craftsmen. The most elegantly carved examples
were made in Salem, particularly by the architect Samuel
McIntire. The details on this piece are based on fashionable
Neoclassical designs.

Hints for Collectors
Masterpieces like this sofa are extremely rare. Modest
interpretations of varying quality are more available. These are
better evaluated when compared with fine museum examples
such as this. Beware of simplified flat carving or machine-pressed
decoration, which may be a sign of an early 20th-century
reproduction.

Empire sofa

Description
Sofa having exposed cylindrical top rail, with thicker center
section and leaf-carved urns at ends; scroll-carved brackets
below urns. Upholstered back and straight-fronted seat. Front
seat rail rounded. Upholstered arms large and cylindrical, with
carved laurel wreath enclosing fabric-covered front of cylindrical
drawer; brass pull. Each cylinder rests on blocklike molded base.
Legs formed by Ionic capitals above gadrooned borders and
tapering plinths fitted into brass shoes on casters. *Variations:*
The back rail may be flat, with inscribed decoration. Legs may
be scroll-shaped. Drawers concealed in arms are rare.

Materials and Dimensions
Mahogany. Brass pulls, feet, and casters. Modern silk damask
upholstery. Height: 34¾". Length: 89½". Depth: 26½".

Locality and Period
Boston. c. 1826–28. Variations made in other centers.

Comment
Empire furniture displays an amazing variety of design, often
inspired by more delicate styles from the beginning of the
century. Although the top rail is a typical Sheraton element, the
classical ornamentation and proportions of the sofa shown here
were popular in the 1820s.

Hints for Collectors
Look for ingenious touches, such as the cylindrical drawers
within bolsters on this sofa, which may enhance the value of a
piece. However, unusual forms are more apt to be Continental
than American, so check such pieces for labels. For example, this
sofa, now covered in reproduction fabric, bears the label of its
original Boston upholsterer.

Empire sofa

Description
Sofa with back topped by exposed straight rail curving up at ends. Top rail, curved side stiles, and straight lower rail frame back cushion bordered with brass tacks. Upholstered arm rails projecting from top rail and serving as upper part of scroll-shaped arms. Arms and seat upholstered except for front edges of continuous armrests and front seat rail; applied ormolu rosettes at ends of arms and winged sphinxes over legs. 2 bolsters. Scroll-shaped legs carved in flat leaf pattern. Brass ball feet. *Variations:* Scroll-end sofas are usually heavier in proportion and have more complex decoration.

Materials and Dimensions
Mahogany, pine, and oak. Ormolu. Brass tacks and feet. Modern upholstery. Height: 33½″. Length: 76½″. Depth: 23″.

Locality and Period
Philadelphia. c. 1815. Variations made in other centers.

Comment
The Empire style took root in the United States shortly after 1800, when classical forms became fashionable. The sofa shown here is based on a Roman couch, with ends raised and legs reduced in size to suit 19th-century tastes. The basic design probably reached these shores via London.

Hints for Collectors
Unusual designs like this sofa, though sometimes expensive, are particularly rewarding to own. Fine carving and ormolu decoration enhance its value. Beware of late 19th- and early 20th-century imitations, which have poorly executed details and are smaller than the originals.

Empire sofa

Description
Scroll-end sofa with exposed top rail having deeply curved ends
and 2 pendant ormolu rosettes. Rail rests on upholstered stiles
forming curved back of arms. Upholstered back with border of
brass tacks. Scroll-shaped arms upholstered over armrests.
Front arm supports carved in fishtail shape, painted in fish-scale
pattern, and looping around at seat rail. Straight-sided seat
outlined in tacks; bolsters at ends. Straight seat rail with bold
brass inlay in Greek key pattern and braces of gilded leaves at
inner corners. Dolphin-shaped legs with gilded heads above
casters. *Variations:* Cornucopias and lion's paws are used more
often as feet. Carved decoration is more common than brass.

Materials and Dimensions
Mahogany, rosewood, maple, ash, and pine. Painted. Gilding.
Ormolu. Brass inlay and casters. Modern upholstery. Height:
34½″. Length: 98½″. Depth: 27″.

Locality and Period
New York. c. 1820. Less elegant versions made in other centers.

Comment
The most elegant Empire-style furniture was usually made in
New York: it was the center of stylish furnituremaking at the
time and attracted fashion-conscious customers from around the
country. The sofa shown here, following a popular design, has
unusually elegant embellishments, such as the brass inlay and
fancifully carved dolphin legs.

Hints for Collectors
Scroll-end Empire sofas range from simple to elaborate in both
overall outline and details. This unusual example would be
toward the top of the price range. Many plainer models are
available, and these are both moderately priced and practical.

Federal cane-back sofa

Description
Cane-back sofa with back topped by convex rail and divided into
3 panels by 2 reeded stiles. Side panels of top rail with pairs of
carved cornucopias tied with ribbon; center panel with sprigs of
laurel. Reeded outer stiles curve to brace arms. Arms curve out
in scroll shape. Armrests with panels of carved sprigs over
caning. Rectangular caned seat covered with long cushion and 2
bolsters. Front arm supports curve down to form part of reeded
curule (X-shaped) legs; other part of legs joined to reeded front
seat rail. Rear legs also curule, joined to front legs by bulbous
stretchers. Ormolu lion's heads at crossing of legs. Ormolu lion's-
paw feet on front legs. Brass casters. *Variations:* Legs are
usually straight and tapered instead of curule.

Materials and Dimensions
Mahogany. Caning. Ormolu mounts. Fabric-upholstered
cushions. Brass casters. Height: 34″. Length: 84¾″. Depth: 23¾″.

Locality and Period
New York. c. 1810.

Comment
Cane-back sofas, high-style pieces favored more in New York
than in other centers, were rare in the early 19th century. The
curule legs were used only on the most elegant sofas and chairs,
and were inspired by ancient stool and chair designs.

Hints for Collectors
Many elegant cane-back sofas, such as the superb example shown
here, have carved panels, but simpler pieces have overall
reeding. These designs were reproduced a century later, but
were rarely well executed. Original caning is rare; recaning does
not significantly affect the value of a piece.

171 China Trade/Empire cane-back sofa or daybed

Description
Cane-back sofa having top rail with carved shell flanked by curving sections; applied rosettes. 3 caned back panels divided by 2 supporting stiles. End stiles conforming to scroll shape of caned arms. Arm supports carved in leaf-and-scroll pattern, with applied rosettes at ends of scrolls. Rectangular caned seat with flat cushion. Caned front protector, removable and fitted over one arm, with sloping top rail ending in carved scroll and rosette. Front seat rail with inscribed linear decoration flanked by applied leaf carving. Tapered legs ring-turned and reeded. Arrow feet. *Variations:* Empire designs of greater or lesser complexity were also made in China.

Materials and Dimensions
Oriental rosewood. Caning. Upholstered cushion. Height: 34″. Length: 92″. Depth: 34″.

Locality and Period
Made in China for export to the West. c. 1840.

Comment
Empire designs executed in China for export to the West generally have more intricate carving than do American examples. The shell and leaves on the sofa shown here, for example, are unlike anything made in American shops, though the piece conforms to Empire designs. The removable front guard converts this sofa into a daybed.

Hints for Collectors
The finest China Trade furniture is usually prized for beautiful carving, but very plain examples do exist. To distinguish Chinese from American designs, note the combination of Western design (usually Empire or Victorian) with Chinese decoration and varieties of wood.

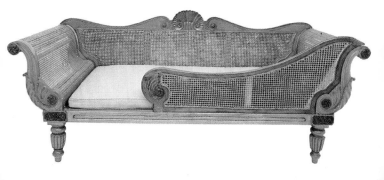

Description
Sofa with curved 3-part back outlined in rounded molding.
Center oval cushion crowned with carved leaves. Curved rails
flanking oval and terminating in swan's-neck curls. Scroll-shaped
arms projecting from back. Curved arm rails above flat-fronted
supports embellished with applied scrolling-leaf design. Seat
plain, rectangular, and upholstered over springs. Legs and front
skirt carved with leaf-and-scroll designs. Scroll-shaped legs on
casters. *Variations:* Empire and Rococo Revival motifs may be
used in various combinations. Scroll-shaped arms are often
bolder. Seat cushion may be loose.

Materials and Dimensions
Mahogany and pine. 1930s fabric upholstery. Iron casters.
Height: 38″. Length: 84″. Depth: 25½″.

Locality and Period
Throughout the United States. c. 1830–50.

Comment
Furniture combining 2 styles is generally called transitional,
although this term misleadingly implies that it was made at a
time when one style was giving way to another, which was not
always so. Transitional designs were more often made by
conservative craftsmen who were unwilling to give up a style
that had gone out of fashion. The sofa shown here was probably
made when stylish craftsmen were producing Rococo Revival
sofas. Such transitional furniture was usually less expensive.

Hints for Collectors
Combinations of Empire and Rococo Revival elements were
common from 1830 to 1860. While fakes of such pieces appear
infrequently, later reproductions—with lighter proportions—
were made from 1890 to 1920.

Rococo Revival sofa

Description
Sofa with curved 3-part back and molded frame. Center oval
cushion flanked by carved leaf-and-scroll ornament. Side sections
curved and angled around seat, continuing into low arms with
curved handholds. Plain seat with rounded edges. Front skirt
curving with bowed center. Front legs modified cabriole shapes
with molded details. Rear legs square and flared back. Plain feet.
Variations: Molded frames may have applied carving on top rails
and front seat rails, and central areas may be more integral parts
of the design. Upholstery may be tufted.

Materials and Dimensions
Walnut and pine. Early 20th-century upholstery over steel
springs. Height: 36″. Length: 61½″. Depth: 25″.

Locality and Period
Throughout the United States. c. 1840–80.

Comment
The Rococo Revival style was first introduced in the 1830s and
flourished for half a century. Examples with simple frames, like
the sofa shown here, were made in all the major furniture
centers as late as the 1880s. The Rococo style was appealing
because of its simple grace, and although no longer the height of
fashion after 1860, it continued to be adapted for the general
public.

Hints for Collectors
The carving on some simple inexpensive sofas is crude, so plain
examples like this one are often preferable. These are quite
plentiful and go well with various types of Victorian furnishings.
Original upholstery is very rare; this sofa may once have been
covered with a damask in a large floral pattern (*see* p. 432).

Rococo Revival laminated sofa

Description
Laminated and upholstered sofa with 3-part back framed by scrolls, shells, and elaborately pierced flora and grapes. End sections of back like tall chair backs; center section wider and lower. Back frame continuing as curved arms. Exposed scroll-shaped handholds. Curved arm supports becoming front legs. Curved front skirt with carved fruit and leaves below plain seat. Front legs cabriole, with carved grapes. Rear legs tapered. Metal casters. *Variations:* Sofas may have solid instead of pierced frames. Framing border may be gadrooned.

Materials and Dimensions
Rosewood and other woods. Laminated. Modern velvet upholstery. Metal casters. Height: 49″. Length: 70″. Depth: 31″.

Locality and Period
Probably made by John Henry Belter, New York. c. 1850. Similar designs made in Philadelphia and Boston.

Comment
New York produced the most elegant Rococo Revival furniture. The sofa shown here had the elaborate carving typical of fine New York cabinetry, though similar work was done in Philadelphia and Boston. The furniture of John Henry Belter was the finest and most elaborate, and only Belter received patents for his lamination processes.

Hints for Collectors
Check elaborate decoration for missing or loose flowers and other carved details; these will detract from the value and appeal of a piece. Count layers of laminated wood visible along exposed edges: Belter used 6 or more layers, his competitors only 3–5. Belter pieces are occasionally labeled.

Rococo Revival painted sofa

Description
Sofa with upholstered 3-part back and painted and gilded frame.
Scroll-and-leaf-carved crestings with pierced centers. End
sections of back like tall chair backs; center section wider and
lower. Tufted back cushion straight in center and curved at tall
ends. Low upholstered arms with exposed scroll-shaped
handholds atop curved arm supports. Front skirt curving down
in center, with carved leaf decoration. Front legs cabriole with
flowers at knees and double-scroll feet. Rear legs plain scroll
shapes. Metal casters. *Variations:* Backs may have more
carving. Rosewood was more common than painted surfaces.

Materials and Dimensions
Mahogany. Painted and gilded. Reproduction tufted upholstery.
Metal casters. Height: 45″. Length: 76″. Depth: 31″.

Locality and Period
Attributed to Alexander Roux, New York. c. 1850.

Comment
American furniture with original overall painting and gilding is
rare. The painted decoration on the Rococo Revival example
shown here was an attempt at greater elegance. This sofa was
probably commissioned from Alexander Roux, one of the more
prominent New York cabinetmakers.

Hints for Collectors
Painted Rococo Revival furniture, although uncommon, reflects
an important decorative tendency of the style. The carving on
this sofa is restrained, but the details are well executed and
display an unusual delicacy. Original paint will have a muted
surface with the patina and weblike crazing that come from age,
while repainted surfaces will appear smooth.

Rococo Revival sofa

Description
Sofa with laminated back in serpentine curve topped by pierced rail. Floral-carved cresting with cartouche flanked by gadrooned sections and scrolled piercework. Top rail curving down and around to sides. Back curved and upholstered. Upholstered arms with curving scroll-carved handholds and arm supports. Front seat rail carved in simple scroll pattern; center cartouche. Cabriole legs; tapered feet on iron casters. *Variations:* Laminated sofas may have more elaborately carved frames.

Materials and Dimensions
Rosewood and other woods. Iron casters. Reproduction damask upholstery. Height: 48½″. Length: 65″. Depth: 35½″.

Locality and Period
Attributed to the firm of J. and J. W. Meeks, New York. c. 1850–60.

Comment
Rococo Revival sofas were made as part of parlor sets that were the height of fashion from the 1840s to the 1860s and continued to be popular in inexpensive versions through the 1880s. The sofa shown here is pierced and laminated in a style associated with the well-known New York workshop of J. and J. W. Meeks. Examples with especially well-executed lamination and more intricate carving than that seen here are usually attributed to John Henry Belter.

Hints for Collectors
There are 3 quality levels of Rococo Revival sofas: in the first 2 are Belter- and Meeks-style laminated sofas, and in the third, sofas made of solid wood bent into Rococo shapes. Since a great price differential exists between these groups, collectors should determine in advance what their budget will allow.

Renaissance Revival sofa

Description
Sofa with tufted back and seat. Back having arched center
topped by curved rail with inscribed and gilded decoration. Urn
finials at rail ends. Pediment above top rail, with cabochon
enclosing oval mother-of-pearl profile in scrolled frame. Side
sections of back curved and upholstered over top rail. Back
ending in molded stiles, with carved projections. Upholstered
arms curving in toward scrolled handholds and supports that are
carved and inscribed. Curved front seat with inscribed
decoration and 3 hanging ornaments. Side rails plain and curved.
Legs trumpet-turned and inscribed. Brass casters. *Variations:*
Renaissance Revival sofas may have simpler turned decoration
without carving.

Materials and Dimensions
Rosewood. Gilding. Mother-of-pearl. Reproduction upholstery.
Brass casters. Height: 45⅞″. Length: 76¾″. Depth: 31″.

Locality and Period
Probably New York. c. 1870. Variations made in other cities.

Comment
Tufting is an upholstering technique used throughout the 19th
century, particularly for Rococo and Renaissance Revival forms.
It serves as an elegant addition to the unusually well-made
Renaissance Revival sofa shown here.

Hints for Collectors
Check whether the ornamentation on Renaissance Revival
furniture was mass-produced. Simple machine-turned elements,
often quite handsome, were easily produced in midwestern
factories, while examples with elegant touches, such as the
carving on this sofa, were handmade by skilled craftsmen in
traditional workshops and are more desirable.

178 Renaissance Revival sofa

Description
Sofa with elaborately sectioned back and gilded and inscribed decoration. Raised center with cresting rail having cabochon flanked by carving. Second rail ending in turned finials. Straight stiles with pyramid-shaped finials. Central tufted cushion outlined with curved molding. Side cushions on back upholstered over top rail and framed on 3 sides by molding. End stiles turned and carved. Arms and lower section of back formed by continuous row of tufted upholstery. Carved arm supports. Straight skirt with flattened shell motif hanging from center. Turned rods connect skirt to lower stretchers. Turned front legs slanting out; hoof feet. Rear legs plain and flared back.
Variations: Similar designs may have caryatids or sphinx heads.

Materials and Dimensions
Walnut and pine. Gilding. Modern velvet upholstery. Height: 45″. Length: 66″. Depth: 27″.

Locality and Period
Made by George Hunzinger and Sons, New York. c. 1870.

Comment
Hunzinger was a manufacturer who also patented a number of folding-chair designs. They were usually based on classical forms even after the Renaissance Revival style was out of fashion. The sofa shown here does not fold up, but the angles of the legs are like those of Hunzinger's folding chairs (90).

Hints for Collectors
Hunzinger and other manufacturers stamped or impressed their names under the seats of most of their products. Marked pieces generally sell at a premium. Renaissance Revival sofas with unusually shaped arms and legs are often more desirable than plainer examples.

Renaissance Revival sofa

Description
Sofa with straight back having raised center upholstered over
top rail and bracketed by ebonized animal heads holding gilded
drapery. Exposed rails mortised into straight stiles with ormolu
mask finials. Upholstered arms supported by ebonized sphinx
heads atop scroll-shaped bodies continuing as corner legs. Plain
skirt with gilded border. 4 front legs, ebonized and gilded,
terminating in hoof feet. 2 plain rear legs. Casters. *Variations:*
Renaissance Revival sofas are generally walnut. A variety of
Egyptian motifs in bright colors were often added.

Materials and Dimensions
Cherry and pine. Ebonized. Ormolu. Modern velvet upholstery.
Brass casters. Height: 43″. Length: 73″. Depth: 32″.

Locality and Period
New York and other centers. c. 1870–85.

Comment
Egyptian motifs were used as alternatives to typical classical
Renaissance Revival elements during the 1870s. These colorful
exotic additions appealed to a public already fascinated by
Napoleon III's resumption of the French archaeological efforts in
Egypt. Little documentation exists to help identify the designers
working in this style. (*See also* 123.)

Hints for Collectors
The great interest in Egyptian design in the 1870s was a renewal
of a vogue that began in the 1820s and 1830s and would be
revived once again in the early 20th century. The earlier designs
were part of the Empire style, while in the 1870s they were
adapted to the Renaissance Revival style. Pieces with Egyptian
motifs are far less common than typical Renaissance Revival
examples and often bring higher prices.

Eastlake settee

Description
Asymmetrical settee with low rectangular back upholstered over top rail. Straight stiles with pairs of inscribed lines. Straight lower back rail. Scroll-shaped ornament bracing stile and back rail. Short rear stile at one end; partly upholstered arm at other end, extending to single front stile. Molded handhold. Inscribed ornament hanging under arm. Rectangular seat. Grooved front skirt; panel of dentils suspended from center. Front legs columnar, with turned capitals and bases. Rear legs square and flared out. Casters. *Variations:* Asymmetrical settees sometimes have an exposed top rail. Decoration may include Oriental or Near Eastern, rather than classical, motifs.

Materials and Dimensions
Walnut and pine. Modern fabric upholstery. Iron casters. Height: 33″. Length: 39″. Depth: 23½″.

Locality and Period
Throughout the United States. c. 1880–90.

Comment
Rectangular shapes arranged in straight lines are characteristic of Eastlake design. Asymmetrical settees were made more angular when adapted to the Eastlake style. The one shown here is unusual because of its classical, rather than Gothic or exotic, decoration. Probably part of a parlor set, this conservative settee was meant for use in a relatively modest home.

Hints for Collectors
Small Eastlake settees such as this piece are relatively common and inexpensive. They are well suited to small apartments and go well with a variety of furnishings. Avoid examples with damaged woodwork or upholstery, since repairs may be costly.

Rococo Revival laminated settee or méridienne

Description
Asymmetrical settee of laminated wood and tufted upholstery.
Curved frame high-backed at one end of elongated seat. Carved
floral and fruit cresting atop rounded scroll border that continues
to seat rail on one side and to molded arm on other. Skirt with
molded convex border on bottom edge. Simple cabriole front legs
terminating in tapered feet. Plain rear legs rounded on 2 sides.
Brass casters. *Variations:* Belter's workshop also produced
settees with piercework frames. Floral cresting may be carved
from a separate piece of wood and applied to the frame.

Materials and Dimensions
Rosewood. Modern silk upholstery tufted in traditional manner.
Brass casters. Height: 38″. Length: 40″. Depth: 27″.

Locality and Period
Made by John Henry Belter, New York. c. 1845–65.

Comment
The méridienne is a type of settee that was part of mid-19th-
century parlor sets, which often included pairs of méridiennes
designed to face each other. While the designation "Belter" is
loosely applied to much Rococo Revival furniture, the carved
flowers and elegant scroll-patterned frame shown here are sure
signs of the New York cabinetmaker's work.

Hints for Collectors
Belter furniture may be identified by the quality of its details; in
general, imitations are less well made. Belter's imitators strove
for obvious elegance by carving elaborate ornament on their
furniture; but instead of Belter's fine roses and fruit, they
resorted to heavily gadrooned borders of leaves or of vines
and grapes.

Empire window seat

Description
Window seat with rectangular upholstered top. Plain flat skirt with mahogany veneer. Simple scroll-shaped legs, broadening toward top, with disks applied on both sides of upper and lower curves. Paired legs resting on simple rectangular platforms with molded ends. *Variations:* Gilded decoration may be used. Legs may have carved details or be turned and reeded. Window seats may have simple arms.

Materials and Dimensions
Mahogany and mahogany veneer. Reproduction wool and linen upholstery. Height: 16¼". Length: 44¾". Depth: 14".

Locality and Period
Attributed to Duncan Phyfe, New York. c. 1837.

Comment
Window seats, introduced in the Federal era, evolved from the simple stools used in the first parlor sets. Made with or without arms, they were generally used in front of windows, against walls, or in the center of rooms. In the piece shown here, the simplicity and heaviness characteristic of late Empire furniture is subtly relieved by the scroll forms and decorative disks, as well as by the carefully selected veneers, which create an almost shimmering surface. Balanced proportions and fine detailing make this window seat exceptional among Empire designs of the 1830s.

Hints for Collectors
Most late Empire pieces are less skillfully made than this window seat, but their plain oversized shapes have a distinctive charm for some collectors. Since few window seats have survived, any Empire example, early or late, should attract a collector's attention.

183 Federal Grecian couch or récamier

Description
Couch with klismos back topped by straight rail in scroll form, with reeded disk at front end. Stiles sloping at 45° angle to seat rails. Caned back panel joined to rectangular cane seat with 2 braces underneath (cushions removed here). Solid panel above rear seat rail, with raised border outlining its curved shape. Scroll form at foot, covered in caning and reeded at ends. Front seat rail reeded, with plain rectangular panels above legs. Plain curved legs with flat sides. Scroll feet. *Variations:* Grecian couches may have carved back panels and legs.

Materials and Dimensions
Mahogany and aspen. Caning. Height: 31″. Length: 71½″. Depth: 25¾″.

Locality and Period
Made by Thomas Needham, Salem, Massachusetts. c. 1820. Variations made in other centers.

Comment
The récamier, or daybed, shown here bears the label of the Salem cabinetmaker Thomas Needham and, like other examples of his work, is relatively restrained. Called a Grecian couch in contemporary descriptions, it is based on Greek or Roman examples, but with shortened legs suited to American taste of the early 1800s. It is a fine expression of the Neoclassical style flourishing at that time.

Hints for Collectors
Simple designs are not easily traced to a city or maker unless, like this couch, they bear a label. Labels may be faked, however, so they should be compared with those on authenticated examples. Advertisements from early newspapers have sometimes been glued on to simulate authentic labels.

Eastlake daybed

Description
Daybed with sloped back topped by scrolled end. Back and deep
seat upholstered over metal springs. Legs flat on 2 sides, with
carved and/or machine-pressed details. Lion's-paw feet. Metal
casters. *Variations:* Late 19th-century daybeds may have
fringed skirts concealing legs or upholstered skirts replacing
legs. Shape of legs may vary considerably. Tufted upholstery
was commonly used.

Materials and Dimensions
Oak. Modern upholstery. Metal springs and casters. Height: 27″.
Length: 73″. Depth: 25″.

Locality and Period
Throughout the United States. c. 1880.

Comment
The daybed shown here may be considered Eastlake in style
because its simple design conforms to Charles Eastlake's notions
about utility and its exposed legs are made of oak, a wood
Eastlake recommended. Though its basic design was adapted
from a classical Empire shape, this daybed is longer and its back
slopes more. It is sometimes called a fainting couch, based on one
practical use, but this name was not given in contemporary
furniture catalogues.

Hints for Collectors
Daybeds are plentiful and usually the least expensive type of
sofa. Original 19th-century upholstery is rare. Furniture like this
might be better appreciated when upholstered in suitable
reproductions of period fabrics. Modern patterns, however, may
be acceptable if reupholstering costs prohibit a more
appropriate choice.

Art Deco chaise longue or daybed

Description
Chaise longue, or daybed, upholstered over wooden frame, metal springs, and legs. Back angled at one end, with rails and stiles cushioned to form rounded upholstered arms. Center of back tufted with vertical pleats. Longer arm extending almost to far end of seat. Straight-sided seat with round ends and braided rope welting. Deep skirt on all sides. Long fringe concealing wooden legs set on casters. *Variations:* Similar daybeds made in the late 19th century have thinner arms and were covered in more ornately tufted Victorian fabrics.

Materials and Dimensions
Mahogany. Silk upholstery and fringe. Metal springs and casters. Height: 34¼″. Length: 65½″. Depth: 30¼″.

Locality and Period
Throughout the United States. c. 1930–40.

Comment
The daybed shown here is a recent example of a form used over a long period. Overstuffed daybeds, chairs, and sofas with inner-spring construction were first introduced in the 1880s and continue to be popular today. The curves of the arms and other elements may vary slightly, but since the basic design remains consistent, the best indicator of age may be the upholstery pattern. The shiny surface and abstract foliate pattern of the fabric on this example are characteristic of American Art Deco.

Hints for Collectors
Like much Art Deco furniture, daybeds in this style are beginning to attract the attention of many collectors. Look for examples with upholstery that is original and in good condition. Remember that silk does not wear well and a piece like this may need recovering after a few years of use (see p. 432).

186

Eastlake conversational sofa or tête-à-tête

Description
Conversational sofa, or tête-à-tête, with 2 seats facing opposite
directions and backs forming S-shaped curve. Top rail
upholstered and tufted, resting on gallery of 12 vase-turned
spindles with low bowls and long necks. Drum-shaped seats with
top upholstery curving over springs in cushions; braided edging.
Straight sides of seats covered in fabric, elaborate braiding,
fringe, and tassels. Straight legs on casters. *Variations:* Seats
are sometimes designed in more complex undulating shapes.

Materials and Dimensions
Maple and pine. Ebonized. Original silk and velvet upholstery
and fringe. Iron inner springs and casters. Height: 25″. Length:
45½″. Depth: 23″.

Locality and Period
Throughout the United States. c. 1885.

Comment
Innovative forms like the tête-à-tête, a 2-seat conversational
sofa, were introduced first in the 1820s and 1830s and became
more common as the century continued. Such unusual designs
fitted easily into the fashionably eclectic décor of the 1880s. The
design shown here is loosely based on the Windsor chair, dressed
up for the occasion with ebonized spindles turned in elegant
patterns and imaginatively flamboyant upholstery. Designed to
be shocking, this piece is nonetheless comfortable and functional.

Hints for Collectors
Unusual sofas like this are rare but in no great demand.
Collectors who like such eccentric pieces should ask dealers
about them, since they may not always be on display. Look for
tassels and fringe in good condition; they are integral parts of the
design and hard to replace.

Modern laminated settee

Description
Sculptural settee built of laminated wooden blocks that have
been carved and polished. 2 rounded chairlike backs connected
by lower middle section. Sloping back flows into arms and
upcurved projecting handholds. 2 cater-cornered seats sculpted
to accommodate sitters. 2 straight, finlike pedestal bases support
seats from front to back. *Variations:* Carved furniture may have
several contrasting woods for added color. Designs may be more
traditional.

Materials and Dimensions
Cherry. Laminated. Height: 31″. Length: 52″. Depth: 30″.

Locality and Period
Made by Wendell Castle, Scottsville, New York. 1973.

Comment
Wendell Castle is one of the foremost contemporary
furnituremakers working in wood. Trained as a sculptor, he
exploits the beauty of his material in essentially functional forms
and a modern idiom. The resulting designs sometimes resemble
those of earlier designers such as Charles Eames (101, 133). His
sculptural shapes and magnificent graining show off the beauty of
wood textures, as seen in the settee—or "2-seater," as he called
it—shown here. Its angled seats are reminiscent of 19th-century
conversational sofas.

Hints for Collectors
Castle is one of a small group of artist-craftsmen at the forefront
of contemporary furniture design. His output has varied over the
years from sculptural forms like this 2-seater to more traditional
designs made of exotic woods. His work, like that of other fine
craftsmen since the 1950s, can be found in galleries featuring
contemporary crafts and may someday become prized antiques.

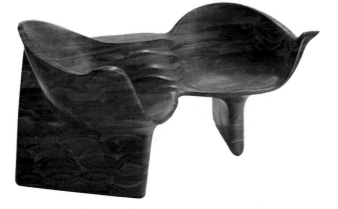

Description
Settee with tubular-steel frame and vinyl-laminated upholstery. Back consisting of 2 rectangular cushions supported behind by upper and lower rails. Upholstery covering metal springs and extending into deep skirt. Tubular upholstered arms projecting from back, then curving downward to form exposed handholds and arm supports that continue as legs. Legs stabilized by U-shaped stretchers at floor level. *Variations:* Full-length sofas of similar design are common. Thickness of cushions varies. Tubular arms and legs may be curved differently.

Materials and Dimensions
Tubular steel. Chrome-plated. Vinyl-laminated fabric upholstery. Height: 33″. Length: 41″. Depth: 34″.

Locality and Period
Designed by Gilbert Rohde for Troy Sunshade Company, New York. c. 1933.

Comment
Tubular steel was introduced as a furniture material in the 1920s by innovative European designers. By the 1930s American designers began using it in simple furniture for kitchens, patios, and playrooms. Gilbert Rohde, designer of the settee, or love seat, shown here, was a pioneer of modern American design who worked closely with progressive manufacturers.

Hints for Collectors
Popularized modern designs such as this settee, though perhaps not as innovative as Bauhaus-inspired examples, do capture the spirit of the period. Such pieces are still inexpensive, but rusty chrome may require potentially costly sanding and replating. Solid fabrics are best for reupholstering, but some flamboyant patterns may also be suitable (*see* p. 432).

Mission-style settee

Description
Settee with back topped by broad plain rail having rounded edges and subtly upcurved ends. Narrow straight stiles. 6 wide slats set into plain lower rail. Arms flat round-edged boards, narrowing toward rear; supported by extensions of front legs, with added curved brace. Rounded handholds. Seat consisting of 13 plain slats protruding just beyond front skirt. Simple board skirt curved down slightly at ends, with single exposed pegs. Rear legs rectangular and flaring back. Paired narrow stretchers, recessed and joining plain side stretchers. *Variations:* Stiles may be thicker and arms flat-edged. Slats may vary in width and number. Seat may be upholstered.

Materials and Dimensions
Oak. Height: 40″. Length: 46″. Depth: 26″.

Locality and Period
Made by Charles Limbert, Grand Rapids. c. 1900–10.

Comment
Oak furniture with simple lines and minimal decoration was very popular in the early 20th century. Contemporary critics named the style Mission, since it was supposedly based on furniture found in California missions. This style was most successfully carried out by Gustav Stickley, but he had many competitors, including Charles Limbert. The Limbert settee shown here was probably meant to be used on a porch.

Hints for Collectors
Limbert's furniture remained close to the simple sturdy designs most admired by collectors today. Its thin stiles, however, seem less appealing than the heavy ones used by Stickley. Exposed pegs or tenon ends are generally the only decorative elements on fine Mission-style furnishings.

Mission-style settee or settle

Description
Settee, or settle, with straight-topped back and arms of equal height. Wide top rails and narrower lower rails mortised into 4 square stiles projecting above rails. 2 cushions serving as backrests. Seat cushion upholstered in imitation leather. Plain seat rails and legs. *Variations:* Vertical slats are commonly used between top and seat rails. Tenons may be visible. Skirt may be deeper.

Materials and Dimensions
Oak. Imitation leather cushions. Height: 32″. Length: 65″. Depth: 26″.

Locality and Period
New York, Grand Rapids, or other furniture centers. c. 1900–15.

Comment
Simple oak settees—wooden benches with backs, called settles by some furnituremakers—were frequently used in parlors, libraries, and halls furnished in the Mission style during the first 2 decades of this century. The example shown here is simpler than most: not only is it lacking vertical slats on the sides and back, but the tenons of the rails do not show. Exposed tenon ends are commonly regarded as a Gustav Stickley hallmark, but many pieces lacking them appeared in his magazine *The Craftsman*, through which he popularized his designs.

Hints for Collectors
Mission-style furniture, made by many manufacturers, may be judged in 2 usually contradictory ways: by its simple functionalism, following Stickley's approach, or by its decorative elements. Both approaches are valid. Do not pay a premium for a piece said to be by a designer such as Stickley unless the attribution is supported by a label or a period illustration.

Description

Settee with back made of 2 parallel flat panels straight along top and bottom and tapered at ends. Central brace behind panels. Stiles curved in front. Arms, projecting straight from stiles, have rounded edges and curve down at handholds. Each arm supported by tapered stile and 2 tapered spindles. Rectangular seat with ropes tied to knobs to support mattress. Seat rails plain and dovetailed together. Cylindrical legs plain and tapered, with rectangular tops. *Variations:* Settees are more often like Sheraton and Windsor models, with top panels on back over rows of spindles or divided sections (192, 193).

Materials and Dimensions

Maple and pine. Homespun upholstery. Horsehair stuffing. Ropes. Height: 32″. Length: 71″. Depth: 27″.

Locality and Period

Massachusetts or New York. c. 1850.

Comment

The settee shown here is a good example of functional Shaker forms blended with fashionable contemporary styles. This design is related to some Sheraton painted Fancy models, but simplified. The back panels and arms, however, have simple details characteristic of Shaker work. Examples by rural non-Shaker cabinetmakers are usually less logical in their simplicity and more affected by elegant styles.

Hints for Collectors

Not every simple 19th-century piece of furniture was made by the Shakers; look for elements such as the plain legs and dovetailed seat rails seen here, as well as overall balanced simplicity. History of use in a Shaker community is also important in identification.

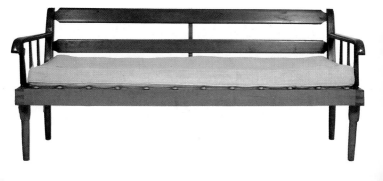

Windsor/Sheraton rocking settee or mammy bench

Description
Rocking bench topped by wide stenciled panel supported by plain rounded stiles and 19 tapered spindles. Arms deeply curved, flat-sided, and thick, with scroll-shaped handholds. Short spindle and rounded stile with painted rings support each arm. Removable guard rail, consisting of 2 stiles and 2 rails, set into holes toward front of seat. Seat curving down in front and slightly hollowed in center. Legs with painted rings, tapered toward top. Flat stretchers in front and back, with linear and stenciled decoration on front one; thin round stretchers on sides. Plain flat-sided rockers. *Variations:* Long settees or benches combined various Windsor and Sheraton elements.

Materials and Dimensions
Ash, pine, and cherry. Painted and stenciled. Height: 32″. Length: 72″. Depth: 22″.

Locality and Period
Throughout the United States. c. 1820–60.

Comment
Because of its guard rail, meant to protect children rocking in it, the bench shown here is popularly called a mammy bench. Examples as simple as this one are hard to localize, since rural shops all over the country produced them. The top panel derives from Sheraton painted Fancy chair designs (40), but the spindles are like those found on Windsor chairs (19).

Hints for Collectors
Country furnishings like this bench were made with many structural and decorative variations. Look for rough elements such as plain heavy seats and legs. Reproductions can be recognized by their fancy or overly delicate details. Examples with original paint are most highly prized.

Sheraton painted Fancy settee

Description
Painted and stenciled settee topped by straight rail curving and
sloping down at ends to form arms with vertical scroll-shaped
handholds. Painted decoration on top rail divided into 5 sections
of pairs of gilded rectangles flanking octagonal frames filled with
flowers, trophies, and symbolic motifs. Rail supported by 4
curved round stiles forming 3 chairbacks, and by 2 front stiles, or
arm supports. Spaces between stiles filled in with columnar slats
supported by lower rail. Cane seat bowed in back and front, and
curving at sides; front decorated with gilded stenciling. 8
columnar legs with arrow feet; center front legs with turned
capitals. Single round stretchers front and back; pairs of deeply
curved stretchers on sides. 2 cross stretchers. *Variations:* Back
and legs may be simpler.

Materials and Dimensions
Maple and tulip. Painted and stenciled. Cane seat. Height: 32¾".
Length: 80". Depth: 19".

Locality and Period
Baltimore. c. 1800–10. Variations made in other centers.

Comment
Sheraton painted Fancy furniture ranges from simple products of
the first factories to finely crafted examples from traditional
workshops. The settee shown here, elegantly conceived and
finely detailed, has been traced to Baltimore, which was a major
center for stylish painted furniture.

Hints for Collectors
Look for signs of elegant craftsmanship, such as curving arms
and carefully cut slats. Fine painting like this is virtually
impossible to duplicate if damaged. Pieces like this are rare and
valuable; less stylish Federal settees are more widely available.

Federal convertible settee

Description
Painted convertible settee with back divided by vertical elements
into 3 sections. Top rail vase-and-ring turned, with stenciled
cylindrical sections. Pairs of slats grooved into 4 stiles. Stiles
curving back, flat in upper area and round below slats. Arms
curving down to scrolled handholds on vase-and-ring-turned
supports. 2-part seat, bottom sliding under top when closed; top
upholstered and outlined with brass tacks. 4 front legs turned
and tapered, joined by ring-turned stretchers. Directly behind, 2
square legs with cylindrical feet and long, straight-sided
stretcher. Round rear legs tapered to feet. Plain stretchers
single in rear and paired on sides. *Variations:* Settees may open
as beds in a variety of ways.

Materials and Dimensions
Maple and pine. Painted and stenciled. Horsehair seat (originally
rush) with modern upholstery. Brass tacks. Height: 33¾".
Length: 80¾". Depth: 24".

Locality and Period
Patented by Chester Johnson, Albany. 1827.

Comment
Redesigning an ordinary settee or sofa so that it may convert
into a bed was an early 19th-century innovation. The convertible
settee shown here loosely resembles earlier Sheraton painted
Fancy chairs (14) as well as Hitchcock designs.

Hints for Collectors
Although much patent furniture is unattractive, it is worth
collecting because it is marked and therefore easily dated. The
patent mark on this sofa is behind the center top rail. Such
innovative pieces attract collectors because they are part of
America's industrial heritage.

William and Mary daybed

Description
8-legged daybed with movable back having arched cresting and
grooved vertical slats. Turned stiles with chains supporting back,
becoming plain stump legs below rush seat. Side stretchers and
that at foot turned in ball-and-ring pattern. Cross stretchers and
that at head simple and tapering. Side legs and those at foot
turned in 3 segments, with elongated bulbous centers and squat
turnip-shaped feet. *Variations:* Backs and turned legs follow a
variety of William and Mary chair patterns. Baluster or caned
backs are more common. Vase-shaped splats were used on the
backs of transitional William and Mary/Queen Anne daybeds.

Materials and Dimensions
Maple. Rush seat. Iron chains. Height: 40″. Length: 69″.
Depth: 24½″.

Locality and Period
Pennsylvania. c. 1720–40.

Comment
Crafted in the Queen Anne as well as William and Mary styles,
daybeds were used more during the Colonial period than at any
later time, though country examples in Chippendale and Federal
styles were also made. The arched cresting and grooved vertical
slats of the daybed shown here follow a popular chair model,
favored particularly in Pennsylvania.

Hints for Collectors
Elaborate English daybeds are generally easier to find than
simpler American versions. Some English examples have more
complex carving; others are plainer, with prominent ring
turnings on the stiles and a simply carved cresting on the back.

Colonial Revival settee

Description
Settee with 2 chair backs. Joined yoke-shaped rails carved in leaf pattern topping 2 pierced and carved splats. 4 leaf-carved stiles flared toward top. Curved arms with molded handholds jutting over curving carved supports set into side seat rails. Straight rails enclosing upholstered slip seat. Skirt with scalloped edge. 3 front legs cabriole, with carved knees and claw-and-ball feet. 2 plain rear legs; tapered feet. *Variations:* Back splats may be solid. Carving may be simpler.

Materials and Dimensions
Mahogany. Fabric upholstery. Metal braces under seat. Height: 37″. Length: 43″. Depth: 23″.

Locality and Period
New York and other furniture centers. c. 1900–20.

Comment
The settee shown here was probably carved by a traditionally trained craftsman, possibly at a large midwestern factory, but more likely at one of the fine smaller New York workshops. Such Colonial Revival furnishings are more elaborate than their 18th-century prototypes, and some of their elements are inconsistent with the originals. This Chippendale-style settee is actually closer to some 18th-century English models.

Hints for Collectors
Colonial Revival furniture is most often well made and functional, but beware of repaired cracks in legs and splats. Examine designs carefully; most have showier details and less careful construction and thus compare unfavorably with the restrained elegance of 18th-century craftsmanship. Finer revival pieces, however, do provide the feel and appearance of Colonial designs, and at a fraction of the cost.

Rococo Revival cast-iron settee

Description
Cast-iron settee with back and arms outlined by rounded
stripping enclosing symmetrical fern-leaf design. Center of back
reinforced by thick leaf clusters projecting above top rail and
concealing a brace. Arms projecting from back and curving in
toward seat. Pierced seat with rounded front edge. Legs curved
in and then out, each pair joined by arched pattern of ferns.
Flattened ball feet. *Variations:* Seats may be wooden.
Neoclassical patterns may be used, sometimes made with thicker
iron.

Materials and Dimensions
Cast iron. Painted. Height: 31″. Length: 44″. Depth: 16″.

Locality and Period
Throughout the United States. c. 1870–80.

Comment
Cast-iron furniture became popular in America in the 1830s and
1840s. Major producers, such as J. L. Mott in New York,
published catalogues showing that the Rococo Revival style
continued as a prime influence on cast-iron designs into the
1870s, particularly for outdoor use. The settee shown here
resembles a model made by the firm of Hanson and Kirk of
Philadelphia in 1874, but similar chairs, settees, and tables were
cast by smaller local foundries all over the country.

Hints for Collectors
Cast-iron furnishings were primarily made for outdoor use. Many
were used in cemeteries and have sometimes been stolen in
recent years, so buy only those pieces with proof of prior
ownership or source. Certain forms have been recently
reproduced; these lack the patina and signs of wear found on
older examples.

Description
Wicker settee with rectangular back slanting away from seat.
Back having curved corners and 2 bands, the top one arched,
across openwork wicker. Rail and stiles covered in basketweave
wicker curving down around arms and armrests; 2 scrolls under
each arm. Wood-framed seat with caned central area. Legs
partially covered by arched wicker skirt. Round legs slanting out
from seat. *Variations:* Basketweave patterns are sometimes
more solid and complex on back. Wicker was woven in dozens of
patterns.

Materials and Dimensions
Wicker. Wood. Cane seat. Painted. Height: 38″. Length: 39″.
Depth: 20″.

Locality and Period
Throughout the United States. c. 1880–1900.

Comment
Wicker, a material used for furniture in America beginning in the
early 19th century, was particularly popular after 1880, when
factories producing wicker furniture flourished. Wicker furniture
was used indoors as well as outdoors, and judging by early
photographs, it was used even in the most elegant rooms. In
early pictures and advertisements, wicker most often appeared
in its natural colors, but was sometimes painted.

Hints for Collectors
Wicker patterns —from the swirling patterns of the turn of the
century to the simpler later designs that reflect the Art Deco
movement—offer collectors a wide variety of choices. Wicker
furnishings like the settee shown here are widely available but
becoming more expensive today, particularly pieces in fine
condition.

Child's country painted storage settle

Description
Small painted storage settle with straight-topped solid back; grained in bold black pattern on Indian-red ground. Projecting wings cut in serpentine curve from top of back to upturned handholds. Solid plank seat hinged over storage area. Straight front skirt between seat and floor. *Variations:* Settles may be made of wainscoting panels. Arms may be cut more simply. Surfaces usually painted without graining.

Materials and Dimensions
Pine. Painted. Iron hinges. Height: 30½". Length: 40". Depth: 15".

Locality and Period
Probably New England. c. 1800–40.

Comment
Dating simple furniture is always difficult. Furniture combining storage space and seating like the settle shown here was common in small rural American houses from the 17th through the 19th centuries. Though gracefully cut wings like these were used since the early 18th century, the fine painted design of this piece suggests an early 19th-century origin. Graining is quite unusual; surfaces were more often painted in solid colors that complemented those of early rooms.

Hints for Collectors
Painted furniture has great charm and is increasingly popular with collectors, who admire its informal grace. But many pine benches have been stripped of their paint or recently repainted. Since the paint is an important part of these pieces, make certain it is original: check for signs of original paint at corners and undersides that may not have been repainted. Also look for a patina and the weblike crazing characteristic of old paint.

Description
Painted storage settle with low back made from plain rectangular plank with rounded corners. Scroll-shaped armrests flank seat. Fixed rear part of seat top made of long plain board. 2 boards hinged at rear, giving access to storage compartment underneath. Rounded overhanging front edge. Skirt made of simple boards forming storage chest. Cutout hole at top of front; simple molding along bottom. Ball feet. *Variations:* Settles may have taller backs. Painting may be more elaborate.

Materials and Dimensions
Pine. Painted. Height: 31″. Length: 66″. Depth: 22″.

Locality and Period
Throughout the United States. c. 1825–50.

Comment
Country pieces are often simple versions of fashionable forms adapted for utilitarian purposes. The basic form of the settle shown here was inspired by Empire settees, but the design was greatly modified to make it a storage piece. The simple back and low curved arms echo fashionable Empire designs; the ball feet, on the other hand, are typical of early 19th-century country furnishings.

Hints for Collectors
Country furniture should bear reasonable signs of age from decades of heavy use; but badly battered pieces, not worth the effort and expense of restoring, should be avoided. Inspect a piece like this to be sure that most, if not all, elements are original, since paint may conceal damaged or recently replaced elements. Replaced hinges, lift tops, and feet are common problems with pieces such as this settle.

Country painted bench

Description
Long bench with top made of 2 plain planks. Plain skirt. Plank legs cut in pointed arches on bottom. Legs reinforced on inner sides with wood blocks just above arches. *Variations:* Examples with turned legs in the 17th-century style were made well into the 18th century. Some solid plank legs are reinforced with bracing from underneath the seat to the inside of the legs. The arches of the plank legs may range from very plain angular shapes to more decorative ones. Benches may be painted a variety of colors.

Materials and Dimensions
Pine. Painted blue. Height: 18″. Length: 84″. Depth: 9″.

Locality and Period
New England. c. 1730–1800. Variations made in other areas.

Comment
Plain long benches may have been used in meetinghouses as well as in homes in the 18th and early 19th centuries. Meant for a simple setting, these sturdy practical pieces were made for a century or more with little change, so that specific dating is difficult.

Hints for Collectors
Besides being difficult to date, early benches are hard to attribute to specific areas. The arched legs and plain skirt of the example shown here are common 18th-century elements, which differentiate original benches from reproductions. Early benches were painted Indian red as well as other colors commonly used in country rooms. Worn paint has more charm than repainted surfaces, which lack the patina of age. Because there is some danger of rot, inspect older benches carefully.

Stools

Stools—chairs without backs or arms—are the oldest and simplest form of seating. They can be strictly utilitarian pieces meant for people seated at various tasks or decorative accessories for stylish interiors. Stools were the most common seating in 17th-century American houses, where chairs were reserved for important members of the household and respected guests. One of the earliest types is the joint stool (204), so named because it is joiner's work of simple mortise-and-tenon construction. Such stools frequently doubled as small tables. Increased use of chairs in the 18th century lessened the dependence on stools, so that Queen Anne and Chippendale stools, even more than earlier examples, are rare and much in demand today.

Stools continued to play an important part in rural life for centuries. Some plain utilitarian examples, such as 3-legged milking stools, are in no particular style and could have been made during any period. More often, no matter how purely functional, country stools do display some stylistic sign of the period in which they were made. On Windsor stools, for instance, the turning of the legs is the best clue to dating. Country stools vary in height to suit particular functions: for example, desks in countinghouses or shops were tall, and early illustrations show that clerks needed high stools to work at such desks. Piano seats that could be revolved to adjust the height were introduced in the late 18th or early 19th century. Though the adjustable mechanism remained much the same throughout the 19th century, styles varied considerably, some being quite elegant. Footstools were fairly common in the 19th century; while most are low and simple, some are higher and more stylish.

During the 19th and 20th centuries, decorative stools were made in all the important styles. Some that are stylistically exaggerated were used as accent pieces in fashionable rooms; others, though just as stylish, were also practical, with storage space under the seat (207). Stools were a regular feature of turn-of-the-century interiors, particularly those furnished in the Mission style, which often included stools with rows of slats on the sides, or wicker stools. Stools were favored by Art Deco and modern designers, who transformed them into sleek geometric forms, either in overstuffed or simplified metal creations. In the 1920s bar stools began appearing in homes when bars became popular in recreation rooms; tubular-steel Art Deco examples, as well as wooden ones in traditional styles, were made in great quantity.

Stools can be both useful and important additions to collections of American furniture. Because early examples are rare, craftsmen over the past 50 years have been tempted to fake them by attaching old legs to spare seats. Fakes or reproductions are usually clumsily made and show little wear from age. Later 19th- and 20th-century stools, unless attributed to well-known designers, are relatively inexpensive and widely available.

Country milking stool

Description
Simple stool with heavy circular top set on round-bottomed base, both made of thick rough-hewn wood; surfaces textured by chisel marks. 3 plain legs of whittled poles flaring out from seat. *Variations:* 4-legged examples were also made. Legs may be turned rather than hand-shaped.

Materials and Dimensions
Pine and elm. Remnants of old paint. Height: 16½″. Diameter of seat: 15″.

Locality and Period
Rural locales throughout the United States. c. 1800–1900.

Comment
Simple country furniture—with obvious signs of handwork, such as chisel marks and rough chips, plus evidence of everyday wear—is difficult to date. A stool like the one shown here, popularly called a milking stool, resembles those in 17th-century Dutch genre paintings as much as those in 19th-century American genre paintings. Though basically a timeless form, the legs here are slanted at an angle characteristic of Windsor stools, and some elements are reminiscent of early 19th-century forms. Some country furnishings, functional items made by unskilled craftsmen, date from as early as the 17th century, but a great majority are from the 19th century.

Hints for Collectors
Authentic rustic furniture should look worn, but make sure these signs of age were not deliberately added to a relatively recent piece. Century-old bruises are often partially smoothed away with age, while blemishes acquired more recently still look raw and fresh. Stools such as this one are inexpensive and can be found in many country shops.

Windsor/Sheraton stool

Description
Stool with circular top molded at edge. Flared legs slightly bulbous at junctures with plain rod stretchers. Feet tapered, cylindrical, and caplike. Handsomely grained wood. *Variations:* Legs are usually more slender and turned with greater restraint. Tops may be plain, with no molding. Similar examples were made of pine or fruitwood and painted, often with stenciled classical embellishments.

Materials and Dimensions
Maple. Height: 22″. Diameter of seat: 10″.

Locality and Period
New England. c. 1800.

Comment
The top of this rural stool is molded in a way that made it serviceable as either a tabletop or seat. The subtlety of design is characteristic of the early 19th century; the legs are carefully turned, even if overly bulbous. In spite of its unusually thick legs, the stool's basic shape combines Sheraton with traditional Windsor design (19). This may be the product of a country chairmaker who operated a workshop or small factory producing a variety of simple furniture.

Hints for Collectors
While the variety of simple stools is endless, they are relatively scarce. Like most Windsors, the stool shown here was constructed of green wood for added strength: legs were inserted into the seat before the wood shrank, so the holes, reduced in size, would clamp the legs tightly. Unlike this deceptively plain stool, reproductions or fakes of rural furniture are most often clumsily made and crude.

William and Mary joint stool or table

Description
Stool with rectangular seat having rounded edges projecting over plain side rails. 4 slanting legs turned in double-vase-and-ring pattern and mortised into seat. Legs having rectangular blocks at junctures with single stretchers, which are turned in pattern similar to legs. Feet turned in simple beehive shape. *Variations:* Overall proportions remain the same, but turnings may be different, with heavier turnings being the earliest.

Materials and Dimensions
Maple and pine. Height: 19¾". Length: 13". Depth: 13½".

Locality and Period
New England. c. 1700.

Comment
Stools like the one shown here, commonly called joint stools, are simple joiner's work that may have served both as seating and as tables, since small tables like this were popular when William and Mary design was most fashionable. This example seems a bit tall for seating, making it better suited for holding objects. Its turnings have the lighter, narrower proportions of the William and Mary style, but their patterns are closer to those of 17th-century oak models.

Hints for Collectors
Practical furnishings like this should show signs of wear on legs and stretchers. Round parts should be more oval than circular in cross section and square tops should have become rectangular, since aging would have caused the wood to shrink in the direction going across the grain. This is a fine and costly piece, but less expensive examples are available. Make certain that such stools are American, since similar pieces were made in England.

Mission-style stool

Description
Rectangular stool with leather-covered cushion set on row of
narrow slats mortised into seat rails. Side rails of seat straight-
edged on top and bottom; front and rear rails straight on top and
arched below. Plain square legs. Row of 4 narrow slats set
between middle and lower rails mortised into legs on short sides;
tenon ends exposed. Front and rear stretchers plain straight
slats. *Variations:* Standard rectangular forms may have more
complex sets of narrower slats as reinforcement and decoration.
Seat rails may be uniformly straight all around.

Materials and Dimensions
Oak. Leather upholstery. Height: 16″. Length: 20″. Depth: 14″.

Locality and Period
Throughout the United States. c. 1900–15.

Comment
Stools were a common part of Mission-style interiors. Besides
being useful, they helped emphasize the informal spirit of the
style. Examples illustrated in Gustav Stickley's magazine *The
Craftsman* tended to be simpler than the one shown here, with
slats set into plain seat rails. Since oak furniture was produced in
volume by manufacturers in Grand Rapids and smaller firms
across the country, undocumented designs are difficult to
attribute.

Hints for Collectors
Magazines and manufacturers' catalogues from the period can
help determine the design and date of a piece. Though basically
sturdy, oak furniture can loosen at the joinings, so check the
joints and materials. If no cracks are present, loose joints can be
glued and clamped. Replacement of elements, easily
accomplished on a simple Mission piece, lowers its value.

Description
Low stool with upholstered rectangular seat. Hooked carpet upholstery fastened by applied rounded molding of tiger maple. Skirt straight and simple. Corners are rectangular blocks veneered in tiger maple. Curved legs intersecting in X (or curule) form. 2 turned stretchers joining lower parts of legs. Scrolled feet. *Variations:* Legs may be thicker and may lack stretchers. Rosewood or mahogany pieces have more elaborate details.

Materials and Dimensions
Maple, tiger maple, and pine. Hooked carpet upholstery. Height: 14". Length: 19". Depth: 15".

Locality and Period
New England or Mid-Atlantic states. c. 1820–40.

Comment
Country Empire furnishings delightfully combine fashionable elements and traditional sturdy restraint. The stool shown here has the curule legs, simply cut out yet stylish, found on some of the most elegant Sheraton and Empire pieces (170). This sort of country furniture appears in folk paintings of the period.

Hints for Collectors
Furnishings made of tiger, bird's-eye, and flame maple are highly prized by collectors and worth substantially more than similar examples in unfigured woods. Because they are so simply detailed, country furnishings are easy to fake. Beware of furniture painted or stained on its undersides, thus preventing you from checking untreated surfaces for the natural darkening that comes with age.

Renaissance Revival lift-top footstool

Description

Ebonized rectangular stool with fringed needlework seat. Skirt straight, with inscribed lines. Cushion lifting up to reveal storage compartment. Trestle base carved at ends and inscribed with classical scroll-carved motifs. Turned stretcher with rectangular center segment. Feet flared out. *Variations:* Renaissance Revival stools are often made of walnut, with inscribed and gilded decoration. Storage compartment under seat is unusual. Tapestry or carpet upholstery was commonly used.

Materials and Dimensions

Ebonized oak or cherry. Berlin-work embroidery. Height: 18". Length: 21". Depth: 12".

Locality and Period

Throughout the United States. c. 1870–90.

Comment

Used in front of chairs or sofas, footstools became popular after 1800. Empire stools were particularly common from 1820 to 1860, followed by various revival-style models such as the one shown here. Judging from its dark ebonized wood, this footstool was probably made after 1870, when exotic influences were strong and ebonized surfaces became fashionable. Furniture from India and the Orient, exhibited at the Philadelphia Centennial Exposition of 1876, had a great effect on American design. The eclectic interiors of the late 1880s featured stools in a variety of styles.

Hints for Collectors

The combination of conservative classical design and innovative detail makes this and similar late Victorian furnishings a fascinating collecting specialty. However, such stools are rare, and any reasonably priced example in good condition is a find.

Gothic Revival footstool

Description
Stool having 2 side boards cut out in trefoil tracery pattern; boards broader at base and tapering to trefoil crown. Plain rectangular footrest joining boards below crown. Turned stretcher at midpoint; similar paired stretchers just above feet. Plain feet curving outward and down. *Variations:* Footrests are often upholstered, and set on lower bases.

Materials and Dimensions
Mahogany with maple stretchers. Height: 24″. Length: 15″. Depth: 12″.

Locality and Period
Throughout the United States. c. 1840–70.

Comment
Footstools were recommended as part of the treatment for such ailments as gout and rheumatism, which required legs to be elevated. Simple designs like the one shown here were made in small as well as large workshops, but few examples of this kind of cutout work bear labels to document their origins. Gothic Revival designs were popular over a long period—from about 1840 to 1880—and small stools were frequently designed in a whimsical style only faintly related to the design of the other furniture in a room.

Hints for Collectors
Simply crafted furniture such as this cutout stool is easily copied. Look for signs of wear, particularly naturally rounded edges. Check that cutout patterns are appropriate to the mid-19th-century Gothic Revival style, which loosely adapted Gothic ornament such as trefoils and pointed arches. Greater accuracy in rendering Gothic motifs is often a sign of late 19th- or early 20th-century workmanship.

Renaissance Revival stool

Description
Painted rectangular stool with low arched sides in shape of open palmettes, filled in with spindles passing through upper rails; painted leaves and scrolls at ends. Seat upholstered in tufted brocade. Rails framed by simple sloping molding with painted band. 2 pairs of crossed (or curule) legs, front and rear, with upper parts ending in painted scroll and leaf; carved shield at crossing, with rosette in center. Animal legs below, with painted leaf-carved knees. Pairs of legs connected by turned stretcher in center. Hoof feet. *Variations:* Overall designs may be simpler, incorporating various classical motifs.

Materials and Dimensions
Probably maple. Painted. Original tufted brocade upholstery. Height: 23¾″. Length: 23″. Depth: 16″.

Locality and Period
Made by Alexander Roux, New York. c. 1865.

Comment
During the Victorian period, besides being used as foot supports, stools frequently served as chairs. The height of the stool shown here suggests that it was intended as a backless chair, probably used as a flamboyant accent piece in a room of more subdued Renaissance Revival furniture. Its style is Neo-Grec (or Neo-Greek), popular in the 1860s and 1870s and having such Greek motifs as columns, foliate scrolls, and palmettes.

Hints for Collectors
Unusually decorative accent pieces like this stool, as well as decorative pedestals, can add distinction and vitality to collections of 19th-century furniture. This is a rare example; other stools from suites of furniture are more common and may be found in small shops or at sales at old houses.

Federal piano stool

Description
Piano stool with circular cushioned seat covered in velvet with welting. Seat height adjusted by cylindrical screw mechanism. Skirt circular and reeded. Tapered legs topped by vase-and-ring-turned capitals above reeded main segment. Platform stretcher, with concave sides, connecting legs and holding cylindrical end of screw mechanism. Ring-turned feet set in brass cups ending in balls. *Variations:* Stools may be plainer, with simple turned legs. Some examples have elegant curved backs.

Materials and Dimensions
Mahogany, pine, and hickory. Brass feet. Velvet upholstery (not original). Height: 20″. Diameter of seat: 14″.

Locality and Period
New York. c. 1800–10. Variations made in other centers.

Comment
Significant numbers of pianos and piano stools were made by American manufacturers in the early 19th century, when Americans were achieving great elegance in the arts, architecture, and design. The piano stool, with its adjustable seat, is the kind of gadget that marked the beginning of an era of invention during which all sorts of innovations were devised for chairs and tables. The reeding on the seat and legs of the example shown here was a Federal motif particularly popular in New York.

Hints for Collectors
Piano stools can be quite appealing, though they may not be the most widely useful of forms concocted during the 19th century. Because they are not much in demand, working examples are often available at bargain prices. Look for fine reeding and brass fittings like those on this elegant piece.

Rococo Revival piano stool

Description
Pedestal-base piano stool with square seat upholstered in silk;
seat height adjustable. Undulating skirt of seat with carved fruit
and leaves at corners and in center of sides. Octagonal pedestal
vase-shaped, hollowed out to hold oversize metal screw for
adjusting seat height. Squat cabriole legs with carved fruit on
knees. Leaf-scrolled feet. *Variations:* Pedestals are frequently
carved in leaf patterns. Roses and fruit are motifs that occur
mainly on the skirts and legs of furniture made by Belter and
other fine craftsmen. Low backs were sometimes added.

Materials and Dimensions
Mahogany. Silk upholstery. Metal screw. Height: 22½″. Length:
15″. Depth: 15″.

Locality and Period
New York, New Orleans, or other fashionable furnituremaking
centers. c. 1840–65.

Comment
Rococo Revival piano stools, featuring screw mechanisms that
adjust the height, were made throughout the 19th century.
Carved flowers and fruit were familiar motifs on fine Rococo
Revival furniture. The stool shown here would have suited a
parlor or music room decorated with Belter or other New York
furniture. Its octagonal pedestal is an Empire element that
Belter himself would probably have avoided.

Hints for Collectors
Most piano stools have skimpy or restrained ornamentation, so a
fashionably carved example such as this is a rarity. Less
attractive Eastlake examples are more common and less costly.
Make sure the adjusting mechanism works, since it may be
difficult to repair.

Description
Circular wicker stool with seat and sides in basketweave pattern. Plain seat with radiating weave. Sides bulging just below top. Legs curving out in saber shape, with broad netlike skirt almost concealing cross stretchers. Plain feet with brass tips. *Variations:* Wicker stools are also made in oval, square, and rectangular shapes. Woven sections often have more complex patterns than the simple basketweave shown here. Colors vary: dark and neutral colors are often original. Unpainted pieces were also popular at the turn of the century.

Materials and Dimensions
Wicker. Ash. Brass feet. Height: 15″. Diameter of seat: 17″.

Locality and Period
Throughout the United States. c. 1900–30.

Comment
Wicker furniture in simple basketweave patterns was frequently used in rooms furnished in the Mission style. Stools played an important part in turn-of-the-century interiors, either as extra seating or, on occasion, for use at dressing tables. Wicker stools are difficult to date since many models, particularly those in basketweave patterns, changed little during the first 3 decades of this century, as is evident in furniture catalogues of the period.

Hints for Collectors
Though labeled wicker furniture is rare, check under the seats of stools and chairs for a maker's label or some mark to help date them. Victorian examples are usually very simple or very elaborate; since the stool shown here is between these extremes, it is more likely a 20th-century piece. Beware of missing bits of wicker that cause an unsightly asymmetry of pattern.

Modern footstool or ottoman

Description
Circular stool fully upholstered except for base. Cushioned top
dome-shaped. Convex sides divided into 3 tiers by horizontal
welting; vertical welting connecting top to base. Lowest tier
tapered. Wooden base plain and circular. *Variations:*
Overstuffed modern furnishings were based on other simple
geometric shapes such as ovals, squares, and rectangles. Either
solid colors or stylish multicolored patterns may be used.

Materials and Dimensions
Fabric-covered pine frame. Walnut base. Height: 20″. Diameter
of seat: 20″.

Locality and Period
Probably designed by Gilbert Rohde, New York, for Herman
Miller, Inc., Zeeland, Michigan. c. 1930–44.

Comment
Modern design was equated with simple design from the 1930s to
the 1950s, when craftsmen using traditional techniques made
furniture that broke with earlier American styles. Some designs
were simplified versions of 18th- and 19th-century forms, while
others were more original. Fully upholstered stools, like the
overstuffed piece shown here, were first made in the 1870s, but
were initially more elaborate in their use of tufting and braids.

Hints for Collectors
Though this stool was probably designed by the well-known
modern designer Gilbert Rohde, it has much in common with the
undocumented popular designs sold in department stores across
the country. Such comfortable pieces, often amusing in their
understated modern shapes but unrelated to the major
progressive trends of the period, are readily available and
reasonably priced.

Art Deco aluminum stool

Description
Oval-topped stool with deep cushion upholstered in leather over springs. Top of cushion rounded, with welting around edge above plain sides. Paired legs are thin U-shaped forms with straight sides and curved bases. *Variations:* Simple modern stools may be based on traditional designs: for example, legs may be versions of straight Neoclassical or curved cabriole forms.

Materials and Dimensions
Aluminum. Leather upholstery. Steel springs. Height: 20″. Length: 21½″. Depth: 15½″.

Locality and Period
Designed by Donald Deskey, New York. c. 1930.

Comment
As designer of the Radio City Music Hall interiors in 1932, Donald Deskey achieved fame as the leading American Art Deco designer. His brand of Art Deco—or Art Moderne, as the American version is often called—was more advanced than that of most American designers of the 1920s, who cautiously transformed traditional designs into modern pieces. Though Deskey was no revolutionary, his streamlined designs and modern materials, as on the stool shown here, were both simple and elegant. His luxurious designs featured a distinctly American combination of German Bauhaus and French Art Deco elements, with rich results.

Hints for Collectors
Many pieces by Deskey are still in use or in storage and have not yet been discovered by collectors. His work can be studied in magazine articles of the period and in the recently restored Radio City Music Hall, especially its luxurious restrooms.

Art Deco tubular-steel bar stools

Description
Tubular-steel bar stools with U-shaped backrest. Circular seat with leather upholstery and welting, set on recessed circular band. 4 straight tubular legs braced on top by seat band. Circular tubular stretcher serving as reinforcement and footrest, with identical one connecting feet for stability. *Variations:* Tubular-steel designs may be square, rectangular, or oval. Back supports may be more complex.

Materials and Dimensions
Tubular and flat steel. Leather upholstery. Height: 39½″. Diameter of seat: 12½″.

Locality and Period
Throughout the United States. c. 1935.

Comment
Tubular steel, introduced as a material for furniture in the 1920s by the more advanced designers of the German Bauhaus, was soon adapted by American designers. It became symbolic of avant-garde furniture design, since the early designs were revolutionary in concept and execution. Subsequent steel designs were based more on traditional forms; the stools shown here, for instance, resemble 18th-century models. Such traditional designs were transformed into decorative, often whimsical geometric shapes that relate the visual result more to Art Deco than to the more radical Bauhaus designs of the 1920s.

Hints for Collectors
Modern furnishings should look new or only slightly worn. While signs of wear are acceptable on 18th-century furniture, most 20th-century pieces look shabby if not in pristine condition. It is common practice for dealers to have modern furnishings relacquered, rechromed, or otherwise refurbished; this is acceptable if necessary and if properly done.

Beds and Cradles

Bed designs have been remarkably consistent over the centuries. They are also conservative, except for some elaborate 19th-century models. Sizes range from small single and children's beds to large double beds. Cradles, also included here, followed similar conservative trends.

Beds

Beds were often the most highly appraised furnishings in Colonial inventories compiled to settle estates, not because of their fine posts and rails but for the elaborate hangings and coverlets that went with them. Sleeping in a bed enclosed by curtains was common, primarily to conserve warmth. Most bed frames themselves were simple, since little wood was left exposed by bedding and hangings. The type most commonly associated with the Colonial era is the tall-post bed with a canopy, or tester. If a bed had low posts, curtains could be suspended from the ceiling.

The basic bed form—four turned posts of varying height held together by plain rails—changed little during the 17th and 18th centuries. Headboards are simply cut and footboards often omitted; the ropes supporting the bedding are fastened to knobs or through holes. The character of the turnings is the best indicator of age and style: rare early examples (195) have thick posts, or stiles, with deep turnings, whereas later pieces (225) have lighter proportions and turnings. Some daybeds—sofas or elongated chairs that doubled as beds—were small beds with matching head- and footboards (222–223). Late 18th-century canopy, or four-poster, beds are usually more elegant and follow period styles. The earliest have cabriole legs. Federal-era examples tend to have reeded or fluted posts at the footboard, straight tapered legs, and, sometimes, painted canopies. Empire beds are characterized by heavy matched head- and footboards; those on sleigh beds (221) are scroll-shaped.

Typical mid-19th-century beds have more exposed woodwork than earlier designs and often display Renaissance Revival, Rococo Revival, or Eastlake decoration. High headboards, lower footboards, and wide side rails are common features; slats usually support the bedding. Some were elaborately carved and decorated by well-known makers such as Herter Brothers and John Henry Belter; others were mass-produced in furniture centers around the country. The basic forms persisted into the 20th century, when many earlier designs were updated to suit later tastes and new materials. Beds made of iron or brass tubing were produced in quantity from 1880 to 1925. Metal beds were later created in the modern style as well. Collectors should always inspect the side rails of a bed to make certain they have not been shortened or lengthened. Because they are cumbersome to display, beds are not frequently stocked by antiques dealers; and when in stock, they are often disassembled. Always make certain a bed has its proper hardware.

Cradles

Simple boxlike cradles, occasionally with a wooden hood at one end, were among the earliest cradles and continued to be made in the 19th century in rural areas. 19th-century cradles included fashionable ones, sometimes based on bed designs (220), and elevated cradles set on trestle bases. The availability of cradles on the market is unpredictable. Some types turn up often; fine early examples and stylish later models are much less common.

Country cradle

Description
Cradle with plain straight sides. Curved cutout handholds at center of separate narrow boards set above wide lower panels. Head- and footboards plain, tapered toward base; headboard topped by 3 curves and footboard deeply curved at top center. Flat plank bottom. Flat-topped rockers with scrolled ends. *Variations:* The earliest American cradles have corner stiles to which the side panels are joined by tongue-and-groove construction. Stiles may be topped by finials. Some examples have a hooded enclosure at one end. Cherry and other woods were also used.

Materials and Dimensions
Pine. Wrought-iron nails. Height: 17″. Length: 36″. Width: 15½″.

Locality and Period
Probably New England. c. 1770–1800.

Comment
Boxlike cradles on rockers were popular throughout most of the 17th and 18th centuries. While the basic design changed only slightly, construction varied from tongue-and-groove to iron-nail techniques. The cradle shown here is a fine late 18th-century model of simple construction and restrained design, with practical cutout handles for carrying. The hoods featured on some examples were necessitated by poorly heated homes.

Hints for Collectors
Pine was the most common wood for cradles in the Colonial era, but cherry and other fruitwoods were also used, particularly by amateur cabinetmakers. Simple cradles are not easily dated, but most were made before 1800; thereafter, fashion became a crucial influence and cradles became more like miniature beds.

Federal trestle-base cradle

Description
Trestle-base cradle flanked by 2 turned stiles topped by urn-shaped finials on chamfered blocks into which flat-sided stretcher is set. Columnar center segments of stiles terminating in blocks fastened to plain cradle stiles by brass mountings. Paired vase-turned spindles flanking lower stiles. Cradle plain and barrel-shaped; reeded edges on ends and sides. Circular head- and footboards flat-bottomed and grooved with concentric circles. 2 pairs of low curved legs, with single rectangular stretcher joining them to form trestle base. *Variations:* Most cradles have flat rather than curving sides.

Materials and Dimensions
Mahogany. Brass. Height: 40″. Length: 40½″. Width: 19″.

Locality and Period
Salem, Massachusetts. c. 1800.

Comment
Fashionable cradles are far less common than simple traditional designs made of local woods. Cradles have generally been little influenced by changing fashions, so that the restrained Neoclassicism of the Federal cradle shown here makes it unusual and important. The curving sides are an early 19th-century innovation, and the reeded edges are linked to the Sheraton style.

Hints for Collectors
Among the many surprises in the field of American furniture, this cradle is one of the more pleasant: every element can be found in other period forms—proving it authentic—but rarely in this combination. If its elements and proportions are correct, collectors should be open-minded enough to recognize the success of an unusual form.

218 Child's Renaissance Revival folding bed or crib

Description
Child's bed with headboard crowned by removable inscribed cartouche. Arched headboard hinged at center and divided into 2 tiers of panels. Upper panels raised and bordered by curved moldings. Vase-and-ring-turned stiles with chamfered blocks at junctures with boards and side rails; stiles topped by acorn finials. Side galleries of 10 turned spindles spanning upper and lower rails. Lower rails hinged for folding. Upper rails rounded on top. Footboard truncated version of arched headboard, with matching stiles. Legs vase-and-ring-turned, tapering to casters. Iron-framed springs to support mattress. *Variations:* Headboard, footboard, and side galleries may be plainer.

Materials and Dimensions
Walnut. Iron-framed springs. Iron casters. Height: 47″. Length: 56″. Width: 32″.

Locality and Period
Throughout the United States. c. 1875–90.

Comment
During the 1870s and 1880s the type of child's bed shown here, commonly called a crib, was often made so it could be folded up for easy carrying and storage. This Renaissance Revival example is quite restrained in its use of classical elements; similar turned spindles were used on Elizabethan Revival pieces a few decades earlier (220).

Hints for Collectors
Children's beds like this one are usually more functional and better-made than modern versions; besides being attractive they are useful and durable. Look for examples with stylish elements that are subtly combined. Check hinges and folding parts carefully, since these have often been damaged.

Turn-of-the-century bentwood cradle

Description
Trestle-base bentwood cradle mounted on stand, with tall stafflike pole at one end to hold curtain. Cradle consisting of 12 loops of flattened bentwood attached along curved spine ending in pointed scroll. Cradle attached to trestle base by knobs and iron screws. 2 sets of wishbone legs joined to ends of lower stretcher to form feet. Added oval loop serving as upper stretcher between legs. *Variations:* Bentwood cradles may be made with more elaborate wooden loops.

Materials and Dimensions
Bentwood (ash or beech). Maple knobs. Iron fixtures. Height (maximum): 77″. Length: 53″. Width: 27″.

Locality and Period
Probably made by Thonet, Austria-Hungary. c. 1890–1910.

Comment
Vintage posters and advertisements show that bentwood furniture was a popular import to this country from Austria-Hungary in the mid-19th to early 20th centuries. Some may have been made in America, but there is no substantial proof of this. Looped designs such as the cradle shown here seem almost Art Nouveau in spirit, even though many examples preceded that style by several decades.

Hints for Collectors
Dating bentwood is difficult and must be done by studying period catalogues and advertisements. In any case, the quality of the design is usually more important than its date. Make sure that the piece is in good condition, since repairing bentwood is troublesome. Bentwood designs, frequently more elaborate than this cradle, allow collectors to choose from a broad variety, ranging from simple to fanciful.

Description
Sleigh-shaped cradle with curved head- and footboards in scroll-end design. Curved top panels set into curved stiles. Flat lower boards joined to stiles by tongue-and-groove construction. Straight lower stiles framing straight broad rails. Long sides with down-curved top rails over 9 spool-turned spindles set into straight-sided lower rails. Short legs. Rockers slightly scrolled. *Variations:* Turned spindles were also used with Gothic or Rococo decoration. All 4 sides may have spindles. More elegant examples have drapery hanging over the lower section.

Materials and Dimensions
Walnut and pine. Painted. Height: 21″. Length: 41″. Width: 18″.

Locality and Period
Throughout the United States. c. 1850.

Comment
19th-century cradles were often designed to match bedroom sets. The spool-turned spindles on the cradle shown here, which is basically Empire in spirit, are an Elizabethan Revival element; the scroll-shaped ends closely resemble the popular Empire sleigh beds. More like a miniature bed, this cradle is an improvement over earlier designs, which were simply boxes for sleeping babies.

Hints for Collectors
During the 19th century, cradles took on increasing decorative importance and were made in most of the styles used to furnish bedrooms. Thus Empire, Gothic Revival, Rococo Revival, and Eastlake cradles are available, though not particularly common, and relatively inexpensive. Some cradles have been converted into low settees by removing one side; however, this destroys their value.

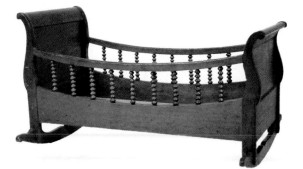

Empire sleigh bed

Description
Single bed with identical head- and footboards topped by curved rounded rails. Rails joining flat-sided scroll-shaped stiles that broaden toward bottom; carved rosette at top and carved scrolls below. Plain panel filling area between top and lower rails. Side rails with carved scroll ornament at ends, and prominent horizontal molding across bottom. Feet flat-sided, curved, and flaring from base of stiles. Outer surfaces veneered. *Variations:* Dimensions vary widely. Some examples may be generously carved or else even plainer.

Materials and Dimensions
Rosewood and rosewood veneer. Height: 37″. Length: 73″. Width: 32″.

Locality and Period
Throughout the United States. c. 1820–50.

Comment
Basically a classical couch adapted as a bed, the sleigh bed was popular in this country from the early to the mid-19th century. Because many are as simple as the one shown here, it is usually impossible to determine a precise origin from their style of decoration. Labeled pieces show that sleigh beds were made in virtually every city with active cabinetmakers, from the East Coast to the Mississippi. While the basic form is Empire, some examples have Rococo or Gothic motifs.

Hints for Collectors
Sleigh beds are common and moderately priced unless they bear the mark of an important maker. Look for labels on the inner side of head- and footboards. Since the carving on these beds is frequently mediocre, many collectors prefer the plainer examples. Fine carving is crisp and bold.

Child's Elizabethan Revival country bed or daybed

Description
Short bed, or daybed, with 4 matching spool-turned stiles supporting turned top rails. 3 slender spool-turned spindles connecting top and lower rails to form identical head- and footboards. Cylindrical top rails tapering smoothly from center bulge. Stiles with chamfered rectangular blocks at rail height. Plain side rails fitted with cross slats to support mattress. Spool-turned legs tapering to plain cylindrical feet. *Variations:* Top rails are often flat. Turnings on stiles and spindles may be more or less elaborate.

Materials and Dimensions
Maple. Horsehair mattress. Height: 24″. Length: 46″. Width: 22″.

Locality and Period
Throughout the United States. c. 1840–60.

Comment
Simple ring turnings, sometimes called spool turnings because they resemble a row of connected spools, were favored for Elizabethan Revival designs of the mid-19th century. The bed shown here is a fine simple piece probably meant for a rural house. The top rails are smoothly turned in an elongated manner that recalls Windsor elements, suggesting the work of a country cabinetmaker rather than a factory.

Hints for Collectors
Country furniture has great appeal for collectors who value relaxed living. The delightful combination of complex and simple elements in this bed makes it both primitive and charming. Check the ends of the side rails on a small bed to be sure they have not been cut down. Sharp or rough-cut ends and fresh-looking unpainted surfaces are signs of such tampering, which lessens a bed's value.

Federal country daybed

Description
Painted daybed with matching ends resembling broadened klismos chair backs. Wide flat top rails with rounded upper edge. Stiles curving out and tapering toward top. Narrow middle slat reinforcing stiles; narrower slat set just below mattress level. 8 boards dovetailed into plain side rails to support mattress. Rectangular legs tapering to plain feet. *Variations:* Chairlike ends may be more elaborate. Legs may be round.

Materials and Dimensions
Maple. Painted. Height: 24″. Length: 71″. Width: 23½″.

Locality and Period
New England. c. 1820–50.

Comment
Plain maple furniture painted or stained to look like mahogany was popular during the first half of the 19th century in rural communities, particularly in New England. The Sheraton daybed shown here is a plain version of a kind of lounge sometimes called a hired-man's bed, since it could serve as a spare bed in an all-purpose room. Though simple, the design reflects then-current fashion in that the head- and footboards are modified klismos chair backs, a form that inspired numerous more stylish Federal designs.

Hints for Collectors
Since simple designs like this daybed are easily faked, check for appropriate signs of wear on feet and slats. Beware of sharp edges, which should have been slightly rounded by a century or more of use. To determine if paint is original, look for cracked areas beneath which an earlier layer of paint may be visible.

Shaker low-post bed

Description
Painted low-post single bed with slightly arched headboard
having cutout sides and 4 corners grooved into stiles. Stiles
topped by rounded finials on chamfered blocks holding ends of
bed rails. Rails plain, with holes for ropes to support mattress.
Legs tapered cylinders, ending in ring turnings. Large
removable casters made of iron and wood. *Variations:*
Headboards may be plainer, without cutout ends. Footboards are
occasionally used.

Materials and Dimensions
Maple. Painted. Iron and wood casters. Rope. Height: 31½".
Length: 75". Width: 36".

Locality and Period
New York State or Massachusetts. c. 1820–60.

Comment
Simply furnished community houses were the centers of Shaker
life. Beds like the one shown here are evidence of the informal
way of life in such houses, where movable furniture made the
space adaptable for many purposes. Though based on plain lines,
Shaker furniture often has graceful touches, showing that there
was room for individualism within the customary forms. Nuances
such as the subtle shaping of the headboard and legs of this
daybed make Shaker furniture continually interesting.

Hints for Collectors
Since a premium is usually paid for any object called Shaker,
make certain a piece deserves the name. If it is unlabeled and
unmarked, look for good craftsmanship and simplified turnings as
well as subtle variation of standard forms. Not everything made
by Shaker craftsmen is successful, so avoid unattractive
examples even if they are authentic.

Federal low-post bed

Description
Painted low-post single bed with arched head- and footboards set into cylindrical stiles crowned with flattened ball finials. Stiles with chamfered blocks containing mortise holes on 2 sides to accommodate tenons of rails. Rails plain except for knobs to fasten ropes to support mattress. Tapered legs. Ring feet. *Variations:* Early examples were made in walnut, mahogany, and other woods. Head- and footboards may be shaped in simple designs, either straight or curved.

Materials and Dimensions
Pine. Painted. Height: 29″. Length: 75″. Width: 41″.

Locality and Period
Pennsylvania. c. 1790–1800.

Comment
Though tester, or canopy, beds were more common, low-post beds were made throughout the 18th century. The design of the legs is a good indication of age: early turned legs are restrained and thicker, while tapered legs like those on the bed shown here are later, Neoclassical examples. Low-post Queen Anne or Chippendale beds often have flattened ball finials like those seen here. Because many of these beds were concealed behind hangings suspended from the ceiling, it was less necessary for their design to keep up with changing fashions.

Hints for Collectors
Federal-era beds are much more common than earlier 18th-century examples, but are fairly costly due to their popularity as daybeds or sofas. Simple pine designs often look older than they actually are and can be mistaken for Queen Anne or Chippendale beds. Head- and footboards were often replaced later; unaltered early beds are generally simple, but not crude.

Federal country folding bed

Description
Folding double bed with simply arched headboard. Concave cutout ends of headboard fitted into short stiles. Stiles with flat-domed finials atop rectangular blocks into which side rails are mortised. Straight-edged side rails, hinged to allow part of frame to fold. Legs tapered and round, with ring-turned capitals. Third pair of legs attached near movable joints. Rail holes for ropes to support mattress. *Variations:* Short canopies may enclose beds when folded. Rails may have knobs instead of holes for attaching mattress ropes.

Materials and Dimensions
Maple. Height: 37½″ (opened). Length: 79″. Width: 52½″.

Locality and Period
New England. c. 1800–30.

Comment
Folding beds were used throughout the 18th century. Some examples appear to date from the William and Mary period, but dating is a problem since the simple turned parts are not very different from those on the later bed shown here. The ring-turned capitals on the legs, much like those on Sheraton painted Fancy furniture, are a sign of this bed's Federal-era origins.

Hints for Collectors
Look for original finish and handsome detailing on simple furniture, such as the ring turnings on the legs and the curved headboard of this bed. There should be appropriate signs of wear on all elements, indicating that none are replacements. Many early beds have been stripped and restained or repainted. If rubbing the stain causes it to come off on your hands, it probably has been applied recently.

Child's Federal canopy bed

Description
Child's 4-poster bed with arched canopy consisting of 2 curved rods reinforced by 5 narrow stretchers and covered with lacy net. Headboard posts plain and tapered, ending in thickened cylinders grooved to hold ends of simple cusped headboard. Columnar posts at foot of bed tapered and ring-turned; set on vase-shaped bases and rectangular blocks into which rails are screwed. Plain side rails with holes for ropes supporting mattress. Baluster-shaped legs ring-turned and set on casters. *Variations:* Posts may be reeded or square.

Materials and Dimensions
Tulip, hard pine, and white pine. Fabric netting. Rope. Iron casters. Height: 64″. Length: 58½″. Width: 35½″.

Locality and Period
Mid-Atlantic states. c. 1780–1800.

Comment
The child's bed shown here epitomizes the simpler fashionable designs popular on the American scene shortly after the Revolution. Posts like these, simply turned on lathes, follow those in the Hepplewhite design book, just as do the more elegantly carved examples. Beds with easily removable arched canopies are often called field beds because they are portable. Net coverings were particularly popular from 1780 to 1820.

Hints for Collectors
Canopies found today are rarely original, but replacements do not lessen the value of beds substantially. Because they are easy to reproduce, check that turned posts are not later substitutions: beware of sharp edges, since 2 centuries of wear should have gently smoothed them.

Chippendale canopy bed

Description
4-poster double bed with straight-sided upholstered canopy.
Plain rectangular rear posts flanking simply cut headboard
(concealed by hangings). Front posts fluted, tapering from base
to ring at capital; shafts ending in rectangular block holding rails,
with brass rosettes concealing bolt heads. Plain rails with holes
for ropes supporting mattress. Cabriole front legs with claw-and-
ball feet. *Variations:* More elegant examples have leaf carving on
knees. Simpler versions have Marlborough legs.

Materials and Dimensions
Mahogany and maple. Brass rosettes. Rope. Reproduction
hangings. Height: 86″. Length: 81″. Width: 59¾″.

Locality and Period
Massachusetts. c. 1760–80. Variations made in other regions.

Comment
The bed shown here is one of a group of outstanding examples
with handsomely curved front legs and claw-and-ball feet carved
in a distinctively Massachusetts manner. Since bed hangings
were very elaborate and expensive in the 1760s, bed frames,
mostly hidden behind the fabric, were often restrained in design.
The canopy and skirt on this bed are reproductions, but the
coverlet is 18th-century painted Indian cotton.

Hints for Collectors
Elegant Chippendale beds are rare, so collectors should be
cautious about potential purchases. Examine claw-and-ball feet
closely, since few later craftsmen have been able to duplicate
them properly. Rails were often lengthened, shortened, or
replaced to change the size of beds; the rails on a fine bed should
be original and unaltered. Check for convincing signs of wear on
them.

Federal canopy bed

Description
4-poster double bed with canopy. Canopy rails molded, gilded, and painted, with ormolu frieze. Silk ceiling with drapery swags suspended all around. Columnar posts tapered, with leaf-carved capitals and fluting interrupted by rings, ending at blocks holding ends of head- and footboards; lower column shaft leaf-carved and fluted. Head- and footboards with angled, scrolled top rails. Straight stiles framing plain panels. Bed rails consisting of flat panels outlined with brass stripping. Corner blocks with brass rosettes covering bolt heads. Leaf-carved legs on brass ball feet and casters. *Variations:* Simpler version may have less fluting and carved detail.

Materials and Dimensions
Mahogany and pine. Painted and gilded canopy frame. Reproduction fabric hangings. Ormolu. Brass decoration, feet, and casters. Height: 98½″. Length: 80¾″. Width: 59½″.

Locality and Period
Attributed to Charles-Honoré Lannuier, New York. c. 1805–19.

Comment
With its matching head- and footboards, the bed shown here is based on Louis XVI designs. The use of mahogany and the elegant, yet subtle, carved decoration is typical of New York craftsmanship of the early 19th century. Charles-Honoré Lannuier was New York's most fashionable cabinetmaker working in the French style.

Hints for Collectors
If more restrained in detail, a bed like this would probably be French rather than American. In this case, though French-inspired, the use of pine and the distinctive carving lead to a firm American attribution.

Eastlake bed

Description
Oversize ebonized bed topped by narrow rectangular canopy
projecting over headboard, with marquetry border of flowers,
leaves, and lines. Carved wreath around marquetry shield
centered in front. Canopy cantilevered from marquetry-
decorated stiles arching at top. Upper headboard with rail set on
6 turned spindles flanking marquetry panel of vase and flowers;
below, second rail crowning long floral-and-ribbon marquetry
panel. Lower section of headboard made of 5 grooved vertical
boards. Molded side rails have floral marquetry bands.
Footboard stiles topped by carved finials above alternating
carved and marquetry blocks. Marquetry panel at center of
footboard flanked by truncated spindles. Turned cylindrical feet.
Variations: Simple carving is more common than marquetry.

Materials and Dimensions
Cherry. Ebonized and stenciled. Marquetry of various woods.
Height: 118″. Length: 89½″. Width: 69½″.

Locality and Period
Made by Herter Brothers, New York. c. 1875–80.

Comment
Even though Charles Eastlake protested against decorative
sham, such as darkly stained woods, mechanical carving, and
flamboyant ornament, some of his followers disregarded his
views. The massive bed shown here is a splendid example of
furniture that both reflects and defies Eastlake's tenets.

Hints for Collectors
Herter Brothers beds are rare; the label, if present, should be on
the back of the headboard. This bed was part of a bedroom suite:
such groups should be kept together and are generally more
valuable when intact.

Eastlake bed

Description
Double bed with rectangular reeded stiles crowned by square
peaked finials projecting above top rail. Top rail with row of
disks on veneered panel. Below, 3 tiles separated by 2 galleries
of knobby spindles atop second reeded rail. Main part of
headboard with alternating grained and reeded planks. Side rails
grained and reeded, with curved braces at headboard. Footboard
a truncated version of headboard, but without tiles and spindles.
Feet with square molding, set on casters. *Variations:* Maple may
be stained or ebonized; cherry was also used. Carved decoration
is more common than tiles.

Materials and Dimensions
Bird's-eye maple. Japanese ceramic tiles. Iron casters. Height:
62½″. Length: 78″. Width: 51½″.

Locality and Period
Made by Herter Brothers, New York. c. 1880–90.

Comment
Herter Brothers, a notable furnituremaker of the Victorian era,
made the bed shown here as part of a bedroom set for
Lyndhurst, Jay Gould's Gothic Revival house in Tarrytown, New
York. This bed follows Eastlake's ideas in being made of planks
cut from local woods. The use of Japanese tiles testifies to the
prevailing interest in exotic design during the 1870s and 1880s.

Hints for Collectors
The range in quality of Eastlake furniture is quite broad. This
restrained bed, elegantly designed and executed, is among the
finest. Like most furnishings by Herter Brothers, the original
price of this bed was likely many times that of Eastlake beds
made in Grand Rapids factories, but its workmanship merits this
price difference, which is even greater today.

Turn-of-the-century oak bed

Description
Double bed with tall rectangular headboard and similar lower footboard. Arched headboard made of plain horizontal panels topped by decorative rail with carved dentil, scroll, and shell motifs. Straight stiles having slightly curved tops. Wooden rails with iron fittings. Flat-topped footboard with contoured skirt. Plain feet. *Variations:* Mass-produced examples were made in many patterns, from Rococo to Oriental, with varying amounts of relief decoration.

Materials and Dimensions
Oak and pine. Iron brackets. Height: 77″. Length: 78″. Width: 59″.

Locality and Period
Probably Grand Rapids. c. 1900–15.

Comment
Turn-of-the-century oak furniture was produced in large furniture factories across the United States, with Grand Rapids as the major center. Designs were selected to be durable and readily reproducible on a mass scale, as well as to attract the largest number of buyers. 18th-century decorative motifs, such as the scrolls and shells on the bed shown here, were frequently applied to the distinctive designs of the 1900–15 period.

Hints for Collectors
Turn-of-the-century oak furnishings followed many trends. Some designs reflect purer, reformist tendencies of the period, while others, like this bed, cater to popular tastes, with extravagant and restrained examples available in both categories. Prices are reasonable and the selection is broad, so select only pieces that are in very good condition.

Eastlake bed

Description
Double bed with tall rectangular headboard crowned by center
panel of disks below fretwork cornice. Top section divided into 3
segments of carved vines, with border of semicircles below. Main
portion of headboard including 3 framed panels set into
horizontal planks. Rectangular stiles with disk finials above
molded and inscribed decoration. Plain side rails with curved
braces at corners. Footboard truncated version of headboard,
topped by flat rail with molded edge. Plain rectangular feet with
protruding chamfered blocks on side. *Variations:* Carved panels
may be more ornate. Stain is often darker.

Materials and Dimensions
Cherry. Iron fixtures. Height: 74″. Length: 79″. Width: 59″.

Locality and Period
Probably Grand Rapids. c. 1880.

Comment
The bed shown here is a popular interpretation of Eastlake
design, decorated more simply to allow for mass production.
Such designs tended to be conservative: the framed panels of this
bed, for instance, were fashionable decades earlier. Renaissance
Revival elements such as disks and moldings were added to this
Eastlake design as a concession to popular taste.

Hints for Collectors
Conservative late 19th-century works combining Renaissance
Revival and Eastlake elements are readily available and
generally inexpensive. Many offer fine detailing and sturdy
construction.

Description
Double bed with tall headboard, topped by curved pediment supported by 2 turned columns and decorated with pointed finial on small panel. Plain stiles with circular finials. Main section of headboard made of grained and plain panels. Rails with iron fittings. Footboard with flat top and curved ends; posts with flat molded tops and square molded feet. *Variations:* Beds may have floral decoration as well as graining. Pediment may be more or less elaborate.

Materials and Dimensions
Pine. Painted and grained. Iron fixtures. Height: 83″. Length: 79″. Width: 59″.

Locality and Period
Possibly Pennsylvania or New England. c. 1875–90.

Comment
Furniture with painted decoration was first mass-produced by factories in Pennsylvania and New England. Although the bed shown here was made after Grand Rapids had become the leading furnituremaking center, it was probably produced at one of the older eastern factories. This type of furniture is often called cottage furniture, for it was inexpensive enough to be used in workers' cottages as well as in the summer cottages of the well-to-do.

Hints for Collectors
Cottage furniture was made and sold in sets, including washstands and dressers, so collectors may wish to look for matching pieces. As it is only just beginning to attract the attention of collectors, painted pine cottage furniture is both plentiful and inexpensive. Look for pieces with good original paint and minimal structural damage.

Rococo Revival bed

Description
Double bed with undulating headboard, footboard, and sides
made of laminated wood. Headboard with elaborate carving of
scrolls, flora, and Cupids above molded rim; back panel curving
down and around to form part of sides. Side rails with carved
protruding centers and upholstered tops; molded lower rim
continuing along bottom of head- and footboards. Footboard a
truncated version of headboard. Curved feet with scrolled
molding. Stretchers spanning width of bed to support specially
shaped mattress. *Variations:* Frames may have less carving and
be in 2, rather than 4, parts.

Materials and Dimensions
Rosewood and other laminated woods. Velvet upholstery.
Height: 75″. Length: 80″. Width: 66″.

Locality and Period
Made by John Henry Belter, New York. c. 1860.

Comment
The bed shown here is an example of the Rococo Revival style at
its most exuberant. In 1856 John Henry Belter received a patent
for a bed frame like this one, but simpler and in 2 parts instead of
4. Although other furnituremakers created similar pieces, when
such beds with undulating sides are exceptionally carved and
made of fine laminated wood, they are generally attributed to
Belter. Some may bear Belter's stamped mark on a cross
stretcher or inner block.

Hints for Collectors
Rococo Revival designs range from relatively simple examples to
those as elaborate as this bed. Collectors with a taste for the
extravagant and a large budget can best find such elegant beds in
the shops of dealers specializing in this field.

Renaissance Revival bed

Description
Double bed with headboard crowned by a cabochon and scrolls atop curving broken pediment. Below, decoration of veneered panels, disks, and carved leaf scrolls. 2 tall veneered posts topped by flattened scroll finials and disks. Side rails with veneered panels and center disks; ends topped by scrolled brackets. Footboard crowned by rounded pediment with center disk, above veneered panel; curved projection below. Low posts of footboard have pyramidal tops, veneered panels, and rectangular feet. *Variations:* Pediments are often straight rather than curving. Additional turned elements are common.

Materials and Dimensions
Walnut and walnut veneer. Height: 105″. Length: 72″. Width: 55″.

Locality and Period
Grand Rapids. c. 1870–80. Variations made in other centers.

Comment
Renaissance Revival beds with turned and simply carved ornament were made in quantity in Grand Rapids factories and shipped all over the country and to Europe. The bed shown here is a good example of elegance that is simply achieved by massive scale and by juxtaposition of rich veneered panels with limited carving.

Hints for Collectors
The elegance of factory-produced Renaissance Revival designs like this bed resulted from their turned parts and veneers, but many examples made in small workshops around the country depended on elaborate carved details. Both types may be well designed, with fine overall lines and artful embellishment.

Rococo Revival bed

Description
Double bed with headboard crowned by arched panel having
applied shell-and-floral carving. 2 pointed molded panels above
rectangular molded frame with stepped corners. 2 tall columnar
posts with urn finials and bases, both having thick bead borders.
Side rails and footboard at same height, with scrolled brackets
above ends, molded panels, and center rosettes. Carved arched
projection above center of footboard. Front posts shorter
versions of rear ones, with Gothic arches cut into columns.
Ringed feet. *Variations:* Carving may be more elaborate. Short
front posts may have built-in rods, which are raised to support a
canopy.

Materials and Dimensions
Walnut. Height: 95″. Length: 74″. Width: 54″.

Locality and Period
Probably New Orleans. c. 1860. Variations from other centers.

Comment
The bed shown here was most likely made in New Orleans, a
center of fine craftsmanship and a thriving port. The history
of New Orleans furnituremaking has yet to be written. Rococo
Revival furnishings, beds in particular, turn up frequently today
in Louisiana, Mississippi, and Alabama, though usually with little
documentation.

Hints for Collectors
Renaissance and Rococo motifs were often combined on furniture
made in the 1850s and 1860s; the purer Rococo Revival designs
usually have the most elegant detailing. Often beds like this have
been altered from 4-poster canopy beds by having their front
posts cut down. Missing bolts or other hardware for holding a
bed together can be difficult to replace.

Description
Tubular-brass double bed with matching head- and footboards of different heights. Top rail straight, with curved corners joined to stiles by ring-shaped capitals. Straight lower rail enclosing 5 slender vertical rods in central portion, with small knobs set at varied heights to create rhythm. Single horizontal rod connecting 2 outer verticals, with center rod passing through it. Plain cast-iron rails to support mattress. Feet with molded rings and casters. *Variations:* Rods may be used in various arrangements. Stiles may have more ornate capitals.

Materials and Dimensions
Tubular brass. Cast-iron bed rails. Iron casters. Height: 61″. Length: 84″. Width: 55″.

Locality and Period
Throughout the United States. c. 1890–1920.

Comment
Brass beds were a staple in modest turn-of-the-century homes. The glitter of tubular brass was meant to compensate for the lack of decoration. Designs were conservative, and manufacturers tended to keep the same models in production for many years. The bed shown here is typical of many produced between 1890 and 1920.

Hints for Collectors
Among the attractions of brass beds were their ease of manufacture and maintenance. Brass needs polishing, but otherwise it does not require much care. Designs should be simple. The many reproductions on the market are generally less sturdy. These will not show wear on feet or casters, and the network of fine lines on the brass, produced by years of polishing, will be absent.

Description
Painted tubular-iron double bed with matching head- and
footboards of different heights. Rails and stiles at right angles,
with corner joints decorated in leaf pattern. Top rails having
center joints in same pattern, connected to thin rods suspended
from corner joints. 6 vertical rods spanning paired horizontal
rods, with molded joints. Straight side and end rails supporting
mattress. Rounded feet. *Variations:* Thin rods may form more
complex patterns.

Materials and Dimensions
Tubular and cast iron. Painted. Height: 51½″. Length: 78″.
Width: 51½″.

Locality and Period
Throughout the United States. c. 1890–1920.

Comment
Simple iron beds of fairly similar design were made in factories
around the country. Though basically functional, the linear
designs of the foot- and headboards were a concession to popular
taste. The fact that iron beds like the one shown here have
matched foot- and headboards, though differing in height,
suggests they were factory products. This design is a very
simplified version of Neoclassical wooden beds made in France
during the 18th century.

Hints for Collectors
Iron beds are sturdy but decorative; their restrained ornament
often creates an elegant impression. Check for rust spots, which
detract from a cast-iron piece and should be removed before
repainting. Many beds such as this were originally painted; worn
paint is quite easy to refurbish, however, and repainting has
little effect on value.

Child's Victorian tubular-iron bed

Description
Small painted tubular-iron bed with matching head- and footboards. Cylindrical stiles with large brass knob finials; block joints at rail height. Thin diagonal rods in X-pattern with rosette in center. Leaf-molded elements at corners where horizontal and vertical rods intersect. Side rails made of L-section iron strips. Plain tubular legs. Circular feet. *Variations:* Headboard may be much taller than footboard.

Materials and Dimensions
Tubular iron. Painted. Brass finials. Cast-iron bed rails. Height: 35½″. Length: 40″. Width: 30½″.

Locality and Period
Throughout the United States. c. 1880–1900.

Comment
Iron beds, first introduced in Europe in the 18th century, did not become common in America until the late 19th century. The bed shown here is typical of the simpler examples. With its discreet ornament on the head- and footboards, it is so much more functional than decorative that it is difficult to assign to any style, such as Renaissance Revival or Eastlake. The shortness of this bed indicates that it was made for a child.

Hints for Collectors
By adding cushions, children's beds may be made into attractive settees. Beware of rust that has recently been covered with paint, since the metal underneath will continue to deteriorate. Though sturdy, iron can be brittle, and repaired cracks may break again. Iron beds are usually substantially less expensive than comparable all-brass ones.

Modern tubular-steel bed

Description
Tubular-steel single bed with matching head- and footboards of
different heights. Straight stiles and top rail formed by
continuous length of tubing with curved corners. Tubular frames
with asymmetrical arrangement of 2 vertical and 2 horizontal
rods. Tubular legs; ring feet. Cast-steel bed rails. *Variations:*
Tubular-steel head- and footboards may have a variety of
symmetrical or asymmetrical linear designs.

Materials and Dimensions
Tubular steel. Cast-steel rails. Height: 37″. Length: 79″. Width:
34½″.

Locality and Period
Throughout the United States. c. 1930–55.

Comment
Furniture made of new materials such as tubular steel became
popular in the 1920s. The bed shown here is a relatively simple
interpretation of earlier brass beds, adapted to modern taste; the
asymmetrical linear design of the tubular head- and footboards is
a popularized version of patterns found in the paintings of Piet
Mondrian. This bed is more decorative and less strictly functional
than tubular-steel designs by architects associated with the
Bauhaus.

Hints for Collectors
Modern furniture ranges from innovative original designs to later
popularized versions that tend to be less severe and more
decorative. Because both are modern does not mean that such
interpretations will complement each other. This bed, for
instance, an expression of modern design but no masterpiece,
would probably be unsuited to a room furnished with purer
modern pieces.

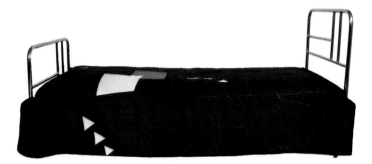

Drop-leaf and Tilt-top Tables

Tables with drop leaves, tilt tops, or concealed leaves form a large, very useful, and versatile group that has evolved since early Colonial days. All have tops that can be adjusted to save space in rooms used for other purposes besides dining.

Drop-leaf Tables

Drop-leaf tables in the William and Mary style have turned legs and, most often, circular tops. Early examples generally display thick turnings on heavy legs. Leaves are often supported by gate legs, which swing out along upper and lower stretchers (246), or by hinged solid braces shaped like a butterfly wing (245). Queen Anne and Chippendale drop-leaf examples, varying in elegance, have cabriole or straight legs. Large-size pieces were commonly used for dining, though some smaller ones, sometimes called breakfast tables, also served this purpose. One elegant 18th-century drop-leaf design is the Pembroke table (261). Pembroke tables continued in the Federal era, but with tapered legs (262); later in the 19th century, Shaker craftsmen created simplified versions. Some of the simplest forms, made by 18th- and early 19th-century rural craftsmen, have plain rectangular drop leaves supported on swinging legs or movable wooden braces (242, 244). Drop-leaf tables with pedestal bases range from elongated rectangular forms, probably used as library or sofa tables during the Federal period, to Empire examples with heavy baluster-shaped bases, used as both center and dining tables. Furnituremakers working in mid-19th-century revival styles did not favor drop-leaf designs, though there were exceptions. The form again became popular at the turn of the century in revival and rustic designs. Later, Art Deco and modern designs appeared (266–267), often with concealed leaves that pull out rather than lift up.

Tilt-top Tables

Tilt-top tables, which can be folded up when not in use, were another basic feature of early American households. Some large country pieces from the 17th to 19th centuries doubled as chairs or storage bins (250–251). Smaller versions, used for such varied purposes as serving tea or holding candles, have fashionably shaped tripod bases; these range from restrained Queen Anne and delicate Federal examples to more elaborate Chippendale pieces. Some, fitted with a so-called bird-cage mechanism, have tops that rotate as well as tilt (254). Tilt-top tables were less common in the Victorian period, except for some highly decorative examples.

Collecting Hints

Since all of these tables have some sort of movable top, make certain that the supports or tilting devices are in good working order. Over the years many tabletops, leaves, and drawers have been replaced; check the undersides for authentic discoloration from aging. Also beware of later hinges and extra screw holes—indicating a leaf has been replaced—as well as such obvious signs of later workmanship as circular saw marks.

Federal country painted drop-leaf table

Description
Painted table with 2 rectangular drop leaves made from narrow planks and fastened by straight iron hinges; planks swing out from skirt to support leaves. Plain plank top. Round legs turned and tapered. Long feet defined by ring turnings at upper ends. *Variations:* Pine was frequently used. Straight square legs, based on Hepplewhite models, were also produced. Brown or gray paint was more common than blue or green; sometimes with grained or marbleized decoration.

Materials and Dimensions
Maple. Painted blue. Iron hinges. Height: 28½". Length: 42½". Depth: 17" (closed); 39" (opened).

Locality and Period
New England. c. 1800–40.

Comment
Painted furniture in Federal designs was made for almost a half century. Some early painted examples were produced at the same time as similar but more fashionable Federal pieces; however, others were made a decade or more after fashions had changed. The round legs on the table shown here were based on Sheraton designs; the thickness of the legs suggests that this table was a late piece and, since it is made of maple, probably fashioned in New England.

Hints for Collectors
Collectors neglected painted furniture until only about a decade ago, so there are still pieces to be found in the Midwest and other areas settled at the beginning of the 19th century. Always check painted surfaces for concealed faults.

Queen Anne drop-leaf table

Description
Table with rectangular top and 2 equal-size drop leaves that have plain straight edges and iron hinges. Top set on rectangular base with straight rails into which legs are mortised; long rails made in 2 parts and hinged by wooden dovetail and pin to enable legs to swing out to support leaves. Straight legs, square in upper part and round below, tapering to raised pad feet. *Variations:* Curved cabriole legs may be used. Round tops were more popular than rectangular ones.

Materials and Dimensions
Mahogany and pine. Iron hinges. Height: 28″. Length: 44½″. Depth: 16″ (closed); 55″ (opened).

Locality and Period
New England. c. 1740–60.

Comment
Large tables with drop leaves, such as the one shown here, were frequently used throughout the Colonial period, when separate dining rooms were very rare: such tables were brought out and opened up for dining, and afterward were pushed back against walls. Mahogany became popular in the Queen Anne period and has been favored for elegant furniture ever since. It was imported from the Caribbean and used particularly in the larger port cities.

Hints for Collectors
Over the years the tops of many 18th-century tables have been replaced, usually ineptly. Check the underside of the tabletop to see if it has the proper discoloration that comes from long exposure to air. Make sure that the screws of the hinges are in their original holes; extra screw holes probably indicate that a leaf has been replaced.

Empire country drop-leaf table

Description
Rectangular table with 2 drop leaves having rounded corners; leaves supported by square rods sliding out from center of skirt on long sides. Top supported on 4 legs mortised into plain skirt. Legs have square upper and lower sections and vase-and-ring-turned center; feet tapered and turned, ending in flattened balls. *Variations:* Leaves may be straight-sided without rounded corners. Turned legs may be tapered. Tables may be painted.

Materials and Dimensions
Pine. Height: 29″. Length: 42½″. Depth: 17″ (closed); 65″ (opened).

Locality and Period
Pennsylvania, the Midwest, or the South. c. 1815–50.

Comment
Country Empire furnishings were simple interpretations of the style fashionable all over the country between about 1815 and 1850. Native woods, such as the pine on the table shown here, were used for such rural products, and were usually stained or painted in contrast to the fashionable urban practice of concealing these woods with elegant veneers. The turned legs of this table are simplified, heavier versions of Sheraton designs; the legs on fashionable Empire pieces are generally more elaborate than those on this country example.

Hints for Collectors
Unadorned country Empire designs have a charm like that of folk portraits because both use the same kinds of simplification. Such pieces are ideal for informal settings but are often as expensive today as urban designs.

William and Mary butterfly table

Description
Table with circular top and 2 butterfly-wing-shaped supports for
drop leaves. Top rests on rectangular base with single drawer
and double-vase-and-ring-turned legs slanting outward from
skirt; feet spool-shaped. Stretchers rectangular and heavy.
Rounded edges on skirt, top, and stretchers. *Variations:* Instead
of butterfly supports, some early drop-leaf tables have gate legs
that pull out to support leaves. Turnings may be thicker or
thinner, as well as more elaborate.

Materials and Dimensions
Cherry, maple, and pine. Height: 26½″. Length: 38″. Depth:
13¼″ (closed).

Locality and Period
New England. c. 1690–1700.

Comment
Although butterfly tables—named for their wing-shaped leaf
supports—were produced in Europe as well as America, most
examples with restrained turnings, such as those on the table
shown here, were made in America. The vase turnings of the
legs here are lighter in proportion than most earlier Pilgrim-style
examples. The angled legs are also more closely associated with
the William and Mary than Pilgrim style. Refinements such as
the finished edges and the delicate turnings suggest a date close
to 1700.

Hints for Collectors
20th-century imitations of this form are always lighter in
proportion and have particularly thin legs. The subtle detailing
on an early piece is seldom successfully duplicated by imitators.
Moreover, later examples have tops made of several boards and
are put together with modern nails or screws.

William and Mary gate-leg table

Description
Gate-leg table with plain top that becomes round when 2 curved
leaves are opened; edges of top are round and leaves are
attached by iron hinges underneath. Center of top set on
rectangular 4-legged structure having plain skirt with cutout
parts to accommodate tops of swing legs. 2 pairs of swing, or
gate, legs support opened leaves. All 8 legs turned in double-
vase-and-ring pattern. Stable legs reinforced by 4 stretchers
turned in block-and-ring design, with notches to hold gate legs.
Worn bun feet. *Variations:* Turnings may be considerably
thicker. Overall proportions range from delicate to bulky.

Materials and Dimensions
Oak base. Maple top. Wrought-iron hinges. Height: 27".
Diameter of top: 44" (opened).

Locality and Period
New England. c. 1700–20. Variations made in New York and
Pennsylvania.

Comment
Gate-leg tables were introduced in America in the 17th century.
In general, thick turnings on thick legs are an indication of early
tables. Such tables were practical in small houses because they
could be folded up to save space. New England examples, like
the one shown here, are usually of maple and are more delicate
than those made in Pennsylvania or New York.

Hints for Collectors
Delicate proportions may be the sign of a turn-of-the-century
reproduction. Wear is the most obvious clue to authenticity, but
if too even or exaggerated, it may have been faked. Beware of
circular saw marks under replaced tabletops.

Colonial Revival drop-leaf table

Description

Table with rectangular top having curved ends and curved drop leaves that open to form circular top. Undulating skirt. 6 legs turned in double-vase-and-ring pattern with blocks at junctures with stretchers. Turned stretchers match legs. Long sides have blocks at junctures with center cross stretchers and middle legs; middle legs have diagonal braces to support opened leaves. Bun feet. *Variations:* Other early American drop-leaf designs were also adapted to 20th-century factory techniques.

Materials and Dimensions

Maple. Height: 30″. Diameter of top: 40½″ (opened).

Locality and Period

Probably Grand Rapids. c. 1920–35. Variations made in other centers.

Comment

Revival design after about 1915 took an interesting turn: manufacturers developed lines of tables and chairs in smaller sizes suitable for the average American home merely by interchanging elements of 17-, 18th-, and early 19th-century styles. Such assembly-line Colonial Revival furniture was sturdy and inexpensive. The wood in the table shown here is probably not top quality, so it was stained dark.

Hints for Collectors

Most, but not all, 20th-century revival furniture is well made. These pieces were scaled down from the originals, making them too delicate for many collectors accustomed to the sturdiness of early American furniture. Variations with carving are less successful than those with turned parts, which were better suited to modern production techniques. Tables like this one are readily available and inexpensive.

Renaissance Revival drop-leaf table

Description
Table with curved drop leaves forming circular top when opened and supported by swinging legs; top covered with baize and framed by wide exposed border embellished with gilded inscribed lines. Skirt has single curved-front drawer on narrow side, decorated with gilded, inscribed linear pattern repeated on long sides. Round legs columnar and tapered, with plain capitals and wide gilded fluting; tapered spool-shaped feet set on casters. Flat cross stretchers curved on sides and decorated with inscribed lines and brass studs; compote-shaped urn in center. *Variations:* Proportions may be heavier, with more elaborate carved ornamentation.

Materials and Dimensions
Walnut and pine. Gilded and stained. Baize. Metal casters. Brass studs. Height: 36½″. Length: 29″. Depth: 27″ (opened).

Locality and Period
Grand Rapids or other furniture centers. c. 1870–80.

Comment
The Renaissance Revival style of the 1860s and 1870s marked the first period in which fine designs were used for mass-produced furnishings. The table shown here did not require a skilled carver or cabinetmaker; nevertheless it is well made and decorated with some imagination. Its light proportions derive from late 18th-century Neoclassical designs.

Hints for Collectors
Flat and colorful surface decoration plays an important part in many Renaissance Revival pieces. Light woods embellished with bronze, enamel, or porcelain plaques and gilded or ebonized details are particularly effective, though such applied decoration is fragile and should be examined carefully.

Queen Anne drop-leaf table

Description
Table with rectangular top having narrow curved ends; 2 curved drop leaves form circular top with rounded edges when opened. Skirt arched on short sides and unfinished on long sides hidden by drop leaves; hinged sections of skirt allow for swinging legs that support opened leaves. Legs tapering and round; plain pad feet. *Variations:* Tops may be rectangular or square when opened. Legs may curve in cabriole shape.

Materials and Dimensions
Mahogany, maple, and pine. Height: 27″. Diameter of top: 38″ (opened).

Locality and Period
Newport, Rhode Island. c. 1740.

Comment
Newport was a center for some of the finest Colonial furniture, but its designs were almost always restrained. The table shown here is typical of Queen Anne design in Newport, with plain legs that are straight rather than curved and a simple arch on the skirt. In general, Queen Anne design throughout the Colonies is restrained when compared to English designs, but elaborate cabriole legs and carved shells on knees of legs were often used outside Newport.

Hints for Collectors
The simplicity that characterized most Queen Anne furniture rarely entails any crudeness. Look for edges shaped in a refined manner and details that are elegantly executed, such as the hinges of the swinging legs. Examine hinges carefully since they may have been broken and replaced over the years; period replacements are perfectly proper, but new hinges may indicate that a leaf or top is a replacement.

Country chair-table

Description
Chair-table with round top made of 2 boards with flattened ends.
Top braced by 2 battens and attached to rear stiles of base by
wooden rod slipped through holes in battens and stiles, allowing
top to swing up and down. Front and rear stiles straight-sided;
stiles tapered to tops and joined by 2 narrow square arms with
rounded handholds projecting over front stiles. Plain legs are
continuations of stiles. Rectangular seat cut out around stiles and
set on plain rails dovetailed into stiles. Single drawer, with plain
front and wooden pull, resting on lower rail. *Variations:* Drawer
may be replaced by simple boxlike storage area with lift top. Top
may be rectangular. Legs are often turned.

Materials and Dimensions
Pine top and maple base. Painted. Height: 33″ (with top down).
Diameter of top: 44″.

Locality and Period
New England. c. 1800–80.

Comment
Chair-tables were first introduced in the 17th century, but
continued to be made in the 18th and 19th centuries for simple
country settings. More functional as tables than as chairs, they
were among many early furnishings conceived as space savers,
since they could be folded up and put out of the way. Maple and
pine were particularly popular in New England.

Hints for Collectors
Dating country furniture is always difficult: to help date pieces,
look for elements that reflect fashionable contemporary styles.
As a rule, pieces became plainer as the 19th century advanced;
the simplicity of the piece shown here as well as its square stiles
suggest a mid-19th-century date.

William and Mary hutch table

Description
Hutch table with oval top that lifts up to reveal rectangular
storage area. Top braced by 2 battens attached to box by 2 rods.
Trestle base consists of 2 solid planks cut in curves below storage
area and set into solid feet with rounded ends. Simple board
stretcher mortised through planks. *Variations:* Similar tables
without storage areas double as chairs when their tops are
positioned vertically. Trestle legs may be cut in complex designs;
some are plain straight planks. Feet may be more elaborately
carved. Simple versions, usually made of thin planks of pine,
were made in the early to mid-19th century.

Materials and Dimensions
Maple and gumwood. Height: 26″. Length: 48″. Depth: 37½″.

Locality and Period
New York. c. 1720.

Comment
Early tables such as the one shown here were used in small rural
interiors, with the tops left up to save space. These tables
doubled as storage bins. The earliest examples were made in the
17th century and featured heavily proportioned, turned legs. The
simple construction and rounded feet suggest that this example
was made before 1725.

Hints for Collectors
Authentic early furniture should have worn or rough spots due to
age. These simple pieces should display traditional construction
techniques, such as the mortise-and-tenon details visible on the
trestle legs, as well as its wrought-iron nails and early wooden
rods. The wood should be thick and worn on all edges.

252 Rococo Revival papier-mâché tilt-top table

Description
Table with scallop-edged, circular tilt top. Molded inner edge of top embellished with gilded foliate decoration; center with painted still life of fruit on table against landscape background. Skirt in scallop-and-scroll design. Pedestal shaped as simple baluster with elongated top and vase-shaped bottom ornamented by gilded leaf-and-scroll design. Base rectangular, with sides curving inward. Block feet with rounded edges. *Variations:* Oval tops are common. The decoration on the tops is frequently more abstract, sometimes with scroll patterns embellished with mother-of-pearl or floral designs.

Materials and Dimensions
Papier-mâché and wood. Painted and gilded. Iron hinge for tilt mechanism. Height: 28″ (with top down). Diameter of top: 25½″.

Locality and Period
Throughout the United States and England. c. 1830–50.

Comment
Most papier-mâché furniture from 1810 to 1870 was made in England. The table shown here is a fine Rococo Revival design decorated a little more simply than most English examples of this period, which suggests that it may be American. One American maker, the Litchfield Manufacturing Company in Connecticut, made various small objects as well as some tables. The paintings on the tops were often based on popular still-life graphics of the period.

Hints for Collectors
Papier-mâché furniture was developed in the mid-19th century and was an ideal medium for making Rococo Revival shapes. Papier-mâché is a relatively delicate material, so check for damage concealed by added patches of paint.

Federal tilt-top candlestand

Description
Candlestand with tilt top elaborately curved at corners and straight in center area of each side; inlaid border on top. Tripod pedestal base with reeded cone. Unusually curved cabriole legs mortised into base. Plain feet. *Variations:* Tops may be oval, octagonal, or rectangular. Pedestal bases may be plain vase shapes or more elaborate with fluting and carved decoration.

Materials and Dimensions
Mahogany. White wood inlay. Height: 32½″ (with top down). Length: 19″. Depth: 14″.

Locality and Period
New England. c. 1800. Variations made in New York, Philadelphia, and the South.

Comment
Federal rooms featured a greater number and variety of small tables than did pre-Revolutionary interiors. The candlestand shown here has an unusually shaped top that is a version of several well-known forms. The Neoclassical design favored during the Federal era was characterized by a lightness of form, delicacy of detail, and classical motifs such as the reeding on this pedestal. Sheraton designs such as this were closer to ancient models than were other Federal designs: this pedestal, for example, is a classical urn shape. New England examples tended to be especially delicate.

Hints for Collectors
Federal furniture is just a little heavier than reproductions made a century later. Make sure that simple details were not mechanically made: for example, early 19th-century fluting should be deeper than that on copies. Hinges should be handmade and not factory-stamped.

Chippendale tilt-top tea table

Description
Tea table with circular tilt top rounded at the edge. Top set on small square support, called a birdcage, made of 2 planks joined by columns at each corner, with a hole in lower plank fitted over tripod base. Turned base in thick baluster shape. Cabriole legs mortised into baluster base; leaf carving on knees. Claw-and-ball feet. *Variations:* New York examples usually have plain tops, while Philadelphia pieces often have scalloped tops. Pedestals may be carved in leaf patterns or fluted.

Materials and Dimensions
Mahogany. Height: 29¼″. Diameter of top: 31½″.

Locality and Period
New York. c. 1760. Similar tables made in Philadelphia.

Comment
Tripod pedestal-base tables with cabriole legs were popular by the 1730s; the claw-and-ball feet and carved knees on the table shown here are later Chippendale elements. Because they were practical, tilt-top tables were common in the 18th century, when furniture was often moved about. Favored by New York and Philadelphia cabinetmakers, the birdcage device allows the top to be rotated as well as tilted. The plain top and baluster and the deep carving on the knees are signs of the table's New York origin.

Hints for Collectors
The top of this table was made from a single board, a typical practice of the period. Check for repaired tops and birdcage mechanisms, which can easily break. As carving added in the 19th century detracts from the value of a table, compare questionable carving with that of unaltered examples.

Chippendale tilt-top candlestand

Description
Candlestand with square top having undulating sides and 2
braces hinged underneath to allow for tilting. Pedestal is turned
tapered column with bulbous top and ring-turned capital. Ring-
turned bulbous base set on cylinder into which 3 legs are
mortised. Narrow legs cut in cabriole design and rounded on
outer surface. Snake feet. *Variations:* Round tops are more
common. Some examples have carved pedestals.

Materials and Dimensions
Mahogany and pine. Height: 32″. Length: 15″. Depth: 15″.

Locality and Period
New England. c. 1770–90.

Comment
Restrained Chippendale designs are often late: the earliest price
book compiled for cabinetmakers in the United States, dating
from the 1790s, lists Chippendale forms and suggests that the
style remained popular in the Federal era. Commonly called
candlestands today, small tables like the example shown here
probably had various functions. They must have been quite
numerous, since many have survived.

Hints for Collectors
Many simple tables are not easily placed in time or locality.
Select one with an overall design and detailing that suits your
collection. Make certain that the top is original: its underside
should show appropriate discoloration from aging. Also check to
see that all the legs are original, since these may have broken off
and been replaced; subtle differences in shape, carving, and
patina will reveal a replacement.

Queen Anne tilt-top table

Description
Table with square top that has wavy sides and rounded edges. Top set on hinged device to allow for tilting. Pedestal vase-shaped and columnar, with straight cylindrical section atop vase having ring turnings on neck and base; pedestal set on cylinder base. 3 legs mortised into base. Cabriole legs thin and rounded on top. Snake feet. *Variations:* Square tops, sometimes with straight sides, were made, but are less common than circular ones. Vases may be turned in more complex patterns. Legs may be thicker.

Materials and Dimensions
Mahogany. Height: 28″. Length: 30″. Depth: 30″.

Locality and Period
Pennsylvania, Connecticut, or the South. c. 1760–90.

Comment
Simple designs like the table shown here are called Queen Anne even when they were made after 1750, the usual cut-off date. The first price book for American craftsmen, compiled in the 1790s, included Queen Anne designs as well as newer ones. The simplicity of this table's pedestal and legs is characteristically Queen Anne, but the shaping of the top and thinness of the legs display the more advanced techniques of the Chippendale or Federal period.

Hints for Collectors
Small late 18th-century tables like this one do not always fit into one stylistic niche, but many complement more easily defined examples. Judge such pieces by their particular design: the combination of simple and naive elements with fashionable ones results in some of the most appealing American designs.

257 Federal double-pedestal drop-leaf table

Description
Table with 2 scalloped elliptical leaves supported by planks that swing out from skirt. Single drawer has gilded bronze rosette-shaped pull with ring handle. Turned drops hang at corners of skirt. 2 pedestal supports, vase-shaped and carved in waterleaf design repeated on legs. Reeded stretcher joining pedestals consists of 2 vase-turned sections connected by 2 hemispheres. Flared legs. Gilded bronze lion's-paw feet on casters. *Variations:* Double-pedestal tables usually have leaves on the short sides instead of the long ones. Pedestals may be turned and reeded, or plain. Strips of ebony or ormolu may be applied on skirts.

Materials and Dimensions
Mahogany and tulip poplar. Bronze hardware. Height: 27″. Length: 41½″ (opened). Depth: 34½″.

Locality and Period
Made in the workshop of Duncan Phyfe, New York. c. 1800–10.

Comment
This table may have been used in a library or as a center table in a drawing room. It is too short—and the leaves are on the wrong sides—for a sofa table. Handsomely carved pedestals, particularly in the waterleaf pattern shown here, are generally associated with Duncan Phyfe, New York's best-known cabinetmaker.

Hints for Collectors
Check elegant Federal designs, such as this one, for signs of weak execution: many Phyfe-inspired reproductions made 50 to 75 years ago have poorly defined carving and darker stains than the originals. Beware of later hinges and pulls as well as marks of later power tools.

Empire drop-leaf table

Description
Table with rectangular top and 2 drop leaves that have cusped corners. Straight skirt with gilded, stenciled lower borders on front and rear, and drops at corners. Baluster-shaped pedestal leaf-carved and set into ring joining base. Cabriole legs carved in elaborate leaf-and-scroll design, terminating in lion's-paw feet on casters. *Variations:* Pedestals and legs may be less embellished, or have pineapple instead of leaf carving. Feet may be gilded or bronzed wood, or gilded brass.

Materials and Dimensions
Mahogany and pine. Painted base. Metal casters. Height: 29½″. Length: 25¾″ (closed); 55¼″ (opened). Depth: 38¾″.

Locality and Period
Made by J. and J. W. Meeks, New York. c. 1825–45.

Comment
Drop-leaf tables were popular in the early 19th century, particularly in New York. The table shown here has the elaborate carving, finely detailed work, and heavy proportions typical of Empire furniture. This design, though not very imaginative, is well executed; it was probably used in one of the many Empire-era middle-class townhouses, where it could double as a center and dining table. It bears the stenciled mark of the well-known Meeks workshop.

Hints for Collectors
Empire pieces produced during the Colonial Revival of the 1890s are recognizable by mechanical-looking carving and lighter proportions than the originals. The stains applied to mahogany at the turn of the century were darker than those used in 1830. The mark of a well-known maker such as Meeks makes a table considerably more valuable.

Chippendale drop-leaf table

Description
Table with rectangular top and 2 plain-edged drop leaves.
Rectangular base with straight finished sides. Long sides have
skirt with extra hinged section mortised to leg that swings out to
support leaf. Cabriole legs with carved leaf decoration on knees;
claw-and-ball feet with talons at right angles to each other.
Variations: Skirts may be arched at short ends. Rare examples
have gadrooning on skirts. Legs may lack carving.

Materials and Dimensions
Mahogany, poplar, and pine. Height: 27½″. Length: 41½″. Depth:
41½″ (opened).

Locality and Period
New York. c. 1755–60. Variations made in other Colonies.

Comment
New York Chippendale tables, including those with elaborate
and skillful carving like that on the knees of the legs shown here,
are heavier in proportion than those from other areas. The
straight skirt, simple curve of the heavy legs, and claw-and-ball
feet with talons at 90° angles to each other are also characteristic
of New York craftsmanship.

Hints for Collectors
American Chippendale furniture is generally more restrained
than most English examples, but simple mahogany pieces may be
difficult to distinguish due to the absence of carving and other
prominent elements. American claw-and-ball feet are more
abstract than those on English examples, which have realistic
talons. Turn-of-the-century reproductions, however, have
schematically carved claw-and-ball feet that lack the vitality
of the originals.

Queen Anne drop-leaf breakfast table

Description
Table with rectangular top and single hinged leaf that is same width as top so that table is square when opened; edge of top is concave and stepped. Skirt straight-fronted and cut in curving outline on lower edge; unfinished rear skirt. Skirt rails are mortised into square upper ends of legs. Cabriole legs with claw-and-ball feet. Single rear leg hinged to skirt section by wooden pin so that it swings out to support leaf. *Variations:* 2 leaves are more common. Opened tops may be round. Pad feet were often used. Skirt may be straight rather than curved.

Materials and Dimensions
Mahogany and pine. Iron hinges. Height: 28″. Length: 30″. Depth: 15″ (closed); 30″ (opened).

Locality and Period
Rhode Island. c. 1750–60. Related designs made in other Colonies.

Comment
Small drop-leaf tables are called breakfast tables because they were often used for serving breakfasts in mid-18th-century bedrooms. The restrained elegance of the example shown here is characteristic of the American Queen Anne style. While its curved skirt is closer to the William and Mary style, the claw-and-ball feet are associated with Chippendale design. The balls are almost oval and the claws stretch over them in a way characteristic of Rhode Island, particularly Newport, cabinetry.

Hints for Collectors
Since they are unfamiliar, rare forms such as breakfast tables should be carefully examined. Extra screw holes or areas on the underside that are not discolored from age suggest that a top or leaf has been replaced.

Chippendale Pembroke table

Description
Table with rectangular top and 2 drop leaves that have flat sides, double-curved ends, and projecting round corners. Skirt has single drawer in short exposed end; plain drawer with keyhole and elegant pull. Drawer slides over straight rail embellished with gadrooning; pierced brackets support rail. Long unfinished sides of skirt have sections hinged on wooden pins to swing out and support leaves. Legs straight, molded, and tapered to projecting square feet. Arched cross stretchers flat-sided and cut in undulating curves with rounded projections between legs and center. *Variations:* Thicker legs are more common. Simpler Pembroke tables have plainer stretchers and leaves with straight ends.

Materials and Dimensions
Mahogany and pine. Brass pull. Height: 27″. Length: 13½″ (closed); 40½″ (opened). Depth: 29″.

Locality and Period
Philadelphia. c. 1770–85. Variations made in other centers.

Comment
Elaborately curved tabletops were a hallmark of the major Philadelphia cabinetmakers. The tapering legs indicate that the piece was made in the 1770s or 1780s, when Neoclassicism was becoming influential. Pembroke tables were used both before and after the Revolution as a decorative but practical form.

Hints for Collectors
The table shown here has the richness characteristic of elegant Chippendale pieces, but simpler tables in this style may have plain leaves and legs. To make certain that a drawer has not been replaced, check to see that its wood, style, and patina match those of the table.

Federal Pembroke table

Description
Table with 2 rectangular drop leaves. Simple top and leaves with straight plain edges; leaves supported by brackets that swing out from skirt. Skirt unfinished under leaves; single drawer at finished narrow end has oval pull and plain rail supporting drawer. Legs tapered and square. *Variations:* Elegant inlaid decoration may be used on legs and tops.

Materials and Dimensions
Walnut. Silver-plated brass pull. Height: 27½". Length: 11½" (closed). Depth: 30½".

Locality and Period
New York, New England, or Pennsylvania. c. 1800.

Comment
The term "Pembroke table" was first used in England in the 1760s and referred to small elegant tables with short rectangular leaves. It was supposedly named after a Countess of Pembroke in Wales, who first ordered it. In America, Pembroke tables were made in the Chippendale style before the Revolution, but were particularly popular in the Federal era. Made in many parts of the young Republic, their place of origin may be difficult to determine; the one shown here was originally acquired in New York State and was very likely a local product. This Hepplewhite example has the simplicity of many earlier pieces, but the tapering legs suggest a post-Revolutionary date.

Hints for Collectors
Simple designs like this one are easier to duplicate than more elaborate pieces. To verify an original, check for proper discoloration from age on the undersides of tops and drawers. Fine Federal tables are readily available, but prices are rapidly approaching those usually paid for 18th-century furniture.

Shaker drop-leaf table

Description
Table with single rectangular drop leaf. Simple top and leaf with plain edges. Single long drawer at narrow end has dovetailed joints and wooden knob for drawer-pull; plain rail supporting drawer. Legs tapered and round. *Variations:* Shaker tables may have 2 leaves and no drawers. Some have square legs.

Materials and Dimensions
Cherry, maple, and pine. Height: 30″. Length: 14″ (closed); 25½″ (opened). Depth: 26″.

Locality and Period
New York or Massachusetts. c. 1820–60.

Comment
Shaker cabinetmakers, whose communities thrived in the 19th century, produced functional and handsome furniture. It is particularly appealing to some collectors because its designs and proportions are in the spirit of the 18th century rather than mid-19th century. The table shown here, made with one leaf for utilitarian purposes, looks at first glance like a Pembroke table made about 1800. However, the plain legs and simple details define it as a later Shaker piece.

Hints for Collectors
The basic simplicity and fine craftsmanship of Shaker furniture distinguish it from other restrained 19th-century forms that are sometimes mistaken for Shaker. Many fine simple examples of the period are much heavier in proportion than Shaker products because they were influenced by the Empire style, which had little effect on Shaker design. Authentic Shaker pieces are far more costly than similar designs of the period.

Turn-of-the-century expandable oak dining table

Description
Dining table with plain square top. 2 leaves under top may be pulled out to expand table. Skirt with inscribed lower border. Legs straight and fluted, tapered down to plain but prominent feet. *Variations:* Basic designs may be plain, embellished with the foliate carving prevalent at the turn of the century, or decorated in styles other than the classicism of this example. Leaves may be concealed in several different ways.

Materials and Dimensions
Oak. Height: 29″. Length: 36″. Depth: 36″ (closed); 60″ (opened).

Locality and Period
Possibly Grand Rapids. c. 1900–10.

Comment
The type of table shown here was made in great numbers after 1860, but oak became the fashionable wood for middle-level furniture only at the turn of the century. The broad fluted legs and the expandable construction of this table were inspired by French Renaissance and Neoclassical designs. This well-made piece was probably the product of one of the better midwestern factories.

Hints for Collectors
The recent popularity of turn-of-the-century oak has tempted some dealers to recondition badly damaged pieces. Furniture can be over-restored, so that basic designs are distorted. Serious collectors interested in original designs should look for gentle wear as a sign that elements have been left intact. However, many people acquire oak furniture more for its sturdiness and low price than for its designs.

Adirondack or rustic gate-leg table

Description
Gate-leg table with narrow rectangular top ending in rounded corners; 2 triangular leaves with rounded edges. Base made of logs without bark; thick legs framing galleries of 11 spindles enclosed by stretchers and rails. 2 legs swing out to support leaves. *Variations:* Surfaces may be bark-covered or bare. The range of designs is similar to that of the more finished Mission-style tables of the period. (*See also* 12 and 321.)

Materials and Dimensions
Oak and hickory. Cast-iron hinges. Height: 33½″. Length: 43½″. Depth: 40″.

Locality and Period
New York State. c. 1900–30. Similar designs made in other furniture centers.

Comment
Furniture created for summer camps in the Adirondacks and elsewhere became fashionable at the turn of the century. Much of it was made by local craftsmen, but some was produced in quantity by large shops. Though intended to look like rustic furniture made by campers, some pieces clearly were the work of experienced furnituremakers who may have been inspired by engravings of rustic 18th-century garden furniture.

Hints for Collectors
As interest in 20th-century rustic furniture has grown and prices have increased, unusual designs such as the ingenious gate-leg table shown here have been brought out of attics and into shops. Look for functional designs with pedestal bases or simple straight legs. Such rustic furniture is still found on porches in older neighborhoods all over the country and may turn up at local yard sales.

Art Deco drop-leaf dining table

Description
Table with plain rectangular top edged with stepped molding.
Single plain drop leaf hinged to top at rear. Rectangular sections
of front legs support top and are joined by recessed front skirt
decorated with sawtooth-pattern veneer along bottom edge.
Rear legs swing out to support opened leaf and are held in place
by latches under leaf. Legs octagonal and tapering to cylindrical
feet, with alternating sides of light and dark veneer. *Variations:*
Drop-leaf tables may be longer. Decorative patterns may be
more complex, with bolder stripes and several colors.

Materials and Dimensions
Mahogany and satinwood veneers over ash. Steel hinges. Height:
30″. Length: 41½″. Depth: 26″ (closed).

Locality and Period
Designed by Herbert Lippman, New York. c. 1925–30.

Comment
In the 1920s and 1930s, small homes and apartments without
dining rooms frequently had drop-leaf or expandable dining
tables that could be pushed against walls or also used as center
tables. The design shown here is one type devised to meet such a
need; it is based on Federal drop-leaf models, but updated by
omitting one leaf and adding veneers in geometric motifs.

Hints for Collectors
Much Art Deco furniture was finished with a special kind of
lacquer: what often appears to be stain is actually lacquer colored
to look like a fashionable wood. This allowed manufacturers to
use any available wood. This lacquer is difficult to match today,
so beware of chipped surfaces that will detract from the visual
effect of Art Deco shapes.

Modern expandable dining table

Description
Table with simple rectangular top having rounded edges. Flat
skirt with beveled edges; side skirts joined to leaves that pull out
and rise into position. Square legs with rounded edges and tops
hidden by skirt. *Variations:* Extension tables usually have tops
that divide and hold separate leaves, or else leaves that slide
under top but remain visible when closed.

Materials and Dimensions
Maple. Bleached. Height: 29½″. Length: 41½″ (closed).
Depth: 30″.

Locality and Period
Designed in New York by Russell Wright for his American
Modern line manufactured by the Conant Ball Company.
c. 1935–40.

Comment
One of the most famous and successful industrial designers from
the 1930s to the 1970s, Russell Wright developed a wide range of
objects for the home, from flatware and ceramics to furniture.
His furniture, such as the table shown here, was often made of
bleached, or blond, wood. Wright's designs were considered
excessively "commercial" by the followers of more innovative
designers.

Hints for Collectors
Works by well-known designers such as Wright are much sought
after by collectors. Many pieces have labels or marks under tops
or on legs; others can be attributed by comparing them to
documented examples. Since the more popular designs were
produced in quantity, they frequently turn up at garage sales
and at shops specializing in modern design.

Library, Tavern, Console, Side, Tea, and Card Tables

This section includes tables designed for specific purposes: library, tavern, console, side, tea, and card tables from the late 17th to the early 20th century. The use to which some were put is certain; library, tea, console, and card tables are all listed as such in early inventories. But the original purposes of some other designs are less clear. The term "tavern table," for example, is a later coinage based on the assumption that these were used in taverns for eating and drinking, yet they were probably also used in various ways in homes.

Library and Tavern Tables
Library tables with pedestal bases were made primarily in the 19th century; some later Mission-style examples are based on these earlier designs, except that their pedestals are transformed into bookcases or flat trestle supports. William and Mary tavern tables, with rectangular tops of various sizes, are functional designs with fashionable turned legs and low stretchers. Some later tables dating from the Queen Anne to Federal periods resemble tavern tables.

Console, Side, and Tea Tables
Tables designed to be placed against walls—console, side, and serving tables—became important forms beginning in the mid-18th century, when elegance was a major factor and paneled walls came into fashion. Console, or pier, tables were designed as architectural embellishments to be placed against a wall between windows, and were particularly popular in the Empire period. In the Federal era, when dining rooms became common, side tables were used as serving tables; if lower and semicircular, side tables also served as extensions for dining tables. Some of the finest had marble tops, which were impervious to spills. Side or serving tables were also made in later styles such as Eastlake and Art Nouveau. Tea tables are finished on all sides and may be used in the center of rooms for serving this fashionable beverage. Queen Anne and Chippendale tea tables were popular, some with galleried edges to prevent china from slipping off. After the Revolution, tea tables all but disappeared as tea prices declined and serving tea lost its glamour.

Card Tables
Card tables, used as side tables when closed, were produced in a wide variety of styles. They became common in the Queen Anne and Chippendale periods, when they had tops that unfolded to be supported on a rear leg (sometimes an added fifth leg) that swings out. The four-legged design persisted in the Federal era; but many had a pedestal base and a top that pivoted 90° when opened. Pedestal-base card tables were also made in the Empire style. Four-legged models with swivel tops were common in later 19th-century revival styles.

Collecting Hints
Condition is very important in considering all forms of tables. Moderate wear is acceptable on antique furniture and a likely sign that a piece is authentic. Excessive wear is less desirable, though such older, heavily used types as tavern tables should be expected to show greater wear. Make sure that tops, particularly hinged sections, and drawers are not replacements taken from similar pieces. Because many early designs were reproduced in the first decades of this century, carefully check the proportions, quality of carved or turned details, hardware, and patina.

Mission-style library table

Description
Library table with rectangular top made of 5 boards with simple straight edges. 2 bookshelves alongside recessed rectangular legs that support top. Narrow vertical slats placed between each pair of legs. 2 shelves project sideways from legs: upper shelf plain; lower shelf with skirt molded in same pattern as base on legs. Sides of shelves formed by square posts enclosing screens of narrow vertical slats topped by narrow rail. Plain legs; bases outlined by strips of straight-edge moldings. 4 stepped rectangular feet. *Variations:* Solid boards, sometimes in conjunction with narrow slats, were used in plainer arrangements by large-scale Mission furnituremakers (277).

Materials and Dimensions
Oak. Height: 28¾″. Length: 66″. Depth: 36″.

Locality and Period
Designed by Frank Lloyd Wright, Chicago. 1908.

Comment
The library table shown here was designed by Frank Lloyd Wright for the Ray W. Evans house in Chicago and is one of a group of pieces by Wright that are interpretations of the Mission style. Wright used straight-lined, functional Mission forms, but added subtle architectural elements such as the moldings on the base and the solid stepped feet of this table. (*See also* 336.)

Hints for Collectors
The architectural details of this table are unusual for Mission-style furniture, but other architects also created fresh interpretations that reflected the decorative tendencies of the period. Such pieces offer interesting contrasts to the typically austere Mission designs and may be overlooked by dealers and collectors looking only for conventional examples.

William and Mary tavern table

Description
Tavern table with rectangular top made of 4 boards grooved into
frame; rounded edges. Straight skirt mortised into legs; single
drawer at short end added about 1760–80. Legs topped by
rectangular blocks and shaped like turned columns broadening to
projecting bases. Rectangular lower blocks of legs mortised to
plain low stretchers. Feet very worn. *Variations:* Similar tables
are often taller. Legs may be turned in vase rather than
columnar shapes.

Materials and Dimensions
Walnut. Height: 25½". Length: 47". Depth: 36".

Locality and Period
The South. c. 1700–25. Variations made in other areas.

Comment
The William and Mary table shown here has been attributed to
the South not only because it was found there but also because
its turned legs are less delicately proportioned than those found
on better-known New England and Pennsylvania examples. This
example is relatively squat, its elements thicker than those on
most William and Mary pieces. Such characteristics are common
on southern examples made by rural cabinetmakers.

Hints for Collectors
William and Mary tables are rare, particularly examples from the
South. Thus, even though the drawer on this table is not as old
as the rest of the piece and the feet have been worn down so that
the table is shorter than it was originally, a serious collector of
southern furniture would not be deterred from buying it. Similar
designs in oak are usually English.

William and Mary tavern table

Description
Tavern table with plain rectangular top having rounded edges and broad overhang on all sides. Single front drawer framed by thin rounded strip; simple wooden pull. Plain skirt. Legs turned in double-vase-and-ring pattern. Plain stretchers, with rounded upper edges, connected to rectangular blocks of legs. Ball feet. *Variations:* Single-drawer tables sometimes have simpler drawer fronts and more complex turned legs. Legs may be slanted (or splayed), terminating in Spanish feet. Some tops are braced by narrow reinforcements grooved into the short ends.

Materials and Dimensions
Maple and pine. Height: 30″. Length: 35″. Depth: 24½″.

Locality and Period
New England. c. 1690–1730.

Comment
The type of table shown here is traditionally called a tavern table, though there is no hard evidence that such tables were used only in taverns. The basic design, with its turned legs and simple stretchers, was used for more than 50 years, and examples with thinner, more delicately turned legs were still being made in the second half of the 18th century. A good design that has always been popular, the tavern table was among the finest creations of rural cabinetmakers in the early 18th century.

Hints for Collectors
Most tavern tables have been much used over the years and show obvious signs of wear, especially on the stretchers and around the drawers. Feet should show sufficient wear, since they wear out first and may have been replaced with new ones. Tops have often been replaced, so check that their wood and patina match those of the skirt.

William and Mary tavern table

Description
Tavern table with octagonal top made from single plank shaped
into rectangle with its corners cut off. Plain skirt with rounded
bottom edges. Rectangular braces supporting tabletop under
long sides of skirt. Slanted legs double-vase-and-ring-turned.
Plain low stretchers, with rounded tops, mortised into
rectangular blocks of legs. Bun feet. *Variations:* Tops may be
rectangular and made of several planks held together by end
boards. Top supports may not be visible. Splay-leg tables may
have Spanish feet and lack stretchers.

Materials and Dimensions
Maple and pine. Height: 25″. Length: 28½″. Depth: 20″.

Locality and Period
New England. c. 1710–20.

Comment
Tavern tables with plain rectangular tops are more common than
those with octagonal ones. Cabinetmakers working in the
William and Mary style lightened the proportions of Pilgrim-
style turned elements and slanted the legs to add a note of grace.
Tables such as the one shown here are sometimes called splay-leg
tables.

Hints for Collectors
Early furniture is rare, but it sometimes turns up in surprising
places. Anecdotes abound about such pieces being used as back-
porch and kitchen furniture until discovered at yard sales by
astute collectors. Examine all parts of a piece of William and
Mary furniture for alterations, which can dramatically lower the
value of a piece.

Federal country table

Description
Table with rectangular top made of planks joined by simple tongue-and-groove construction. Plain board skirt on sides and rear, mortised into tops of legs. Front has narrow rails above and below single drawer. Wide simple drawer with border of rounded molding and small disk-shaped pull in center. Legs square and tapered. *Variations:* Legs may be plain and straight or turned; possibly reinforced by plain stretchers. Maple pieces were sometimes painted.

Materials and Dimensions
Maple. Pine and other secondary woods. Brass pull. Height: 26½". Length: 45". Depth: 20".

Locality and Period
New England. c. 1800–20.

Comment
Simple furniture like the table shown here is regarded as country furniture, though much of it was probably made in urban furniture centers. The records of many cabinetmakers of the period show that their work ranged from such plain country designs to more elegant ones. This simple table was made to be functional rather than decorative and may have been used in a kitchen, shop, or office. Its plain brass drawer-pull is characteristic of early 19th-century furniture.

Hints for Collectors
The best simple furniture has subtle details such as the tapering legs and the border around the drawer on this table. Since simple furniture is easy to imitate, this is an area where fakery is common. Turn a piece upside down and take the drawer out: the wood under the top should be uniformly darkened from age and should not have circular saw marks made by a rotary saw.

Queen Anne country table

Description
Table with rectangular top edged by convex molding and
fastened to skirt by flat wooden braces. Plain skirt has molded
lower edge. 2 drawers of unequal sizes with simple brass pulls
and molded edges. Legs topped by square sections and ring
turnings over tapering cylinders curving out to pad feet.
Variations: Equal-size drawers are more common. Legs may be
curved in cabriole shape.

Materials and Dimensions
Walnut and pine. Brass pulls. Height: 28¾". Length: 48¼".
Depth: 33¼".

Locality and Period
Pennsylvania. c. 1750–1800. Variations made in other areas.

Comment
The table shown here is not as early as it first appears. Although
pad feet, simple drawers, and overall simplicity suggest an
earlier date, the brass pulls and the simply turned legs indicate a
date closer to 1800. Country pieces like this are difficult to date
because country cabinetmakers were conservative and usually
used elements already out of fashion. The heavy proportions and
use of walnut are clues to this table's Pennsylvania origin. Plain
country pieces from other areas are more often made of maple or
pine, and many, particularly those from New England, are
lighter in proportion.

Hints for Collectors
Simple country furnishings were usually heavily used and may no
longer be in acceptable condition or have perhaps been over-
restored. Make certain the drawers fit well, since they have
often been replaced with those from other pieces.

Description
Table with rectangular top; shallow gallery, made of strips of wood, rounded on upper edge. Recessed drawer suspended from top, with plain sides and dovetailed joints; simple round wooden pull. Legs, forming X's on sides, taper from center to ends. Single stretcher connecting intersections of legs; stretcher thicker in center and at ends. *Variations:* Larger tables also had galleried tops for seeds. Many seed tables look like 18th-century pedestal-based candlestands with shallow galleries.

Materials and Dimensions
Maple and pine. Height: 22½". Length: 22¾". Depth: 15¾".

Locality and Period
New York or New England. c. 1820–60.

Comment
Shaker furniture is distinguished by functional and restrained design partly inspired by 18th-century forms. Shaker craftsmen deliberately avoided the heavier ornate fashions of the 1820s to 1860s. The seed table shown here, so simple to make and so practical, is surprisingly rare because of its X-patterned legs. The seed industry was an important source of income for the Shakers, and they used such tables to sort seeds and put them in envelopes.

Hints for Collectors
A typical Shaker piece is simply designed, well finished, and without superfluous ornament. Since many reproductions of good quality are still made, collectors should not confuse these with original Shaker pieces. Look for the proper patina and beware of crisp edges, which should have been softened by a century of wear.

Shaker trestle table

Description
Trestle table with rectangular top made of 2 long boards with slightly rounded edges. Top braced by long rectangular reinforcement and short cross braces on underside. 2 wishbone-shaped trestle supports broaden at top and base and have gently rounded edges. Pairs of legs arching out to floor, terminating in projecting flat feet. 6 iron diagonal braces are later additions. *Variations:* Shaker trestle tables may have different kinds of wooden or metal bracing for the legs. Stretchers may also be used.

Materials and Dimensions
Maple and oak. Wrought-iron braces. Height: 29½". Length: 72". Depth: 31".

Locality and Period
New England or New York. c. 1820–60.

Comment
The table shown here exemplifies Shaker craftsmanship before 1860, which consistently favored simplicity of design. With its very plain top and simple supports that are smoothed and rounded into an almost sculpturesque appearance, the design is practical and handsome, echoing traditional designs while anticipating modern Scandinavian furniture of the 1950s.

Hints for Collectors
Look for a combination of subtle detailing and striking understatement in the best Shaker furniture. Not every simple 19th-century piece was made in a Shaker community: beware of frills such as carved or molded details—which were scorned by the Shakers—when paying a premium price for a supposedly Shaker article.

Art Deco side or console table

Description
Console table with rectangular top painted green on sides.
Recessed skirt covered by undulating wrought-iron strip. Top
set on rectangular pillar, with front ends chamfered and
lacquered. Wrought-iron strips, angled from chamfered ends of
pillar, curve down from tabletop and end in scrolls set on flat
platforms on table base. Rectangular base with painted
chamfered edges. Flat square feet. *Variations:* Iron and wood
were also combined in more traditional pieces of the period.

Materials and Dimensions
Maple. Painted. Wrought-iron braces and skirt. Height: 28½″.
Length: 42″. Depth: 13¾″.

Locality and Period
Designed by Jules Bouy, New York. c. 1930.

Comment
Jules Bouy was trained in Belgium and was best known for his
metalwork and lamps. The table shown here, part of a dining
room set (*see also* 148), was used both as a side table and as an
extension to a dining table, just as some side tables had been
used for both purposes during the Federal era. This table,
remarkably simple in its materials and shape, achieves some
degree of elegance through its iron braces and painted trim.

Hints for Collectors
American Art Deco pieces can be distinguished from their
French counterparts by their more economical use of decorative
elements such as paint, lacquer, and metalwork. Many simple
crisp designs of the 1920s and 1930s have stains and lacquers that
are difficult to restore. Select a restorer who is aware of the
problems involved in repairing modern materials.

Mission-style library trestle table

Description
Library table with rectangular top made of 4 boards joined by splines, with plain outer edges. Top set on 2 shaped rails atop pairs of plain boards ending in feet shaped like top rails. Shelf made of 2 boards mortised through legs and arched at ends, with keys as reinforcements on outside. *Variations:* Rectangular tables with shelves often have drawers. Square legs are more common than the flat board legs seen here.

Materials and Dimensions
Oak. Height: 28″. Length: 48″. Depth: 30″.

Locality and Period
Probably designed by Gustav Stickley, New York. c. 1900–15.

Comment
Gustav Stickley's Mission-style designs represented a revolt against machine-made furniture. They were related to the designs of the Arts and Crafts movement of the late 19th century in England, but they differed in that Stickley's strictly functional furniture was designed less for art's sake and was based more closely on the sturdy and primitive forms found in medieval furniture. Stickley's designs were executed in a factory outside Syracuse, but he also provided designs for home production through his magazine *The Craftsman*. Designs such as the one shown here were simple enough to be carried out by amateurs.

Hints for Collectors
Mission oak designs, ranging from factory products to homemade creations, are quite sturdy and now attract many collectors. Check the underside of a tabletop or chair seat for a label or maker's mark; if present, it will add to the value of the piece. Mission furniture came with light or dark stains; original finishes are preferable.

Empire mirrored console or pier table

Description
Console or pier table with straight-edged marble top. Straight skirt with gilded lyres at front ends and elaborate swan-and-scroll design in center. 2 Ionic capitals on plain columns in front, 2 engaged columns behind. Mirrored back. Thick shelf curved in front with leaf border on top and leaf-and-rosette design in front. Gilded acanthus-leaf carving on front legs; ball feet topped by rings. *Variations:* Marble columns may be used; also lion's-paw feet. Ormolu, rather than gilding, was often used on skirt. White marble tops were most common.

Materials and Dimensions
Mahogany and poplar. Painted and gilded. Marble top. Mirror. Height: 36½". Length: 42". Depth: 18".

Locality and Period
Possibly designed by Charles-Honoré Lannuier, New York. c. 1810. Variations made in other centers.

Comment
The console or pier table was a standard Empire form from about 1810 to 1840. Often used in a hall or placed between windows in a parlor, it was also the right height for use in a dining room as a serving table. New York examples, such as the one shown here, were often simply designed but featured elegant ormolu or painted decoration. In Philadelphia, designs were more elaborate, with scrolls replacing columns and bottom shelves cut in more complex patterns. (*See also* 229.)

Hints for Collectors
Do not be misled by Empire Revival designs from the end of the 19th century: they are usually very simple, with rough carving, and sometimes with drawers, which are very rare on examples from 1810–40.

Art Nouveau side table

Description
Side table with plain rectangular top edged with concave molding and projecting over skirt. Skirt forms arched bracket with legs; brackets on long sides have carved leaf decoration; short sides have 2 applied disks. 2 turned balusters suspended from skirt to shelf below; shelf straight on 3 sides and curved on fourth. Gallery of straight spindles topped by molded rail mortised into legs above shelf at one end and under shelf at other end. Straight legs with inscribed outlines. Feet rounded and leaf-carved; casters. *Variations:* Carving may be more elaborate.

Materials and Dimensions
Oak. Iron casters. Height: 31½″. Length: 36″. Depth: 18″.

Locality and Period
Grand Rapids. c. 1900–10. Variations made in other centers.

Comment
Oak was the most popular wood for turn-of-the-century furniture, and manufacturers used it for virtually every style. The carving and straight legs on the table shown here suggest the influence of the international Art Nouveau style, tempered to suit American tastes: the table is heavier in proportion than typical Art Nouveau pieces and the gallery is a familiar element derived from exotic American designs of the 1880s and 1890s.

Hints for Collectors
Vintage oak furniture is currently enjoying a renaissance, in part because it is sturdier and more practical than today's department-store furniture. This has resulted in much reworking of damaged oak furniture to make it more salable. Examine joints as well as the overall design to see that elements have not been replaced or added.

Description
Ebonized side table with rectangular top edged by curved
stepped molding. Straight skirt embellished with flat-carved
frieze and mortised into legs. Curved piecework brackets
connecting skirt and legs. Legs turned in elongated ball-and-ring
patterns in central section; straight-sided and scroll-shaped in
lower part. Galleried side stretchers with blocks and turned
spindles; stretchers mortised to narrow plank shelf with
matching gallery. Square feet on iron casters. *Variations:*
Ebonized tables may have bamboo- or vase-turned elements.

Materials and Dimensions
Maple and pine. Ebonized. Iron casters. Height: 29″. Length:
30¼″. Depth: 19″.

Locality and Period
Probably New York. c. 1880. Variations made in other cities.

Comment
Ebonized tables from the 1880s reflect the reform ideas of
Charles Eastlake; they are often called Anglo-Japanese since
they follow an Orientalizing trend that was part of the English
Aesthetic Movement. Though simply made, the table shown here
may well have been the product of one of several New York
furnituremakers who kept up with the latest fashions during the
1870s and 1880s.

Hints for Collectors
Collectors may learn about ebonized Eastlake furniture from the
illustrated catalogues published by manufacturers and retailers
beginning in the 1870s; such catalogues may be available at
libraries and museums specializing in Victorian decorative arts.
Beware of tables that have been simplified by the removal of
damaged galleries or finials.

Eastlake side table

Description
Side table with rectangular top having molded overhanging
edges. Base made of 4 legs with rectangular tops mortised to
skirt. Side panels and front drawer grooved in linear pattern and
supported by molded rails; 2 brass drawer-pulls. Grooved
triangular brackets connecting rails and legs. Legs turned in
tapering columnar or trumpet shape, with bulbous ring-turned
capitals and set of rings in middle. Lower rectangular blocks of
legs mortised to block-turned stretchers. Side stretchers hold flat
shelf with cutout arched ends. Spool-turned feet. *Variations:*
Leg turnings may be simple or more complex.

Materials and Dimensions
Walnut and pine. Brass pulls. Height: 29½″. Length: 30″. Depth:
19½″.

Locality and Period
Grand Rapids, New York, or other centers. c. 1875–90.

Comment
Conservative furnituremakers working in the Eastlake style
diluted this innovative approach with classical elements: the
columnar legs on the table shown here are close to those found on
earlier Renaissance Revival tables, but instead of having
inscribed leaves as capitals, it has lathe-turned rings. Its maker
utilized his machines to achieve simple decoration instead of
trying to imitate Renaissance Revival carving.

Hints for Collectors
Look for outstanding designs based on the Eastlake furniture
approach: according to Eastlake, simple cherry or oak designs
with turnings and no carving are most desirable. However, many
American examples, including this one, were made of different
woods. Wood type, in any case, is less important than design.

Queen Anne country tea table

Description
Tea table with plain rectangular top having sharp straight edges. Skirt with 2 simply curved arches on each side. Ends of skirt mortised into legs; visible reinforcing pegs holding tenons in mortise holes. Single long drawer on a narrow side of skirt, with small round pull. Legs turned and slanted, with rectangular tops and simple ring turnings; legs flaring out just below skirt and tapering to bun feet. *Variations:* Country tables made of maple were frequently painted. Tops are sometimes thicker, with raised borders to suggest a tray. Legs may be thicker, and feet in plain pad shapes.

Materials and Dimensions
Maple. Height: 32″. Length: 26″. Depth: 16″.

Locality and Period
New England. c. 1730–90.

Comment
The table shown here is a fine example of a country tea table made in the spirit of the Queen Anne style. Simple 18th-century tables such as this may be difficult to date. The skirt is arched in a way that was popular in the 1720s, but most of the details are too plain and delicate for this early date.

Hints for Collectors
Country furniture is more valuable when it has its original paint or stain. If you wish to restore this color, check for remnants of early paint or stain. Country furniture is generally less expensive than the finest fashionable pieces, but in recent years important country pieces have been commanding higher prices than many high-style examples.

83 Queen Anne country tea table

Description
Tea table with oval top having rounded edges and set on rectangular base. Skirt rails straight-bottomed but cut at corners in stepped pattern to emphasize legs mortised to them. Legs turned and tapered below rectangular top sections. Small pad feet. *Variations:* Similar designs have rectangular tops, or circular tilt tops on pedestal bases. Skirts may be arched. Legs may be cabriole, with larger pad feet.

Materials and Dimensions
Maple. Height: 26″. Length: 34″. Depth: 27″.

Locality and Period
New England. c. 1740.

Comment
The simply made country table shown here displays the straight skirt, pad feet, and overall lightness of the Queen Anne style, combined with old-fashioned William and Mary elements, such as the cutout skirt corners and turned legs, to suit rural taste. This is a typical product of rural New England cabinetmakers, who adapted fashionable details but could not afford to expend too much time on pieces.

Hints for Collectors
The authenticity of simple 18th-century furniture is more open to question than are high-style pieces; since it was easily made, it is easy to fake or alter. Examine the undersides of tops for signs of recent manufacture, such as raw wood or freshly stained surfaces, and check for correct proportions and authentic Colonial construction. Fakes rarely capture the consistent grace of the early rural pieces.

Description
Side table with top having curved sides, projecting corners, and arched front. Skirt repeats shape of top, but concave front corners hold tops of legs; veneered borders and elaborate graining on skirt. Round legs with fluted tops in front and plain rectangular tops in rear. Legs have ring-turned capitals and reeded main sections tapering to lower rings. Flattened balls top cylindrical feet. *Variations:* Side tables often have marble tops. Carved capitals on legs were frequently used. Straight-sided examples were also common.

Materials and Dimensions
Mahogany, mahogany veneer, and pine. Height: 34″. Length: 45½″. Depth: 18″.

Locality and Period
Massachusetts. c. 1800.

Comment
The side table is a relatively tall table intended to stand against a wall as a pier table in a hallway or as a serving table in a dining room. The example shown here has round reeded legs typical of Massachusetts tables. The basic shape was inspired by Sheraton designs and was included in price books published by cabinetmakers in England and America.

Hints for Collectors
Unusual forms like this tall side table, though not easily found, add to the scope of a collection. Check for signs of age, such as the cracking of veneer due to shrinkage of the base wood to which it is glued (*see* cover). If a side table has a marble top, make sure it is original: the underside of the marble should have a discolored outline from the frame, and if the top has been replaced, this outline would be lacking or askew.

Federal side table

Description
Side table with half-oval marble top; edge of top rounded and stepped. Curved skirt with inlaid decoration set in 4 wide panels flanking narrow central area; oval outlines in wide panels and light-colored cross-shaped motif in center. Legs square and tapered, with inlaid bellflower ornament. Plain feet. *Variations:* Federal tables are often more elaborate, with round legs and some carving.

Materials and Dimensions
Mahogany and pine. Variegated black and white marble. Height: 32″. Length: 45″. Depth: 17½″.

Locality and Period
New York. c. 1795–1810.

Comment
Marble-topped Federal-era tables are rare; the example shown here was inspired by Hepplewhite designs. Though restrained in ornamentation, this table is nonetheless a very elegant example of Federal design. The inlaid decoration on this piece is strongly suggestive of New York craftsmanship: the bellflower decoration is similar to that found on the legs of sideboards and card tables known to have been made by New York cabinetmakers.

Hints for Collectors
Semicircular tables, usually with wooden tops and about 28″ tall, were often designed to serve several purposes: they could be used in parlors as pier tables, or in dining rooms as side and serving tables or as table ends to be added to dining tables for large parties. This piece is particularly rare and valuable because it is taller than most examples and marble-topped.

Federal card table

Description
Card table with semicircular top that flips open to complete circle. Plain edge with inlaid borders. Curved skirt has 3 sections, with inlaid border along lower edge and 3 rectangular outlines. Skirt has 2 inlaid pateras framed by lightwood rectangles above legs. Single drawer outlined by center panel; octagonal brass handle. Skirt panels mortised into legs. Single rear leg swings out to support top. Square tapered legs topped by small inlaid disks; vertical borders. Plain feet. *Variations:* Inlays are generally more complex. Fifth leg may be added to support top. Bracket-reinforced Marlborough legs and other Chippendale elements may be incorporated.

Materials and Dimensions
Mahogany. Possibly also maple and pine. Lightwood inlay. Brass handle. Felt. Height: 28¾″. Length: 36″. Depth: 18″ (closed).

Locality and Period
Rhode Island. c. 1785–1800. Variations made in other centers.

Comment
Round card tables inspired by Hepplewhite designs are rare because Americans favored more complex shapes during the Federal era. Nonetheless, some circular card tables were made in Boston, New York, Philadelphia, and Rhode Island. Rhode Island examples are most elegant because of their fine inlay, often more elaborate than that on the table shown here.

Hints for Collectors
Round Hepplewhite card tables from America may be easily confused with those from England. Check the secondary woods: pine was most commonly used in this country, while oak and ash were more prevalent in England. American inlay is usually crisper in outline than English inlay.

Renaissance Revival card table

Description
Card table with folding top having molded stepped edge; straight sides flanked by curves with projecting triangles at corners. Open top rotates 90° to be securely positioned. Front skirt decorated at center with shell-scroll-leaf motif; bottom edge curved and molded. Rectangular corner panels with projecting molding. Tapering columnar legs with large carved capitals and lower ring turnings. Ball feet on casters. *Variations:* Carved decoration may vary considerably.

Materials and Dimensions
Walnut. Brass casters. Fabric-covered inner top. Height: 30″. Length: 36″. Depth: 17¾″ (closed).

Locality and Period
New York, Boston, or Salem, Massachusetts. c. 1850.

Comment
The Renaissance Revival style was introduced about 1850 as an alternate to the Rococo Revival; furniture in the newer style was often decorated in high relief, as on the table shown here. The finer examples in the style may have been made in New York, a center of fashionable furniture production, but there were skilled cabinetmakers in Boston and Salem as well as other cities. This table is a combination of true Renaissance motifs with Neoclassical designs. Positioning the open top by a 90° rotation was a practical innovation often seen on 19th-century card tables.

Hints for Collectors
Renaissance Revival furniture is not in great demand, so excellent examples are available at reasonable prices to collectors who hunt for them. This table is an unusually fine piece, against which potential acquisitions might be measured.

Federal card table

Description
Card table with folding top having curved projecting center area and rounded projecting corners. Top finished at edges, with rounded molding enclosed by straight strips above and below. Rear leg swings out to support opened top. Rounded legs fluted at top and set into round corners of skirt; vase-and-ring-turned capitals. Legs reeded and tapering to arrow feet. *Variations:* Carved leaf ornaments may be used on the capitals or upper legs just under the top. Tops and skirts may be subtly curved across the entire front. Rare examples have carved panels in the center of their skirts.

Materials and Dimensions
Mahogany and white pine. Height: 29″. Length: 36″. Depth: 16″ (closed).

Locality and Period
Boston. c. 1795–1820. Similar models made in other centers.

Comment
Originally called square card tables, designs like the one shown here followed a Sheraton model that was fashionable in Boston and Salem. Card tables were never more popular than in the Federal era, when they had delicate lines and handsome graining. Tastes changed after 1815 and square card tables were produced with thicker legs and wider reeding.

Hints for Collectors
Since these tables are relatively common, collectors should be selective and look for interesting and balanced details. This table is particularly successful because of its light reeding and gracefully turned capitals. Such slender legs are, however, easily cracked or broken and must be checked for repairs that may not hold.

Queen Anne tea table

Description
Rectangular tea table with plain top bordered by shallow gallery
that is concave inside and convex outside. Plain skirt with half-
round molding around lower edge. Cabriole legs plain, with
sharp edge at corner curving down from knee. Slipper feet.
Variations: Galleries may be convex on the inside as well as
outside. Pad feet may be used instead of slipper feet.

Materials and Dimensions
Mahogany. Height: 26¼″. Length: 29½″. Depth: 19½″.

Locality and Period
Newport, Rhode Island. c. 1730–60.

Comment
Tea tables were particularly popular in the mid- and late 18th
century. The Queen Anne version shown here is restrained but
very elegant: the curve of the gallery, the profile of the molding
around the skirt, and the cut of the legs are all subtle details that
might be overlooked. All are signs of the fine craftsmanship
characteristic of Newport, one of the major 18th-century
cabinetmaking centers.

Hints for Collectors
The graceful lines of restrained American pieces are often
lacking in English examples that are their Old World equivalents.
Americans used mahogany as well as cherry and a few other local
woods for simple elegant furniture, while English cabinetmakers
often used oak. Queen Anne tea tables as fine as this one are not
common. Collectors should bear this and other elegant 18th-
century examples in mind so as not to mistake more primitive
19th-century pieces for the high-style originals.

Queen Anne card table

Description
Card table with top leaf hinged in rear. Concave sides and front of top, with rounded edges and projecting round front corners. Opened top covered with baize; circular depressions at corners to hold glasses, and oval ones for counters. Recessed skirt follows outline of top. Front panel forms drawer front that pulls forward from underneath. Rear leg hinged to skirt with wooden pin to allow it to swing out to support opened leaf. Legs simplified cabriole forms. Flared pad feet. *Variations:* Skirts and knees of legs may have carved embellishments.

Materials and Dimensions
Mahogany and pine. Baize-covered top. Height: 28″. Length: 32″. Depth: 16″ (closed).

Locality and Period
Philadelphia. c. 1740–60. Variations made in other Colonial centers.

Comment
Identifying a table with a simple design and little or no carving or detailing can be complicated. The table shown here closely follows an English Queen Anne model, but the curve of the top is like that on other, more obviously American tables, and the use of pine as a secondary wood also supports this American attribution. Plain cabriole legs as straight as these are found on tables made in New England as well as Philadelphia, although the top is distinctively Philadelphian in outline.

Hints for Collectors
Check secondary woods where there is a problem of attribution: American pieces almost always use pine. Beware of imitations since simple designs like this Queen Anne table are easily copied and have been reproduced since about 1910.

Chippendale 5-legged card table

Description
Card table with top leaf hinged in rear. Straight sides and front of top, with round projecting front corners (corners have circular depressions on inner side to hold glasses when top is opened). Recessed skirt with arched lower edge on sides; double arch in front with carved shell in center. Unfinished skirt in rear with extra section dovetailed to fifth leg so that it can swing out to support opened leaf. Legs with rectangular tops mortised into skirt panels. Cabriole legs with leaf carving on knees. Claw-and-ball feet. *Variations:* Skirt may conform to the outline of the top. Examples with 5 legs are rarer than those with 4.

Materials and Dimensions
Mahogany and pine. Height: 28″. Length: 33″. Depth: 16″ (closed).

Locality and Period
Philadelphia. c. 1760–70. Variations made in New York and other Colonies.

Comment
The products of many major Colonial furniture centers are recognizable by certain consistent characteristics. The Philadelphia origin of the table shown here is suggested by its overall appearance, and specifically by the depth of the skirt, the large overhang of the top, the curve of the cabriole legs, and the squat balls and detailing of the claws of the feet.

Hints for Collectors
Make sure all parts of a Chippendale table are solid. Legs that curve strangely may have been broken, and a dark finish may conceal a glued repair. Hinged tops may have been replaced: both portions of a top should match in wood, patina, and shaping.

Chippendale 5-legged card table

Description
Card table with top leaf hinged in center. Undulating sides and front with rounded edges and projecting square front corners. Opened top covered with felt, with square depressions at corners to hold candles, and oval ones for counters. Recessed skirt follows outline of top; added molding as lower border. Fifth leg swings out to support opened leaf. Cabriole legs with leaf carving at knees. Claw-and-ball feet. *Variations:* Sides may be more or less curved. 4-legged card tables were more common outside of New York. Legs may be straight in Chinese Chippendale style.

Materials and Dimensions
Mahogany, poplar, and maple. Felt. Height: 28″. Length: 34″. Depth: 33″ (opened).

Locality and Period
New York. c. 1765. Variations made in other Colonial centers.

Comment
Card games for 4 players, particularly whist, were very popular in the 18th century. Although card, or gaming, tables were made in England beginning in the 17th century, pre-Revolutionary American examples like the one shown here are rare, and are usually in the Queen Anne style. New York craftsmen produced the sturdiest and handsomest card tables, many with 5 legs.

Hints for Collectors
Though rare and valuable, fine Chippendale card tables are available from time to time at finer antiques shops around the country. Condition is extremely important in fashionable 18th-century furniture; handsome surfaces undergo a natural aging process that cannot be duplicated.

Rococo Revival card table

Description
Card table with plain folding top having undulating sides and
stepped molding along edge; hinged in center and felt-covered
when opened. Curved skirt with scrolled lower edge and carved
leaf motif in center front; rear skirt plain. Single half-length
drawer concealed on side. Carved cabriole legs curving in 2-part
molded scroll design. Front legs joined to similar rear legs by top
rails and curving stretchers. Rear legs on brass casters swing
out to support unfolded top. *Variations:* Tops usually turn 90°
when opened, making swinging legs unnecessary.

Materials and Dimensions
Rosewood. Felt. Brass casters. Height: 30″. Length: 46″. Depth:
32″ (opened).

Locality and Period
Made by Charles Badouine, New York. c. 1850.

Comment
Charles Badouine was a highly successful cabinetmaker whose
workshop produced a variety of very fashionable Rococo Revival
furniture. The card table shown here is unusual because of its
swinging cabriole legs meant to support the opened top; it is a
fine expression of the style that predominated in elegant homes
all over the country during the mid-19th century.

Hints for Collectors
Rococo Revival designs ranged from restrained to elaborate.
This superb table, elegant yet not flamboyant, is pure Rococo. It
is beautifully executed and a good indicator of the high quality
that collectors should seek. Some collectors may prefer Rococo
designs with less delicate lines and more floral carving, which
have their own particular charm.

Empire double-pedestal-base card table

Description
Double-pedestal-base card table with rectangular top made of 2 hinged leaves to be turned 90° when opened. Top has undulating molded edge. Skirt conforms to outline of top and is veneered on front and sides; narrow edge of contrasting veneer. 2 trestlelike supports, flat-sided in front and rear, curving in outline on sides, and shaped in silhouette like dolphins with 2 scrolled fins. Supports set on flat-sided curving legs reinforced by arched stretcher with urn finial and floral carving in center and drop below. Casters. *Variations:* Skirt may be boxlike with an enclosed bottom, and may have added decorative elements such as gadrooned molding. Supports and bases are sometimes more complexly curved.

Materials and Dimensions
Mahogany, mahogany veneer, and pine. Brass casters. Height: 29½″. Length: 34½″. Depth: 19″ (closed).

Locality and Period
Throughout the United States. c. 1830–50.

Comment
Standard Empire designs became more curvilinear in the 1830s and 1840s as the Empire style was being replaced by the Rococo Revival; the table shown here has elements of both styles. Its embellishments were easily executed; sawing rather than carving was used to produce the curvilinear elements.

Hints for Collectors
The value of relatively simple Empire furniture like this table depends heavily on its condition, because its basic effect requires finely grained surfaces without any chips or other damage. Whereas a patina is usually appealing on earlier designs, many Empire designs demand near-pristine condition.

Federal lyre-base card table

Description
Lyre-base card table with rectangular top having its corners cut off; veneered straight edges. Opened top turns 90°. Skirt plain but veneered, with brass-strip molding along lower edge; boarded at bottom to create shallow storage area. Double-lyre support with leaf-carved scrolls ending in flowers; brass rods as lyre strings. Lyres set on 4-legged base having rectangular center block with chamfered corners; block has raised panels and upper edge covered with brass-strip molding. Legs curving down and angled from chamfered corners; carved in waterleaf pattern and tapering. Lion's-paw feet on casters. *Variations:* Lyres may be simpler. Legs may have fluting and no carving. Feet may be brass. Details may be ebony instead of brass.

Materials and Dimensions
Mahogany, mahogany veneer, pine, and cherry. Brass details and casters. Height: 29¾". Length: 35⅞". Depth: 17⅞" (closed).

Locality and Period
New York. c. 1815. Variations made in other centers.

Comment
The type of card table shown here was particularly popular in New York, where the contrast between brass and dark wood was favored. New York cabinetmakers also favored plain surfaces contrasted with intricate waterleaf carving, as seen here.

Hints for Collectors
After decades of being relatively ignored, Federal furniture at its most elegant is attracting collectors again. The next decade should offer great opportunities to acquire some of the finest Federal examples as heightened interest and prices bring more and more pieces on the market.

Empire pedestal-base card table

Description
Pedestal-base card table with rectangular top having rounded front corners and molded edges. Hinged top unfolds and swings 90° to function as card-table top. Concave skirt encloses shallow storage area for cards and counters, accessible when top is turned. Plain pedestal shaped as tapered column with molded collar at juncture with base. 4-sided base concave at front and rear, serpentine on sides, with projecting squared corners. Flattened ball feet large and squat. *Variations:* Pedestals may be more elaborate and vase-shaped, sometimes carved in pineapple or leaf pattern. Skirt may be flat.

Materials and Dimensions
Mahogany and mahogany veneer over pine. Brass hinges. Height: 28″. Length: 34¾″. Depth: 17″ (closed).

Locality and Period
New York, Philadelphia, Boston, or other centers. c. 1825–40.

Comment
Among Empire designs for card tables, pedestal-base models like the one shown here were among the most popular. A restrained but heavy form, it was an ideal expression of the style. An awareness of current fashions began to spread in the 1820s, so elegant but modestly priced tables like this were produced in quantity.

Hints for Collectors
Empire designs reproduced or adapted at the end of the 19th century are deceptive, so check the undersides of the top and base for such signs of factory manufacture as metal braces and circular saw marks. Mediocre designs are often as expensive as fine ones, so weigh the merits of a table's construction, design, and decoration.

Empire pedestal-base card table

Description
Pedestal-base card table with rectangular top having rounded
corners and veneered border. Hinged top swings 90° when
opened. Edges of top have brass line inlays; opened top baize-
covered. Recessed skirt with brass inlay along lower edge and
ormolu ornament of Cupid in chariot pulled by swans in center.
Skirt covered on bottom to enclose storage space. Pedestal is
plain tapered column with textured ormolu collar at bottom.
X-shaped base with circular ends; band of brass inlay in
continuous X pattern, flanked by line inlays above and below.
Cylindrical feet with gilded leaf-and-ring design, set on casters.
Variations: Decoration may be simpler, with stenciled ornament.

Materials and Dimensions
Rosewood. Brass inlay and ormolu. Gilding. Baize covering.
Brass casters. Height: 29½". Length: 34½". Depth: 17" (closed).

Locality and Period
Possibly made by Duncan Phyfe, New York. c. 1825.

Comment
The bold simple lines of the Empire card table shown here
suggest the influence of the Restauration style that flourished in
France from 1815 to 1830. The striking brass inlays, though
uncomplicated, are evidence of highly skilled craftsmanship, so it
is tempting to attribute this table to the finest workshop in New
York, that of Duncan Phyfe.

Hints for Collectors
Empire design is often disconcerting to a modern eye because its
scale is so much heavier than most American furniture,
particularly contemporary design. If possible, look for details as
fine as those on this exceptional table. Light proportions are
often a sign of a later revival piece.

Center, Coffee, End, and Related Tables

Center tables—round, oval, rectangular, or shaped medium-size tables finished on all sides so they may be used in the center of a room—are mainly a 19th-century form, whereas coffee and end tables date from the 20th century.

Center Tables

Center tables provide evidence of the shift from function to decoration that occurred during the last century. During the 17th and 18th centuries, even the most sumptuous American tables were conceived with function as the main consideration. However, the elaborate decoration and massive scale of the center tables first introduced in the Empire era made them the focal points of rooms, where they were clearly designed to complement the architecture. In later works the ornamental aspect is given even more attention, so that flamboyant Rococo and Renaissance Revival center tables are among the most elaborate ever made. The more elegant 19th-century center tables, often marble-topped, have intricate carving or turnings, ebonized and gilded decoration, and ingenious combinations of classical, exotic, and naturalistic motifs.

Center tables were generally part of parlor sets. Double-duty center tables, also serving as dining or sofa tables, were introduced in the first half of the 19th century, when many homes lacked separate dining rooms. Wicker was also used for all-purpose tables; first made in the 1840s, they remained popular into the 20th century and were usually mass-produced. Simple iron-wire and Mission-style tables were produced about the turn of the century. In the 1920s and 1930s, designers and manufacturers experimented with new materials such as metal and glass in modern shapes inspired either by innovative Bauhaus models or more traditional Art Deco forms.

Coffee, End, and Related Tables

In the 18th and for most of the 19th century, round or oval tables used in front of sofas were made full height. Toward the end of the last century, eclectic interiors often had low trays or stands in the Moorish or Chinese style placed in front of sofas or near chairs. After 1915, these were replaced by low coffee tables in the prevailing revival styles. Art Deco and modern designers in particular favored low coffee tables, frequently with glass tops, indicating that a major purpose was for serving beverages. End tables for flanking sofas and holding lamps are another relatively recent invention, primarily part of 20th-century parlor sets.

Collecting Hints

Center, coffee, and related tables from the 19th and 20th centuries are available in varied styles and levels of elegance. Most Eastlake, turn-of-the-century oak, Art Deco, and modern forms are readily found. Long-neglected early and mid-19th-century designs, particularly pieces attributed to important makers working in the Empire and revival styles, have been attracting more and more collectors in recent years.

Eastlake center table

Description
Center table with rectangular marble top having molded edges and chamfered corners. Top projects over similarly shaped skirt decorated with incised panels flanking center rosette. Cutout valance with 2 turned drops suspended from center of each side. Central pedestal turned in cylinder-and-vase shape, joined to 4 scroll-shaped legs arching to support top; rosettes near junctures with column. Lines and dots incised on upper sections of legs; panels of veneer on lower sections of legs. Feet decorated with rosettes; iron casters. *Variations:* Scroll-shaped legs are often simpler.

Materials and Dimensions
Walnut and walnut veneer. Marble. Iron casters. Height: 29½".
Length: 28½". Depth: 20½".

Locality and Period
Grand Rapids or other factory centers. c. 1875–90.

Comment
The simple construction of the table shown here, with its 4 cutout scroll-shaped legs braced into a center pedestal, suggests that it was produced on an assembly line. Its decoration is effective because the incised linear patterns and flat relief carving are executed with some precision. While this kind of design is commonly called Eastlake, the rosettes and the use of veneers reflect the Renaissance Revival style.

Hints for Collectors
Eastlake furniture is readily available in most parts of the country and, particularly the factory products, relatively inexpensive. Many mass-produced examples are quite well made and based on fine designs. Look for pieces with good proportions and original finish.

Renaissance Revival center table

Description
Oval center table with inlaid floral medallion in center of top, framed by elaborate linear border; edge molded and ebonized. Skirt with panels having ebonized borders and inscribed gilded decoration. Legs on long sides vase-shaped and reinforced by complex turned brackets attached to drops on skirt; turnip feet. Legs on short sides cabriole, with ebonized and gilded caryatids on knees; tapered square feet. Cross stretchers support urn at center. *Variations:* Tops are often painted. Legs of a table are usually alike; simpler brackets.

Materials and Dimensions
Walnut and walnut veneer. Satinwood inlay. Ebonized and gilded. Height: 29½". Length: 40½". Depth: 26½".

Locality and Period
The Midwest, probably Grand Rapids. c. 1870–85.

Comment
Renaissance Revival furnishings fall into 2 categories: those employing traditional techniques such as fine carving and marquetry, and those employing innovative decorative and construction techniques. The table shown here is one of the latter, since its complex decoration was a product of ingenious turning and cutting rather than fine craftsmanship.

Hints for Collectors
Some of the best Renaissance Revival designs are those with flat surfaces and linear decoration, and colors that are an integral part of the design. For instance, the gilding and ebonizing on this table highlight important elements of its decoration. Prices for Renaissance Revival tables range from inexpensive to moderate, depending on condition, decoration, and attribution.

Rococo Revival center table

Description
Oval center table with marble top rounded on upper edges and
set into molded frame. Skirt with laminated pierced leaves and
scroll border. Cabriole legs embellished with carved scrolls and
flora. Cross stretchers made of 2 carved winged dragons, with a
center urn topped by a striated acorn finial and resting on a
flattened ball foot. *Variations:* Tables may have more complex
piercework as well as fruit and floral motifs carved on the skirt
and stretchers; the most elaborate examples were made by John
Henry Belter.

Materials and Dimensions
Walnut. Marble top. Height: 30″. Length: 49″. Depth: 32″.

Locality and Period
Probably made by J. and J.W. Meeks or another New York
workshop. c. 1850–60.

Comment
The Rococo Revival style flourished in America from about 1840
to 1870, and tables such as the one shown here are among its
most distinctive creations. A new technique for using laminated
wood resulted in elegantly carved furniture that was more
elaborate than contemporary European examples that were
closely based on 18th-century designs.

Hints for Collectors
This table, probably by the Meeks workshop, is simpler than
similar pieces by John Henry Belter, who was the major
innovator in the Rococo Revival field. Belter's pieces are in
greater demand and therefore fetch higher prices than those by
his competitors.

Eastlake center table

Description
Oval center table with curved, ormolu-framed marble top. Skirt carved in pierced foliate pattern; acorn-shaped drops hanging from 4 corners of skirt. Baluster-shaped pedestal, with braces joining the center pedestal to smaller turned and carved vertical supports. Carved scrolls reinforce braces and rest on 4 projecting feet. Base X-shaped and elaborately carved. *Variations:* Elegant ebonized tables were more often rectangular. Flat carving was more common than carving in high relief.

Materials and Dimensions
Walnut. Ebonized. Stained highlights. Marble with ormolu. Height: 29″. Length: 41″. Depth: 23″.

Locality and Period
Throughout the United States. c. 1870–80.

Comment
The combination of Oriental and Western motifs in the table shown here is typical of innovative designs of the 1870s and 1880s, when the design reforms of Charles Eastlake were most influential. Its pedestals and scrolls are classical, but the foliate ornament and ebonizing are Oriental in inspiration. The maker of this elegant table used Eastlake-style ornamentation—such as the projecting braces—but ignored Eastlake's emphasis on simplicity and the honest handling of materials. Eastlake would have objected, for example, to the ebony stain.

Hints for Collectors
Elaborate examples of late 19th-century furniture are rarely fakes or reproductions, but beware of pieces drastically altered by repairs, particularly by replaced drops or inserted pieces of carving. Check that flat decoration is consistently well executed.

Empire center table

Description
Center table with circular top having various types of marble (called specimen marble) inset in geometric pattern radiating from center circle. Marble framed by stenciled ring and gadrooning. Skirt rounded, with gilt-brass leaf border on bottom edge. Pedestal plain and bulbous at top; plain and gadrooned rings top vase-shaped section, which is leaf-carved and highlighted by gilding. Bottom of pedestal with turned rings fitted into textured ormolu collar. Flat tripod base with curving sides and stenciled stepped rim on top. 3 ebonized lion's-paw feet with carved scrolls and casters. *Variations:* Plain marble tops are more common. Carved pedestals may be more complex.

Materials and Dimensions
Mahogany. Gilt brass. Marble. Ebonized, gilded, and stenciled. Brass casters. Height: 29¾". Diameter of top: 35".

Locality and Period
Made by Antoine-Gabriel Quervelle, Philadelphia. c. 1830.

Comment
The center table was a standard form in the Empire parlor, with round tops and pedestal bases most popular. Antoine-Gabriel Quervelle, an outstanding Philadelphia craftsman of the period, followed the fashion but added elements—such as the specimen marble top, with various types of inset marble, and the restrained leaf carving—to make the table shown here particularly elegant. More ordinary versions have coarser carving in more flamboyant patterns.

Hints for Collectors
Look for restraint in Empire designs. Beware of Empire Revival furniture of the late 19th century, which has crude carving, overly elaborate ormolu mounts, and elongated overall designs.

Empire center table

Description
Center table with gray circular marble top. Wide skirt stenciled with flat leaf borders. Round pedestal, upper section plain, lower section with large carved and gilded acanthus leaves. Flat tripod base with curving sides. 3 large lion's-paw feet decorated with scroll-and-leaf ornament. *Variations:* Marble tops may be white, green, or black. Skirts are sometimes plain. Pedestals may be baluster-shaped and more elaborately carved. 4 legs are more common than 3.

Materials and Dimensions
Mahogany, mahogany veneer, and pine. Marble. Gilding. Height: 33″. Diameter of top: 29½″.

Locality and Period
New York. c. 1815–40. Variations made in other centers.

Comment
American Empire furniture was heavier in proportion than the Sheraton and Hepplewhite designs that preceded it, and center tables epitomized the new approach. At a time when fashionable furnishings were being made available to more and more people, pieces were made with varying degrees of elegance and flamboyance. The table shown here strikes a note of obvious elegance, but lacks the subtlety of many of Duncan Phyfe's tables.

Hints for Collectors
Center tables were used in almost every parlor of the Empire period, but since many were discarded later in the 19th century, when Empire parlor sets went out of style, they are harder to find than Empire chairs; look for them at estate sales of property long owned by a single family.

Turn-of-the-century oak expandable dining table

Description
Expandable table with circular top that divides in center to hold leaf. Skirt recessed under rounded edge of top. Cylindrical pedestal base with ring around bottom. 4 cabriole legs with lion's-paw feet. *Variations:* Round oak tables often have more elaborate detailing. Pedestals may be carved in leaf patterns and may divide when table expands. Legs may have carved fur and leaf motifs.

Materials and Dimensions
Oak. Height: 28″. Diameter of top: 38″ (closed).

Locality and Period
Grand Rapids. c. 1900–15.

Comment
Turn-of-the-century oak furniture has become much sought after because of its practicality. Employing the latest technology of the time, it was produced efficiently and in strong designs that were very salable. Because expandable tables had been introduced before 1850, the form was well known when this table was manufactured.

Hints for Collectors
Turn-of-the-century oak was made in a variety of designs. The most significant and desirable examples are those influenced by the Arts and Crafts movement in the so-called Mission style. The most elaborate oak designs, more eclectic than any of the preceding revival styles, are not particularly popular with sophisticated collectors of the furniture of this period, though they are popular enough today to invite reproductions. Pieces with simple straight lines, following the Arts and Crafts principles of Gustav Stickley, are more desirable. Avoid examples which have oak veneered over pine.

Empire expandable dining table

Description
Expandable table with circular top that divides in center to hold leaf. Skirt recessed under molded edge of top; straight lower border protruding from skirt. Base consisting of 4 clusters of columns set on small platforms and separated by vertical planks. Columns with brass capitals and bases. Thick platform with 4 curved sides and molded upper rims. Base also divides when leaf is added. *Variations:* Other early expandable tables have cylindrical bases. Bases may be plain or more ornately decorated.

Materials and Dimensions
Mahogany and pine. Brass fittings. Height: 31½″. Diameter of top: 52″ (closed).

Locality and Period
Possibly New York. c. 1830–50.

Comment
Early expandable tables are rare and, if unlabeled, difficult to attribute unless similar documented examples are known. The columns and overall design of the table shown here are clearly of the Empire period, though probably late since expandable tables were a later innovation. It is similar to some center tables of the period and may have been used in the parlor of a small house that had no dining room.

Hints for Collectors
Check the inner mechanism on tables for makers' marks. The proper Empire proportions of this unlabeled example distinguish it from similar late Victorian tables, which imitated the Empire styling but not its fine details.

Description
Table with flat circular top framed by shallow gallery; hole in center holds aluminum reflector for light bulb (circular frosted-glass cover missing). 4 cylindrical brass legs set on flat-sided, X-shaped base. Trumpet-shaped center pedestal concealing lamp. *Variations:* Tables from the 1930s and 1940s may have lamps situated elsewhere—for example, below their tops or projecting above tops. Tables may also have built-in ashtrays, storage areas, and even fish tanks.

Materials and Dimensions
Mahogany. Brass. Aluminum reflector. Height: 30″. Diameter of top: 36″.

Locality and Period
New York or other furniture centers. c. 1930–40.

Comment
Brass and aluminum were frequently used for simple mass-produced Art Deco furniture from the end of the 1920s until World War II. Some examples were made in quantity, others in limited numbers, but most were made inexpensively. The stark forms were inspired by Cubist paintings and complemented the streamlined interiors of the period.

Hints for Collectors
The best Art Deco designs are flamboyant and daring. The table shown here is a good example—a curious combination of table and lamp that must have seemed innovative until its novelty wore off. Brass and other metals may tarnish, so they should be maintained carefully. The absence of the circular piece of frosted glass that covered the light bulb of this table is not a serious defect, as it can easily be replaced.

Modern lacquered table

Description
Lacquered table with simple circular top and straight edges.
3 flat boards, set at 120° angles to each other, support top and
circular center shelf. Supports bend at bottom and meet in
center, resting on tripod base of rectangular boards. Square feet
with rounded outer edge. *Variations:* Lacquer in different colors
and metal inlays were sometimes used.

Materials and Dimensions
Pine or hardwood. Lacquered. Height: 23½″. Diameter of top:
29½″.

Locality and Period
New York. c. 1935–50. Variations designed in other centers.

Comment
Simple modern design of the 1930s evolved from 2 trends, the
very decorative Art Deco and the more functional Bauhaus. The
table shown here depends on Art Deco precedents, but is simpler
than the fashionable designs of the 1920s. Furniture like this was
designed by architects and industrial designers and came from
cabinetmaking shops, many in New York and some in the
Midwest, as well as from factories producing fine furniture
rather than purely commercial pieces.

Hints for Collectors
One test to apply to modern design is its consistency. This table
is consistent, avoiding the extraneous details often added by
larger manufacturers who appealed to a large conservative public
and thus compromised the work of their designers. Look under
the top for a label; otherwise it is difficult to attribute a piece to a
specific maker, unless it resembles a documented example.
Beware of pieces that have recently been lacquered to make
them more salable on today's market.

Art Deco glass center table

Description
Table with circular glass top resting on 3 curved glass legs. Legs
set at an angle into circular wooden base having flat surfaces
painted with black lacquer. Table may be disassembled.
Variations: Glass and lucite were sometimes used together.
Tripod bases may be more decoratively curved.

Materials and Dimensions
Glass. Ash painted with lacquer. Height: 26½". Diameter of top:
30".

Locality and Period
Made for Modern Age, a New York retailer. c. 1930–55.

Comment
Glass, a new material for furniture, was used for its shock appeal
on the table shown here, although the design itself is relatively
conservative. Its basic form is related to Empire or Regency
examples in which the supports are leaf-shaped. This table was
made for Modern Age, a prominent New York retailer of
advanced furniture designs. At the time this table was made,
however, the Art Deco style was already being replaced in the
vanguard of modern design by the more innovative work of the
Bauhaus designers and their American followers.

Hints for Collectors
Conservative modern furniture such as this table, though
possibly contradictory in nature, represents an important aspect
of American design from the 1930s to 1950s that is usually
overlooked. Unlike the highly durable and utilitarian Bauhaus
designs, many Art Deco pieces must be handled with care,
particularly if lacquered or glass. Lacquer damage is costly
to repair.

Modern glass-topped table

Description
Table with circular glass top set on steel base. Square base made of straight narrow rails. Legs round and plain. *Variations:* Glass-topped tables may have wooden or plastic bases. Top may be square and rest on X-shaped base. Unpainted stainless steel may be used.

Materials and Dimensions
Glass. Tubular steel painted black. Height: 26¼". Diameter of top: 36".

Locality and Period
New York or other furniture centers. c. 1938–60.

Comment
Simple modern designs are not easily dated: they evolved from the Bauhaus designs of the late 1930s and became staples for more than 20 years. The table shown here is restrained but, because of its breakable glass top, not functional. This distinguishes it from the utilitarian tradition of the German Bauhaus and places it, though it is more abstract, equally in the tradition of Art Deco design.

Hints for Collectors
Since modern designs are usually difficult to date and attribute, a selection should depend on condition and purity of form. A piece should be in as perfect condition as possible, without the signs of age that are acceptable in antique furniture. Consider the influences of the period—from Bauhaus to Art Deco—and determine which direction is most interesting. Examples as clean in outline and as restrained in decoration as this table are the most desirable. Beware of tables with glass tops taken from other pieces.

Description

Iron-wire table with thick circular wooden top having stepped
molded edge. Top set on 4 legs, each made of 2 wires bent into
modified cabriole outline with fasteners at narrow knees. Simple
cross stretchers. Legs end in twisted sections opening into pad-
shaped loop feet. *Variations:* Wire legs may be twisted into
different designs, including some closer to cabriole shape. Tops
may be plywood.

Materials and Dimensions

Oak. Iron wire and brackets. Height: 30″. Diameter of top: 24½″

Locality and Period

Chicago, New York, or other furniture centers. c. 1900–20.

Comment

Popularly known as an ice-cream parlor table, this form was used
in restaurants and other public places beginning about the turn
of the century. A nearly indestructible table, it was produced
throughout the country. This simple utilitarian piece has an Art
Nouveau look because the wire legs are as delicate as the sinuous
forms of French Art Nouveau furniture. Some improved models
were patented, but most makers produced thousands of these
tables without ever striving for innovation. The design of the
table shown here is restrained, but there is an amusing echo of
the Queen Anne style in the cabriole legs and in the backs of the
matching chairs (98).

Hints for Collectors

Repairs on these relatively inexpensive tables can be costly, so
be sure to check their condition. These tables and the matching
chairs were made in a number of patterns, so collectors may mix
such wire furniture as they wish or obtain a matching set.

Turn-of-the-century wicker table

Description
Table with circular top covered with basketweave wicker
bending over edges to form arcaded skirt, with rounded arches
between legs. 4 wicker-covered legs round and slanted outward;
cross stretchers similar to legs. Iron caps on feet. *Variations:*
Wicker was painted in a wide range of colors or left natural.
Basketweave patterns may be more complex.

Materials and Dimensions
Wicker and ash. Painted white. Iron caps on feet. Height: 28½".
Diameter of top: 25".

Locality and Period
New England, New York, or other centers for wicker.
c. 1880–1930.

Comment
Imported Oriental furniture made of rattan inspired American
manufacturers to produce wicker objects made either of local
twigs or of Asiatic rattan and bamboo. Starting in the 1840s,
wicker was made in simple designs, and these, along with more
curvilinear designs, continued to be popular into the 20th
century. The simple table shown here was probably made in one
of the larger factories in New England or New York around the
turn of the century.

Hints for Collectors
Wicker furniture is available in both simple and elaborate
designs, offering collectors many options for matching it to other
furnishings. Most pieces have been repainted, but this is not a
major drawback since original paint or varnish has seldom
survived; pieces with original natural finish should not be
repainted. Check under the top for labels—although they are
very rare—to determine the date and locality of a piece.

Mission-style card table

Description
Table with circular 2-piece top joined by splines and by battens underneath, with 4 copper insets to hold glasses. 4 square legs slant outward, with broad cross stretchers mortised through. *Variations:* Similar Mission tables were designed for purposes other than card-playing, such as small dining tables with drop leaves and circular center tables with lower shelves.

Materials and Dimensions
Oak. Metal reinforcements. Copper insets. Height: 29½″. Diameter of top: 38″.

Locality and Period
Probably made by Stickley Brothers, Grand Rapids. c. 1900–15.

Comment
Mission-style furniture was designed for informal settings in city as well as country homes. Oak was practical because of its strength, and Mission design was particularly utilitarian. The firm of Stickley Brothers was well acquainted with the design concepts of Gustav Stickley since it was operated by 2 of his brothers, George and Albert. But Stickley Brothers added elements intended to appeal to a wider audience, such as the copper insets for glasses on the table shown here. Moreover, the production techniques used in their factory were based more on practical economics than on Gustav's design philosophy.

Hints for Collectors
Mission furniture offers collectors a broad range of designs, from austere to highly decorative. Gustav Stickley's designs are the most severe and original, while those of his brothers are more popularized and available. Labeled examples by any of the Stickleys are much sought after and are becoming costly; these may still be bought inexpensively, however, in some rural shops.

Modern coffee table

Description
Low table with plain circular top covered with walnut veneer;
straight edge all around. Top set on 4 severely tapered, round
legs covered with leather upholstery; simple screw construction
attaching legs to top. *Variations:* Tables may have marble, glass,
or other kinds of veneered tops, which may be rectangular. Legs
may be oval instead of round, set at angles to the top, and not
covered with leather.

Materials and Dimensions
Pine and walnut veneer. Ash legs covered in leather. Height:
17″. Diameter of top: 30″.

Locality and Period
Made by Herman Miller, Inc., Zeeland, Michigan. c. 1935–45.

Comment
As one of the first manufacturers to concentrate on quality in
modern design, Herman Miller, Inc. worked with designers and
architects from around the country. It had made traditional
furnishings before aligning itself with innovative designers at the
start of the Depression. The firm's pioneer designer was Gilbert
Rohde, who headed a group that led conservative Zeeland into
the avant-garde of contemporary design.

Hints for Collectors
Condition is extremely important in modern furniture since its
visual effect depends on the interaction of its sleek unembellished
surfaces. Miller pieces often bear labels under tops or on legs. If
in doubt about the identification of a piece, check decorating
magazines from the 1930s and 1940s for advertisements and
articles illustrating similar designs. Consistent well-balanced
design is the hallmark of fine Miller work as well as that of its
best competitors.

Art Deco glass-topped coffee table

Description
Table with oval top of blue mirrored glass set into simple wooden frame. Long shallow drawer is suspended from center of skirt and pushes through to open at either end; plain drawer fronts. Plain narrow panels at short sides. 4 legs joined to skirt are flat rectangular boards rounded at tops. 3 tiers of bands, mortised into legs just below drawer, loop around all sides. 2 balls connect bands below each drawer front. *Variations:* Small tables with blue glass tops were made in many rectangular or circular shapes, often with simply molded frames.

Materials and Dimensions
Maple. Blue glass. Height: 17″. Length: 38″. Depth: 18¾″.

Locality and Period
Grand Rapids or other furniture centers. c. 1930–45.

Comment
Blue mirrored glass, frequently used on tabletops, might be taken as the symbol of the popular version of Art Deco sold in American department stores in the 1930s. Tables like the one shown here were inexpensive yet handsome and fashionable. The sleek and ingeniously simple shapes of these mass-produced wares are in marked contrast to more elegant Art Deco furniture produced with consummate craftsmanship by traditionally trained cabinetmakers working in fine workshops.

Hints for Collectors
Collectors should think twice about mixing finely crafted, elegant Art Deco pieces with popularized versions, since this will show neither type to its advantage. Art Deco designs should be in near-perfect condition for the proper visual effect. Restoration of some pieces has special problems: the dark stain used over the maple on this table, for instance, may be difficult to match.

Modern lacquered coffee table

Description
Low table with thick symmetrical top having flat lacquered surfaces, concave sides, and rounded corners. Flat legs angled from corners of top. Legs have curved outer sides; fastened to top by brackets. *Variations:* Coffee tables may be kidney-shaped. Other examples display simpler geometric shapes.

Materials and Dimensions
Mahogany and pine. Lacquered. Height: 15″. Length: 41½″. Depth: 35½″.

Locality and Period
Designed by Paul Frankl, New York. Produced by Johnson Furniture Company. c. 1949.

Comment
Paul Frankl was a major figure in the modern design movement in this country from the 1920s until his death in 1958. The Austrian-born architect and furniture designer was responsible for many impressive designs, first geometric in outline, and later curvilinear like the table shown here. His work was a continuation of the decorative approach introduced with Art Deco, in which painting and sculpture were major sources of innovation, a tendency very different from the more functional approach of the German Bauhaus.

Hints for Collectors
Works attributed to major designers through either characteristic elements or period documentation are readily available and most desirable. Knowledgeable collectors may be able to do research on an anonymous design, make an attribution, and thus enhance the value and interest of a piece.

Modern lacquered end table

Description
Lacquered double-tiered table with small square top. Curved board supporting top and continuing as semicircle touching base at midpoint. Lower rectangular shelf supported by short end of semicircle and braced to center of long end. Semicircular section secured by rectangular metal brace to plain rectangular platform. 2 long narrow feet. *Variations:* Geometric table designs usually combine square and circular shapes in various ways, often with glass or metal elements.

Materials and Dimensions
Pine or hardwood. Lacquered. Metal brace. Height: 26″. Length: 26¾″. Depth: 12″.

Locality and Period
New York, Grand Rapids, or other centers. c. 1928–55.

Comment
Simple designs executed in materials such as lacquered wood, metal, and glass were introduced in the late 1920s as a development of the Art Deco style; the major difference was their omission of the lavish traditional craftsmanship characteristic of the finest Art Deco work. The lacquered surface of the end table shown here replaces the veneers and carving used by the earlier generation of craftsmen and reflects the taste for sleeker surfaces that look machine-made.

Hints for Collectors
Look for unusual modern designs in which the overall shape works well with the lacquered, glass, or metal surfaces. There were many levels of modern design: some pieces were executed by small workshops that employed traditionally trained cabinetmakers, while others were made in factories.

Modern lacquered end table

Description
Lacquered double-tiered table with straight-sided rectangular top partly covered by glass inset. Top set on 4 plain rectangular posts attached to shelf same size as top; short ends of shelf have deeper skirt. Plain narrow legs connected on 2 sides at floor level by stretchers. *Variations:* Straight-sided elements may be arranged in other geometric patterns. Tables may be lacquered in neutral or bright colors. Inset may be leather.

Materials and Dimensions
Pine or hardwood. Lacquered. Glass inset. Height: 22½".
Length: 30". Depth: 19".

Locality and Period
New York, Grand Rapids, or other centers. c. 1935–50.

Comment
Modern geometric designs continued to be mass-produced until after World War II. Surfaces were often lacquered to resemble bleached wood, but sometimes bright colors were used to emphasize the basic shapes. The table shown here is disarmingly simple and looks as though it might have been hammered together from a few 2-by-4's. It may have been produced by one of the larger manufacturers, since they specialized in lacquered surfaces.

Hints for Collectors
Simple modern designs are difficult to identify since few examples were marked or labeled, and the possibility of 2 companies producing very similar work is great. Pieces such as this table are readily available in used-furniture stores and small antiques shops. They are still inexpensive but will surely become more costly in the near future.

Stands, Pedestals, Work, Sewing, and Other Small Tables

Small tables such as stands and occasional tables usually served multiple purposes. Pedestals and work or sewing tables, however, were designed for single purposes.

Stands

Though commonly referred to as candlestands today, little pedestal-base tables held plates or cups as often as candles. Such stands, first introduced in 17th-century America, were made throughout the 18th century in all major styles. (For tilt-top examples, see the first section of tables, 253–256.) Simple stands and small tables were particularly popular in rural interiors from the William and Mary period through Shaker times and later. Federal-era examples, with delicately turned pedestals usually set on tripod bases, vary greatly in height and the size of tops, indicating they were intended for varied uses. Victorian stands, sometimes serving as pedestals, were made in a large variety of designs and styles. At the beginning of this century, Mission-style and Arts and Crafts designers favored small rectangular stands suitable for holding houseplants, among other uses.

Pedestals and Small Tables

Another type of small table, designed for a more limited purpose, is the pedestal. Pedestals were a late 19th-century phenomenon expressing the manners and taste of the period. In the 1870s and 1880s, called the Gilded Age by Mark Twain, many Americans joined Europeans in touring the world and bringing home artworks. American-made bronzes as well as plaster statuary by John Rogers were found in many homes. All these art objects required pedestals for display. Renaissance Revival and exotic pedestals with Oriental or Middle Eastern ornament were most popular. Medium-size all-purpose, or occasional, tables were also used for holding statues and lamps.

Work and Sewing Tables

Work tables are another popular American form; most commonly associated with the Federal period, they were made throughout the 19th century. These small tables, used for sewing and a variety of pastimes, are not always distinct from other types of tables, except for their comparative smallness and their drawers or storage space for small items. Some examples are clearly designed for sewing, with small compartments for needles and thread or with bags attached for fabrics (340–342). Federal work tables range from elegant high-style models to simpler country designs. Pedestal-base forms include restrained Federal examples and bulkier Empire pieces. Later in the century, wickerwork sewing tables were used in eclectically decorated interiors. During the Colonial Revival of the early 20th century, manufacturers made small tables similar to work tables but incorporating earlier Colonial elements; these were usually called end, lamp, or bedside tables (343).

Collecting Hints

Small stands, pedestals, and work tables appeal to collectors who value useful furnishings. Stands and pedestals range from simple country and Mission-style examples to restrained fashionable designs and flamboyant Victorian creations. Work tables offer collectors many forms and varying degrees of elegance. After decades of relative neglect, Federal work tables and stands are beginning to attract collectors and command high prices, causing the entry of some of the finest pieces onto the market. Late 19th-century tables are still relatively inexpensive, except for outstanding designs or those attributed to well-known makers.

Arts and Crafts stand

Description
Small square table with raised marble top. Marble framed by flat rails mortised together, with ends left open and outer edges rounded. 3 contrasting square pegs set in diagonal lines at corners of top; pairs of pegs in center of top rails. Legs straight and plain except for 3 pegs. Stepped skirt; 2 inscribed lines follow outline of skirt. Stretchers stepped on upper edge and joined to legs by single pegs. *Variations:* Tops may be plain, not marble. Oriental-inspired details such as the stepped skirt and stretchers seen here may be omitted.

Materials and Dimensions
Mahogany. Marble. Ebony pegs. Height: 16⅛". Length: 12⅝". Depth: 12⅝".

Locality and Period
Designed by Charles Sumner Greene of the architectural firm of Greene and Greene, Pasadena, California. 1908.

Comment
The Greene brothers carried Arts and Crafts design a bit further than did Gustav Stickley. Whereas Stickley's simple furniture depended on austere lines and traditional construction techniques, Greene and Greene achieved a restrained elegance in their finely detailed, almost sculptural designs. The Oriental details and ebony pegs on the small table shown here were hallmarks of these California designers. (*See also* 81, 82.)

Hints for Collectors
The supply of Greene and Greene designs is limited since they were custom-made for the firm's houses in southern California, but pieces like this stand are excellent examples of some of the key decorative tendencies within the broader Arts and Crafts and Mission movements.

Mission-style stand

Description
Small table with square top made of 2 planks battened together; corners chamfered to hold flat angled legs. Arched ends of legs protruding over top; straight-sided legs joined to top by round-topped screws. Geometric floral disks inscribed and painted on upper legs. Cross stretchers mortised through legs. Tapered feet. *Variations:* Tables may be simpler, with no decoration and plain square legs.

Materials and Dimensions
Oak. Height: 19½″. Length: 14″. Depth: 14″.

Locality and Period
New York, Grand Rapids, or other centers. c. 1900–15.

Comment
Although Grand Rapids and New York were centers for Mission-style furniture, small tables like the one shown here are hard to place, since they are simple enough to have been made in either a factory or a smaller workshop anywhere in the country. This example is more decorative than most of Gustav Stickley's Mission-style products. This decorative Arts and Crafts approach was taken by many artist-craftsmen as well as manufacturers who popularized Stickley's Mission style. The visible screws suggest large-scale factory production.

Hints for Collectors
Mission-style furniture offers more variety in design than is generally realized. Decorative designs such as this table are avoided by those collectors who prefer Stickley's innovative austerity, but others view them as part of a fascinating trend reflecting the Art Nouveau style that flourished at the time. Moreover, such pieces are generally far less expensive than similar identified Stickley designs.

Mission-style stand

Description
Small table with octagonal top screwed onto 4 legs. Legs are flat boards broadening toward top and foot. Cross stretchers mortised through legs and held in place by keys. *Variations:* Small Mission tables come with tops in a variety of shapes, with simplest forms most in demand. Straight-sided legs are more common than the cut legs seen here.

Materials and Dimensions
Oak. Height: 18¼″. Length: 16¾″. Depth: 16¾″.

Locality and Period
Mass-produced in Grand Rapids or other furniture centers. c. 1900–15.

Comment
Mission oak furniture was often made with the simple construction techniques used on early American pieces, but some elements, such as the visible tenons on the lower parts of the legs on the table shown here, were purely decorative. Tables like this were designed by inventive craftsmen working for small shops or large factories. The legs are based on plain designs by Gustav Stickley, but are more decorative, suggesting that the manufacturer was attempting to make the piece more salable.

Hints for Collectors
Check simple oak furniture to see if it is the work of an artist-craftsman or a factory: metal screws and clamps under the top are signs of a factory product. as is the lack of rough handmade surfaces. The work of the better-known Mission-style makers—for instance, Stickley, Roycroft, and Limbert—attracts the most collectors, but some factory products are just as fine.

Arts and Crafts rustic stand

Description
Bark-covered and painted stand with square top framed by
straight-edged border projecting over base. Base broadening
toward bottom, with 4 solid sides cut in cusped arches below.
Flat borders dividing each side into 3 horizontal parts. Flat
applied tulips in upper sections, with 3 cutout petals exposing
unpainted wood underneath. Tapered feet. *Variations:* Tops may
be smaller; bases straight rather than tapering. Surfaces may be
rougher.

Materials and Dimensions
Pine and birch bark. Painted. Height: 18″. Length: 11¼″. Depth:
11¼″.

Locality and Period
Probably New York State. c. 1900–20. Also the Midwest.

Comment
The birch bark on the stand shown here suggests that it was
made in the Adirondacks region, where hunting and fishing
lodges often had rustic furnishings designed to look as if they had
been made at the sites; camps in the Midwest had similar
furniture. The shape of this stand reflects the blocky forms
prevalent in Mission-style furniture of the period. The idea of
making furniture out of unfinished logs and branches is related to
the turn-of-the-century Arts and Crafts movement as well as to
18th-century rustic garden furniture (12).

Hints for Collectors
Turn-of-the-century rustic furniture, often derived from popular
Mission forms, is most available in regions that served as
summer resorts early in the century; small tables are especially
available and inexpensive. Make sure that the bark is intact,
since it is difficult to restore properly.

322 Federal country candlestand or small table

Description
Small table with simple rectangular top. Pedestal base baluster-shaped and plain. 4 unadorned cabriole legs with rounded upper sides; legs joined to base by mortise-and-tenon technique. *Variations:* Most stands or small tables have tripod bases. Pedestals may be turned in various patterns, with minor changes in proportions. Tables may have tilt tops.

Materials and Dimensions
Tiger maple. Height: 26″. Length: 19½″. Depth: 16″.

Locality and Period
New England. c. 1800–20.

Comment
It is sometimes difficult to determine the function of small tables, some of which were used as candlestands, kettle stands, or tea tables. The 4 legs are an unusual feature on the stand shown here, which resembles many tripod versions. The curve of the legs is similar to that on Hepplewhite examples, but the baluster shape of the pedestal base resembles earlier 18th-century examples. The use of maple and the combination of traditional and fashionable designs was typical of the work of rural New England cabinetmakers.

Hints for Collectors
Simple designs are easily imitated and some turn-of-the-century country versions are passed off as period pieces. Most recent copies are poorly made. The top should be smooth on the underside, even though some authentic country pieces have rough surfaces. Modern circular saw marks on the underside of the top and modern screws and nails are the most obvious signs of a reproduction.

William and Mary country candlestand or small table

Description
Small table with galleried round top set on simple columnar
pedestal. Thick disk base supported by 4 legs set at angles. Legs
turned in double-vase-and-ring pattern cut off at vase to form
feet; gilded rings. *Variations:* Simple tables often have tops that
are plain rather than galleried. Turnings on the legs may be
simpler.

Materials and Dimensions
Maple. Painted black and gold. Height: 28″. Diameter of top:
15¼″.

Locality and Period
New England. c. 1720–50.

Comment
Small tables were first made in 17th-century America. Popularly
called a candlestand today, the table shown here probably served
broader functions in the 18th century. Maple tables were often
painted or stained: the black paint with gold trim on this example
is characteristic of late 18th-century work, when the piece was
probably repainted. Simple construction was all-important in
rural cabinetmaking, but is often misunderstood today. A table
such as this was originally purely functional; now its country look
seems highly decorative.

Hints for Collectors
Simple early forms like this small table are often overlooked by
collectors. Though rare, such pieces do turn up, whether in
family attics or elegant shops. Check country pieces carefully
since many are recent copies; beware of examples with regular
turnings that have crisp details and those without suitable wear
on tops, legs, and particularly bottoms of feet.

Shaker candlestand

Description
Tripod-base candlestand with plain circular top braced to simple tapered pedestal. Rounded pedestal with capital on top and plain bottom. Cylindrical base into which 3 legs are dovetailed. Legs are thin boards cut in cabriole shape with rounded top surfaces. Snake feet. *Variations:* Some Shaker tables of this type have more elaborately curved pedestals; others are simpler, with flat bases. When the top is rectangular and has a gallery around it, the table was used to sort seeds; sometimes drawers were suspended from the top.

Materials and Dimensions
Pine top. Maple base. Height: 30″. Diameter of top: 16″.

Locality and Period
New York or Massachusetts. c. 1830–60.

Comment
The simple design of the table shown here is from the early Shaker period; a similar table was made at the Chatham, New York, Shaker community about 1830. The design is based on Federal tables made at the beginning of the 19th century, but modified to suit the utilitarian needs of a Shaker community. Shaker designs were conservative and remained unchanged through most of the 19th century. It was not until the end of the century that Shaker communities made furniture that might be described as Victorian in character.

Hints for Collectors
A collector should study Shaker furniture in museums and books before paying a premium for a supposed Shaker piece. Shaker simplicity is characterized by finer detailing than that displayed by other simple contemporary pieces. Similar designs made outside the Shaker communities should cost considerably less.

Federal candlestand

Description
Tripod-base candlestand with circular top having low gallery around outer edge. Turned pedestal with cylindrical upper section, vase-and-ring middle, and cylindrical base into which 3 legs are mortised. Legs are thin boards cut in cabriole shape with rounded outer and inner edges. Snake feet. *Variations:* Pedestals may be columnar and turned in various patterns. Tops may be set on hinges for tilting. Gallery around top may be lacking.

Materials and Dimensions
Maple and tiger maple. Height: 26″. Diameter of top: 15″.

Locality and Period
New England. c. 1800–20.

Comment
Small pedestal tables on tripod bases were made throughout the 18th century as well as during the first decades of the 19th century. Though they must have functioned as candlestands, contemporary records rarely refer to them as such. 18th-century examples usually have vase-shaped columns that are simpler than the one shown here, and the ring in the lower section is a clear sign that this table was made in the early 19th rather than the 18th century. The thin flat legs, instead of fuller carved ones, provide another clue to its Federal-era origin. Like most conservative designs made of maple, this table was probably produced in New England.

Hints for Collectors
This is an easy form to copy and it has been widely reproduced. Look for overall signs of wear and for evidence of handwork, such as the gentle smoothing of coarse chisel marks, especially under the base of the pedestal.

Federal candlestand

Description
Tripod-base candlestand with small circular top having molded gallery. Turned pedestal with leaf-carved capital, vase-shaped reeded middle, and leaf-decorated urn. Cylindrical base holding 3 legs. Legs curving down, with bellflower carving on outer surface. Feet small and square. *Variations:* Shorter pedestals are more common, some with less carved decoration.

Materials and Dimensions
Mahogany. Height: 36″. Diameter of top: 9¾″.

Locality and Period
Salem, Massachusetts. c. 1800–10. Variations made elsewhere in New England.

Comment
Early descriptions often refer to candlestands like the one shown here as pillar-and-claw tables because of their long central columns set on clawlike bases. While there were earlier examples of small tables, a wide assortment of forms became increasingly popular during the Federal period. This piece is taller than most candlestands, which are 27″ to 30″ high. The reeding and delicate leaf carving, characteristic of Neoclassical design, reflect the Sheraton influence on American furniture at the beginning of the 19th century.

Hints for Collectors
Even though this candlestand is unusually tall, its well-executed details and logical proportions attest to its authenticity. Do not reject unusual pieces if their overall style and details are appropriate to the period. Their rarity, in fact, may make them more valuable.

Country ratchet-base candlestand

Description
Candlestand with octagonal top set on toothed stile. Stile fitted through slot in rail connecting 2 lower stiles. Toothed stile set into midrail and held at varying heights by hinged diagonal catch. X-shaped base. *Variations:* Ratchet-base stands are often set on tripod base. Tops may be square or circular.

Materials and Dimensions
Oak and maple. Height: 36″. Length: 11½″. Depth: 11½″.

Locality and Period
New England or Midwest. c. 1700–1900.

Comment
Ratchet-base stands like the one shown here, crude in construction but ingenious, are a type of rural furniture that is virtually impossible to date. Though their worn surfaces often suggest 18th-century manufacture, such stands lack the subtle details commonly associated with such furniture. The adjustable top probably was handy in working situations for which the height needed to be raised or lowered to direct the candlelight.

Hints for Collectors
The charm of crude furniture derives largely from its worn surfaces. Make sure that the wear is overall and not artificially created: worn surfaces should be smooth, not covered with rough lines from a later file or sandpaper. In the 1920s collectors often used rustic candlestands, cobbler's benches, and other rustic pieces for purely decorative purposes; and since they prized the crude look of such furniture, they unknowingly often settled for fakes. Most collectors today no longer equate country furniture with primitive workmanship.

Renaissance Revival pedestal

Description
Pedestal with rectangular top having rounded corners and textile covering fastened with brass tacks. Curved front skirt with ebonized decoration, inscribed lines, and gilding. 2 brackets curving from top to center of pedestal. Upper section of pedestal turned in baluster shape, ebonized, and gilded in abstract leaf pattern; lower section tapered and fluted. Round base with geometric decoration. 4 hoof feet. *Variations:* Pedestals may be more closely based on classical designs. Openwork forms and Oriental or exotic motifs were often used.

Materials and Dimensions
Walnut. Ebonized and gilded. Textile covering. Brass tacks. Height: 36½″. Length: 15¼″ (top). Depth: 10¼″ (top).

Locality and Period
Throughout the United States. c. 1870–90.

Comment
Pedestals became increasingly popular in the late 19th century as more and more sculpture was displayed in American homes. Since the Renaissance Revival pedestal shown here has no carving or inlay, it was probably produced in a factory. Its design is based on classical models modified in a manner common about 1880. Ebonized surfaces were frequently used for classical as well as Orientally inspired designs.

Hints for Collectors
Renaissance Revival pedestals, very popular a century ago, are not common today and are often overlooked by dealers and collectors when they do turn up. Some examples are more substantial than this one, which was probably used in a small-scale room along with other classically inspired or ebonized furnishings.

Renaissance Revival table

Description
Small oval table with white marble top having molded edges and resting on frame with similar moldings. Base has turned cylindrical center column with 4 legs dovetailed into its top and bottom; flattened ball pendant below. Flared legs are flat boards grooved on outer side and ending in cabriole shape. *Variations:* Silhouette of legs and grooving may vary, but this is a standard type of table made in great quantities.

Materials and Dimensions
Walnut. Marble. Height: 28½″. Length: 21¾″. Depth: 16¼″.

Locality and Period
Factories in Grand Rapids and throughout the United States. c. 1870–90.

Comment
The table shown here demonstrates the virtues of factory-made furniture, with parts that are elegantly cut yet easily assembled. This table may have been made in Grand Rapids, or in a large factory in almost any part of the country with a convenient lumber and power supply.

Hints for Collectors
Many reproductions of this table were made in the 1930s and some are still being made at small factories in the South. Reproductions may look convincing, but they are often lower and have more complex details with sharp edges that, on originals, would have become rounded from a century of wear. Look for dirt and discoloration from age on the underside of original marble tops as well as wear on the top frame caused by the weight of the marble.

Eastlake upholstered-top table

Description
Small table with circular top upholstered with embroidered fabric fastened with brass tacks. Fabric skirt in deeply scalloped pattern. Base has turned cylindrical center support stabilized by horizontal spokes joined to turned vertical spokes, all ebonized and having gilded rings and bell-shaped brass drops. 2 sets of larger horizontal spokes joined to 4 legs. Turned legs topped by finials. Ring-turned feet flaring out. *Variations:* Turned parts may resemble bamboo more closely. Tops may be simple trays or covered with rug fragments.

Materials and Dimensions
Maple. Ebonized and gilded. Wool embroidery. Brass tacks and drops. Height: 28″. Diameter of top: 16″.

Locality and Period
Probably New York. c. 1880. Variations made in other cities.

Comment
The table shown here was inspired by exotic sources: the fabric cover for the top is Middle Eastern in style; the pattern of the turned supports is Oriental. Such combinations suited those designers who were reacting against the emphasis on European models in earlier 19th-century design. This form is more decorative and less functional than most designs in Charles Eastlake's influential book, *Hints on Household Taste*, but its linear design follows Eastlake's suggestions.

Hints for Collectors
Small tables like this are often found today in the attics of elegant old houses, to which they were relegated between 1910 and 1930 when fashion turned to simpler designs in reaction to such Victorian extravagances. The more desirable examples have their original finish and fabric coverings.

Renaissance Revival pedestal

Description
Pedestal with square top covered in felt and edged with stepped molding. Top projects over partly ebonized skirt with gilded border in suspended arch design. Skirt has circular inlaid medallion of classical vase on each side, flanked by inscribed gilded leaves. Skirt resting on cylinder set on straight-sided pedestal with columnar corners that have boxlike capitals, gilded fluting, ring-turned bases, and domed drops below; narrow center panels of inlaid flora. Pedestal narrows at base. Square base with sloping ebonized sides; lower edges cut out to form legs. *Variations:* Pedestals may be simpler, more tapered forms, with more inscribed decoration. Height may be lower.

Materials and Dimensions
Walnut and pine. Ebonized and gilded. Felt. Satinwood inlay. Height: 41¼". Length: 20½". Depth: 20½".

Locality and Period
Grand Rapids or other factory centers. c. 1870–85.

Comment
During the 1870s—a period Mark Twain called the Gilded Age—the American middle class was becoming richer, and a sign of newly acquired wealth was the increase in the number of artworks displayed in homes. Pedestals like the one shown here usually held small statues or ceramics. Renaissance Revival pedestals, emphasizing inlays and contrasting woods, were designed to complement Renaissance-style rooms.

Hints for Collectors
Pedestals were luxury items that often had elegant detailing. Look for elaborate examples that successfully combine such various forms of decoration as paint, inlay, and gilding. Excellent workmanship may be found at modest prices.

Eastlake parlor table

Description
Table with plain square top edged with convex inscribed molding. Top projecting over plain straight skirt; convex molding forming lower edge of skirt. 4 legs slanting out from central core under top; reinforced by curved brackets suspended from corners of top. Tops of legs are rectangular above long spiral-turned sections ending in turned rings and blocks; blocks with inscribed rosettes. Square shelf bordered by stepped molding. Thick brackets curve under shelf from lower legs. Cylindrical feet on casters. *Variations:* Turned legs are sometimes plainer. The slanted legs seen here were popular, and came with or without brackets.

Materials and Dimensions
Cherry and oak. Iron casters. Height: 30½″. Length: 24″. Depth: 24″.

Locality and Period
Grand Rapids. c. 1880–1900. Variations made in other centers.

Comment
Simple square parlor tables with slanted legs were made in quantity after 1880. The turnings on the legs of the example shown here were inspired by the Renaissance models that appealed to Charles Eastlake and his followers as well as to less fashionable designers working for major American manufacturers.

Hints for Collectors
This was a popular form in the 1880s, but it has never been valued enough to be worth faking. Many variations of the basic design were produced, so look for an appealing example, such as this one, that has interesting detailing and is in good condition.

Eastlake parlor table

Description
Table with thick square top edged with complex molding. Legs slanted, with upper section turned in broad spiral pattern and lower section turned in vase-and-ring design. Square shelf with scalloped edges, set just below middle of legs. Tapered feet fitted into shoes of brass claws clutching glass balls. *Variations:* Square tops may be fabric-covered. Legs may be completely spiral-turned or simpler, with plain tapered feet.

Materials and Dimensions
Oak. Brass and glass feet. Height: 28″. Length: 24″. Depth: 24″.

Locality and Period
Grand Rapids or other furniture centers. c. 1880–1900.

Comment
Small tables were made in increasing numbers after 1880, when crowded eclectic interiors of overstuffed sofas and wicker chairs became fashionable. The table shown here has 17th-century European elements, particularly the spiral-turned legs, that were popular beginning in the 1870s. The glass ball feet suggest a date after 1880, when they began to be used by Louis Comfort Tiffany's decorating company. This type of table was called a gypsy table in some early catalogues; more recently it has been called a lamp table.

Hints for Collectors
Oak was a popular furniture wood for more than 50 years, so be careful in dating a piece: the wood was used for Eastlake designs of the 1870s as well as for eclectic turn-of-the-century designs. Some examples have fabric-covered tops and legs that unscrew for easy transport. These tables were widely made and are not difficult to obtain today.

Description
Rectangular 3-tiered table with long stiles mortised into rails supporting shelves. Top has straight grooved edges. 2 lower shelves plain-edged and fitted around stiles. Stiles have reeded vase-and-ring-turned main sections, with blocks at shelf level. Single drawer below lower shelf, enclosed by plain panels; 2 round stamped-brass pulls. Drawer area has plain rectangular stiles. Legs are squat reeded vases with rings above and below. Tapered feet fitted into brass shoes on brass casters. *Variations:* This is a rare form in American furniture; English versions are better known, often with more elaborate stiles.

Materials and Dimensions
Mahogany and pine. Brass pulls and casters. Height: 39″. Length: 23″. Depth: 15″.

Locality and Period
New York. c. 1800–20. Variations made in Philadelphia, Boston, and other furniture centers.

Comment
New Yorkers at the beginning of the 19th century were cosmopolitan and often favored European forms that were not common on the American scene. The Sheraton-style dumbwaiter shown here, a highly utilitarian serving table, was based on an English design. The general restraint of this design and its details suggest a New York origin.

Hints for Collectors
Check the secondary woods on furnishings not commonly made in this country: if pine or tulip poplar was used, the piece is probably American; the English favored ash. In most cases, American versions of a form have simpler lines and details.

Eastlake plant stand

Description
Square 3-tiered plant stand with plain top having elaborately
molded edge. Straight skirt with low-relief decoration. Skirt
mortised into rectangular stiles. Stiles become turned columnar
forms with thick center areas. Second shelf having low gallery
with grooved border enclosing relief panels. Middle tier mortised
into rectangular blocks of stiles. Heavy lower shelf mortised to
lower stiles turned as above but longer. Scroll feet flat-sided,
with square bottom. *Variations:* Decoration may be more exotic.
Stands may be painted or made of light wood instead of being
ebonized.

Materials and Dimensions
Maple or ash. Ebonized. Height: 32¾". Length: 14". Depth: 14".

Locality and Period
New York. c. 1875–95. Variations made in other centers.

Comment
Ebonized wooden furniture was popular in the New York area in
the late 19th century. The angularity and novel motifs of designs
like the plant stand shown here were expressions of the
American reform movement that has been associated with the
English designer Charles Eastlake. Combined with the Eastlake
angularity are the equally popular exotic or Oriental touches on
the example illustrated, such as the ebonizing, the motifs on the
panels, and the turned stiles.

Hints for Collectors
Look for outstanding detailing in small Eastlake-style tables,
which rarely have makers' marks. The foremost New York
cabinetmakers produced some of the finest tables in this style;
work almost as stylish was produced in Boston and Philadelphia.

Mission-style stand

Description
Tall stand with solid square top showing plain edges projecting over recessed skirt. Skirt bordered by straight projecting molding that continues on tops of legs. 4 square legs flanked by pairs of thin slats connecting skirt and lower shelf. Square shelf with straight molding going around legs to form gallery. Legs tapering from shelf to feet. *Variations:* Similar forms may have more slats and no decorative moldings.

Materials and Dimensions
Oak. Height: 35¾". Length: 15½". Depth: 15½".

Locality and Period
Designed by Frank Lloyd Wright, Chicago, for the Francis Little house in Peoria, Illinois. c. 1902.

Comment
Frank Lloyd Wright designed simple forms distinguished from the mainstream Mission style by unusual decorative additions such as the moldings on the stand shown here. Although distinctive, Wright's furniture from the turn of the century was made of oak, the wood popular with the reformers of the period. His designs have characteristics that make them forerunners of Art Deco designs of the 1920s. (*See also* 134, 157, 268.)

Hints for Collectors
Look for variations of the Mission style by designer-architects such as Wright as well as by small shops making furniture for them. Such pieces were directly influenced by the Arts and Crafts movement of the beginning of the century. Early Wright pieces such as this table are most desirable and costly; later designs from the 1940s and 1950s were sometimes produced in quantity and are usually less expensive.

Late Victorian wicker sewing stand

Description
Rectangular wicker stand in basketweave pattern. Upper basketlike section has a hinged top with plain wooden frame. Diamond decoration woven on top, front, and back; handles on sides. Looped skirt below. Wooden legs covered with wicker in repeating ball design. Lower shelf enclosed by basketweave gallery topped by looping; half-diamond design on front and back. Plain flaring feet. *Variations:* Upper sections may be uncovered. Woven patterns may be more complex.

Materials and Dimensions
Wicker. Hickory or ash. Brass hinges. Height: 30½". Length: 15½". Depth: 12¾".

Locality and Period
New England or other wicker-producing centers. c. 1880–1910.

Comment
Used both indoors and outdoors in the late 19th century, wicker was often found in the elegant parlors of the 1880s, which displayed an eclectic mixture of furnishings. Inspired first by Oriental imports and often using a variety of Oriental materials, wicker furniture factories sprang up all over America. Some of the largest producers, such as the Wakefield Rattan Company in Massachusetts, were located in New England.

Hints for Collectors
Wicker was used to create a wide variety of objects, from chairs and settees to baby buggies. A collection of wicker should balance restrained utilitarian pieces, like the sewing stand shown here, with more flamboyant designs. 19th-century wicker furnishings, such as this example, were often left in natural colors or simply lacquered or stained, which is preferable to the bright painted colors often seen today.

Empire drop-leaf sewing or work table

Description
Sewing or work table with rectangular top and 2 drop leaves bordered by half-round molding. 3 drawers with veneered fronts: top and bottom drawers straight-fronted, with keyholes and 2 elaborate brass pulls on lower drawer; middle drawer curved and plain. Square pedestal widening toward bottom. Base with concave sides, chamfered at corners. 4 hairy lion's-paw feet on casters. *Variations:* Arrangement of drawers varies; top drawer may be compartmentalized to store sewing equipment. Pedestals were sometimes round and turned or carved. Some examples have legs; also bags for fabric hanging from lower drawers.

Materials and Dimensions
Mahogany and mahogany veneer over pine. Brass hardware and casters. Height: 28½″. Length: 17″ (closed); 37″ (opened). Depth: 20″.

Locality and Period
New York or other major furnituremaking centers. c. 1815–40.

Comment
After the American Revolution, sewing or work tables were first made in Neoclassical Federal designs, followed by Empire as well as Gothic and Rococo Revival versions. Empire designs, whether plain like the example shown here or embellished with more carving, typically display heavily proportioned elements.

Hints for Collectors
Empire sewing or work tables are fairly common, so collectors should be selective. Craftsmen of the Empire era sometimes did hasty and inferior work, resulting in pieces poor in design and construction. Avoid examples with peeling veneer, warped leaves, and carving that is chipped or cracked.

Federal work table

Description
Work table with rounded sides and straight front and back. Lift top plain-edged, except for flat central projection; top hinged at rear and opening onto sectioned interior. Top third of cabinet veneered, with false drawer having 2 lion's-head pulls. Section below drawer level recessed slightly and covered by tambourlike reeding. Brass-knobbed central door opening onto 2 shelflike pull-out trays. Rounded ends contain wells reached through top. Base with reeded vase set into cylinder. 4 reeded legs curving from center cylinder to floor. Carved lion's-paw feet. *Variations:* Interiors may be more elaborately sectioned. Vase may display more carving.

Materials and Dimensions
Mahogany and pine. Brass pulls. Height: 30½″. Length: 28″. Depth: 14½″.

Locality and Period
New York. c. 1805–20. Variations made in other centers.

Comment
The restrained lines and stylish yet simple decoration of this piece (referred to in period records as an astragal-end work table) used to be considered hallmarks of the work of Duncan Phyfe. But recent research has shown that Phyfe's contemporaries crafted similarly elegant details. A genuine Phyfe table, however, still commands the highest price.

Hints for Collectors
Work tables are useful for storing small objects and are often moderately priced. Federal examples have a wide variety of shapes and elegant details. Veneered surfaces must be carefully handled since they can crack from rough treatment or drastic changes in humidity, and restoration is difficult and costly.

Federal draped sewing table

Description
Oval sewing table with concave center areas in front and back.
Hinged top opens to storage area. Veneered skirt just under top;
taffeta drapery below skirt. Round legs extend over fabric-
covered storage area; freestanding portions of legs are tapered,
with rectangular blocks at bottom of storage area. Ring turnings
and balls above cylindrical feet. *Variations:* Some Federal
sewing tables have drawers or hanging fabric bags, as well as
small compartments for needles and thread. Tables may be
kidney-shaped or rectangular.

Materials and Dimensions
Mahogany. Modern taffeta. Height: 28″. Length: 24½″. Depth:
14½″.

Locality and Period
Philadelphia. c. 1795. Variations made in other centers.

Comment
The sewing table was one of several types of small tables
introduced in the Federal era. Delicate in detail as well as
proportion, these tables complemented the classically styled
tables, chairs, and sofas found in Federal rooms. The concave
curves on the sides of the Philadelphia table shown here were
inspired by more elegant, kidney-shaped Sheraton models. The
simple, classically proportioned ring turnings on the legs make
this table an exemplary Federal design.

Hints for Collectors
Many simple pieces have undergone structural changes over the
years. If a sewing table has storage compartments in drawers,
make sure these are not later additions. Original fabric covering
in good condition is extremely rare; appropriate reproduction
material does not lower the value of a piece.

Federal sewing table with fabric bag

Description

Sewing or work table with rectangular top rounded at corners to conform to shape of round legs supporting them. All sides veneered. Front has 3 narrow drawers with round brass pulls. Lowest drawer opening to suspended fabric bag with smaller bottom board. Legs ring-turned alongside drawers; below, plain vase-shaped capitals set atop reeded tapering sections ending with ring turnings and tapered cylinders. Ball feet. *Variations:* Legs may be leaf-carved or plain. Surfaces are sometimes embellished with inlays. Fabric bags are often omitted.

Materials and Dimensions

Mahogany, mahogany veneer, and pine. Brass pulls. Silk bag. Height: 30½". Length: 18". Depth: 14".

Locality and Period

Salem, Massachusetts. c. 1805. Variations made in other centers.

Comment

Though tables like the one shown here were called square work tables in early accounts, most are actually rectangular. This example, like many others, has legs that continue along the full height of the piece. Sheraton designs such as this one were more popular in Salem than elsewhere. The fabric bag for storing sewing materials was favored in the early 19th century.

Hints for Collectors

Sheraton-influenced Federal designs are often most appealing when decorated by both fine graining and delicate carving. This simple piece is a fine example of Neoclassical elegance. Exceptional Federal pieces are still available, but collectors should be prepared to pay handsomely for them. On the other hand, such small tables were easily stored away and may still be found in many New England attics and barns.

Rococo Revival sewing table

Description
Sewing table with sarcophagus-lid lift top that is flat with concave sides and projecting molded edges. 2 drawers with plain grained fronts and oval escutcheons. Single drawer below, tapering in on all sides. Interior of top area with 9 compartments veneered in bird's-eye maple; drawers similarly veneered. Cabriole legs with elaborately carved knees. Leafy scroll feet on casters. *Variations:* Simpler examples may have stretchers. Curving legs may be plain or fancily carved.

Materials and Dimensions
Rosewood. Maple veneer. Brass casters and pulls. Height: 32″. Length: 22″. Depth: 17″.

Locality and Period
Made by Mitchell and Rammelsberg, Cincinnati. c. 1860.

Comment
Sewing tables like the one shown here were produced in many parts of the United States, including New York, where one was made by John Henry Belter. The firm of Mitchell and Rammelsberg, whose mark appears on this example, was one of the most prominent manufacturers during the latter half of the 19th century. In 1860 the *History of Manufactures* reported that this factory utilized modern production methods similar to those used by Grand Rapids factories.

Hints for Collectors
New York and New Orleans were the major centers for Rococo Revival furniture. The Cincinnati origin of this sewing table, however, suggests that the style flourished in other parts of the country as well. Craftsmen operating on a smaller scale than Mitchell and Rammelsberg produced equally appealing tables that were less restrained in shape and carved decoration.

Colonial Revival end table

Description
Small table with rectangular top having complex molded edges.
Top resting on 4 stiles. Front stiles are engaged columns with
ring-turned capitals and bases as well as vertical veneers
simulating fluting. Rear stiles plain and rectangular. Plain panels
on 3 sides. Front has 2 drawers with molded borders and brass
pulls. Valanced skirt projecting forward on 3 sides. Simple
cabriole legs. Pad feet. *Variations:* Similar small tables were also
made in Pilgrim, William and Mary, and Federal styles.

Materials and Dimensions
Mahogany and ash. Brass pulls. Height: 29½″. Length: 19″.
Depth: 14½″.

Locality and Period
Probably Grand Rapids. c. 1920.

Comment
Colonial Revival design took root at the turn of the century and
in the next few decades developed into a richly eclectic, popular
style. At first many designs closely followed 18th-century
prototypes, but ingenious designers soon began to adapt Colonial
elements to contemporary needs. The end table shown here is an
eclectic mixture of various 18th-century styles.

Hints for Collectors
Colonial Revival furniture was made in several grades. Much of
it was manufactured in Grand Rapids and was among the
sturdiest produced anywhere. Though primarily made to have
sales appeal, many Grand Rapids designs were carefully
conceived and well executed. Since it is a largely unexplored
field, Colonial Revival furniture is generally low-priced, even
when of fine quality.

Federal work table

Description
Work table with veneered rectangular top having plain edges
projecting over skirt. Plain side and back panels and front rails
mortised into square stiles that become tops of legs. 2 drawers
have handsomely veneered fronts with 4 brass lion's-head pulls
and center keyholes. Round legs with ringed capitals and long
reeded section ending at single ring. Tapered feet set in brass
shoes on brass casters. *Variations:* Drawers may be smaller.
Shelf may be set between legs.

Materials and Dimensions
Mahogany and mahogany veneer over pine. Brass hardware and
casters. Height: 30″. Length: 20″. Depth: 15″.

Locality and Period
New York. c. 1800–15. Variations made in other northeastern
cities.

Comment
Richly grained mahogany tables as restrained as the example
shown here are very often of New York origin. Inspired in part
by the Sheraton design book, the simplicity and elegance of this
table are typically American and particularly characteristic of
New York work. Empire designs are sometimes similarly plain,
but with legs that are heavier in proportion.

Hints for Collectors
Federal furniture offers collectors a wide variety of choices, from
flamboyant to restrained examples. This is an example of great
restraint, revealing an important aspect of Federal design. Many
collectors, however, prefer pieces embellished with inlays or
carving. Beware of paint used to conceal missing bits of veneer.
Slender legs should be checked for repaired fractures.

Federal work table

Description
Work table with 2 drawers and rectangular top. Drawers have beautifully grained fronts, brass escutcheons, and bold rosette pulls with ring handles. Legs with ring-turned capitals atop wide spiral turnings. Ring-turned tapered feet ending in casters. *Variations:* Drawer fronts may be more elaborate and have molding. Legs may have floral or foliate decoration. Tops may be shaped or have curved corners.

Materials and Dimensions
Mahogany and pine. Brass hardware and casters. Height: 29″. Length: 20½″. Depth: 18½″.

Locality and Period
Massachusetts. c. 1820. Variations made in other states.

Comment
The work table was a popular form in the Federal era. The simple design shown here was inspired by Sheraton models; earlier examples from about 1800 have more delicately tapered legs. In Massachusetts, particularly in Salem, delicate Sheraton designs were updated after 1815 through the adoption of thicker legs and carving in higher relief. This was a restrained response to the demands of changing tastes, which at the same time inspired more fashionable furnituremakers to make the dramatic shift from Sheraton to Empire designs.

Hints for Collectors
Many turn-of-the-century reproductions were more smoothly finished than the Federal originals, which were made well but simply. Shallow fluting and drawer interiors made of polished maple are other signs of later copies. Check for replacement hardware, which is often rougher, thinner, and less carefully stamped.

Federal country painted work table

Description
Painted work table with plain-edged rectangular top. Plain skirt. Single drawer with elaborately curved front resembling flamboyant Empire moldings; lower edge curving in to allow for grip to open drawer. Legs turned and tapered. Dumbbell-shaped feet. *Variations:* Tapered legs may be square or turned in various patterns. Drawer fronts are usually simple straight panels with appropriate pulls.

Materials and Dimensions
Pine. Painted. Height: 31″. Length: 21½″. Depth: 17″.

Locality and Period
Possibly Pennsylvania. c. 1820–40.

Comment
Painted furniture is often less stylish than that made of fine woods. The unusual molded drawer front on the table shown here is a fashionable touch on an otherwise simple design. Commonly referred to as side tables or bedside tables in recent years, such designs were called work tables in sources from the period. Because this table is so simply made and decorated, it probably was a product of an early furniture factory in Pennsylvania, where painted surfaces had great appeal.

Hints for Collectors
Work tables were made in a wide variety of designs, although the basic shape—small and rectangular-topped, with long legs—was constant. Judge a design by its gracefulness; avoid those too heavy for today's tastes. A moderately worn look of age, called a patina, is preferable to repainted surfaces. The demand for country designs has markedly increased in recent years and prices have risen accordingly.

Federal country painted dressing or work table

Description
Painted dressing table with rectangular top having plain edges painted with linear motif. Curved splashboard has scroll ends and painted pears and leaves. Single drawer with plain front painted in elongated rosette pattern at either side; stylized leaf design surrounding circular stamped-brass pull. Legs straight, square, and tapered, with painted rosette pattern above simple linear motif. Plain feet. *Variations:* Tables may be up to twice as long as this example. Colors range from white to dark green and black, with stenciled or freehand decoration.

Materials and Dimensions
Pine. Painted. Stamped-brass pull. Height: 32½". Length: 18". Depth: 19".

Locality and Period
Probably New England. c. 1825–40. Variations made in other centers.

Comment
Early 19th-century price books, intended to assist the furniture trade in some larger American cities, might have described the piece shown here as a work table; however, the rear splashboard suggests it was probably a dressing table or washstand. Much painted furniture was produced in the Federal era because it could be made from inexpensive pine or mixed woods and because the prevailing Neoclassical style favored painted wood.

Hints for Collectors
Since paint can conceal breaks and repairs, check surfaces carefully. Decoration that was added later is generally inappropriate and confusing. Check undersides as well as corners of drawers to see if the original color has been changed.

Checklist for Identifying Styles

Pilgrim Style: 17th century

Proportions Massive.

Essential elements Turned columnar stiles and legs. Turned spindles. Broad slats. Some inset wainscot paneling. Seats: cane, rush, leather, or needlepoint. Tabletops made of wide heavy boards.

Primary woods Oak; sometimes maple or hickory for turned parts. *Secondary woods* Pine, ash, maple, hickory, or others.

Notable forms Chairs: slat-back, Wainscot, Carver, Brewster, and Cromwell. Joint stool. Simple bench. Tables: trestle-base and gate-leg. Chair-table. Low-post bed.

William and Mary Style: 1690–1725

Proportions Tall and slender.

Essential elements Stiles, rails, and legs in scroll, columnar, or spiral shapes. Crisp slender turnings, often vase- or trumpet-shaped. Elaborate carving in low relief. Feet: ball, bun, or scroll (Spanish). Elegantly grained surfaces; some veneered or painted. Split balusters (or bannisters) on chair backs. Seats: cane, rush, or leather.

Primary woods Walnut or maple. *Secondary woods* Pine or others.

Notable forms Chairs: tall-back, bannister-back, and easy. Daybed. Low-post bed. Tables: large and small gate-leg, butterfly, tavern, and tea.

Queen Anne Style: 1725–1750

Proportions Broad but delicate.

Essential elements Curved and subtly carved parts. Carved motifs, primarily shells. Yoke-shaped top rails and solid vase-shaped splats on chairs; upholstered horseshoe-shaped seats. Cabriole legs. Feet: pad, slipper, trifid, and, later, claw-and-ball.

Primary woods Walnut; also maple, cherry, or, later, mahogany. *Secondary woods* Maple, pine, ash, cedar, beech, tulip, or others.

Notable forms Splat-back chair. Upholstered easy chair, sofa, and settee, often with arched backs. Low-post and canopy beds. Tables: card, tea, drop-leaf, side, candlestand, and others.

Chippendale Style: 1750–1780

Proportions Broad but delicate.

Essential elements Curved and elaborately carved parts. Carved motifs such as scrolls, shells, and acanthus leaves. Cabriole and Marlborough legs. Claw-and-ball feet. Fretwork decoration. Yoke-shaped top rails with upturned ends on chairs. Pierced chair splats, sometimes with Gothic arches, flora, and trefoils. Upholstered seats with straight sides. Some gadrooned skirts on tables and chairs.

Primary woods Mahogany; sometimes walnut, maple, or cherry. *Secondary woods* Maple, pine, ash, cedar, beech, tulip, or others.

Notable forms Splat-back and ladder-back chairs. Upholstered easy chair, sofa, and settee, often with arched backs. Tables: tea, card, drop-leaf, Pembroke, and tilt-top. Low-post and canopy beds.

Federal Style: 1780–1820

Proportions Slender and delicate.

Essential elements Geometric overall shapes. Flat and simplified classical ornament, such as pateras, bellflowers, urns of flowers, columns, feathers, and patriotic symbols; executed in low relief, inlay, veneer, or paint. Legs: tapered and round or square, or saber; sometimes reeded. Spade or arrow feet. Vase- or lyre-shaped pedestal bases on tables.

Primary woods Mahogany; satinwood or other contrasting veneers. *Secondary woods* Pine or others.

Notable forms Chairs: shield-back, oval-back, square-back, klismos, Martha Washington, and painted Fancy. Sofa with straight-topped or arched back. Grecian couch. Tables: work or sewing, large dining (extension or sectional), side, pier, and serving. Low-post and canopy beds.

Empire Style: 1815–1840

Proportions Massive and bulky.

Essential elements Bold carving in high relief, emphasizing outline instead of detail. Oversized classical motifs. Structural scroll components and heavy geometric shapes. Stenciling or gilded brass or bronze decoration. Handsome veneers. Saber or curule legs. Feet: large scroll, ball, or carved animal. Solid vase-shaped splats on some chairs. Marble tops and heavy pedestal bases on tables.

Primary woods Rosewood or mahogany; also handsomely grained maple; pine, birch, or other local woods for country pieces. *Secondary wood* Beginning in the Empire period, pine became almost standard.

Notable forms Klismos chair. Scroll-end sofa and settee. Récamier and méridienne. Ornamental center table; mirrored-back pier table. Sleigh and canopy beds.

Country and Shaker Furniture: 1690–1900

Proportions Depending on period and style of country furniture, but slender and delicate for Shaker pieces.

Essential elements Simplified shapes, traditional construction, and minimal decoration, all derived from fashionable designs of the 17th to 19th centuries. Turned or cutout parts. Rush, splint, tape, or cane seats. Often painted.

Woods Pine, maple, or various local fruitwoods or softwoods.

Notable forms Slat-back and other chairs. Stool. Bench. Settle. Low-post bed. Cradle. Drop-leaf, tea, work or sewing, and other tables.

Windsor Furniture: 1730–1830

Proportions Medium to delicate.

Essential elements Interlocking turned or cutout parts. Chair and settee backs with a series of plain spindles enclosed by a curved or straight top rail. Saddle- or shield-shaped seat. Angled legs. Turned stretchers. Often painted.

Woods Several used for each piece, typically pine and maple with hickory, ash, or birch.

Notable forms Chair. Stool. Settee. Occasionally tables.

Gothic Revival Style: 1840–1880

Proportions Medium to large.

Essential elements Gothic motifs such as tracery, arches, rose windows, and quatrefoils. Bold turned or cutout parts. Spiral or spool turnings (in Elizabethan style).

Woods Walnut; also mahogany, rosewood, cherry, or oak.

Notable forms Tall-back chairs, some with upholstered backs. Footstool. Bed. Sofa and settee. Extension and center tables.

Rococo Revival Style: 1840–70

Proportions Medium to large.

Essential elements Curving overall shapes. Bold and naturalistic piercework or solid carving of flowers, fruit, and leaves framed by scrolls. Cabriole and scrolled legs. Tufted upholstery and inner springs. Marble table tops. Laminated wood used on some pieces. Forms sometimes adapted in cast iron.

Woods Mahogany or rosewood; also walnut for lower-priced pieces.

Notable forms Balloon-back and upholstered-back chairs. Fully upholstered sofa with serpentine back, méridienne, settee, and tête-à-tête. Side and center tables. Elaborate beds.

Renaissance Revival Style: 1850–1880

Proportions Medium to large.

Essential elements Rectilinear shapes. Prominent Renaissance and Neoclassical motifs such as columns, pediments, cartouches, rosettes, and carved masks; also plaques in porcelain, bronze, or mother-of-pearl. Occasional Egyptian motifs. Veneer panels, often framed by applied molding. Inscribed linear decoration. Turned or cutout parts on factory pieces; carving or elaborate inlay on finer examples. Forms sometimes adapted in cast iron.

Woods Walnut; also ash or pine for less expensive pieces.

Notable forms Upholstered chair and sofa. Stool. Bed. Extension and center tables. Pedestal.

Eastlake Style: 1870–1890

Proportions Medium and delicate.

Essential elements Simple rectilinear shapes. Geometric or floral ornament, often carved in low relief. Inscribed linear decoration. Turned spindles and stiles. Inset panels. Scroll-cut brackets. Middle or Far Eastern motifs. Some ebonizing.

Woods Oak, walnut, cherry, or maple.

Notable forms Chair. Sofa. Stool. Bed. Side and center tables. Pedestal.

Colonial Revival Style: 1890–1925

Proportions Narrower and more slender than 18th-century originals.

Essential elements Traditional 18th-century motifs and shapes, rendered more schematically. Some modern construction techniques such as metal braces.

Woods Oak; or traditional high-style woods such as mahogany and walnut.

Notable forms Most Colonial types.

Art Nouveau Style: 1895–1910
Proportions Elongated.
Essential elements Sinuous elongated forms. Elaborate carving or inlay. Floral, curving, and various organic motifs.
Woods Oak for mass-produced pieces; mahogany, rosewood, maple, or exotic woods such as amboyna for elegant examples.
Notable forms All types.

Mission/Arts and Crafts Styles: 1900–1925
Proportions Squat and boxy.
Essential elements Simple rectilinear forms. Rows of vertical or horizontal slats across chair and settee backs. Exposed tenons, sometimes secured by wooden pegs or keys. Leather upholstery. More decoration on examples in the Arts and Crafts tradition.
Wood Oak.
Notable forms Chair. Settee. Bench. Settle. Small and large tables.

Art Deco Style: 1925–1945
Proportions Small to medium.
Essential elements Bold geometric shapes based on traditional forms. Simplified geometric ornament.
Materials Pine or maple for less expensive lacquered or painted pieces; mahogany, walnut, or more exotic woods for finer examples. Sometimes metal or glass.
Notable forms Overstuffed armchair, sofa, and ottoman. Dining-room and kitchen sets. Side, coffee, and end tables. Beds. Other distinctive forms.

Modern (or Bauhaus) Style: 1925–1950
Proportions Small to medium, generally delicate.
Essential elements Innovative forms. Industrial materials. Minimal decoration.
Materials Tubular steel and other metals. Pine for lacquered or painted pieces; teak, mahogany, or rosewood for luxurious pieces. Plywood. Plastic.
Notable forms All types, particularly the chair with cantilevered seat.

List of Plates by Style

Art Deco
Chairs: 89, 134–137, 139, 148, 154, 158, 159. Daybed: 185.
Stools: 214, 215. Tables: 266, 276, 306, 308, 314.

Art Nouveau
Chairs: 107, 151. Table: 279.

Arts and Crafts
Chairs: 81, 82. Stands: 318, 321.

Bentwood
Chairs: 83, 92, 147. Cradle: 219.

Cast Iron and Brass
Beds: 238–240. Chairs: 93, 95, 96. Settee: 197.

China Trade
Chairs: 48, 86. Sofa: 171.

Chippendale
Bed: 228. Chairs: 61, 62, 65–71, 143, 145, 149. Sofas: 161, 162.
Tables: 254, 255, 259, 261, 291, 292.

Colonial Revival
Chairs: 15, 16, 18, 37, 55, 57, 64, 127. Settee: 196. Tables: 247,
343.

Country
Bed: 226. Bench: 201. Chairs: 4, 5, 7–9, 17, 33, 34, 53, 54, 69, 70.
Cradle: 216. Daybed: 223. Settles: 199, 200. Sofa: 163. Stools:
202, 206. Tables: 242, 244, 250, 272, 273, 282, 283, 322, 323, 327,
346, 347.

Eastlake
Beds: 230, 231, 233. Chairs: 47, 73, 90, 125, 126, 129–131.
Daybed: 184. Settee: 180. Sofa: 186. Tables: 280, 281, 298, 301,
330, 332, 333, 335.

Elizabethan Revival
Cradle: 220. Daybed: 222.

Empire
Bed: 221. Chairs: 45, 46, 51, 52, 106. Cradle: 220. Daybed: 171.
Settle: 200. Sofas: 167–169, 171, 172. Stool: 206. Tables: 244, 258,
278, 294, 296, 297, 302, 303, 305, 338. Window Seat: 182.

Federal (Sheraton and Hepplewhite)
Beds: 225–227, 229. Chairs: 10, 13, 14, 19, 20, 39–44, 72, 75–79,
146, 150. Cradle: 217. Daybeds: 183, 223. Settees: 160, 192–194.
Sofas: 163–166, 170. Stools: 203, 210. Tables: 242, 253, 257, 262,
272, 284–286, 288, 295, 322, 325, 326, 334, 339–341, 344–347.

Gothic Revival
Chairs: 80, 111, 112. Stool: 208.

Hepplewhite
See Federal.

Mission
Chairs: 11, 155–157. Settees: 189. Settle: 190. Stool: 205.
Tables: 268, 277, 312, 319, 320, 336.

Modern
Bed: 241. Chairs: 99–105, 133, 138, 147. Settees: 187, 188.
Stool: 213. Tables: 267, 307, 309, 313, 315–317.

Pilgrim
Chairs: 38, 140, 141.

Queen Anne

Chairs: 34, 53, 54, 56, 59, 60, 63, 142, 144. Tables: 243, 249, 256, 260, 273, 282, 283, 289, 290.

Renaissance Revival

Beds: 234, 236. Chairs: 74, 94, 110, 114, 115, 120–124, 128. Crib: 218. Sofas: 177–179. Stools: 207, 209. Tables: 248, 287, 299, 328, 329, 331.

Rococo Revival

Beds: 235, 237. Chairs: 49, 50, 93, 95, 113, 116–119. Settees: 181, 197. Sofas: 172–176. Stool: 211. Tables: 252, 293, 300, 342.

Rustic

Chair: 12. Table: 265.

Shaker

Bed: 224. Chairs: 1–3, 6, 31. Settee: 191. Tables: 263, 274, 275, 324.

Sheraton

See Federal.

Victorian

Bed: 232. Chairs: 91, 127, 132, 152, 153. Tables: 252, 264, 304. *See also* Gothic Revival, Renaissance Revival, Rococo Revival, Elizabethan Revival, Eastlake, Cast Iron and Brass, and Wicker.

Wicker

Chairs: 84, 85, 87–89. Settee: 198. Stool: 212. Tables: 311, 337.

William and Mary

Chairs: 7, 8, 33, 35, 36, 108, 109. Daybed: 195. Stool: 204. Tables: 245, 246, 251, 269–271, 323.

Windsor

Chairs: 13, 14, 19–30, 32. Settee: 192. Stool: 203.

–

Upholstery Guide

Since upholstery covers as much as 90 percent of the surface area of many chairs, sofas, and other forms of seating, it is a crucial element in virtually every style. The earliest American furniture was rarely upholstered, but when it was, the upholstery consisted of simple cloth, needlework, embroidery, or leather. In the 18th and early 19th centuries, elegant imported fabrics were employed to cover high-style pieces. Later in the 19th century, more and more fabrics woven in American factories were used. Since upholstery is meant to suit the character of a piece, it is important to check the correlation of the covering material and its pattern—in the appropriate scale—with the

Pilgrim
Needlework fabric, called turkeywork (*1*), resembling Middle Eastern rug patterns; plain rough-textured wool or silk; also leather. *See* 140.

William and Mary
Silk in oversize floral patterns (*2*); velvet in large Baroque patterns (*3*); wool in solid colors with elaborate fringe; leather, sometimes with stamped designs. *See* 108.

Queen Anne
Waterstained wool or other plain woven textiles; flamestitch needlework pattern (*4*); crewelwork in large pictorial or floral designs (*5*); silk or wool damask; painted or printed cotton; also some leather. *See* 56, 60, 144.

Chippendale
Silk or wool (damask or brocade) in large Rococo floral, foliate, and scroll patterns (*6*); cotton prints, such as pastoral scenes (*7*); embroidered fabrics; wool or leather. *See* 67, 70, 143, 145, 162.

decorative style. Original upholstery is very rare on period furniture, however, and the upholstery found on many antique chairs and sofas is often badly worn or unsuitable. A good solution for such pieces is the use of reproduction fabrics; fortunately, these are widely available.

To help you choose upholstery materials and patterns, we have illustrated and described some popular examples here. All the major styles are represented except Mission, since the typical solid textured fabric or leather of that style does not need illustration. For further guidance, check the color plates listed at the end of each of the following descriptions.

Early Federal

Silk or wool with delicate waterstained, wavy, or classical
patterns; silk in small repeating pattern or stripes (*8*);
silk brocade or damask in floral, bough, and lattice patterns (*9*);
cotton prints in light-scale designs; plain solid-color cloth.
See 75–78, 160.

Late Federal

Silk or satin in classical patterns, such as feathers and baskets of
flowers (*10*), as well as animals or medallions with classical
figures (*11*). *See* 164, 170.

Empire

Silk damask in bold, large-scale classical designs, such as
columns and vines (*12*), or in repeating patterns of stylized
flowerheads and medallions or urns (*13*); solid silk with applied
stripes; solid velvet. *See* 167–168, 182.

Gothic Revival

Needlework in small repeating Gothic pattern (*14*); printed
cotton or woven damask or brocade in architectural patterns;
sometimes leather. *See* 113.

Rococo Revival

Silk or wool (damask or brocade) in Rococo pattern of flowers
and scrolls (*15*, *16*); woolen prints; a variety of rich solid-color
fabrics. *See* 116, 119, 175–176.

Renaissance Revival

Silk or wool in symmetrical, Neoclassical (Louis XVI) floral, foliate, and ribbon patterns (*17*) or with architectural elements, medallions, or flower urns (*18*); carpetlike pile fabric or tapestry for folding chairs; velvet and other solid-color fabrics. *See* 120, 126, 177, 207.

Eastlake

Silk, wool, or cotton in delicate Japanese, Near Eastern, or medieval motifs (*19*); Arts and Crafts patterns such as those by the English craftsman William Morris (*20*); carpetlike pile fabric in printed patterns. *See* 128–129.

Art Nouveau

Silk (damask or brocade) or tapestry in elongated, stylized floral or curvilinear patterns (*21*, *22*). *See* 122.

Art Deco

Wool, silk, or cotton in geometric patterns influenced by Cubism (*23*) or in oversize floral patterns (*24*); solid fabrics with contrasting welting. *See* 154, 159, 185.

Modern

Wool, cotton, silk, or synthetics printed or woven in simple schematic or abstract patterns (*25*), often influenced by Bauhaus fabric design; also solid-color materials. *See* 138–139.

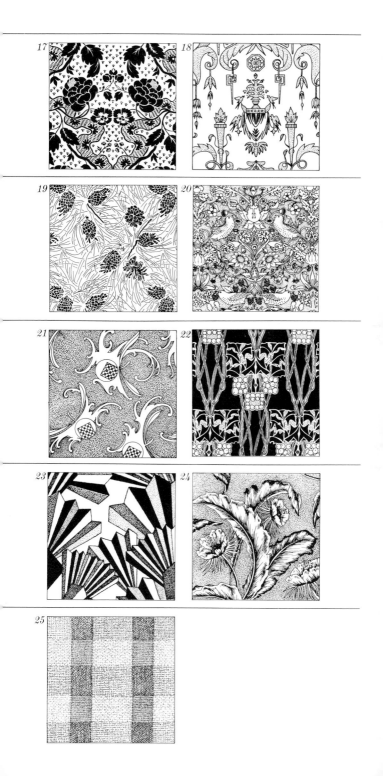

Public Collections

Most large art museums exhibit American furniture. In addition, many of the historic houses, buildings, and restoration villages that are open to the public have fine examples. The sources listed below indicate significant permanent collections.

New England
Connecticut Hartford: Wadsworth Atheneum. New Haven: Yale University Art Gallery.
Maine Columbia Falls: Ruggles House. Ellsworth: Colonel Black Mansion. New Gloucester: The Shaker Museum.
Massachusetts Andover: Addison Gallery of American Art, Phillips Academy. Boston: Museum of Fine Arts; The Society for the Preservation of New England Antiquities. Deerfield: Historic Deerfield. Hancock: Hancock Shaker Village. Milton: China Trade Museum. Sturbridge: Old Sturbridge Village.
New Hampshire Manchester: The Currier Gallery of Art.
Rhode Island Providence: Museum of Art, Rhode Island School of Design.
Vermont Shelburne: Shelburne Museum.

Mid-Atlantic Region
Delaware Winterthur: Henry Francis du Pont Winterthur Museum.
District of Columbia Department of State Diplomatic Reception Rooms; National Museum of American History, Smithsonian Institution; The Octagon House; Renwick Gallery of the National Museum of American Art, Smithsonian Institution; The White House.
Maryland Baltimore: Baltimore Museum of Art; Maryland Historical Society.
New Jersey Newark: Newark Museum and the Ballantine House.
New York Albany: Albany Institute of History and Art. Cooperstown: New York State Historical Association. Garrison: Boscobel. Old Bethpage, Long Island: Old Bethpage Village. Old Chatham: The Shaker Museum. Rochester: The Margaret Woodbury Strong Museum. Tarrytown: Sleepy Hollow Restorations. Utica: Munson-Williams-Proctor Institute.
New York City The Brooklyn Museum; Cooper-Hewitt Museum, Smithsonian Institution's National Museum of Design; Dyckman House and Museum; The Metropolitan Museum of Art; Morris-Jumel Mansion; Museum of American Folk Art; Museum of the City of New York; Museum of Modern Art; The New-York Historical Society; Old Merchant's House; Abigail Adams Smith Museum.
Pennsylvania Philadelphia: Fairmount Park Historic Houses; Independence Hall; Philadelphia Museum of Art.

South
Alabama Mobile: The Fine Arts Museum of the South.
Florida Winter Park: The Morse Gallery of Art.
Georgia Atlanta: The High Museum of Art.
Louisiana New Orleans: Longue Vue Center for Decorative Arts.
Missouri Kansas City: William Rockhill Nelson Gallery and Atkins Museum of Fine Arts. St. Louis: St. Louis Art Museum.
North Carolina Winston-Salem: Museum of Early Southern Decorative Arts.
South Carolina Charleston: Historic Charleston.
Virginia Norfolk: Chrysler Museum at Norfolk. Richmond: Virginia Museum of Fine Arts. Williamsburg: Colonial Williamsburg; The Abby Aldrich Rockefeller Collection of American Folk Art.

Midwest

Illinois Chicago: Art Institute of Chicago; Chicago Historical Society.

Indiana Indianapolis: Indianapolis Museum of Art.

Iowa Amana: Amana Villages.

Michigan Dearborn: Greenfield Village and Henry Ford Museum. Detroit: Detroit Historical Museum; Detroit Institute of Arts.

Minnesota Minneapolis: Minneapolis Institute of Arts.

Ohio Cincinnati: Cincinnati Art Museum. Cleveland: Cleveland Museum of Art; Western Reserve Historical Society. Toledo: Toledo Museum of Art.

Wisconsin Milwaukee: Milwaukee Public Museum; Villa-Terrace Museum of the Decorative Arts.

Rockies, Southwest, and West Coast

Arizona Tucson: Arizona Historical Society.

California Los Angeles: Hollyhock House; Los Angeles County Museum of Art. Oakland: The Oakland Museum. Pasadena: Gamble House. San Diego: San Diego Museum of Art. San Francisco: M. H. de Young Memorial Museum, Fine Arts Museums.

Colorado Denver: The Denver Art Museum.

Kansas Lawrence: Helen Foresman Spencer Museum of Art, the University of Kansas.

Nebraska Omaha: Joslyn Art Museum.

Texas Dallas: Dallas Museum of Fine Arts. Houston: The Bayou Bend Collection, Museum of Fine Arts.

Washington Seattle: Seattle Art Museum.

Glossary

Acanthus leaf
Foliate decoration used in classical architecture; adapted as motif in furniture design, usually carved on knees of Chippendale cabriole legs and on pedestal bases of Empire tables.

Aesthetic movement
English artistic movement from about 1860 to 1890, wherein the design of all objects was elevated to the level of the so-called fine arts. Japanese and other exotic influences were combined with traditional furniture design. Influential in America in the 1880s.

Anthemion
See Palmette.

Applied ornament
Carved or shaped decoration, usually wood or metal, glued or nailed to furniture; appears on elegant Chippendale pieces and in a succession of 19th-century styles.

Arcade
Architectural element of a series of arches supported on columns. The series of columns is called a colonnade.

Arrow foot
Tapered cylindrical foot separated from leg by turned ring.

Art Deco
Decorative style originating in France in the 1920s, characterized by geometric shapes, stylized ornament, and fine traditional craftsmanship. Popularized in America in the 1920s and 1930s. The streamlined 1930s version is often called Art Moderne.

Art Moderne
See Art Deco.

Art Nouveau
Turn-of-the-century decorative style originating in France, characterized by elongated forms usually ornamented with sinuous curves, stylized flowers, and other Japanese-inspired motifs. Less influential in America than in Europe.

Arts and Crafts movement
Late 19th-century artistic movement in England, based on William Morris's ideal of simple medieval handwork and rejection of mechanized Victorian design. Influential in America from 1900 to 1920, it includes functional oak furniture in the Mission style.

Ball foot
Spherical turned foot most popular in the William and Mary period; also used on some Empire pieces.

Baluster
A vase-turned, columnar element usually used to support a stair rail; also called bannister. Adapted as motif in furniture design when split in 2 and used in a vertical series on a chair back.

Baroque
The major style of 17th-century Europe, characterized by scrolls, elaborate ornament, and inventive use of classical motifs. Reflected in the American William and Mary style.

Batten
A strip of wood, used to prevent warping, attached at right angles to the grain of planks forming a tabletop or other element.

Bauhaus
German school of art and design, founded in 1919, where innovative work in architecture and the decorative arts was undertaken. Its inventive forms and new materials have been influential in America since the 1920s, inspiring so-called "modern" designs.

Beading
A narrow half-round molding or series of adjacent beadlike balls used as decoration.

Bellflower
Classical floral motif of a series of 3 or 5 narrow pointed petals in bell shape, carved or inlaid.

Bentwood
Steamed and bent strip of wood, often tubular, used in furniture construction. Technique perfected by Michael Thonet (1796–1871) in Austria-Hungary.

Beveled
See Chamfered.

Boss
Small applied wooden decorative device, usually round or oval.

Bracket
Shaped wooden or metal support, usually in the form of a right angle.

Brocade
Elegant fabric woven with a raised design; often silk.

Bun foot
A squat version of a ball foot, flattened slightly on top and more on the bottom.

Burl
Protruding growth on a tree that, when sliced, reveals beautiful graining. Used as veneer on American William and Mary furniture as well as on 19th-century pieces.

Butterfly table
Table having drop leaves held up by swinging supports in the shape of a butterfly wing.

Cabochon
A carved ornament, oval or round, resembling a convex uncut jewel, from which the name derives.

Cabriole leg
Curving furniture member resembling an animal leg. In Queen Anne style, usually with pad foot; in Chippendale style, claw-and-ball foot most common.

Camel-back
High-arched (humplike) upholstered back of a sofa; typical of Queen Anne, Chippendale, and Federal examples.

Cane (or Caning)
Tightly woven strips of rattan used first in America about 1690 for chair seats.

Canopy
Framework topping tall-post bed, usually draped with fabric. Sometimes called a tester.

Canted
Term describing an angled or oblique element.

Cantilevered
Term for a projecting element supported at only one end by a vertical member.

Capital
The enlarged top of a column, often carved, adapted from classical architecture and used as furniture decoration on legs and stiles.

Cartouche
An ornate Rococo framing motif with scrolled edges, used on Chippendale and various 19th-century revival-style pieces.

Chamfered
Having a flat area made by cutting away a corner or edge formed by 2 surfaces at right angles to each other.

Chinese taste
A phrase used by Thomas Chippendale to describe many of his Chinese-inspired decorative elements.

Chippendale style
Furniture style named for London cabinetmaker Thomas Chippendale (1718–79) and inspired by designs published in his *Director* (1754–62). Basically Rococo, the style includes Gothic and so-called Chinese elements. Prevalent in America from 1750 to 1780, where it was more conservative than in England.

Classical style
Style of design inspired by Greek and Roman art and architecture, most influential in America in Federal-era and Empire designs.

Claw-and-ball foot
Endpiece consisting of the claw of a bird or dragon grasping a ball flattened on the bottom, often on a Queen Anne, Chippendale, or Colonial Revival cabriole leg.

Colonial Revival Style
Style in furniture and architecture that imitated or freely interpreted American designs from the Pilgrim to Federal eras. Begun in the 1880s, it became the dominant style of the early 20th century.

Column
Classical pillar consisting of a capital, cylindrical shaft, and base; often used as design motif on Chippendale, Federal, Empire, and Renaissance Revival furniture.

Corbel
Decorative bracket, derived from structural element in architecture.

Cornice
The horizontal molding or group of moldings at the top of a piece of furniture.

Country furniture
Simple designs of the period between the late 17th and mid-19th centuries; usually made by rural craftsmen, though occasionally by urban cabinetmakers.

Cresting
The carved decoration on the top rail of a chair, sofa, or daybed.

Curule legs
X-shaped legs based on Roman chair design, used on Federal and other classically inspired furnishings.

Cusp
Pointed contour formed by 2 intersecting arcs.

Damask
Richly patterned fabric, usually of silk, linen, or wool.

Dentil molding
Classical motif consisting of a series of small rectangular blocks projecting like teeth.

Dovetail joint
Joining of 2 boards at right angles to each other by interlocking flared tenons, thought to resemble a dove's tail.

Drop
Wooden decorative element, often urn- or bell-shaped, hanging from the skirt of a table or seat rail of a chair.

Drop-leaf table
Table with hinged leaves that can be raised to enlarge the top. In this category are butterfly, gate-leg, and Pembroke tables.

Ears
Up-curved ends of top rail, usually on Chippendale chairs.

Eastlake style
Style named after English architect and designer Charles Lock Eastlake (1836–1906), whose *Hints on Household Taste* (1868) advocated reform of furniture design. American pieces from 1870 to 1890, rectilinear and frequently displaying exotic motifs, reflected the Eastlake approach.

Ebonized
Term for wood stained black to resemble ebony, often for contrasting color; used in America in the William and Mary period and the 19th century.

Empire style
Early 19th-century French Neoclassical style inspired by furniture made for Napoleon; widely adopted in Europe and America (1815–40).

Escutcheon
Decorative plate surrounding a keyhole, usually of brass, but sometimes of ivory in the Federal era.

Fancy chair
Painted chair in Neoclassical style, usually Sheraton, popular 1790–1850. Decoration is often stenciled and painted.

Federal style
American style of the early Republic (1780–1820), influenced by English Neoclassicism of Robert Adam, George Hepplewhite, and Thomas Sheraton.

Finial
Turned or carved ornament, ranging from simple egg shape to flaming urn, atop a stile or other vertical member.

Fluting
A series of narrow grooves, usually vertical, used in ancient architecture on columns; later used in Europe and America to decorate classically inspired furniture; the reverse of reeding.

Fretwork
Openwork or pierced ornament, usually geometric, found on friezes, galleries of tables, stretchers, and brackets on legs; popular on Chinese-influenced Chippendale furniture.

Gadrooning
Carved ornamental edging consisting of a series of slanted convex sections; particularly popular on Chippendale furniture made in New York and Philadelphia.

Gallery
Decorative raised border usually along the edge of the top of a table; used with Chippendale, Federal, and later styles.

Gate leg
Swinging gatelike support for a drop leaf, made of 2 legs joined together by upper and lower stretchers; most common on William and Mary tables.

Gilded
Decorated with thinly applied gold leaf or gold paint.

Gothic style
European architectural style of the 12th to 15th centuries. Major Gothic revival in American architecture and design occurred 1840–60, and again in the 1870s.

Greek key
Ornamental band found on classically inspired furniture, consisting of repeated square hook shapes formed by intersecting horizontal and vertical lines. Sometimes called meander pattern.

Hepplewhite style
Neoclassical style named for English furniture designer George Hepplewhite (d. 1786); popular in America during the Federal era.

Inlay
Design made of small pieces of contrasting colored wood or other materials set into recesses carved out of a solid surface; used particularly on Queen Anne, Federal, Renaissance Revival, and Eastlake furniture.

Inscribed
Carved or engraved with linear decoration.

Key
Interlocking element set through an exposed tenon; a medieval joinery technique used on some Mission-style furniture.

Klismos
Ancient Greek chair form characterized by a broad top rail and curved stiles and legs; revived in the late 18th and early 19th centuries.

Knee
The upper convex curve of a cabriole leg.

Lacquering
Decorative process of applying successive layers of varnish to wood; ancient Oriental finishing technique introduced to the West in the 17th century.

Laminated wood
Superimposed layers of wood veneer glued together; grains of adjacent layers arranged perpendicularly. Used extensively by John Henry Belter in the 19th century and later by Charles Eames.

Lattice
Open framework made of crisscrossed wood or metal strips, often in a diamond pattern.

Marlborough leg
Straight-sided leg introduced as in the Chinese taste by Thomas Chippendale.

Marquetry
Decorative technique in which elaborate patterns are formed by inserting shaped pieces of wood or other contrasting materials into a veneer applied to another surface.

Medallion
Round, oval, square, or octagonal plaque, painted or carved with decorative figures.

Molding
Continuous strip of wood, of rounded or more complex profile, used as a decorative relief band.

Mortise-and-tenon construction
Technique for joining 2 pieces of wood: the mortise is a cavity, usually rectangular, and the tenon, a protruding end shaped to fit the cavity.

Ormolu
Bronze or brass to which a thin layer of gold has been applied, popular in Rococo and Neoclassical styles for furniture mounts.

Pad foot
Simple rounded foot, sometimes set on a disk; favored on Queen Anne cabriole legs.

Palmette
Fan-shaped ornamental motif resembling either a palm leaf or a loose cluster of honeysuckle flowers. A band of palmettes is called an anthemion.

Patera
Oval or circular ornament carved or inlaid in patterns of Roman origin. Sometimes only a segment of the circle may be used.

Patina
Mellow and worn aspect a surface acquires through age; highly desirable quality on most antique furniture.

Paw foot
Foot carved to resemble an animal paw, usually a lion's.

Pediment
Triangular or arched cresting above a building or doorway or on a piece of furniture. Called a broken pediment when sides do not converge at an apex.

Peg
Wooden pin passing through both units of a mortise-and-tenon joint to bind them together.

Piercework
Openwork design particularly characteristic of Chippendale and Federal chair splats and Rococo Revival carving.

Pilaster
Rectangular column projecting about one quarter of its ordinary depth from a surface; used as an ornamental detail on furniture.

Pilgrim style
Term describing 17th-century American furniture based on medieval, Renaissance, and 17th-century European designs.

Plinth
Block forming the base on which a column or pedestal rests.

Quatrefoil
Gothic decorative motif of 4 lobes arranged in an abstract floral design.

Queen Anne style
English furniture style displaying curving Rococo elements and fine carving; dominant American style from 1725 to 1750.

Rail
Horizontal structural component usually connecting the stiles across the back of a chair or sofa and also framing a seat.

Rattan
Palm stems used as material for making wicker furniture.

Reeding
Thin convex moldings, usually vertical, used to decorate round legs and bedposts on classical-style furniture; the reverse of fluting.

Relief carving
Decoration formed by carving away the background to produce projecting figures or forms; called low relief when only slightly projecting and high relief when more deeply cut.

Renaissance style
European art and architecture style of the 15th to 17th centuries. Major American revival style of 1850–70 which freely adapted Renaissance forms; reappeared in the 1890s.

Rococo style
Ornate style originating in France in the 18th century and evolving from the Baroque style. It was a whimsical interpretation of mainly classical designs, characterized by carved shells and S-shaped curves. The Queen Anne style was a restrained version, and the Chippendale a more elaborate version of the Rococo. A major Rococo revival occurred in America in 1840–60.

Rosette
Circular floral design, sometimes simplified and abstract.

Rush
Stems of a grasslike marsh plant woven into chair seats, usually on American country examples, from the 17th through 19th centuries.

Saber leg
Classically inspired leg curving sharply outward and generally tapered.

Saddle seat
Seat shaped like a saddle to fit the human form, used especially on Windsor chairs, occasionally on more elegant furniture.

Scroll
Spiral decorative form resembling a partially rolled paper scroll.

Secondary wood
Wood used for any unexposed parts of furniture, usually an inexpensive softwood such as pine.

Serpentine
Contour of a wavy surface, particularly one having a convex center flanked by concave ends.

Settle
Country bench with high back and arms of solid wood; seat is often hinged to allow access to storage space beneath.

Sheraton style
Neoclassical style named for English furniture designer Thomas Sheraton (1751–1806); popular in America during the Federal era.

Skirt
Plain or valanced element suspended from the rail of a chair seat or table.

Slat
Flat narrow band of wood, often set in a horizontal series across the back of 17th-century chairs and later country versions; sometimes used to support seat cushions or mattresses in other styles.

Slipper foot
A pointed and elongated variation of the pad foot found mostly on Queen Anne furniture.

Slip seat
Removable upholstered seat slipped or inserted into an open chair frame; found on Queen Anne, Chippendale, and Colonial Revival examples.

Snake foot
Narrow elongated foot swelling slightly upward before pointed end; found on Queen Anne, Chippendale, and some Federal tripod-base tables.

Spade foot
Tapered rectangular foot commonly found on Hepplewhite pieces.

Spanish foot
Scrolled foot with curving vertical ribs; used on turned legs in the William and Mary and the Queen Anne periods.

Spindle
One of a series of slender turned rods set in vertical rows to fill in chair backs and galleries.

Splat
Flat vertical element in the center of a chair back. Usually vase-shaped on Queen Anne and Chippendale chairs; also pierced on the latter.

Spline
Thin strip of wood set into deep grooves to fasten boards or planks.

Splint
Thin oak or hickory strips interlaced to form a chair seat; popular since the 17th century.

Stenciling
Painted decoration applied through a cutout pattern, commonly used on country and later mass-produced furniture.

Stile
Vertical structural member usually framing the back of a chair or sofa; often called a post if turned.

Stretcher
Turned rod, or plain or cutout slat, used to reinforce legs.

Tape seat
Seat woven from sturdy cotton strips; characteristic of Shaker chairs.

Tenon
See Mortise-and-tenon construction.

Tête-à-tête
S-shaped settee with 2 catercornered seats; also called a conversational sofa.

Tongue-and-groove construction
Construction technique for joining 2 pieces of wood. The groove is a long narrow channel; the tongue, a projection shaped to fit the channel.

Tracery
Gothic decorative element consisting of thin interlacing strips of cut wood or molding.

Trefoil
3-lobed Gothic decorative motif.

Trestle
Table support of medieval inspiration, consisting of 2 or more inverted T or Y shapes braced by a stretcher or brackets.

Trifid foot
3-lobed endpiece of a Queen Anne cabriole leg; also called a drake foot.

Turning
Wood shaped by applying a chisel to it while it is rotated on a lathe. Common turned shapes are: ball, ring, spiral, sausage, rope, spool, trumpet, vase, and combinations of these.

Turnip foot
Ball foot with a small collar at its base.

Valance
Symmetrical cutout shapes, usually curved, decorating the lower edge of a seat or table rail; also, drapery of a bed canopy.

Veneer
Thin sheet of decoratively grained wood glued to the surface of inferior or inexpensive wood, such as pine. Used in William and Mary, Queen Anne, Federal, Empire, and later 19th-century furniture.

Waterleaf
Carved ornament based on the laurel leaf; Neoclassical counterpart of the acanthus leaf.

Welting
Tape or covered cord sewn into the seams of upholstered furniture for reinforcement and decoration.

Wicker
Furniture woven of rattan, willow, bamboo, or other imported or local grasses.

William and Mary style
Late English version of the Baroque style, characterized by carved scroll shapes and turned elements, named for the English monarchs (reigning jointly 1689–94). American version thrived about 1690–1725.

Bibliography

Andersen, Timothy J. et al.
California Design 1910
Pasadena, California: California Design Publications, 1974
Reprinted Santa Barbara, California, and Salt Lake City, Utah: Peregrine Smith, Inc., 1980.

Andrews, Edward Deming and Faith
Religion in Wood: A Book of Shaker Furniture
Bloomington, Indiana, and London: Indiana University Press, 1966.

Bishop, Robert
Centuries and Styles of the American Chair 1640–1970
New York: E.P. Dutton, Inc., 1972.
How to Know American Antique Furniture
New York: E.P. Dutton, Inc., 1973.

Bjerkoe, Ethel Hall
The Cabinetmakers of America
Garden City, New York: Doubleday & Co., Inc., 1957
Reprinted Exton, Pennsylvania: Schiffer Publishing, Ltd., 1981.

Butler, Joseph T.
American Antiques, 1800–1900: A Collector's History and Guide
New York: The Odyssey Press, 1965.

Cathers, David M.
Furniture of the American Arts and Crafts Movement, Stickley and Roycroft Mission Oak
New York: New American Library, 1981.

Clark, Robert Judson et al.
The Arts and Crafts Movement in America
Princeton: Princeton University Press, 1972.

Comstock, Helen
American Furniture: Seventeenth, Eighteenth, and Nineteenth Century Styles
New York: The Viking Press, 1962.

Corbin, Patricia
All About Wicker
New York: E.P. Dutton, Inc., 1978.

Crossman, Carl L.
A Design Catalogue of Chinese Export Paintings, Furniture, Silver & Other Objects, 1785–1865
Salem, Massachusetts: Peabody Museum, 1970.

Downs, Joseph
American Furniture: Queen Anne and Chippendale Periods in the Henry Francis du Pont Winterthur Museum
New York: The Macmillan Co., 1952.

Elder, William Voss
Maryland Queen Anne and Chippendale Furniture of the Eighteenth Century
Baltimore: The Baltimore Museum of Art, 1968.

Fairbanks, Jonathan, and Bates, Elizabeth Bidwell
American Furniture 1620 to the Present
New York: Richard Marek Publishers, 1981.

Fales, Dean A., Jr.
American Painted Furniture 1660–1880
New York: E.P. Dutton, Inc., 1979.

Fitzgerald, Oscar P.
Three Centuries of American Furniture
Englewood Cliffs, New Jersey: Prentice-Hall, Inc., 1981.

Gusler, Wallace B.
Furniture of Williamsburg and Eastern Virginia, 1710–1790
Richmond, Virginia: Virginia Museum of Fine Arts, n.d.

Hanks, David
Innovative Furniture in America: From 1800 to the Present
New York: Horizon Press Publishers, 1981.

Hillier, Bevis
The World of Art Deco
New York: E.P. Dutton, Inc., 1981.

Horner, William Macpherson, Jr.
Blue Book, Philadelphia Furniture, William Penn to George Washington
Philadelphia: privately printed, 1935.

Hummel, Charles F.
A Winterthur Guide to American Chippendale Furniture: Middle Atlantic and Southern Colonies
New York: Rutledge Books/Crown Publishers, Inc., 1976.

Kane, Patricia E.
300 Years of American Seating Furniture: Chairs and Beds from the Mabel Brady Garvan and Other Collections at Yale University
Boston: New York Graphic Society, 1976.

Kassay, John
The Book of Shaker Furniture
Amherst, Massachusetts: University of Massachusetts Press, 1980.

Ketchum, William C., Jr.
The Catalog of American Antiques
New York: Rutledge Books, 1977; revised 1980.

Kirk, John T.
Early American Furniture: How to Recognize, Buy, and Care for the Most Beautiful Pieces—High Style, Country, Primitive, and Rustic
New York: Alfred A. Knopf, 1970.
The Impecunious Collector's Guide to American Antiques
New York: Alfred A. Knopf, 1975.

Kovel, Ralph and Terry
American Country Furniture: 1780–1875
New York: Crown Publishers, Inc., 1965.

McClelland, Nancy
Duncan Phyfe and the English Regency
New York: Dover Publications, Inc., 1980.

McClinton, Katherine Morrison
Collecting American Victorian Antiques
New York: Charles Scribner's Sons, 1966
Reprinted Des Moines, Iowa: Wallace-Homestead Book Company, 1978.

Makinson, Randell L.
Greene & Greene: Furniture & Related Designs
Santa Barbara, California: Peregrine Smith, Inc., 1979.

Meader, Robert F. W.
Illustrated Guide to Shaker Furniture
New York: The Greystone Press, 1950
Reprinted New York: Dover Publications, Inc., 1972.

Metropolitan Museum of Art
Nineteenth Century America: Furniture and Other Decorative Arts
New York: New York Graphic Society, 1971.

Miller, Edgar G., Jr.
American Antique Furniture. 2 vols.
New York: Dover Publications, Inc., 1966 (Reprint of 1937 ed.).

Montgomery, Charles F.
American Furniture: The Federal Period 1785–1825
New York: The Viking Press, 1966.

Morse, John D., ed.
Country Cabinetwork and Simple City Furniture
Charlottesville, Virginia: University of Virginia Press, 1970.

Nutting, Wallace
Furniture of the Pilgrim Century. 2 vols.
Framingham, Massachusetts: Old America Company, 1921, 1924
Reprinted New York: Dover Publications, Inc., 1965.
Furniture Treasury. 3 vols.
Framingham, Massachusetts: Old America Company, 1928–1933
Reprinted New York: The Macmillan Co., 1948, 1954.

Ormsbee, Thomas Hamilton
Field Guide to Early American Furniture
Boston: Little, Brown & Co., 1951.
Field Guide to American Victorian Furniture
Boston: Little, Brown & Co., 1952.

Otto, Celia Jackson
American Furniture of the Nineteenth Century
New York: The Viking Press, 1965.

Page, Marian
Furniture Designed by Architects
New York: Whitney Library of Design, Watson-Guptill Publications,
1980.

Rice, Norman S.
New York Furniture Before 1840
Albany, New York: Albany Institute of History and Art, 1962.

Santore, Charles
*The Windsor Style in America: A Pictorial Study of the History &
Regional Characteristics of the Most Popular Furniture Form of 18th
Century America, 1730–1830*
Philadelphia: Running Press, 1981.

Schiffer, Herbert F. and Nancy
Woods We Live With
Exton, Pennsylvania: Schiffer Publishing, Ltd., 1977.

Schwartz, Marvin D.
American Furniture of the Colonial Period
New York: The Metropolitan Museum of Art, 1976.
Country Style
Brooklyn, New York: The Brooklyn Museum, 1956.

Schwartz, Marvin D.; Stanek, Edward J.; and True, Douglas K.
The Furniture of John Henry Belter and the Rococo Revival
New York: E.P. Dutton, Inc., 1981.

Shea, John G.
Antique Country Furniture of North America
New York: Van Nostrand Reinhold Co., 1975.

Stickley, Gustav
*Craftsman Homes: Architecture and Furnishings of the American Arts
and Crafts Movement*
New York: Dover Publications, Inc., 1979 (Reprint of 1909 ed.).

Tracy, Berry B.; Johnson, Marilynn; Schwartz, Marvin D.; and Boorsch,
Suzanne
Nineteenth-Century America: Furniture and Other Decorative Arts
New York: The Metropolitan Museum of Art, 1973.

Warren, David B.
*Bayou Bend: American Furniture, Paintings and Silver from the Bayou
Bend Collection*
Houston: Museum of Fine Arts, 1975.

Watson, Aldren A.
Country Furniture
New York: Harper & Row Publishers, Inc., 1974.

White, Marshall S.
Wood Identification Handbook
New York: Charles Scribner's Sons, 1981.

Where to Buy Antique Furniture

Throughout America, antique furniture is available at thousands of shops, shows, flea markets, house sales, and auctions. Each source has its advantages and disadvantages.

Shops
Most antiques are sold by dealers. These professionals are usually glad to share their knowledge with customers. In an antiques shop or at a dealer's home, you have time to examine a piece thoroughly, and you rarely need to make an immediate decision to buy. Since there are dealers specializing in virtually every field and in every price range, you are sure to find one who suits your taste and budget.

Shows
Antiques shows take place regularly in communities of all sizes and give collectors a chance to meet many dealers at one time. Because many collectors come to these shows, dealers usually exhibit their finest wares there, making it somewhat easier for collectors to find objects that are hard to locate. But most antiques shows last only a day or two, and since several collectors are often interested in the same item, decisions must be made rather quickly.

Flea Markets and House Sales
At flea markets, the sellers are rarely professionals. Most of the merchandise is inexpensive, unidentified, or sometimes even new. Here you must depend almost totally on your own knowledge. The same is true of house sales: whether a tag, yard, garage, or private sale, buyers must be able to distinguish between true bargains and overpriced odds and ends.

Auctions
Auctions, ranging from those at city auction houses to backyard or country affairs, offer a considerable quantity of objects in one place. The unpredictability that makes an auction so exciting, however, is also its major drawback. Buyers have only moments to decide upon a bid, and prices are set by the interest generated in the people who happen to be on hand. Buying at auction requires patience and self-restraint. A particular auction may not offer the specific object you are seeking, and it may be wise to wait until you find exactly what you want at a future sale. (*See* pp. 454-455 for hints on how to buy at auction.)

Shopping Hints
No matter where you buy, be cautious. Although dishonest practices are rare, any seller may occasionally be guilty of poor judgment or excessive optimism; deliberate deceptions are far less common than honest mistakes. Deal with the most reputable people you can find, and if you suspect that an object is not what it is said to be, don't buy.

Buying at Auction

Most collectors eventually try buying at auctions. The lure is understandable, for tales abound of detecting rare pieces concealed by coats of paint and dirt, or sought-after objects that fetch half their predicted price. Most of these tales date from the 1920s to 1940s, when bargains were commonplace. Auctions today are attended by an army of sophisticated collectors and dealers, well-schooled in what to look for and how much to pay. The best tool in buying—no matter where—is a knowledge of furniture styles, construction methods, and current market prices. And at auction, knowing the rules of the game can help prevent costly mistakes.

How an Auction Works
An auction is a sale of objects to the highest bidders. The seller, or the consignor, offers goods to prospective buyers through his agent, the auctioneer. The bidder offering the most money for a given item buys the "lot" (one piece or a group of pieces sold together). The auctioneer always tries to stimulate bidding and to get the highest price, since he (or his firm) generally receives a percentage of the sale as payment or commission.

The Viewing and Other Preliminaries
The first step toward informed bidding is to attend the viewing before the auction, an advertised period of a few hours or days during which the objects offered may be examined by the public. Never bid on something unless you have checked it thoroughly at the viewing. Compare what you see with the information given in the catalogue, if one is available. If you have any question about an object, its attribution, or its condition, talk to the auctioneer or the firm's specialist in that field. If a catalogue is not available, carry a small notebook to jot down the lot number and other information about the object, particularly its condition. If you feel uncertain about the auctioneer's or your own judgment about a piece, especially an expensive one, you may wish to hire a consultant—often a dealer who, for a fee, will advise you or sometimes even bid for you.
The viewing is also a good time to find out what form of payment the auctioneer requires. Some will take only cash or certified checks; others will accept personal checks with proper identification, or credit cards.

The Sale
At most larger auctions, the auctioneer will provide estimated price ranges for the pieces in the sale. These are usually printed in the auction catalogue or on a separate list. Though pieces quite often sell for more or less than the estimates, these should give you some idea of what the auctioneer expects a piece to fetch. Also, many large auction houses allow a seller to set a "reserve" on a lot—the price below which it will not be sold, frequently close to the low estimate. If bidding does not reach this minimum, the lot will be withdrawn and returned to the consignor for a small handling fee.
Decide in advance the price you are willing to pay for a particular lot. The Price Guide section of this book provides general guidelines and prevailing market price ranges to help you set your own bidding limit.
The best place to sit at an auction is toward the rear, where you can best see what is going on. There are two customary ways to bid—by raising a hand or by using the numbered paddle sometimes furnished by the auctioneer. Listen closely because the bidding is often extremely rapid. When your pre-established

price limit has been reached, stop. This is the key to wise auction bidding.

Patience and persistence are required, since at every auction some pieces may sell for more or for less than most people anticipate. There is almost always a "sleeper" or two, particularly just after or even just before a high-priced lot has captured the attention of the audience.

At many auction houses, someone who has attended the viewing but cannot be present at the auction itself can leave a bid with the personnel. Such bids will be treated as the maximum the absentee bidder is willing to spend, so that if there is little competition when the auction house bids for you, the final price you pay may be far less than your top bid. An out-of-town collector who has seen an auction catalogue but cannot attend the viewing and auction may sometimes be allowed to place a bid by telephone, but such blind bidding is not recommended unless the bidder delegates someone to examine the object for him prior to the sale.

Collecting Your Purchases

The fall of the gavel and the cry "sold" mark a successful bid. Now the buyer must pay for the purchase and remove it from the auction premises. Large auction houses will ship items for a fee; most auctioneers do not have such services, however, and the buyer is responsible for transporting a purchase within a stated time limit.

Price Guide

Sooner or later, every experienced collector will buy a piece of furniture for less than its true market value. More often, however, novices pay more than they should because they are unfamiliar with current prices. To recognize a bargain and to avoid buying unwisely, it is vital to understand today's marketplace. In the last twenty years, interest in antiques and collectibles has grown tremendously, making it increasingly difficult to keep abreast of current values. As certain styles or types of furniture become popular and as inflation continues, the prices for some may double or triple within a few years, while less popular pieces may fall behind the rate of inflation. To follow these trends, collectors should keep informed about prices being asked by dealers or fetched at auction.

Dealers' prices are the most accurate guide to what is happening on the market. Because dealers must remain competitive, their prices tend to become relatively uniform over a period of time. Today many collectors look to auctions as the ultimate price determinant, for they do offer dramatic evidence of the market in action. A piece is presented, all bidders compete as equals, and the highest bidder gets the piece. Actually, it is not that simple. Anyone who has observed two bidders competing for an object knows that such competition can drive prices well above a reasonable figure. The added attraction of objects with fancy pedigrees may also distort auction records. On the other hand, auction prices can be unrealistically low if, for some reason, attendance at the sale is poor or if doubt is cast on the authenticity of a piece. Yet auction results do reflect long-term market trends. In the late 1970s, for instance, the fact that Mission-style furniture suddenly began to fetch high prices at auction signaled its new popularity.

This price guide is based on auction records as well as on consultations with dealers and knowledgeable collectors. But remember that a price guide is only that—a guide: no two objects are identical and no two buying situations are the same. The prices listed here are national averages. Collectors should note that some types of furniture may be more popular and therefore more costly in one part of the country than in another. Thus, turn-of-the-century oak furniture generally brings higher prices on the West Coast than in the East, and Victorian items are more in demand in the South than in the North. An even more important variable is whether a maker's mark is present. A good Federal chair without such a mark may bring $2000; but if it bears the mark of a famous maker, it may fetch $15,000 or more.

Condition is important in determining the value of a piece. If a piece is in poor and irreparable condition, whether from unintentional damage or deliberate alterations, it will be worth only a fraction of its listed price. The prices given here assume that each piece is in good condition, with no major restoration, even if the particular example illustrated shows some damage. Before you buy a repaired, altered, or damaged piece, be sure to adjust the price given here accordingly.

The style and quality of a piece greatly affect its value. Pieces in highly desirable styles will almost always be more costly than those in other styles. Every style has a wide range of prices, however, and fine designs with exceptional decoration will command high prices regardless of style. The price ranges listed in this guide take into account both the style and the potential range in quality of the type of piece illustrated.

Scarcity also affects prices. Some rare period pieces are almost impossible to price accurately. For example, there are so few 17th-century Wainscot or Cromwell chairs that they seldom come on the market; and when they do, competition is likely to be so great that prices may take a tremendous leap from one sale to the next. The same is true of a one-of-a-kind or specially commissioned piece from any period. Moreover, many kinds of Colonial Revival or modern furniture have never been sold at major auction houses, so that there are no recorded prices for them.

Sometimes a period style suddenly captures the public's fancy, and prices rise accordingly. When interest in it diminishes, prices usually fall. These sporadic trends are hard to predict. Currently Art Deco and other 20th-century pieces, for instance, are becoming increasingly popular, especially in metropolitan areas, where new fashions catch on most quickly. Although many of these pieces were mass-produced and are still abundant, they may command exceptional prices, particularly in city stores. The ranges given here reflect not only those urban prices but also what you may expect to pay in a country store or at a rural auction.

Finally, and most important, the items priced here stand for a class of similar pieces, so the prices refer to the general types, not merely to the specific pieces shown.

Slat-back and Spindle-back Chairs

Country slat-back and Windsor chairs are much sought after by collectors who prize their sturdy construction and simple, traditional design. Slat-back chairs range from early, Pilgrim-style examples with thick posts and deep turnings, which may sell for more than $10,000, to unattributed Mission-style chairs that are frequently found for about $50 to $200. Ordinary slat-and spindle-back chairs from the 18th and 19th centuries, generally good buys, sell for prices in the low hundreds, with the following exceptions: early bannister-back chairs often fetch upward of $2000; and labeled Shaker slat-back chairs dating from as late as the second half of the 19th century are frequently priced in the high hundreds or, for an unusual design such as a revolving spindle-back chair, in the thousands. Sheraton Fancy chairs and other painted examples begin as low as $100 when they are from the mid-19th century and may climb to about $2000 for finer examples from about 1790–1820.

Windsors are among the most widely collected chairs on the market today. While some early 19th-century chairs such as rod-back and arrow-back Windsors can be found for under $100, most earlier pieces sell for $500 to $5000. Windsors with original paint bring a premium; and unusual forms, such as writing-arm models, may command prices in excess of $10,000. Much less expensive are mass-produced turn-of-the-century oak chairs, which often combine Pilgrim-era and Windsor design; these generally sell for $100 to $300.

1 Shaker rocking chair $500–700
2 Shaker dining chair $400–650
3 Shaker side chair $200–600
4 Child's slat-back highchair $250–750
5 Slat-back rocking chair $275–450
6 Shaker armchair $450–800
7 William and Mary slat-back side chair $400–800
8 William and Mary slat-back side chair $1500–3000

9 Slat-back Great chair $8000–12,000
10 Federal comb-back rocking chair $300–600
11 Mission-style side chair $50–250
12 Child's rustic rocking chair $50–125
13 Windsor/Sheraton painted Fancy side chair $125–250
14 Windsor/Sheraton painted Fancy side chairs $100–250 each
15 Colonial Revival side chair $100–250
16 Colonial Revival press-back rocking chair $225–350
17 Boston or Salem rocking chair $150–350
18 Colonial Revival press-back side chair $100–175
19 Windsor/Sheraton side chair $80–200
20 Windsor/Sheraton side chairs $60–150 (left); $100–350 (right)
21 Windsor fan-back side chair $1000–4500
22 Windsor comb-back armchair $5000–10,000
23 Windsor low-back armchair with writing arm $5000–12,000
24 Windsor hoop-back armchair $2000–6000
25 Windsor continuous-arm armchair $2000–5000
26 Windsor braced loop-back armchair $2500–8000
27 Windsor loop-back rocking chair $400–1200
28 Windsor loop-back side chair $300–1500
29 Windsor rod-back side chair $700–2500
30 Windsor rod-back side chair $200–750
31 Shaker revolving chair or revolver $1750–3500
32 Windsor highchair $150–350
33 William and Mary country corner chair $1500–3500
34 Queen Anne country corner chair $1000–3500
35 William and Mary bannister-back armchair $800–2500
36 William and Mary bannister-back side chair $1000–3000
37 Colonial Revival Great or Brewster chair $300–1000
38 Pilgrim-style Great or Carver chair $10,000–15,000
39 Sheraton painted Fancy armchair $1000–1800
40 Sheraton painted Fancy side chair $500–1500
41 Sheraton painted Fancy side chair $100–200
42 Sheraton painted Fancy side chair $800–2000

Splat-back, Shield-back, and Related Chairs

Fashionable chairs with carved openwork backs, dating from the 18th and early 19th centuries, are recognized by collectors as classic examples of fine American craftsmanship. Although stratospheric prices—$25,000 or even much more—may be expected for the most elaborate examples, particularly those attributed to well-known makers, plainer versions may sometimes be found for under $1000. Federal designs at every quality level still cost less than half the amount commanded by comparable Queen Anne and Chippendale chairs, though Federal prices have risen markedly during the past decade.

The large sums collectors are willing to pay for high-style 18th-century chairs have led many craftsmen to reproduce them: such so-called Colonial Revival pieces are among the least expensive chairs on the market today; they often sell for $50 to $200, making them likely alternatives for collectors who cannot afford the 4- or 5-figure prices of the originals. Many later 19th-century chairs—such as Empire klismos models and Rococo Revival balloon-backs—are also relative bargains at $100 to $300. Simple Eastlake chairs are even greater bargains, usually selling for $75 to $200. On the other hand, some hand-crafted, early 20th-century pieces are one-of-a-kind and justifiably costly.

43 Federal cane-seated side chairs $2000–6000 each
44 Federal arm and side chairs $6000–12,000 (left);
    $4000–8000 (right)
45 Empire side chair $200–800
46 Empire side chair $150–650
47 Eastlake side chair $85–250
48 China Trade armchair $1000–2500
49 Rococo Revival balloon-back side chair $85–300
50 Rococo Revival balloon-back side chair $100–350
51 Empire side chair $125–175
52 Empire armchair $225–350
53 Queen Anne country side chair $2000–3500
54 Queen Anne country side chair $1700–3000
55 Colonial Revival side chair $50–100
56 Queen Anne leather-back side chair $3000–5000
57 Colonial Revival side chair $125–400
58 Georgian Revival side chair $150–400
59 Queen Anne side chair $8000–25,000
60 Queen Anne corner chair $15,000–25,000
61 Chippendale corner chair $10,000–30,000
62 Chippendale armchair $10,000–25,000
63 Queen Anne armchair $15,000–25,000
64 Colonial Revival armchair $300–700
65 Chippendale side chair $2500–9000
66 Chippendale side chair $4000–20,000
67 Chippendale side chair $3000–9000
68 Chippendale side chair $2500–8000
69 Chippendale country side chair $1500–3000
70 Chippendale country side chair $8000–20,000
71 Chippendale ladder-back side chair $1500–2500
72 Federal square-back armchair $2000–5000
73 Eastlake side chair $85–150
74 Renaissance Revival side chair $200–700
75 Federal shield-back side chair $4000–8000
76 Federal truncated shield-back side chair $4000–5500
77 Federal shield-back side chair $2000–5000
78 Federal shield-back side chair $6000–15,000
79 Federal square-back armchair $2500–5000
80 Gothic Revival side chair $800–1500
81 Arts and Crafts armchair $3000–15,000
82 Arts and Crafts armchair $3000–15,000

Wicker, Bentwood, and Metal Chairs

Wicker, bentwood, and metal chairs offer collectors a wide
variety of designs and, since these are new collecting specialties,
they can be had fairly inexpensively. Particularly varied are
wicker chairs, which are priced less by age than by design and
condition (original finish, for instance, is always preferable).
Prices for typical examples range from $100 to $700, while
unusual designs may bring more than $1000 and fine pieces
imported from China in the early 19th century may fetch even
more. Bentwood chairs, first imported from Europe in the second
half of the 19th century, generally cost $100 to $500, making
them relative bargains since new bentwood chairs can cost as
much as this.

Innovative 19th-century metal chairs—such as folding chairs and
platform rocking chairs—sell for anywhere from $100 to $750,
depending on the maker and design, though some patented
innovative forms may be more costly. Cast-iron garden chairs, on

the other hand, are fairly uniformly priced in the low hundreds, and turn-of-the-century ice-cream parlor chairs sell in the $25-to-$150 range. Modern metal chairs are often difficult to price: while most sell for a few hundred dollars, some examples attributed to well-known designers may exceed $500, and common, mass-produced chairs are often priced under $100.

83 Turn-of-the-century bentwood side chair $100–250
84 Victorian wicker rocking chair $250–500
85 Child's Victorian wicker rocking chair $225–450
86 China Trade bamboo armchair $2000–3000
87 Turn-of-the-century wicker corner chair $350–1250
88 Late Victorian wicker armchair $200–450
89 Child's Art Deco wicker armchair $100–150
90 Eastlake folding armchair $150–650
91 Turn-of-the-century highchair $100–200
92 Turn-of-the-century bentwood highchair $150–350
93 Rococo Revival iron-spring rocking chair $500–2500
94 Renaissance Revival folding iron armchair $250–750
95 Rococo Revival cast-iron side chair $75–250
96 Late Victorian cast-iron armchair $125–350
97 Turn-of-the-century iron-wire side chair $25–100
98 Turn-of-the-century iron-wire armchair $75–150
99 Modern steel-wire side chairs $100–450 each
100 Modern steel-wire armchair $150–450
101 Modern fiberglass-and-iron armchair $125–400
102 Modern tubular-steel roundabout armchair $175–450
103 Modern tubular-aluminum side chair $150–400
104 Modern tubular-steel side chair $75–250
105 Modern tubular-steel armchair $50–200

Upholstered-back and Related Wooden-back Chairs
The prices in this group are as varied as the chairs themselves, with some of the rarest and most costly examples included alongside some of the least expensive. The majority are 19th-century upholstered chairs, ranging from Empire to Victorian revival styles and usually selling for amounts in the $100-to-$700 range. The quality of the carving or other decoration is a measure of the value of most upholstered chairs, so that examples with mediocre machine-made decoration will sell for $100 to $200. The label of a well-known maker will greatly increase the value of a piece: for instance, a Rococo Revival chair by John Henry Belter may sell for $1500 to $3000, while a similar unattributed design may be found for $800 or less. Original upholstery also enhances the value of a piece.

20th-century designs in this group range from wooden kitchen and overstuffed chairs, selling for $50 to $400, to elegant pieces attributed to major designers and selling for $2000 or more. Mission-style rocking or Morris chairs may cost as little as $200, but prices can soar to $8000 or more for an unusual design by Gustav Stickley. Similar premiums are commanded by such names as Louis Comfort Tiffany, Charles Sumner Greene, and Frank Lloyd Wright; modern classics by them may approach $10,000.

Even more expensive are rare 17th-century Wainscot and Cromwell chairs, which usually command anywhere from $10,000 to $40,000. William and Mary chairs are somewhat more common and generally sell for $3000 to $6000, but beware of turn-of-the-century reproductions, which should cost less than a tenth as much as originals. Queen Anne and Chippendale easy, or wing, chairs are among the most sought-after upholstered chairs, and their $10,000-to-$40,000 price range reflects this. Federal-era upholstered chairs are a bit more affordable at $1000 to $6000, though rare works by an esteemed carver such as Samuel McIntire may justify higher prices.

106 Empire side chair $250–600
107 Art Nouveau side chair $150–400
108 William and Mary leather-upholstered side chair $3000–5000
109 William and Mary caned side chair $4000–6000
110 Renaissance Revival side chair $125–300
111 Child's Gothic Revival side chair $150–550
112 Gothic Revival side chair $175–550
113 Rococo Revival side chair $200–500
114 Renaissance Revival revolving desk chair $350–600
115 Renaissance Revival armchair $250–450
116 Rococo Revival side chair $800–3000
117 Rococo Revival side chair $500–1500
118 Rococo Revival armchair $350–750
119 Rococo Revival armchair $300–650
120 Renaissance Revival armchair $350–750
121 Renaissance Revival miniature or child's armchair $250–350
122 Renaissance Revival armchair $450–850
123 Renaissance Revival armchair $600–1200
124 Renaissance Revival platform rocking chair $200–450
125 Eastlake folding armchair with footrest $250–750
126 Eastlake folding armchair $250–350
127 Colonial Revival platform rocking chair $200–450
128 Renaissance Revival side chair $200–600
129 Eastlake side chair $375–650
130 Eastlake side chair $150–250
131 Eastlake plywood armchair $100–250
132 Turn-of-the-century Savonarola armchair $100–250
133 Modern laminated side chair $250–550
134 Art Deco side chair $1000–4000
135 Child's Art Deco chair $125–300
136 Art Deco side chair $300–2000
137 Art Deco kitchen chair $25–75
138 Modern side chair $75–250
139 Art Deco side chair $50–150
140 Pilgrim-style Cromwell or Farthingale side chair $10,000–40,000
141 Pilgrim-style Wainscot chair $25,000–40,000
142 Queen Anne easy chair $10,000–20,000
143 Chippendale easy chair $20,000–40,000
144 Queen Anne easy chair $25,000–50,000
145 Chippendale upholstered armchair $3000–15,000
146 Federal upholstered Martha Washington armchair $2000–15,000
147 Modern upholstered bentwood armchair $200–600
148 Art Deco leather-upholstered armchair $250–1000
149 Chippendale leather-upholstered armchair $5000–20,000
150 Federal upholstered armchair or bergère $4000–6000
151 Art Nouveau upholstered armchair $10,000–20,000
152 Victorian upholstered horn armchair $300–750
153 Victorian platform rocking chair $250–650
154 Art Deco bamboo armchair $100–350
155 Misson-style rocking chair $200–1000
156 Misson-style easy or Morris chair $350–5000

157 Mission-style armchair $2000–7500
158 Art Deco overstuffed corner chair $150–450
159 Art Deco overstuffed armchair $100–350

Sofas, Daybeds, Settees, Settles, and Benches

Seating furniture for two or more people ranges from simple country benches, available for as little as $100, to a wide variety of high-style sofas. Some of the latter, particularly those from the 18th century, are among the rarest and most costly pieces of American furniture. For collectors of substantial means, there are Queen Anne and Chippendale sofas for $40,000 to well over $100,000, fine Federal models in the $4000-to-$40,000 range, or later Rococo Revival examples by John Henry Belter for $20,000 or more. Collectors looking for inexpensive sofas should focus on mass-produced Rococo Revival, Renaissance Revival, and Eastlake examples, which may be had for as little as $200; late Empire sofas at $500 or less; or Federal country pieces for $500 to $1000. As a rule of thumb, sofas sell for at least twice as much as related chairs.

Settees and daybeds are usually less expensive than sofas, though sometimes harder to find. An Eastlake settee or tête-à-tête may cost no more than $100 to $200; some factory-made Mission-style settees or Art Deco daybeds are also in the same price range. On the other hand, collectors may have to pay upward of $5000 for a small Belter settee or for a handmade example by a well-known modern craftsman such as Wendell Castle. Early daybeds may also be costly: William and Mary, Queen Anne, and Chippendale versions are generally priced at $2000 to $10,000. In contrast, late Empire and Victorian daybeds are often bargains at $100 to $300.

Original upholstery is rare on any antique sofa, daybed, or settee and makes a piece more desirable. Similarly, shabby or inappropriate upholstery can make a would-be bargain a liability, since reupholstering may be more costly than the piece itself.

160 Federal camel-back settee $5000–10,000
161 Chippendale camel-back sofa $100,000–200,000
162 Chippendale camel-back sofa $20,000–120,000
163 Federal country sofa $500–1000
164 Federal square-back sofa $4000–8000
165 Federal square-back sofa $4500–8500
166 Federal square-back sofa $20,000–35,000
167 Empire sofa $2000–5000
168 Empire sofa $1000–7500
169 Empire sofa $20,000–40,000
170 Federal cane-back sofa $10,000–40,000
171 China Trade/Empire cane-back sofa or daybed $2000–4500
172 Empire/Rococo Revival sofa $200–500
173 Rococo Revival sofa $500–1200
174 Rococo Revival laminated sofa $20,000–25,000
175 Rococo Revival painted sofa $2500–5500
176 Rococo Revival sofa $5000–7000
177 Renaissance Revival sofa $1200–3500
178 Renaissance Revival sofa $2500–3500
179 Renaissance Revival sofa $2000–3000
180 Eastlake settee $100–250
181 Rococo Revival laminated settee or méridienne $5000–7000
182 Empire window seat $500–3000
183 Federal Grecian couch or récamier $4000–12,000

184 Eastlake daybed $100–350
185 Art Deco chaise longue or daybed $100–450
186 Eastlake conversational sofa or tête-à-tête $650–850
187 Modern laminated settee $2000–10,000
188 Modern tubular-steel settee or love seat $200–750
189 Mission-style settee $150–450
190 Mission-style settee or settle $400–2000
191 Shaker settee $2500–4500
192 Windsor/Sheraton rocking settee or mammy bench $1000–1500
193 Sheraton painted Fancy settee $2000–5000
194 Federal convertible settee $1500–2500
195 William and Mary daybed $3000–8000
196 Colonial Revival settee $500–800
197 Rococo Revival cast-iron settee $300–400
198 Late Victorian wicker settee $450–750
199 Child's country painted storage settle $750–2500
200 Empire country storage settle $250–550
201 Country painted bench $100–250

Stools

Though stools are the simplest form of seating furniture, they are remarkably varied in style, shape, and price. One of the most common is the milking, or work, stool. Such sturdy country pieces from the 18th and 19th centuries usually sell for $25 to $100. Windsor versions, however, are far rarer than typical country stools and may command as much as $2000. Early high-style stools, from the William and Mary to Chippendale periods, are in even greater demand and are very costly; these turned or carved pieces often sell for $5000 to $15,000 because of their rarity. Top-of-the-line Federal stools, also scarce, generally sell for $1000 to $2000.

Far more affordable are later 19th-century stools, but prices do vary widely. A simple cutout Gothic Revival or Eastlake example may bring less than $100, while a rare and sophisticated piece in the Greek or Egyptian Revival style may cost as much as $1000, and a fine Rococo Revival version even twice as much. 20th-century bar and other stools, made of aluminum or tubular steel, are readily available for $50 to $200; examples by well-known modern designers, however, will bring considerably more. Among the least expensive stools are unattributed Mission-style oak stools and Victorian wicker models, which can be had for as little as $50. Art Deco and other 20th-century upholstered ottomans are widely available at $25 to $100.

202 Country milking stool $25–75
203 Windsor/Sheraton stool $1000–2000
204 William and Mary joint stool or table $5000–15,000
205 Mission-style stool $85–250
206 Empire country stool $85–175
207 Renaissance Revival lift-top footstool $100–200
208 Gothic Revival footstool $75–200
209 Renaissance Revival stool $300–1000
210 Federal piano stool $1000–2000
211 Rococo Revival piano stool $600–1500
212 Early 20th-century wicker stool $85–150
213 Modern footstool or ottoman $25–150
214 Art Deco aluminum stool $200–750
215 Art Deco tubular-steel bar stools $150–300 each

Beds and Cradles

Early American beds from the 17th and 18th centuries are very rare, so that when Queen Anne and Chippendale examples do come onto the market, they command high prices. Beds from the 19th century, on the other hand, are widely available, affordable, and popular with collectors. Factory-made Eastlake examples are among the least expensive, usually selling for $250 to $900. Rare and highly decorative Eastlake beds by major makers such as Herter Brothers, however, may sell for three times as much. Renaissance Revival beds display a similarly wide range of prices, from $250 for a later mass-produced piece to as much as $5000 for a finely carved example from a fashionable workshop. The most costly Victorian beds are those in the Rococo Revival style by John Henry Belter, with prices exceeding $50,000 if particularly elaborate. Far more reasonable and popular are turn-of-the-century cast-iron or brass beds: typical prices are $150 to $750, depending on size and style. The most collected 20th-century beds are Art Deco wooden and modern tubular-steel designs, selling at $200 to $1000, while Colonial Revival beds are bargains at $100 to $300.

Collectors seeking earlier 19th-century beds may choose among various types of low- and high-post Federal beds, available at $800 to $3000. Prices for Empire sleigh beds begin at about $500, but climb steeply into the high thousands for elaborate examples with impressive attributions. High-style 18th-century beds are costly—about $3000 to $6000 for low-post models and upward of $10,000 for elegant canopy beds.

Cradles are more limited in variety than are beds. Most common are simple country examples, sometimes with wooden hoods, at $200 to $400 or even less. The least expensive Victorian cradles are brass cradles, at $100 to $200. Those in the various mid-century revival styles generally cost $200 to $750. Prices for stylish Federal or Empire models range from $750 to $2500. Equally expensive are the elaborate and highly desirable bentwood swinging cradles from the turn of the century; these may command as much as $3500.

216 Country cradle $200–400
217 Federal trestle-base cradle $2000–2500
218 Child's Renaissance Revival folding bed or crib $300–750
219 Turn-of-the-century bentwood cradle $1000–3500
220 Empire/Elizabethan Revival cradle $400–750
221 Empire sleigh bed $750–2500
222 Child's Elizabethan Revival country bed or daybed $250–450
223 Federal country daybed $800–1200
224 Shaker low-post bed $2000–3500
225 Federal low-post bed $800–1200
226 Federal country folding bed $2000–6000
227 Child's Federal canopy bed $4500–7000
228 Chippendale canopy bed $10,000–35,000
229 Federal canopy bed $9000–20,000
230 Eastlake bed $2500–6000
231 Eastlake bed $1200–2500
232 Turn-of-the-century oak bed $400–750
233 Eastlake bed $500–900
234 Renaissance Revival bed $250–500
235 Rococo Revival bed $30,000–60,000
236 Renaissance Revival bed $1500–3000
237 Rococo Revival bed $2500–3500

238 Turn-of-the-century tubular-brass bed $350–1000
239 Turn-of-the-century tubular-iron bed $150–750
240 Child's Victorian tubular-iron bed $150–350
241 Modern tubular-steel bed $300–1000

Drop-leaf and Tilt-top Tables

As is the case with most furniture, the earliest types of drop-leaf tables are the most costly. William and Mary butterfly tables bring anywhere from $15,000 to $40,000, and gate-leg tables of the same period cost $5000 to $20,000. Turn-of-the-century Colonial Revival reproductions of early drop-leaf tables, however, are plentiful at only a few hundred dollars or less. Other good buys are plain country drop-leaf designs, sometimes with original paint: early 19th-century examples fetch $150 to $900, while late 18th-century country tables and later Shaker pieces cost at least twice as much. Victorian drop-leaf tables, in a variety of styles, are relative bargains at $150 to $500.

Quite appealing and often moderately priced are small Pembroke tables, which begin at about $500 for Federal examples but climb to $5000 or more for earlier Chippendale designs. Other early drop-leaf tables can be very expensive. Large or medium-size Queen Anne and Chippendale models bring anywhere from $2000 for simple designs to as much as $40,000 for the most elegant examples.

Federal pieces are less costly, although an authentic Duncan Phyfe drop-leaf library table (or virtually any Phyfe table) can seldom be found for under $4000. Empire designs are still less expensive, with a general range of $250 to $2000. Turn-of-the-century expandable oak tables generally sell for $150 to $750; while Art Deco and modern drop-leaf or expandable tables have a similar price range, those attributed to well-known designers may cost more than $1000.

Tilt-top tables have a similarly wide range of prices and are quite popular with collectors. Queen Anne, Chippendale, and Federal pieces are priced for the most part at $500 to $6000. Rural chair-tables, having large tilt tops, range from 19th-century models at $1000 to $2000 to early 18th-century versions at $3000 to $7000.

242 Federal country painted drop-leaf table $175–750
243 Queen Anne drop-leaf table $2800–3800
244 Empire country drop-leaf table $250–850
245 William and Mary butterfly table $15,000–40,000
246 William and Mary gate-leg table $10,000–20,000
247 Colonial Revival drop-leaf table $200–350
248 Renaissance Revival drop-leaf table $400–1000
249 Queen Anne drop-leaf table $3500–10,000
250 Country chair-table $1200–3000
251 William and Mary hutch table $3000–6000
252 Rococo Revival papier-mâché tilt-top table $200–750
253 Federal tilt-top candlestand $500–1500
254 Chippendale tilt-top tea table $3000–6000
255 Chippendale tilt-top candlestand $700–2500
256 Queen Anne tilt-top table $1000–3000
257 Federal double-pedestal drop-leaf table $4000–10,000
258 Empire drop-leaf table $900–2500
259 Chippendale drop-leaf table $4000–7000
260 Queen Anne drop-leaf breakfast table $20,000–40,000
261 Chippendale Pembroke table $5000–10,000
262 Federal Pembroke table $550–1200

263 Shaker drop-leaf table $1200–2000
264 Turn-of-the-century expandable oak dining table $150–350
265 Adirondack or rustic gate-leg table $200–450
266 Art Deco drop-leaf dining table $300–1000
267 Modern expandable dining table $400–1000

Library, Tavern, Console, Side, Tea, and Card Tables

The tables covered in this section are highly varied in form and price, ranging from $400 Victorian card tables to $60,000 Queen Anne tea tables. Among the earliest are tavern tables, which are most often in the William and Mary style and command $1500 to $7500. High-style Federal side tables usually range from $1000 to $6000. While some Empire side tables may be found for about $500, elegant designs may soar as high as $4000 to $6000. On the other hand, Renaissance Revival and Eastlake side tables are common at $150 to $750.

Tea tables, dating almost exclusively from the 18th century, generally bear price tags of $3000 to $10,000, though a superb piece may cost $25,000 to $60,000. Card tables, originating in the Queen Anne era, similarly range from $4000 for plain country examples to $60,000 for finely carved masterpieces. Federal card tables are more abundant and somewhat less expensive—$1000 to $7500. Empire card tables are not in great demand; most cost $250 to $1000, though elegant examples may occasionally fetch as much as $10,000. Card tables were less common by the Victorian era; ordinary examples will bring no more than $400, but a fine Rococo Revival example may sell for $3500 or more. Library tables were a 19th-century development, but early 20th-century models are most available. Small oak examples seldom cost more than $300; a Mission-style piece, however, will be priced at $500 to $1500, and a fine library table by a major designer such as Frank Lloyd Wright will probably exceed $5000.

268 Mission-style library table $5000–20,000
269 William and Mary tavern table $2000–7000
270 William and Mary tavern table $3000–6000
271 William and Mary tavern table $4500–6000
272 Federal country table $500–1200
273 Queen Anne country table $2000–3500
274 Shaker seed table $1000–2200
275 Shaker trestle table $2500–10,000
276 Art Deco side or console table $400–1000
277 Mission-style library trestle table $500–2000
278 Empire mirrored console or pier table $4000–8000
279 Art Nouveau side table $250–450
280 Eastlake side table $200–750
281 Eastlake side table $150–500
282 Queen Anne country tea table $3000–6000
283 Queen Anne country tea table $4000–8000
284 Federal side table $1000–4000
285 Federal side table $3000–25,000
286 Federal card table $3000–7500
287 Renaissance Revival card table $400–1200
288 Federal card table $2000–3500
289 Queen Anne tea table $40,000–60,000
290 Queen Anne card table $15,000–25,000
291 Chippendale 5-legged card table $20,000–35,000
292 Chippendale 5-legged card table $40,000–60,000
293 Rococo Revival card table $1500–3500

294 Empire double-pedestal-base card table $250–450
295 Federal lyre-base card table $3000–9000
296 Empire pedestal-base card table $250–750
297 Empire pedestal-base card table $6000–10,000

Center, Coffee, and End Tables

The tables in this section—all from the 19th or 20th century—
are popular with collectors and generally inexpensive. Among
the better buys are factory-made Eastlake center tables, readily
available at $250 to $500. Handsome Renaissance Revival center
tables, often mass-produced and embellished with turnings
rather than carving, range from $500 to $2000. The best Empire
tables, rich in marquetry, inlay, or ormolu, may command $5000,
but simpler pieces are available at $500 to $1000. Late 19th-
century oak tables are common and inexpensive at $300 to $750,
though Mission-style examples, especially those made by Gustav
Stickley, are much sought after and may cost $1000 or more.
Collectors with modest budgets may also wish to focus on turn-
of-the-century wicker or iron-wire tables, which may often be
purchased for as little as $100. Collectors with a taste for the
extravagant, on the other hand, may seek out a Rococo Revival
center table from the workshops of J. and J. W. Meeks or John
Henry Belter. The former will cost $4000 to $12,000; the latter,
perhaps $40,000 to $60,000.

20th-century coffee and end tables are just beginning to attract
collectors' attention. Those made to appeal to popular tastes,
such as lacquered or glass-topped pieces, are good investments
at $100 to $300. Elegant, austere examples combining steel and
glass sell for anywhere from $200 to $1000, while fine wooden
pieces by important designers may be priced at $2000 or more.

298 Eastlake center table $250–450
299 Renaissance Revival center table $600–2000
300 Rococo Revival center table $4000–60,000
301 Eastlake center table $2000–3500
302 Empire center table $1500–5000
303 Empire center table $500–1500
304 Turn-of-the-century expandable oak dining table $450–750
305 Empire expandable dining table $1500–3500
306 Art Deco table with built-in lamp $250–800
307 Modern lacquered table $150–600
308 Art Deco glass center table $300–1000
309 Modern glass-topped table $150–500
310 Turn-of-the-century iron-wire table $100–150
311 Turn-of-the-century wicker table $100–250
312 Mission-style card table $200–1000
313 Modern coffee table $200–750
314 Art Deco glass-topped coffee table $150–400
315 Modern lacquered coffee table $600–2000
316 Modern lacquered end table $100–300
317 Modern lacquered end table $100–400

Stands, Pedestals, Work, Sewing, and Other Small Tables

These small tables are quite common and, in general, moderately
priced. Colonial homes had a wide variety of stands: early tripod-
base candlestands may be expensive, with Queen Anne and
Chippendale pieces commanding $2000 to $5000, and ratchet-base
country stands from the same period bringing $500 to $1500.

Many stands date from the Federal era, and their prices are fairly consistently between $800 and $2000, though the finest examples will be higher.

Work or sewing tables are another popular type of small table. The earliest and most costly are Federal-era examples, which range from about $500 for plain country models, to $6000 to $12,000 for pieces by important cabinetmakers such as Duncan Phyfe; most Federal work tables, however, are in the $1000 to $2000 range. Empire work tables are less popular and can be found for as little as $100 to $400, while Victorian pieces range from $300 to $800 for well-made Rococo and Renaissance Revival tables to only $100 to $250 for wicker ones. Bargains may be found among the many Colonial Revival tables on the market, selling for $100 to $250.

Several other kinds of small stands or tables date from the Victorian era. Oak pieces are most common and readily available at $75 to $350; Mission-style oak tables sell at the top of this price range, or even higher if they bear the label of a major maker. Arts and Crafts stands are often inexpensive, and rustic examples made of bark and branches may be found in the $75-to-$200 range. Pedestals for statuary or vases were a Victorian phenomenon: simple oak pedestals are available at $100 to $300, but elaborate Renaissance Revival or Eastlake pieces may be twice as expensive.

318 Arts and Crafts stand $3000–8000
319 Mission-style stand $75–200
320 Mission-style stand $100–350
321 Arts and Crafts rustic stand $75–200
322 Federal country candlestand or small table $1200–2500
323 William and Mary country candlestand or small table $2000–5000
324 Shaker candlestand $1200–2000
325 Federal candlestand $1000–2000
326 Federal candlestand $1500–3000
327 Country ratchet-base candlestand $800–1500
328 Renaissance Revival pedestal $200–450
329 Renaissance Revival table $200–350
330 Eastlake upholstered-top table $350–700
331 Renaissance Revival pedestal $250–600
332 Eastlake parlor table $100–300
333 Eastlake parlor table $125–350
334 Federal dumbwaiter or serving table $2000–6000
335 Eastlake plant stand $150–250
336 Mission-style stand $2000–7000
337 Late Victorian wicker sewing stand $150–250
338 Empire drop-leaf sewing or work table $125–300
339 Federal work table $5000–12,000
340 Federal draped sewing table $4000–10,000
341 Federal sewing table with fabric bag $3000–8000
342 Rococo Revival sewing table $500–1000
343 Colonial Revival end table $100–250
344 Federal work table $800–1500
345 Federal work table $400–800
346 Federal country painted work table $400–600
347 Federal country painted dressing or work table $1000–2000

This Price Guide and the preceding essay on Where to Buy Antique Furniture were written by William C. Ketchum, Jr.

Picture Credits

The Metropolitan Museum of Art, New York City: Cover (purchase, funds from various donors, 1976), 70 (gift of Mrs. J. Insley Blair, 1943), 74 (gift of Mrs. D. Chester Noyes, 1968), 78 (Friends of the American Wing Fund, 1962), 108 (gift of Mrs. Russell Sage, 1909), 113 (Edgar J. Kaufmann Charitable Foundation Fund, 1968), 140 (bequest of Mrs. J. Insley Blair, 1952), 151 (gift of Mr. and Mrs. Georges Seligmann, 1964), 157 (Emily C. Chadbourne Bequest, 1972), 162 (gift of Mrs. Louis Guerineau Myers, in memory of her husband, 1972), 166 (Fletcher Fund, 1926), 167 (gift of Mrs. William W. Hoppin, 1948), 169 (Friends of the American Wing Fund, 1965), 170 (gift of C. Ruxton Love, 1960), 176 (gift of Mr. and Mrs. Lowell Ross Burch and Miss Jean McLean Morron, 1951), 177 (gift of Josephine M. Fiala, 1968), 182 (purchase, L. E. Katzenbach Gift, 1966), 209 (Edgar J. Kaufmann Charitable Foundation Fund, 1969), 230 (gift of Paul Martini, 1969), 289 (Rogers Fund, 1925), 297 (Edgar J. Kaufmann Charitable Foundation Fund, 1968), 302 (Edgar J. Kaufmann Charitable Foundation Fund, 1968), 336 (Emily C. Chadbourne Bequest, 1972).

Judith and James Milne, Inc., New York City: 13, 17, 27, 163, 201–203, 223, 242, 321.

Morton's Auction Exchange, New Orleans: 221, 236, 237.

Alan Moss Studios, New York City: 102, 103, 133, 135, 136, 214, 215, 266, 267.

New York State Museum, Albany, New York: 41, 42, 94, 175, 194.

Oak 'N Stuff Antiques, New York City: 16, 18, 264, 304, 333.

Peabody Museum, Salem, Massachusetts: 40.

Private Collections: 3, 10, 29, 45, 62, 68, 75, 77, 81, 82, 144, 145, 199, 255, 260, 261, 263, 282, 284, 288, 290, 291, 324, 334, 339, 344, 347.

Pat Sales Antiques, New York City: 5, 19, 20, 30, 250, 272.

Secondhand Rose, New York City: 89, 101, 154, 158, 188, 213.

Shaker Community, Inc., Pittsfield, Massachusetts: 2, 6, 31, 191, 224, 274, 275.

The Margaret Woodbury Strong Museum, Rochester, New York: 37, 55, 58, 64, 80, 83, 85, 87, 90, 92, 93, 112, 119, 123–126, 128–131, 148, 155, 174, 178, 179, 185, 186, 219, 220, 247, 248, 276, 279, 280, 298–301, 303, 328, 330–332.

Robert Stuart, Limington, Maine: 4, 246.

Van der Hurd Studio, New York City: 104, 138, 139, 147, 159, 241, 307–309, 313, 315–317.

Westchester Auction Galleries, Yorktown Heights, New York: 52, 172, 189, 196, 218, 343.

The Henry Francis du Pont Winterthur Museum, Delaware: 23, 161, 183, 193, 227, 229, 295.

Yale University Art Gallery, New Haven, Connecticut: 141 (gift of John E. Bray).

Drawings

Dolores Santoliquido: pp. 38, 43–44, 432–437, 440–449.

Paul Singer, Alan Singer, and Tuula Fischer: pp. 20–23, 32–33, 36–37, 50–55, 426–429.

Mary Jane Spring: pp. 10–19, 24–31, 34–35.

Index

Numbers in boldface refer to color plates. Numbers in italics refer to pages.

Staff

Prepared and produced by Chanticleer Press, Inc.
Publisher: Paul Steiner
Editor-in-Chief: Gudrun Buettner
Senior Editor: Milton Rugoff
Managing Editor: Susan Costello
Project Editor: Michael Goldman
Assistant Editor: Constance V. Mersel
Art Director: Carol Nehring
Art Assistant: Ayn Svoboda
Marketing: Carol Robertson
Production: Helga Lose, John Holliday
Picture Library: Joan Lynch, Edward Douglas
Visual Key Symbols: Paul Singer
Drawings: Dolores Santoliquido, Mary Jane Spring, Paul Singer
Design: Massimo Vignelli

The Knopf Collectors' Guides to American Antiques

Also available in this unique full-color format:

Chests, Cupboards, Desks & Other Pieces
by William C. Ketchum, Jr.

Glass Tableware, Bowls & Vases
by Jane Shadel Spillman

Quilts, Coverlets, Rugs & Samplers
by Robert Bishop